Restoring Faith in Reason

With a New Translation of the Encyclical Letter

FAITH AND REASON

of Pope John Paul II

Together with a Commentary and Discussion

Edited by Laurence Paul Hemming and Susan Frank Parsons

University of Notre Dame Press
Notre Dame, Indiana

Published in the United States in 2003 by
University of Notre Dame Press
Notre Dame, Indiana 46556
www.undpress.nd.edu

First published in 2002 by SCM Press
9–17 St Albans Place, London N1 0NX
www.scm-canterburypress.co.uk

SCM Press is a division of SCM-Canterbury Press Ltd

Library of Congress Cataloging-in-Publication Data

Fides et ratio. English.

Restoring faith in reason : with a new translation of the Encyclical letter, Faith and reason of Pope John Paul II : together with a commentary and discussion / edited by Laurence Paul Hemming and Susan Frank Parsons.

p. cm.

Includes bibliographical references and index.

ISBN 0-268-03067-7 (pbk. : alk. paper)

1. Faith and reason—Christianity. 2. Catholic Church.—Doctrines—Papal documents. 3. Reason—Religious aspects. 4. Knowledge, Theory of (Religion) I. Hemming, Laurence Paul. II. Parsons, Susan Frank. III. Title.

BT50.F5313 2003
231'.042—dc21 2003050729

∞ *This book is printed on acid-free paper.*

Contents

Acknowledgments

The new translation offered here of the Holy Father's encyclical letter *Fides et ratio* is not in any way intended to supplant the official English translation, released simultaneously with the definitive Latin text in 1998. The editors of this text are grateful to the great number of people who in one way or another have been involved in the preparation of this volume since work began on it in 1999. In the first place we must thank Archbishop Vincent Nichols of Birmingham for his unobtrusive encouragement of this project throughout its development. We are profoundly indebted to Fr Anthony Meredith SJ for his contribution towards the work of translating the text of *Fides et ratio*. We would like to thank Fr John Moffat SJ and Fr Richard Barrett for their advice at the earlier stages of the work. Gratitude is owed Sr Francis North IBVM for her meticulous and invaluable advice on both Latin and English as the translation progressed. We also thank Dr Martin Stone of King's College, University of London, for his thorough scrutiny of the final draft of the translation.

We are grateful to others who worked on the translations in this volume. We would like to thank Fr Philip Endean SJ (assisted by Kirsten Weissenberg) for his work as translator and editor of the contribution from Professor Eilert Herms. If the translations are the better for their work, the editors take full responsibility for remaining mistakes or infelicities.

We must express our gratitude to Fr James McEvoy, Dean and Professor of the Department of Philosophy in the National University of Ireland at Maynooth for the Commentary that accompanies the translation of the Encyclical. We are indebted to the contributors to the discussion in the volume: to Dr Wayne J. Hankey, Carnegie Professor of Classics and member of King's College at Dalhousie University, Nova Scotia; Professor Dr Eilert Herms of the Evangelische-Theologische Fakultät at the University of Tübingen; Nicholas Lash, Norris-Hulse Professor Emeritus of the Divinity Faculty of Cambridge University; Dr Aristotle Papanikolaou, Assistant Professor in the Department of Theology at Fordham University; His Excellency Archbishop Angelo Scola, Patriarch of Venice, who, during his time as Rector of the Pontifical

Lateran University kindly provided invaluable advice and encouragement in the formation of this volume; Monsignor Robert S. Sokolowski, Professor in the School of Philosophy of the Catholic University of America; and Dr Janet Soskice, Reader in the Divinity Faculty of Cambridge University.

We are grateful to the Prior, Fr Edmund Power OSB and Professor Dr James Leachman OSB of the College of the Pontifical Athenaeum of Sant' Anselmo, Rome, for permission to use the image of St Anselm reproduced on the front cover of this work.

Lastly, we wish to thank Alex Wright and all those at SCM Press for their help in the production of the volume.

Preface

LAURENCE PAUL HEMMING
SUSAN FRANK PARSONS

'And Pilate said to him "What is truth?" '.[1] Truth is the lot of philosophy, and yet, for Christians, we can hardly be surprised that the question of the meaning of truth arises in this way, as a question posed by Pontius Pilate in the course of the trial of Jesus, in the course of the events that lead to his crucifixion. Pilate frames the question in the Greek of the New Testament as much as if it had been asked by Aristotle or Plato. Pilate asks, 'What is . . .', the very question that characterizes the beginnings of philosophy among the Greeks.[2] What truth is, as a question that receives its very answer in the person of Jesus, that he is the Christ, the Son of the Living God, lies at the heart of the events of the Triduum, the three days through which the salvation of humanity unfolds. What our human relation to the truth itself is, also lies at the heart of these events – the ways in which we are implicated and folded in to the death and resurrection of the Lord. Jesus Christ is the fulfilment and revelation of the truth – this is why he was sent: indeed, his very claim to be this is what prompts Pilate's question at all.[3] Yet Jesus' claim to be 'the Truth' does not belong to philosophy, and is not the matter of the contemplation of wisdom nor even of a rational or dialectical enquiry. His claim belongs to faith; to know its truth is in virtue of believing it to be given by God, and for the salvation of humankind.

Truth is philosophy's lot, both inasmuch as it genuinely enquires into what truth indeed is, as much as when it declares (as some contemporary philosophers have done) that what truth is unfolds as a question to which no founding answer can be given.

Even this conclusion is reached in the face of – and in the face of the occlusion of – the whole history of the human engagement with truth. In

---

[1] Jn 18:38: *λέγει αὐτῷ ὁ Πιλᾶτος, τί ἐστιν ἀλήθεια.*

[2] *τί τὸ ὄν* – what is this being, in so far as it is?

[3] Jn 18:37. 'Jesus answered, "You say that I am a king. For this I was born, and for this I have come into the world, to bear witness to the truth. Every one who is of the truth hears my voice".'

his extended treatment of the unfolding of the history of philosophy, especially in the West, the Holy Father notes that 'as a consequence of the crisis of rationalism, something akin to *nihilism* has appeared'.[4] A number of responses to the Encyclical have pursued this aspect of his discussion, not least in the essays in this volume.[5] Other commentators also have understood the contemporary response of Christianity to nihilism as a resistance of nihilism. It is in this context that a 'philosophy of being' must be undertaken. To what extent, therefore, must any future philosophy of being take into account and work through the questions raised by Martin Heidegger's understanding that the discipline and practice of metaphysics has, and holds within itself and from its very outset in Plato, the propensity towards the nihilism which eventually comes to prevail in the history of philosophy? Heidegger captures this in a sharp and provocative phrase that spans almost the entire history of philosophy in the West, when he says that 'the metaphysics of Plato is not less nihilistic than the metaphysics of Nietzsche'.[6] Nevertheless this provocation serves to remind us that metaphysics in and of itself is not Christian and cannot through its own efforts be redemptive.

A philosophy of being alone, without God and through God's self-revelation, surely cannot save us. Is it not for this very reason that the Encyclical is rightly cautious in repeating the insight of Pope Pius XII that 'the Church does not have a philosophy of her own, nor does she select a particular one to the detriment of others'?[7] The question of how God is understood in thinking is one that remains for every philosophy and indeed every philosopher. It can never be worked out independently of those to whom salvation is addressed – which means it can never be a mere formula, a *philosophical* 'answer' or piece of reasoning, true at all times and in all places, independently of faith.

The Christian experience of Christ as the truth, that truth is fully revealed personally, means that truth itself is no mere binary, no mere opposition to falsehood. To claim that truth is solely an evaluative function in the working out of logical propositions or computations is something very new. This is an absolutization of truth, but it is not the absolute truth, nor the truth of Him who is absolute. To understand truth in this way, and to import its distinctions into the realm of faith is

---

[4] *Fides et ratio*, §46.

[5] See also V. Possenti, *Filosofia e Rivelazione. Un contributo al dibatto su ragione e fede* (Rome: Città Nuova, 1999) especially Chapter 3. ET E. L. Paparella, *Philosophy and Revelation: A Contribution to the Debate on Reason and Faith* (Farnborough: Ashgate, 2001).

[6] M. Heidegger, *Die seinsgeschichtliche Bestimmung des Nihilismus* in *Nietzsche*, Vol. 2 (Gesamtausgabe 6.2) (Frankfurt: Klostermann, 1997) [1961], p. 309. 'Die Metaphysik Platons ist nicht weniger nihilistisch als die Metaphysik Nietzsches.'

[7] *Fides et ratio*, §49.

to tread the paths that lead to various kinds of fundamentalism, of which the biblical is only one. The Greeks already knew that the truth was something which had to be struggled for to be known. Truth must be taken to the heart as well as through the mind. What they understood as the false – τὸ ψεῦδος – is not the mere opposite of truth, but something which at the same time as hiding the truth also depends on the truth in order to hide it. It is in this way that we can speak of someone taking up a false identity, or acting as an impostor. If truth is not binary, neither is it relative. Freedom towards the truth is not freedom to use the truth as I will, or to pick and chose what will be true for me. Truth is not at my disposal, but it is something into whose province I have to bring myself, often in ways that are not easy, and in which the things I cherish are risked, or have even to be given up. This struggle for truth is one with which I might have to engage for a time, and then perhaps lay down again, only to take it up later when I can re-enter it more deeply – or perhaps not be able to lay it down, if there is something the truth of which I must know because some aspect of my life depends upon it.

Truth is disclosed in the encounter with it. In this the Incarnation is central – for the non-believer must first be free with regard to his or her encounter with truth, to discover first that Jesus comes among us as a man among men and women. This is not the whole truth of who Jesus is, but it opens ways and paths to discovering the deeper meanings of the truth that he reveals. The freedom of the one who cannot yet believe is always that he will have encountered part of the truth, and in not yet delivering himself over to it fully, neither to be disbarred from what it is of the truth he has already discovered. If truth is compelling, it cannot compel in order to be so, but must draw towards itself, whilst always holding within itself the freedom that should he choose, the one addressed can walk away down the by-ways and paths that – if they lead toward the truth – also lead away from it.

The Latin term *probare* is often translated as 'to prove', but it does not really mean this. Rather it means, to demonstrate through the work of the mind what is already the case. In this sense, *probare* does not mean to prove a theorem, and only secondarily relates to the production of proofs. Primarily it means to bring myself, by means of the mind and by rigorous reflection, into what can be known. In this sense we cannot prove incorrigibly that God exists (as has sometimes been claimed), but we can demonstrate how, and by what ways, we come to know this to be true.

In beginning his Encyclical Letter *Fides et ratio*, the Holy Father identifies the human being – man himself – as that one who searches for truth, and who does so in the context of the world in which he finds himself. A world given socially as well as naturally, a world which makes something

of him, as much as he is called to co-operate with it and have a hand in its building up and making. In the Encyclical John Paul II develops a theme which he sums up by saying '*the understanding of faith* demands the assistance of a philosophy of being'.[8] At the same time he draws to the fore again the figure of St Thomas Aquinas, saying of him that 'his is truly a philosophy of being'.[9] The phrase 'philosophy of being' may be taken in more than one sense. In so far as it refers to human being, it means the way we live and are disclosed by the world in which we find ourselves. In so far as it concerns who we are, it also concerns how we understand ourselves to belong to God. St Thomas is always cautious of how we undertake the enquiry into our relation to God. Thus even when he considers the question of whether it is necessary that every being be created and so caused by God,[10] he does so only after having considered the God of revelation in his three persons as Trinity, and only because we may suppose 'in accord with the Catholic faith, that the world has not existed from eternity but had a beginning of its duration'.[11] In other words we may only work out (*probare*) the answers to these questions after the data of faith have been given and we have given ourselves over to them. From these things given, the others follow.

In the person of St Thomas we find an exemplary and remarkable encounter with the tradition of philosophical reflection. Thoroughly schooled in the Mediaeval encounter with Plato and Neoplatonism, nevertheless he drew the most remarkable energy from his enquiry into Aristotle, for whom philosophy was the science of being in so far as it is being.[12] Even though Aristotle calls this science not only 'first philosophy' but also 'theology', Aquinas is careful to distinguish *this* theology from the theology proper to faith or holy teaching.[13] Aquinas strives to place the unfolding of truth as he has received it and as he engages it within the mystery of the God who reveals himself in Christ for the salvation of humankind. It is to this task that the Encyclical *Fides et ratio* calls us again, and it is for this reason that the call made is itself a personal one, in the person of the Pope himself. In this, the Holy Father follows on a

---

[8] *Fides et ratio*, §97.

[9] *Fides et ratio*, §44.

[10] Cf. Aquinas, *Summa Theologiae*, Ia, Q. 44, art. 1. 'Utrum sit necessarium omne ens esse creatum a Deo.'

[11] Aquinas, *De aeternitate mundi*, art. 1. '. . . secundum fidem catholicam, quod mundus durationis initium habuit'. Cf. *On The Eternity of the World,* trans. C. Vollert SJ, L. H. Kendzierski and P. M. Byrne (Milwaukee: Marquette University Press, 1964), p. 18.

[12] Aristotle, *Metaphysics*, 1026 a 32.

[13] Cf. Aristotle, *Metaphysics*, 1026 a 20; Aquinas, *Summa Theologiae*, Ia, Q. 1, art. 1 resp. ad. 2. '. . . unde theologia quae ad sacram doctrinam pertinet, differt secundum genus ab illa theologia quae pars philosophiae ponitur'.

path in which St Thomas is indeed an exemplar, and to which we too are called.

We do not enter the consideration of wisdom and reflective reason from nowhere, or from some anterior place of faith which privileges us with regard to wisdom's practice and so leads us to bestow upon it a status it could not otherwise have had. Rather, faithful or not, we have always been formed already and are already taking as self-evident the disciplines and practices of thinking which surround us and constitute the world in which we find ourselves. These always bear the human longing for truth even as they seek to provide for its resolution, and so they bear us along into the midst of the world's cry for redemption in shaping and giving shape to all that we undertake. Our philosophical conceptions are carried even into the liturgy by which the Church celebrates the mystery of this redemption. Cardinal Joseph Ratzinger has noted how the two modern tendencies – of pure subjectivity, and of the priority of the will, threaten the very genius of the liturgy itself by preventing our reception of the truth as love. This is, if you like, how we unwittingly bring the very dissolution of the world itself to the foot of the cross, and so to the place of redemption. Yet wisdom and truth will here find their unravelling and their consummation, as they – and so we – are called into question by the sacramental actions of love. The very power of the liturgy to effect this presence of us to the mystery of redemption, to hand us over to the coming of Christ to the world, is the resolution of everything that threatens it. It is only in passing through these threats to their dissolution that 'all this perhaps can thereby help us to overcome the unbounded inflation of subjectivity, and to recognise again that a relationship with the Logos who was at the beginning saves the subject, that is, the person'.[14]

If Pilate asks, 'What is truth?', we too are called to this question, and called to ask it most deeply in the very place he asked it, in entering the mysteries of our salvation, at the threshold of our journey through the Triduum. This journey is undertaken above all in our worship, through the liturgy, where once and time again we are ourselves made present to the singular sacrifice of Christ and his victory over death, and where we are enjoined to his body. How we undertake and reflect on our asking of this question in this place is determined by who we know ourselves to be, and so in our asking of it, we take up our places at the Seat of Wisdom where the truth which is love comes to matter.

---

[14] Joseph Cardinal Ratzinger, *Der Geist der Liturgie: Eine Einführung* (Freiburg: Herder, 2000), p. 133. ET J. Saward, *The Spirit of the Liturgy* (San Francisco, CA: Ignatius Press, 2000). 'All dies kann vielleicht dazu helfen, daß die maßlose Übersteigerung des Subjekts überwunden und wieder erkannt wird, daß gerade die Beziehung auf den am Anfang stehenden Logos auch das Subjekt, nämlich die Person, rettet.'

This book is the first in what we hope will be a number of studies which, in different ways, and from a variety of perspectives, will pay generous heed to the questions which *Fides et ratio* has raised. These will be informed by a desire for the mutual engagement of the disciplines of theology and philosophy in the problematic areas of current debate at the highest and most serious level of scholarship. Such may constitute an ecumenical renewal of the work of philosophical theology, both as an illumination of the foundations of faith and as an apologetic for faith that may be heard by those in search of truth. This work is inspired by the Holy Father's assurance that 'by insisting on the truth of faith, we can both restore to contemporary men and women a true confidence in their capacity for reflecting and can also inspire philosophers to regain and develop the proper dignity of their discipline'.[15] That we should find ourselves gathering again in friendship at the table of divine mercy, as scholars in other times and places have done, in order to understand the human way of belonging to God and of bearing the difference God is to the world, is the hope into which the Encyclical releases us, so that Christ may be known among all peoples.

[15] *Fides et ratio*, §6.

Abbreviations

AAS	*Acta Apostolicae Sedis, Commentarium officiale*
ASS	*Acta Sanctae Sedis*
CCL	*Corpus Christianorum Latinorum*
DS	Denzinger, Henry and Schönmetzer, Adolf (eds.), *Enchiridion symbolorum definitionum et declarationum de rebus fidei et morum*
PG	*Patrilogia Graeca* (J. P. Migne, ed.)
PL	*Patrilogia Latina* (J. P. Migne, ed.)
SC	*Sacrosanctum concilium, Constitution of Vatican II*

LITTERAE ENCYCLICAE
FIDES ET RATIO
IOANNIS PAULI PP. II SUMMI PONTIFICIS
CUNCTIS CATHOLICAE ECCLESIAE EPISCOPIS
DE NECESSITUDINIS NATURA INTER UTRAMQUE

Venerabiles in Episcopatu Fratres,
salutem et Apostolicam Benedictionem!

FIDES ET RATIO binae quasi pennae videntur quibus veritatis ad contemplationem hominis attollitur animus. Deus autem ipse est qui veritatis cognoscendae studium hominum mentibus insevit, suique tandem etiam cognoscendi ut, cognoscentes Eum diligentesque, ad plenam pariter de se ipsis pertingere possint veritatem (cfr *Ex* 33:18; *Ps* 27[26]:8–9; 63[62]:2–3; *Io* 14:8; *1 Io* 3:2).

PROOEMIUM
"NOSCE TE IPSUM"

1. Fieri quidem potest ut, tam in Orientis orbe quam in Occidentis solis plaga, iter quoddam dignoscatur quod, progredientibus saeculis eo usque hominum genus perduxerit ut cum veritate paulatim congrediatur seque cum illa componat. Hoc quidem iter sic explicatum est – neque aliter accidere potuit – intra prospectum quendam singularis hominum conscientiae: quo namque plenius res orbemque cognovit homo, eo magis ipsemet cognoscit se unica in sua natura, eodemque tempore instans fit interrogatio de significatione rerum suaeque ipsius exsistentiae. Quidquid se nobis obicit veluti cognitionis nostrae argumentum, hanc ipsam ob causam evadit vitae nostrae elementum. Admonitio illa *Γνῶθι σεαυτόν* in superliminari inscripta erat Delphis in templo, principalem ut veritatem testificaretur quae minima omni homini

ENCYCLICAL LETTER
FAITH AND REASON
OF THE SUPREME PONTIFF POPE JOHN PAUL II
TO THE BISHOPS OF THE CATHOLIC CHURCH
ON THE NATURE OF THE RELATIONSHIP BETWEEN THEM

Venerable Brothers in the Episcopate,
health and the Apostolic Blessing!

FAITH AND REASON seem to be like two wings by which the human spirit is raised up toward the contemplation of truth. It is God himself who implanted in the minds of men and women an inclination for knowing the truth and an inclination for knowing him, so that knowing and loving him, they may likewise attain the whole truth about their very selves (cf. *Ex* 33:18; *Ps* 27[26]:8–9; 63[62]:2–3; *Jn* 14:8; *1 Jn* 3:2).

INTRODUCTION
'KNOW YOURSELF'

1. It is possible, in fact, both in the Eastern and Western world, for us to discern a journey by which, as the ages progress, humanity has gradually been led in the company of truth and come to terms with it. This journey has thus been explained – and it could never have happened otherwise – within the particular perspective of the unique self awareness of man: for in that perspective the more man comes to know the world and its affairs, the more he learns to understand himself in his own uniqueness, and with that there presses upon him the urgent desire to find out about the meaning of reality and of our existence. Whatever offers itself to us as a proof of our own knowledge becomes for that very reason a part of our own lives. The admonition *know yourself* was carved over the portal in the temple of Delphi in order to witness to this primary truth, a truth which had to be taken as a minimum rule for every

sumenda erat regula quicumque inter res creatas se extollere cupiebat veluti "hominem" scilicet "sui ipsius cognitorem".

Candidus intuitus veteres in annales luculenter aliunde demonstrat, variis in orbis regionibus multiplici humano distinctis cultu, exsistere eodem tempore principales illas interrogationes quibus vita designatur hominum: *Quis egomet sum? Unde venio? Quoque vado? Cur mala adsunt? Quid nos manet hanc post vitam?* Haec quaesita reperiuntur in sacris Israelis scriptionibus, at insunt etiam scriptis *Veda* necnon *Avesta*; detegimus ea in operibus Confutii atque Lao-Tze, quemadmodum in praedicatione virorum Tirthankara ipsiusque Buddhae; exsistunt similiter ex Homeri carminibus ac tragoediis Euripidis et Sophoclis, perinde ac philosophicis in Platonis et Aristotelis tractatibus. Hae nempe interrogationes sunt quae ex illa communi profluunt inquisitione de sensu ipso quo numquam non hominis animus inquietatur: ex responsione vero, quae talibus redditur rogationibus, directio pendet quae vitae humanae est imprimenda.

2. Aliena sane non est Ecclesia, neque esse potest, hoc ab inquirendi opere. Ab eo enim tempore, cum intra Paschale Mysterium postremam accepit de hominis vita veritatem uti donum, facta est illa vicissim peregrina per semitas orbis ut Christum Iesum esse praedicet "viam veritatem et vitam" (cfr *Io* 14:6). Diversa inter officia, quae hominibus ea offerat oportet, unum illud nimirum esse intellegit sibi plane proprium: *Veritatis diaconiam.*[1] Hoc officium, una ex parte, facit ut credens ipsa communitas particeps evadat communis illius operae qua homines attingere student veritatem;[2] altera vero ex parte, obstringitur communitas illa officio ut nuntia fiat rerum certarum quas cognovit, licet sibi conscia sit omnem veritatem captam unam dumtaxat stationem esse plenam ad illam veritatem quae ultima in Dei revelatione ostendetur: "Videmus enim nunc per speculum in aenigmate, tunc autem facie ad faciem; nunc cognosco ex parte, tunc autem cognoscam, sicut et cognitus sum" (*1 Cor* 13:12).

---

[1] Iam primis Nostris in Litteris Encyclicis *Redemptor hominis* inscriptis ediximus: "Inde huius muneris Christi, prophetae, participes facti sumus et ex eodem munere cum eo servimus veritati divinae in Ecclesia. Officium circa hanc veritatem assumptum etiam idem valet atque eam amare et curare, quo penitius cognoscatur, ita ut ad eam, cum tota vi salvifica, qua pollet, cum splendore, quo nitet, cum profunditate simul et simplicitate, quibus distinguitur, propius accedamus". §19: *AAS* 71 (1979), 306.

[2] Cfr Conc. Oecum. Vat. II, Const. past. de Ecclesia in mundo huius temporis *Gaudium et spes*, §16.

human being, that is, for anyone who wished to raise himself up within creation as 'man' does so as 'one who knows himself'.

An honest inspection of the ancient evidence demonstrates that shining through the variety of human cultures in different regions of the world there exist those primary questions by which human life is marked out: *Who Am I? Where do I come from? Where am I going? Why do evils appear? What remains to us after this life?* These questions may be found in the sacred writings of Israel and also in the Veda and the Avesta. We discover them in the works of Confucius and of Lao-Tze, and likewise in the preaching of the Tirthankaras and in that of the Buddha himself. Similarly, they are present in the songs of Homer and the tragedies of Euripides and Sophocles, just as they are in the philosophical works of Plato and Aristotle. These questions are the ones, of course, which flow from that common investigation concerning meaning itself by which the spirit of man is never left undisturbed: the direction given to human life depends upon the response which is given to these questions.

2. The Church is no stranger to this work of investigation, nor could she ever be. From the moment when, from within the Paschal Mystery, she received the ultimate truth about human life as a gift, she in her turn was made a pilgrim upon the highways of the world in order to preach that Jesus Christ is 'the way, and the truth, and the life' (*Jn* 14:6). Among the various duties which she is bound to offer to humanity, there is one in particular that is understood as clearly her own, the *diakonia of truth*.[1] On the one hand she carries out this office so that the believing community itself may share in this common struggle by which humanity seeks to attain to truth;[2] and on the other hand this community is constrained to the duty of proclaiming the certainties which she knows, while conscious herself that every truth arrived at is just one stopping-place on the way to that fullness of truth which will be shown forth in the final revelation of God: 'for now we see in a mirror dimly, but then face to face. Now I know in part; then I shall understand fully' (*1 Cor* 13:12).

---

[1] In our first Encyclical Letter *Redemptor hominis* we wrote: 'We have become sharers in this mission of the prophet Christ, and in virtue of that mission we together with Him are serving divine truth in the Church. Being responsible for that truth also means loving it and seeking the most exact understanding of it, in order to bring it closer to ourselves and others in all its saving power, its splendour and its profundity joined with simplicity.' John Paul II Encyclical Letter *Redemptor hominis* (4 March 1979) (London: Catholic Truth Society, 1979) §19.

[2] Cf. Second Vatican Council, Pastoral Constitution on the Church in the Modern World *Gaudium et spes*, §16 in A. Flannery OP, (ed.), *Vatican Council II: The Conciliar and Post-Conciliar Documents* (Grand Rapids, MI: Eerdmans, 1992), p. 916.

3. Multiplices sunt facultates quibus uti potest homo ut veritatum cognoscendarum foveat progressionem, unde exsistentiam suam humaniorem reddat. Inter has *philosophia* eminet, quae recta adiuvat ut et interrogatio ponatur de vitae sensu et ei responsio iam adumbretur: quapropter unum ipsa reperitur nobiliorum hominis munerum. "Philosophiae" vox Graecam ad originem "sapientiae amorem" designat. Etenim nata philosophia est atque eo tempore enucleata quo coepit se ipsum homo interrogare de rerum causis finibusque. Diversis quidem formis modisque demonstrat philosophia ad ipsam hominis naturam pertinere veritatis cupiditatem. Innata est eius menti illa proprietas ut de rerum percontetur causis etiamsi responsiones paulatim inde redditae in formam quandam ingrediuntur quae diversas cultus humani species inter se complere manifesto ostendit.

Impulsio vehemens illa, quam ad efformationem progressionemque culturae in orbe Occidentali adhibuit philosophia, facere haud debet ut obliviscamur quatenus ipsa quoque pervaserit vias etiam humanae vitae concipiendae ex quibus Orientalis etiam vivit orbis. Cuique enim populo nativa est atque pristina sapientia quae, tamquam verus animi culturarum thesaurus, eo tendit ut exprimatur et rationibus potissimum philosophicis maturetur. Quam sit hoc verum inde etiam comprobatur quod principalis quaedam philosophicae scientiae figura, nostris etiam temporibus, deprehendi potest in iis postulatis quibus leges Nationum et civitatum informantur ad socialem vitam moderandam.

4. Quidquid autem id est, notetur oportet sub uno nomine diversas latere significationes. Praevia igitur explicatio necessaria evadit. Concupiscens extremam vitae veritatem homo adipisci, illas universales studet comparare cognitiones quae ei facultatem dant melius se comprehendendi ulteriusque progrediendi ad se perficiendum. Fundamentales hae notiones illa ex *admiratione* emanant quam rerum creatarum contemplatio in eo excitat: rapitur enim homo stupens quod se in rerum universitatem videt insertum cum aliis sui similibus consociatum quibuscum etiam communicat sortem. Iter hinc incipit quod illum pervehet ad novos usque cognitionis orbes detegendos. Nisi obstupescens miraretur homo, in repetitionem quandam sterilem recideret ac, paulatim, facultatem amitteret vitae reapse personalis ducendae.

Speculandi potestas, quae humani propria est intellectus, adiuvat ut, philosophicam per industriam, figura enucleetur exactae cogitationis

3. There are many resources which men and women can deploy to foster the progress of the knowledge of truth so that life is made more human. Standing out among these is *philosophy*, which when properly constituted, is a direct help in posing the question about the meaning of life and sketching an answer to it. For this reason, philosophy is numbered among the nobler gifts of man. The word 'philosophy', according to its Greek origin, signifies the 'love of wisdom'. Indeed philosophy was born and came to expression at the moment when man began to pose questions about causes of things and their purposes. In fact, in sundry ways and forms, philosophy shows that the desire for truth belongs to the very nature of man. Innate in his mind is that propensity to enquire into the causes of things, even as the answers gradually emerging take on a particular form that clearly shows how the diverse cultures of humanity complement one another.

This powerful impulse which philosophy has brought to the formation and progress of culture in the Western world should not allow us to forget how central has been its influence on the various ways human life is understood in the Eastern world. Every people has its own native and original wisdom which, as a true treasury of the spirit of cultures, seeks to be expressed and to develop in forms of reasoning which are above all philosophical. The truth of this is also confirmed in that the basic forms of the philosophical discipline, even today, can be detected in the principles used by nations and states for the organizing of social life.

4. Nonetheless, it should be noted that a single term conceals a variety of meanings. A preliminary explanation is therefore necessary. The one who is desirous of attaining the ultimate truth about life strives to acquire those universal elements of knowing which give him the ability to understand himself better and which lead to the advancement of his own perfection. These fundamental conceptions arise from that wonder which the contemplation of created realities excites in him. Man is seized with awe to see that he has been placed in the universe, in fellowship with others like himself with whom he also shares a common lot. This is the beginning of the journey which will lead him to discover new realms of knowledge. Without this sense of wondering amazement, man would subside into deadening routine and would bit by bit lose the power of leading a properly personal life.

The power of speculation, which is proper to the human intellect, with the aid of philosophy helps the formation of an exact reflection, and so a

sicque ordinata exstruatur disciplina logico affirmationum consensu atque solido doctrinarum contextu distincta. Hanc propter rationem, variis in cultus humani formis diversisque pariter aetatibus, fructus percepti sunt qui elaborandis veris cogitationum modis profuerunt. Ad historiae fidem factum est ut istud induceret ad unam dumtaxat philosophiae viam confundendam cum tota philosophica disciplina. Constat vero, his in casibus, certam quandam exsistere "superbiam philosophicam" quae suos attollere audeat oculos longe prospicientes at imperfectos ad interpretationem aliquam universalem. Re vera quodque philosophiae *corpus*, quantumvis reverendum sua in summa et amplitudine sine ullis abusibus, agnoscere debet principatum philosophicae *cogitationis*, ex qua et suam ducit originem et cui congruenter serviat necesse est.

Hoc modo, quamquam mutantur tempora cognitionesque progrediuntur, agnosci licet quasi nucleum quendam philosophicarum notionum, quae nonnumquam adsunt in hominum cogitantium historia. Cogitentur verbi gratia, principia non contradictionis, finalitatis ac causalitatis nec non cogitatum personae veluti subiecti liberi et intellegentis eiusque facultas Deum veritatem bonumque cognoscendi; cogitentur pariter nonnullae normae morales praecipuae quae omnium item sunt communes. Haec aliaque argumenta demonstrant, variis doctrinarum praetermissis scholis, corpus exsistere cognitionum in quibus introspici potest genus quoddam spiritalis hominum patrimonii. Ita fit ut ante oculos quasi *philosophiam implicitam* reperiamus cuius principia quisque homo se possidere sentiat, tametsi sub forma omnino universali neque conscia. Quoniam communicantur hae notiones quadamtenus ab omnibus, ipsae efficere debent medium quoddam punctum quo diversae philosophicae scholae confluunt. Quotiens ratio percipere valet atque exprimere prima et universalia vitae principia indeque recte consectaria propria deducere ordinis logici et deontologici, totiens appellari potest ratio recta sive, quemadmodum antiqui loquebantur, *ὀρθὸς λόγος*.

5. Sua ex parte facere non potest Ecclesia quin magni officium rationis aestimet ad proposita illa consequenda unde ipsa hominum vita dignior reddatur. Etenim in philosophia viam ipsa conspicatur cognoscendi principales veritates hominum vitam tangentes. Eodem tempore, philosophiam iudicat instrumentum pernecessarium ut fidei intellectus altius inquiratur atque Evangelii veritas iis impertiatur qui eam nondum cognoverunt.

logical coherence of assertions is built up through an ordered discipline, distinguished by a firm body of teachings. For this reason, in the various forms of human culture and equally in different ages, fruits have been gathered which have been of benefit in developing genuine approaches to reflection. In practice this has led people to confuse one way of philosophizing with the entire philosophical discipline. Very clearly in such cases a certain 'philosophical pride' exists, which looks out with eyes that have a long but faulty vision and assumes it has found some universal interpretation. Indeed the *body* of philosophy, though it demands great reverence both for its height and its breadth, provided it contains no abuses, must recognize that which is the basis of all philosophical *reflection*, from where it draws its origin and which it must serve appropriately.

In this way, despite changing times and an increase in knowledge, we may still admit a sort of nucleus of philosophical ideas, which are regularly present in the history of human reflection. Consider, for example, the principles of non-contradiction, of finality and causality, as well as the concept of the person as a free and intelligent subject, and of her capacity to know God, the truth and the good. Consider as well certain moral norms, above all those which are common to everyone. These and other arguments indicate that, without going into the doctrines of the various schools, there exists a body of knowledge into which we can look as a kind of spiritual heritage of humanity. This means that before our own eyes we may discover something like an *implicit philosophy*, the principles of which anyone might feel that they possessed, albeit in a general and unconscious way. Since these conceptions are shared in some way by everyone, these same conceptions can effect a certain middle point at which the diverse philosophical schools converge. Whenever reason successfully perceives and expresses the first and universal principles of life and from there correctly deduces conclusions of a logical and deontological order, then it may be called right reason or, as the ancients called it, *ỏrthòs lógos*.

5. On her part the Church can do no other than have a high esteem of the duty of reason in pursuit of those aims through which the life of man is rendered more worthwhile. For she sees in philosophy itself a way of knowing those principal truths which touch upon the life of man. At the same time, the Church judges philosophy to be an indispensable instrument for acquiring a deeper understanding of faith and for communicating the truth of the Gospel to those who as yet do not know it.

Similia igitur Decessorum Nostrorum coepta prosecuti, cupimus etiam Nos ad hoc peculiare rationis humanae opus convertere oculos. Eo praesertim impellimur quod novimus his maxime temporibus veritatis ultimae inquisitionem saepius obscuratam videri. Haud dubitatur quin philosophiae recentiori laudi tribuatur quod mentes iam in hominem ipsum intenduntur. Hinc initio facto, quaedam ratio interrogationum plena ulterius propulit hominis cupiditatem plus plusque cognoscendi atque singula multo altius. Ita doctrinarum formae implexae exstructae sunt quae suos variis in cognitionis provinciis protulerunt fructus, progressui nempe faventes tum culturae tum historiae. Anthropologia, logica disciplina, scientiae naturales, historia et sermo . . . , immo quodam modo universitas cognitionis humanae est assumpta. Effectus re percepti suadere aliunde non debent ut obscuretur quod ipsa ratio, ad investigandum uno solo ex latere hominem uti subiectum intenta, videtur esse omnino oblita eundem hominem semper invitari ut ad veritatem se transcendentem progrediatur. Deficiente habitudine ad illam, quisque homo exponitur arbitrio soli suo atque ipsius velut personae condicio in eo est ut regulis unis pragmaticis aestimetur quae suapte natura experimentis innituntur, cum perperam credatur technicam artem necessario debere reliquis rebus dominari. Sic sane accidit ut, cum melius hanc intentionem ad veritatem exprimere deberet, gravata contra onere tot notitiarum ratio humana in se replicaretur atque de die in diem minus intuitum suum attollere in altiora posset ut veritatem exsistentiae consequi auderet. Recentior philosophia, omittens suas perquisitiones in ipsum "esse" dirigere, opus suum in cognitionibus hominum collocavit. Non ergo extulit facultatem quae homini data est veritatis cognoscendae, sed extollere eius limites maluit et condiciones.

Multiplices hinc enatae sunt agnosticismi et relativismi formae quibus eo usque provecta est philosophica investigatio ut iam in mobili veluti scepticismi universalis tellure pererraret. Recentius praeterea variae invaluerunt doctrinae illuc tendentes ut etiam illae veritates imminuantur quas homo se iam adeptum esse putaverat. Licita sententiarum varietas iam indistincto concessit pluralismo, principio niso omnes opinationes idem prorsus valere: unum hoc est signorum latissime disseminatorum illius diffidentiae de veritate, quam hodiernis in adiunctis deprehendi passim licet. In idem diffidens iudicium incidunt etiam quaedam vitae notiones ex Oriente profectae; in iis, enim, veritati negatur propria eius indoles, cum pro concesso sumatur pari modo veritatem diversis indicari in doctrinis, vel inter se contradicentibus. Hoc in rerum prospectu cuncta ad opinationem quandam rediguntur. Percipitur quasi motus quidam

Pursuing, therefore, the similar initiatives of our Predecessors, we also wish to turn our gaze toward this particular work of human reason. We are impelled to do so by the fact that, at the present time especially, we know that the search for ultimate truth is too frequently obscured. This is without prejudice to the fact that modern philosophy is often praised because it focuses our minds upon man itself. From this starting-point, a complete system of questioning propels the desire of humanity to know more and more, and to know it ever more deeply. Complex systems of thought have thus been constructed, producing results in the different fields of knowledge while fostering both the progress of culture and of history. Anthropology, logic, the natural sciences, history, rhetoric, etc. – indeed in some way the whole universe of human knowledge has been involved. Yet the positive results perceived must not obscure the fact that reason itself, intent upon investigating man from one angle only, as a subject, seems to have forgotten that the same man is always invited to progress toward a truth which transcends himself. Deprived of this habit, any man is thereby exposed to the tyranny of his own will, and the condition of the person becomes such that he is judged simply in terms of pragmatic norms which of their very nature rely upon experiments, it being perversely supposed that every thing else is under the control of technique. Thus it not infrequently happens that, despite the fact that the human mind ought to express this attitude to the truth, it is weighed down by factual knowledge and has instead turned back on itself, so that almost every day it becomes less able to lift its eyes to higher things and so courageously pursue the truth of existence. More recent philosophy in its failure to interest itself in 'being' has laid all its emphasis on human knowledge. Instead, therefore, of exalting the capacity given to man for recognizing the truth, it has preferred to accentuate his limits and conditions.

Thus many forms of agnosticism and relativism were spawned, and the result has been that philosophical research wanders around in the uncertain soil of universal scepticism. Moreover, different teachings tending in that direction have recently gathered strength, so that even those truths which man had already thought to be certain have been diminished. A legitimate plurality of views has already yielded to a vague pluralism, based upon the assumption that all positions have the same value: this is one of the widely diffused signs of a diffidence about truth which can be observed everywhere in modern times. Even certain conceptions of life brought from the East betray this diffidence; denying to truth its real character, when, for instance, it is assumed that truth reveals itself equally in conflicting teachings, or even among those which are self-contradictory. In this view of things, everything is reduced to opinion. A

fluctuans: cum hinc philosophica investigatio iam in illam viam se inserere potuit, quae propiorem eam reddit ad hominum vitam eiusque formas expressas, illinc tamen eadem inquisitio explicare iam vult deliberationes exsistentiales, hermeneuticas vel linguisticas quae alienae sunt a fundamentali hac quaestione de veritate cuiusque hominis vitae, exsistentiae atque Dei ipsius. Quapropter in homine nostrae aetatis, neque tantummodo quosdam apud philosophos, iam emerserunt affectus alicuius diffidentiae passim disseminatae nulliusque fiduciae de permagnis hominum cognoscendi facultatibus. Falso cum pudore quis contentus fit veritatibus ex parte et ad tempus, quin interrogationes radicales ponere iam contendat de sensu extremoque vitae humanae fundamento, in singulis hominibus et in ipsa societate. Brevi: spes iam interiit fieri posse ut talibus interrogationibus decretoriae responsiones reddantur.

6. Ecclesia vigens auctoritate illa, quae ei obtingit quod Revelationis Iesu Christi est custos, confirmare cupit huius meditationis necessitatem super veritate. Hanc ipsam ob causam in animum induximus appellare tum vos Veneratos in Episcopatu Fratres quibuscum annuntiandi communicamus munus "in manifestatione veritatis" (2 *Cor* 4:2) tum etiam philosophos atque theologos quorum est diversos veritatis perscrutari aspectus, tum etiam homines omnes adhuc quaerentes, ut nonnullas participemus cogitationes de itinere quod conducit ad veram sapientiam, ut quicumque in pectore amorem ipsius habeat, rectam ingredi valeat viam ut eam consequatur, in eaque quietem reperiat suis a laboribus spiritalemque laetitiam.

Ad hoc inceptum Nos adducit conscientia in primis quae verbis Concilii Vaticani II significatur cum Episcopos esse adfirmat "divinae et catholicae veritatis testes".[3] Testificandae igitur veritatis officium est concreditum nobis Episcopis, quod deponere haud possumus quin simul ministerium acceptum deseramus. Fidei veritatem confirmantes, nostrae aetatis hominibus reddere possumus veram fiduciam de propriis cognoscendi facultatibus ipsique philosophicae disciplinae praebere provocationem ut suam plenam recuperare valeat explicareque dignitatem.

Alia Nos quoque permovet causa ut has perscribamus deliberationes. Litteris in Encyclicis *Veritatis splendor* inscriptis animorum intentionem direximus ad quasdam "doctrinae catholicae fundamentales veritates

[3] Const. dogm. de Ecclesia *Lumen gentium*, §25.

sort of instability is evident: since on the one hand, philosophical enquiry had already allowed itself to take the road which brings it closer to human life and its varied expressions, on the other, this same enquiry plunges into existential, hermeneutic, or linguistic discussions which are quite foreign to this fundamental question of the truth of each man's life, and of the existence of God himself. Hence not just some philosophers, but the men and women of our time have been subject to an increasing distrust and lack of confidence in the existence of the great cognitive capacities of the human mind. A certain false modesty has made them content with partial and provisional truths so that they no longer strive to pose radical questions about the meaning and ultimate foundation of human life, both individually and collectively. In short, the hope that philosophy might be able to provide definitive answers to these questions has dwindled.

6. The Church, vibrant with the authority which she has in virtue of her being guardian of the Revelation of Jesus Christ, wishes to insist upon the need for this meditation upon truth. For this reason we have decided first of all to call upon you, Venerable Brothers in the Episcopate, with whom we share the duty of making clear 'the manifestation of the truth' (2 *Cor* 4:2), and secondly upon philosophers and theologians whose vocation it is to explore different aspects of the truth, and finally upon all of those who are still seeking it; so that we may share some thoughts about the way which leads to true wisdom, and so that whosoever has a heartfelt love of truth might enter upon the right road that confers it and may find in it a rest from labours and a spiritual joy.

We are led to begin this task, conscious first of all of the words of the Second Vatican Council when it affirms that the Bishops are 'witnesses to divine and catholic truth'.[3] The duty to bear witness to the truth is therefore entrusted to us Bishops, a task which we can hardly renounce without deserting the ministry we have received. By insisting on the truth of faith, we can both restore to contemporary men and women a true confidence in their capacity for reflecting and can also inspire philosophers to regain and develop the proper dignity of their discipline.

There is a further reason which leads us to expand our thoughts on this subject. In the Encyclical Letter *Veritatis splendor* we directed thoughtful attention to certain 'fundamental truths of Catholic doctrine which, in

---

[3] Second Vatican Council, Dogmatic Constitution on the Church *Lumen gentium*, §25 in Flannery, (ed.), *Vatican Council II*, p. 379.

quae in periculo versantur deformationis vel negationis ob rerum adiuncta aetatis nostrae".[4] His Litteris pergere cupimus easdem meditationes ulterius persequi, mente videlicet conversa ad argumentum ipsius *veritatis* eiusque *fundamentum* quod spectat ad *fidem*. Etenim negari non potest hoc celerium et implicatarum mutationum tempore iuniores praesertim, ad quos pertinet ventura aetas et de quibus ea pendet, illi exponi sensui sive persuasioni se certis privari fundamentalibus principiis ad quae referantur. Necessitas alicuius solidi firmamenti, in quo vita singulorum hominum societatisque exstruatur, vehementius persentitur praesertim quotiens necesse est comprobare partialem naturam propositorum quae res transeuntes ad gradum alicuius ponderis tollunt, dum decipiunt potestatem ipsam assequendi verum vitae sensum. Ita profecto evenit ut multi suam vitam ad ipsum praecipitii marginem producant, nescientes interea quid ultra maneat. Inde hoc nempe accidit quod nonnumquam ii, quos munus fere proprium obstringebat ut culturae formis fructus proferrent suarum deliberationum, oculos a veritate abstraherent, cum laboris successum subitum praeferrent patientis inquisitionis labori earum rerum quae vivendo sunt experiendae. Strenue igitur pristinam suam vocationem recuperare debet philosophia cuius grave est officium cogitationem humanam informare nec non humanum ipsum cultum, perpetuo revocando homines ad veritatis perquisitionem. Hac omnino de causa non solam necessitatem sensimus, verum etiam morale officium ut de hoc argumento eloqueremur, ut hominum genus, limen tertii millenni christiani aetatis supergressurum, magis conscium sibi facultatum magnarum reddatur quae illi sunt concessae seque renovato animi fervore dedat salutis explendo consilio in quod ipsius est inserta historia.

CAPUT I
SAPIENTIAE DIVINAE PATEFACTIO

Iesus Patris revelator

7. Omni meditationi quam perficit Ecclesia subiacet conscientia apud ipsam nuntium depositum esse qui suam trahat originem ex Deo ipso (cfr 2 *Cor* 4:1–2). Haud ex propria consideratione provenit haec conscientia etiam profundissima quam hominibus ea praebet, verum ex verbi Dei in fide receptione (cfr *1 Thess* 2:13). Ad vitae nostrae uti credentium

[4] *Veritatis splendor*, §4: *AAS* 85 (1993), 1136.

the present circumstances, risk being distorted or denied'.[4] In this Letter, we intend to pursue this thought further, by turning our mind to the theme of *truth* itself and on its *foundation* in relation to *faith*. For it cannot be denied that in this time of such swift and complex changes, younger people, to whom the future belongs and upon whom it depends, are particularly exposed to the sense or conviction that they are bereft of certain fundamental principles to which they may refer. The need for a solid foundation, in which the life of individuals and of human society may be built up, becomes all the more pressing when it is necessary to prove the partial nature of those propositions which bring transient things to a level of seriousness, while they cast into doubt the very power itself of attaining the true meaning of life. For this reason many people take their lives to the very edge of the precipice, quite ignorant of what awaits them. What often happens is that those whose particular duty it is to express the fruits of their investigations in the forms provided by culture, avert their eyes from truth, since they prefer quick results to the toil of patient enquiry into those things which make life worth living. Philosophy must, therefore, recover its original vocation and realize the grave duty which is the formation of human reflection as well as human culture itself, forever recalling humanity to the search for truth. All this will explain why we feel not only the need, but also the moral duty, to address this theme, so that the human race, about to cross the threshold of the third millennium of the Christian era, may be more conscious of the great resources given to it and may commit itself with renewed fervour of spirit to fulfilling the plan of salvation in which history has unfolded.

CHAPTER I
THE DISCLOSURE OF DIVINE WISDOM

Jesus, revealer of the Father

7. Underlying every meditation which the Church undertakes is the awareness that she is the bearer of a message which takes its origin from God himself (cf. *2 Cor* 4:1–2). This deep awareness that she offers to men and women is a fruit not of her own reflections, but derives from the word of God received in faith (cf. *1 Thess* 2:13). At the origin of our life as believers a certain encounter takes place, unique in its nature, which issues in the disclosure of a mystery, hidden in the ages and now revealed

[4] John Paul II, Encyclical Letter *Veritatis splendor* (6 August 1993) (London: Catholic Truth Society, 1993), §4.

originem congressio quaedam, sui generis unica, invenitur quae mysterii a saeculis absconditi designat illuminationem (cfr *1 Cor* 2:7; *Rom* 16:25–26), quod autem nunc aperitur: "Placuit Deo in sua bonitate et sapientia seipsum revelare et notum facere sacramentum voluntatis suae (cfr *Eph* 1:9), quo homines per Christum, Verbum carnem factum, in Spiritu Sancto accessum habent ad Patrem et divinae naturae consortes efficiuntur".[5] Hoc est plane gratuitum opus quod a Deo proficiscitur et ad homines pervenit ut illi salvi fiant. Tamquam amoris fons Deus se cupit cognosci atque cognitio quam illius habet homo omnem perficit aliam notitiam quam mens eius assequi potest de propriae exsistentiae sensu.

8. Doctrinam fere verbatim repetens, quam Concilii Vaticani I Constitutio *Dei Filius* exhibet, rationemque ducens principiorum in Concilio Tridentino propositorum Constitutio Concilii Vaticani II *Dei Verbum* ulterius produxit saeculare iter *intellectus fidei*, Revelationem ad doctrinae biblicae institutionisque totius patristicae lucem ponderando. Concilii Vaticani I participes supernaturalem revelationis divinae extulerunt indolem. Negabat censura rationalistica, quae eo ipso tempore adversus fidem movebatur secundum falsas lateque disseminatas opinationes, omnem cognitionem quae rationis naturalium potestatum non esset consecutio. Hoc quidem Concilium induxit ut vehementer inculcaret ultra omnem rationis humanae cognitionem, quae suapte natura ad Conditorem usque agnoscendum progredi valeret, cognitionem etiam reperiri quae fidei propria esset. Haec cognitio veritatem exprimit quae fundamentum invenit in Deo sese revelante quaeque veritas est certissima quandoquidem Deus nec fallit nec fallere cupit.[6]

9. Docet itaque Concilium Vaticanum I veritatem ex philosophica deliberatione perceptam atque Revelationis veritatem non confundi neutramque earum alteram reddere supervacaneam: "Duplicem esse ordinem cognitionis non solum principio, sed obiecto etiam distinctum: principio quidem, quia in altero naturali ratione, in altero fide divina cognoscimus; obiecto autem, quia praeter ea, ad quae naturalis ratio pertingere potest, credenda nobis proponuntur mysteria in Deo abscondita, quae, nisi revelata divinitus, innotescere non possunt".[7]

---

[5] Conc. Oecum. Vat. II, Const. dogm. de divina Revelatione *Dei Verbum*, §2.

[6] Cfr Const. dogm. de fide catholica *Dei Filius*, III: *DS* 3008.

[7] Const. dogm. de fide catholica *Dei Filius*, IV: *DS* 30015; memoratum etiam in Conc. Oecum. Vat. II, Const. past. de Ecclesia in mundo huius temporis *Gaudium et spes*, §59.

(cf. *1 Cor* 2:7; *Rom* 16:25–26): 'it pleased God in his goodness and wisdom to reveal himself and to make known the mystery of his will (cf. *Eph* 1:9), by which men and women, through Christ, the Word made flesh, might have access to the Father in the Holy Spirit and become sharers in the divine nature'.[5] This action is the entirely gratuitous work of God, initiated by him and coming to us for our own salvation. Like a fountain of love, God desires to make himself known; and the knowledge which man has of him perfects all the conceptions which the mind can attain concerning the meaning of its own existence.

8. The decree of the Second Vatican Council, *Dei Verbum*, repeats, almost verbatim, the language employed by the First Vatican Council in its decree *Dei Filius*, and that in its turn was simply an exposition of the principles laid down in the Council of Trent. What the Second Vatican Council adds in the age-old journey of *understanding of the faith* is its relating the truth of Revelation to the whole biblical and Patristic tradition. The Fathers of Vatican I laid great stress on the supernatural nature of divine revelation. Rationalist criticism, which at that time was stirring against the faith according to false but widely disseminated claims, was denying all knowledge which could not be arrived at by the natural powers of reason. This fact forced the Council strongly to insist that a knowledge could be found, proper to faith, which is beyond all natural human knowledge, even though that natural knowledge can advance to the knowledge of its creator. This knowledge expresses a truth which finds its foundation in God revealing himself, a truth which is absolutely certain, seeing that God can neither deceive nor be deceived.[6]

9. Thus the First Vatican Council teaches that the truth perceived by philosophical deliberation and the truth of Revelation are not to be confused, neither do they render one another superfluous or invalid: 'there exists a twofold order of knowledge, distinct not only as regards their source, but also as regards their object. With regard to the source, they are distinct because in the one we find it by natural reason, in the other by divine faith. With regard to the object, because besides those things which natural reason can attain, there are proposed for our belief mysteries hidden in God which, unless they are divinely revealed,

[5] Second Vatican Council, Dogmatic Constitution on Divine Revelation, *Dei Verbum*, §2, in Flannery, (ed.), *Vatican Council II*, pp. 750 f.

[6] First Vatican Council, Dogmatic Constitution on the Catholic Faith *Dei Filius*, §3 in N. Tanner SJ, (ed.), *Decrees of the Ecumenical Councils*, 2 vols. (London: Sheed & Ward, 1990) II, p. 807.

Quae Dei testimonio innititur fides atque supernaturali gratiae utitur adiumento, re vera ad alium pertinet ordinem ac philosophicae cognitionis. Sensuum enim haec perceptioni adnititur nec non experientiae ac se sub intellectus solius lumine movet. Philosophia atque scientiae in naturalis rationis versantur ordine, dum contra a Spiritu illuminata et gubernata fides agnoscit in ipso salutis nuntio "gratiae et veritatis plenitudinem" (cfr *Io* 1:14) quam per historiam patefacere decrevit Deus semelque in sempiternum per Filium suum Iesum Christum (cfr *1 Io* 5:9; *Io* 5:31–32).

10. In Concilio Vaticano II Patres intendentes in Iesum Revelatorem mentes, voluerunt naturam revelationis Dei salutiferam collustrare in historia, cuius hoc modo proprietatem ita significaverunt: "Hac itaque revelatione Deus invisibilis (cfr *Col* 1:15; *1 Tim* 1:17) ex abundantia caritatis suae homines tamquam amicos alloquitur (cfr *Ex* 33:11; *Io* 15:14–15) et cum eis conversatur (cfr *Bar* 3:38), ut eos ad societatem secum invitet in eamque suscipiat. Haec Revelationis oeconomia fit gestis verbisque intrinsece inter se connexis, ita ut opera, in historia salutis a Deo patrata, doctrinam et res verbis significatas manifestent ac corroborent, verba autem opera proclament et mysterium in eis contentum elucident. Intima autem per hanc Revelationem tam de Deo quam de hominis salute veritas nobis in Christo illucescit, qui mediator simul et plenitudo totius revelationis exsistit".[8]

11. In tempus propterea inque historiae annales se interserit Dei revelatio. Immo evenit Iesu Christi incarnatio "in plenitudine temporis" (cfr *Gal* 4:4). Duobus ideo milibus annorum post illum eventum necesse esse rursus adseverare istud arbitramur: "Christiana in fide praecipuum habet pondus tempus".[9] Intra tempus namque profertur in lucem totum creationis ac salutis opus at in primis elucet per Filii Dei incarnationem vivere nos et iam nunc id antecapere quod ipsius temporis erit complementum (cfr *Heb* 1:2).

Quam veritatem homini Deus concredidit de eo ipso eiusque vita in tempus itaque se introducit nec non in historiam. Semel quidem in perpetuum enuntiata est in mysterio Iesu Nazareni. Hoc eloquentibus quidem verbis edicit Constitutio *Dei Verbum*: "Postquam vero multi-

---

[8] Conc. Oecum. Vat. II, Const. dogm. de divina Revelatione *Dei Verbum*, §2.

[9] Litt. Ap. *Tertio millennio adveniente* (10 Novembris 1994), §10: *AAS* 87 (1995), 11.

cannot be known'.[7] Faith, indeed, which relies upon the witness of God and uses the help of divine grace, does belong to another order than that of philosophy. This latter relies upon sensory perception and experience and is under the influence of reason alone. Philosophy and the sciences belong to the order of natural reason. Faith, on the other hand, is enlightened and guided by the Spirit and recognizes in the very proclamation of faith 'the fullness of grace and truth' (cf. *Jn* 1:14). This God decided to declare once and for all through his Son Jesus Christ (cf. *1 Jn* 5:9; *Jn* 5:31–32).

10. In the Second Vatican Council the Fathers directed their attention to Jesus the Revealer, and wished to illustrate the saving nature of divine revelation in history, describing it in this appropriate way: 'in this Revelation the invisible God (cf. *Col* 1:15; *1 Tim* 1:17), out of the abundance of his love, speaks to men and women as friends (cf. *Ex* 33:11; *Jn* 15:14–15) and lives among them (cf. *Bar* 3:38), so that he may invite and take them into fellowship with himself. This economy of Revelation is realized by the inner unity of the deeds and words: as a result the deeds wrought by God in the history of salvation manifest and confirm the teaching and realities signified by the words, while the words proclaim the deeds and bring to light the mystery they contain. By this Revelation, then, the deepest truth about God and human salvation is made clear to us in Christ, who is the mediator and at the same time the fullness of all revelation'.[8]

11. God's revelation, therefore, makes itself present in time and in the annals of history. Indeed the incarnation of Jesus Christ occurred in the 'fullness of time' (*Gal* 4:4). Two thousand years after this event we think it necessary to insist once again that 'in the Christian faith time has a fundamental importance'.[9] For it is within time that the whole work of creation and salvation comes to light and above all it is clear that we live through the incarnation of the Son of God, and even now already anticipate what time will bring to perfection (cf. *Heb* 1:2).

God has committed this truth about himself and his life to man in time, and so has brought himself into history. This was clearly revealed once and for all in the mystery of Jesus of Nazareth. This truth is eloquently

---

[7] First Vatican Council, Dogmatic Constitution on the Catholic Faith *Dei Filius*, §4 in Tanner, (ed.), *Decrees of the Ecumenical Councils*, II, p. 808; quoted also in the Second Vatican Council, Pastoral Constitution on the Church *Gaudium et spes*, §59 (cf. Flannery, [ed.], *Vatican Council II*, p. 963).

[8] Second Vatican Council, Dogmatic Constitution on Divine Revelation *Dei Verbum*, §2 in Flannery, (ed.), *Vatican Council II*, p. 751.

[9] John Paul II, Apostolic Letter *Tertio millennio adveniente* (10 November 1994) (London: Catholic Truth Society, 1994), §10.

fariam multisque modis Deus locutus est in Prophetis, 'novissime diebus istis locutus est nobis in Filio' (*Heb* 1:1–2). Misit enim Filium suum, aeternum scilicet Verbum, qui omnes homines illuminat, ut inter homines habitaret iisque intima Dei enarraret (cfr *Io* 1:1–18). Iesus Christus [. . .], Verbum caro factum, "homo ad homines" missus, "verba Dei loquitur" (*Io* 3:34), et opus salutare consummat quod dedit ei Pater faciendum (cfr *Io* 5:36; 17:4). Quapropter Ipse, quem qui videt, videt et Patrem (cfr *Io* 14:9), tota sui ipsius praesentia ac manifestatione, verbis et operibus, signis et miraculis, praesertim autem morte sua et gloriosa ex mortuis resurrectione, misso tandem Spiritu veritatis, Revelationem complendo perficit".[10] Efficit itaque populo Dei historia haec iter quoddam ex toto percurrendum, ita ut revelata veritas omnem suam plene aperiat continentiam ob Spiritus Sancti continuam actionem (cfr *Io* 16:13). Id rursus Constitutio *Dei Verbum* docet cum adfirmat: "Ecclesia, volventibus saeculis, ad plenitudinem divinae veritatis iugiter tendit, donec in ipsa consummentur verba Dei".[11]

12. Locus ita evadit historia ubi comprobare possumus Dei acta pro hominibus. Nos enim attingit ille in iis quae nobis maxime sunt familiaria et ad demonstrandum facilia, quia cotidiana nostra constituunt adiuncta, quibus submotis haud possemus nosmet ipsos intellegere.

Permittit Dei Filii incarnatio ut perennis ac postrema summa videatur completa quam ex se profecta hominum mens numquam fingere sibi valuisset: Aeternum ingreditur tempus, Quod est Omne absconditur in parte, Deus hominis suscipit vultum. Christi in Revelatione igitur expressa veritas iam nullis circumscribitur artis locorum et culturarum finibus, verum cuivis viro et feminae aperitur quae eam complecti voluerit veluti sermonem penitus validum qui vitae tribuat sensum. In Christo omnes homines iam accessum habent ad Patrem; sua namque morte ac resurrectione Ipse vitam aeternam dono dedit quam primus respuerat Adamus (cfr *Rom* 5:12–15). Hanc per Revelationem ultima exhibetur homini de propria vita veritas deque historiae sorte: "Reapse nonnisi in mysterio Verbi incarnati mysterium hominis vere clarescit" adseverat Constitutio *Gaudium et spes*.[12] Extra hunc rerum conspectum mysterium vitae singulorum hominum manet aenigma insolubile. Ubi reperire valet homo responsiones illis permoventibus interrogationibus,

---

[10] Conc. Oecum. Vat. II, Const. dogm. de divina Revelatione *Dei Verbum*, §4.
[11] Conc. Oecum. Vat. II, Const. dogm. de divina Revelatione *Dei Verbum*, §8.
[12] Conc. Oecum. Vat. II, Const. dogm. de divina Revelatione *Dei Verbum*, §22.

expressed in the constitution *Dei Verbum*: 'after God had spoken in various different ways in the Prophets, "most recently in these days he has spoken to us through his Son" (*Heb* 1:2). For he has sent his Son, the eternal Word, who enlightens all men, that he might dwell among them and tell of the intimate truth about God (cf. *Jn* 1:1–18). Jesus Christ . . . the Word made flesh, sent as "a man to men", "speaks the words of God" (*Jn* 3:34) and completes the work of salvation the Father gave him to do (*Jn* 5:36; 17:4). Therefore, whoever sees him sees the Father (cf. *Jn* 14:9), the one who, by means of his total presence and self revelation, by his signs and miracles, especially by his death and glorious resurrection, and finally by dispatching the Spirit of truth, completes Revelation by fulfilling it.'[10] For the people of God, therefore, this history becomes a path to be pursued to the end, so that through the continuous action of the Holy Spirit revealed truth should completely open up its contents. This again is the teaching of the Constitution *Dei Verbum*, when it affirms that 'the Church, as the ages pass by, is always on the move towards the fullness of divine truth, until the words of God are fulfilled'.[11]

12. History therefore becomes the arena where we are able to confirm the deeds of God for the sake of men and women. He touches us in the things which we best know and can easily verify, because they constitute the circumstances of our everyday life, without which we would hardly be able to understand ourselves.

The incarnation of the Son of God allows the expression of the perfect and complete whole which the mind of man desires, but could never fashion for himself: the Eternal enters time, Who is Whole is concealed in the part, God takes on human face. This means that the truth expressed in the Revelation of Christ is circumscribed by no narrow limits of places or of cultures. Instead every man and woman has opened up to them, should they wish to embrace it, the definitive statement which is to give sense to life. In Christ all men and women already have access to the Father; by his own death and resurrection he gives freely that eternal life which Adam once spurned (cf. *Rom*5:12–15). Through this Revelation the ultimate truth about his own life and the end of history is displayed before us: 'only in the mystery of the Incarnate Word is the mystery of man revealed' as *Gaudium et spes*

---

[10] Second Vatican Council, Dogmatic Constitution on Divine Revelation *Dei Verbum*, §4 in Flannery, (ed.), *Vatican Council II*, p. 751.

[11] Second Vatican Council, Dogmatic Constitution on Divine Revelation *Dei Verbum*, §8 in Flannery, (ed.), *Vatican Council II*, p. 754.

verbi gratia de dolore atque innocentis cruciatu ac de morte, nisi illo sub lumine quod ex mysterio passionis mortis resurrectionis Christi profluit?

Coram arcano – ratio

13. Non tamen oblivisci licebit Revelationem mysteriis abundare. Sane quidem cuncta sua ex vita Iesus vultum Patris revelat utpote qui venerit ut intima Dei enarraret;[13] verumtamen quam habemus talis vultus cognitio semper designatur incompleta quadam ratione atque etiam nostrae comprehensionis finibus. Sinit una fides nos in mysterium ingredi intimum, cuius congruentem fovet intellectum.

Docet Concilium quod "Deo revelanti praestanda est oboeditio fidei."[14] Perbrevi hac sed densa affirmatione principalis quaedam fidei christianae declaratur veritas. Dicitur, in primis, fidem esse oboedientiae responsionem Deo. Id poscit ut Ille sua agnoscatur in divinitate, sua in transcendentia supremaque libertate. Deus qui facit ut ipse cognoscatur ob suae absolutae transcendentiae auctoritatem, secum etiam adfert credibilitatem eorum quae revelat. Sua fide *adsensum* suum huiusmodi testificationi divinae tribuit homo. Hoc significat eum plene integreque agnoscere rerum revelatarum veritatem, quoniam ipse se pignus illarum exhibet Deus. Veritas haec, quae homini conceditur neque ab eo exigi potest, in contextum se introducit cuiusdam communicationis singularis inter personas rationemque ipsam humanam impellit ut ei se aperiat eiusque altam percipiat significationem. Hanc ob causam actus ille, quo nos Deo committimus, semper ab Ecclesia tamquam tempus habitus est cuiusdam electionis fundamentalis, qua tota involvitur persona. Usque ad extremum intellectus ac voluntas exercent spiritalem suam naturam ut subiecto humano permittatur actum perficere quo uniuscuiusque libertas pleno modo vivatur.[15] In fide proinde non adest dumtaxat praesens libertas: etiam postulatur. Immo, ipsa fides unicuique facultatem dat suam enuntiandi meliore ratione libertatem. Aliis verbis: libertas non in

---

[13] Cfr Conc. Oecum. Vat. II, Const. dogm. de divina Revelatione *Dei Verbum*, §4.

[14] Cfr Conc. Oecum. Vat. II, Const. dogm. de divina Revelatione *Dei Verbum*, §5.

[15] Concilium Vaticanum I, ad quod superior haec prolata refertur sententia, docet fidei oboeditionem opus postulare tum intellectus tum voluntatis: "Cum homo a Deo tamquam creatore et Domino suo totus dependeat et ratio creata increatae Veritati penitus subiecta sit, plenum revelanti Deo intellectus et voluntatis obsequium fide praestare tenemur" (Constitutio dogm. de fide catholica *Dei Filius*, III; *DS* 3008).

declares.[12] If we stand outside this vision of the world, the mystery of individual men and women remains an insoluble enigma. Where indeed could man discover answers to the disturbing questions, for example, about the sorrow, suffering, and death of the innocent, except under the light which flows from the mystery of the passion, death and resurrection of Christ?

Before the hidden – reason

13. It should not be forgotten that Revelation abounds in mysteries. Indeed throughout his whole life Jesus reveals the face of the Father in that he came to expound on the secret things of God.[13] Even so the knowledge we possess of this face is always incomplete, both because of its own inner nature and because of the limits of our own understanding. Faith permits us to enter the inner mystery and from there develop a coherent comprehension.

The Council teaches that 'to the God who reveals himself must be given the obedience of faith'.[14] By this brief but pregnant affirmation a very important truth of the Christian faith is made clear. First of all it is stated that faith is the obedient response to God. It demands of us that he be acknowledged in his divinity, his transcendence, and his total freedom. The God who brings about his own recognition because of the authority of his absolute transcendence at the same time makes the content of his revelation credible. In this way man by his faith owes his own *assent* to the divine testimony. This shows that he fully and integrally accepts the truth of things revealed, because God offers himself as their guarantee. This truth, which is granted to man and cannot be demanded by him, set within the context of interpersonal communication, compels human reason to open itself to it and to grasp its deep meaning. For this very reason the act whereby we commit ourselves to God has always been considered by the Church to be a moment of fundamental choice which involves the whole person. To the very end the intellect and the will exercise their spiritual character so that the human being is capable of acting in such a way that he may live with complete freedom.[15] Therefore, it is

[12] Second Vatican Council, Pastoral Constitution on the Church *Gaudium et spes*, §22 in Flannery, (ed.), *Vatican Council II*, p. 922.

[13] Second Vatican Council, Dogmatic Constitution on Divine Revelation *Dei Verbum*, §4 in Flannery, (ed.), *Vatican Council II*, p. 751.

[14] Second Vatican Council, Dogmatic Constitution on Divine Revelation *Dei Verbum*, §5 in Flannery, (ed.), *Vatican Council II*, p. 751.

[15] The First Vatican Council, to which the quotation above refers, teaches that the obedience of faith requires the engagement of the intellect and the will: 'Since human beings are totally dependent on God as their creator and lord, and created reason is completely subject to uncreated truth, we are obliged to yield through faith to God the revealer full submission of intellect and will' (First Vatican Council, Dogmatic

electionibus contra Deum impletur. Quomodo enim verus libertatis usus iudicari posset nulla sese aperiendi voluntas ad id quod sinit homines se totos explicare? Credendo namque persona humana actum suae vitae significantissimum complet; hic enim veritatis certitudinem adsequitur veritas in eaque vivere decernit.

In rationis adiumentum, quae mysterii quaerit intellectum, etiam signa praesentia in Revelatione occurrunt. Adiuvant ea ut altius perquiratur veritas utque mentem ex sese intra mysterium scrutari valeat. Quidquid id est, signa haec, si altera ex parte maiorem tribuunt rationi humanae vim quia sinunt eam propriis viribus, quarum ipsa est invidiosa custos, intra mysterium investigare, ex altera vero parte eam incitant ut eorum veluti signorum naturam transgrediatur ut ulteriorem percipiat significationem eorum quae in se continent. In iis ideoque iam abscondita subiacet veritas, ad quam dirigitur mens et a qua seiungi non potest quin simul signum ipsum illi praebitum deleatur.

Quadamtenus revertimur ad *sacramentalem* Revelationis rationem atque, nominatim, ad eucharisticum signum ubi individua unitas inter rem ipsam eiusque significationem permittit ut mysterii capiatur altitudo. In Eucharistia revera praesens adest ac vivus Christus, suo cum Spiritu operatur, sed, quemadmodum praeclare sanctus Thomas edixit, "Quod non capis, quod non vides, animosa firmat fides, praeter rerum ordinem. Sub diversis speciebus, signis tantum, et non rebus, latent res eximiae".[16] Refert idem philosophus Blasius Pascal: "Sicut Christus Iesus ignotus inter homines fuit, ita manet veritas eius, communes inter opinationes, sine ulla exteriore distinctione. Sic etiam Eucharistia restat inter panem communem".[17]

Fidei cognitio, demum, mysterium non exstinguit; illud evidentius dumtaxat reddit demonstratque veluti necessarium vitae hominis elementum: Christus Dominus "in ipsa Revelatione mysterii Patris Eiusque amoris, hominem ipsi homini plene manifestat eique altissimam eius vocationem patefacit",[18] quae nempe ea est ut vitae trinitariae Dei particeps fiat.[19]

---

[16] *Sequentia* in sollemnitate Sanctissimi Corporis et Sanguinis Domini.
[17] *Pensées*, §789 (ed. L. Brunschvicg).
[18] Conc. Oecum. Vat. II, Const. past. de Ecclesia in mundo huius temporis *Gaudium et spes*, §22.
[19] Cfr Conc. Oecum. Vat. II, Const. dogm. de divina Revelatione *Dei Verbum*, §2.

not that in faith freedom merely happens to be present: it is required by it. In fact faith itself gives to each of us the power of expressing individual freedom on far better grounds. To put it another way: freedom is not expressed in choices made against God. For how can the refusal to be opened up to that which allows men and women to come to complete self-understanding be judged a true use of freedom? And thus by believing, the human person accomplishes the most meaningful act of her life, for here the certainty of truth is attained in that one who decides to live by it.

To help reason, which seeks to understand the mystery, there are indications provided by Revelation itself. These facilitate a deeper understanding of the truth and aid the mind to extend itself more profoundly into the truth. What all this means is that these signs, on the one hand, give a greater force to human reason, since they allow it by its own powers, powers reason guards jealously, to enquire into mystery; and on the other hand, they hasten reason to move beyond these signs and so to grasp the higher meaning of the things which the signs contain. The hidden truth, therefore, is already concealed in these signs toward which the mind is directed and from which it cannot separate itself, without at the same time erasing the very sign which is given to it.

In a sense, then, we are returned to the *sacramental* basis of Revelation, and expressly to the eucharistic sign wherein the indivisible unity between the reality itself and its signification permits us to grasp the depths of the mystery. In the Eucharist, the present and living Christ is really there, working with his Spirit; yet, as St Thomas wrote so well: 'a lively faith beyond the power of the human mind confirms what you can neither grasp nor see. Beneath different appearances, signs and not things, wondrous truths lie hidden'.[16] The same point too is made by the philosopher Blaise Pascal: 'As Christ Jesus was unknown among men and women, so too the truth about him remains, among familiar modes of thought, without any external distinction. So, too, the Eucharist remains among common bread'.[17]

Finally the knowledge faith offers does not destroy the mystery. Rather it makes it more evident and proves it to be almost a necessary element of human life. Christ the Lord 'in the very Revelation of the Father and of his love, fully manifests man to man himself and makes clear his high

Constitution on the Catholic Faith *Dei Filius*, §3 in Tanner, [ed.], *Decrees of the Ecumenical Councils*, II, p. 807).

[16] Cf. Roman Missal, *Sequence* for the Solemnity of the Body and Blood of the Lord.

[17] B. Pascal, *Pensées (d'après l'édition de L. Brunschvicg)* (London: J. M. Dent, 1913), §789.

14. Verum novitatis prospectum recludunt ipsi scientiae philosophicae doctrinae binorum Conciliorum Vaticanorum. In hominum historiam inducit Revelatio necessitudinis punctum quoddam quo carere non potest homo, si ad suae vitae comprehendendum mysterium pervenire voluerit; aliunde vero haec cognitio continenter ad Dei refertur mysterium quod plane exhaurire mens non valet, sed dumtaxat percipere et in fide complecti. Intra haec duo tempora peculiare habet ratio humana spatium suum unde investigare ei licet atque comprehendere, quin tamen nulla alia re circumscribatur nisi finita natura suae indolis coram Dei infinito mysterio.

Quapropter in historiam nostram Revelatio infert aliquam veritatem, universalem atque ultimam, quae hominis mentem incitat ne umquam consistat; immo vero, eam impellit ut suae cognitionis fines perpetuo dilatet, donec ea omnia se perfecisse intellegat quae in ipsius erant potestate, nulla praetermissa parte. Ad hanc autem deliberationem adiuvare nos festinat unum ex fecundissimis ingeniis maximeque significantibus in generis hominum historia, ad quem virum honorifice se convertunt tam philosophia quam theologia: sanctus Anselmus. Ille Cantuariensis Archiepiscopus sic sententiam suo in *Proslogion* eloquitur: "Ad quod cum saepe studioseque cogitationem converterem atque aliquando mihi videretur iam capi posse quod quaerebam, aliquando mentis aciem omnino fugeret, tandem desperans volui cessare, velut ab inquisitione rei, quam inveniri esset impossibile. Sed cum illam cogitationem, ne mentem meam frustra occupando, ab aliis, in quibus proficere possem, impediret, penitus a me vellem excludere, tunc magis ac magis, nolenti et defendenti se coepit cum importunitate quadam ingerere. [. . .] Sed heu! me miserum, unum de aliis miseris filiis Evae, elongatis a Deo! Quid incoepi? Quid effeci? Quo tendebam? Quo deveni? Ad quid aspirabam? In quibus suspiro? [. . .] Ergo, Domine, non solum es id quo maius cogitari nequit, sed es quiddam maius quam cogitari possit. Quoniam namque valet cogitari esse aliquid huiusmodi; si tu non es hoc ipsum, potest cogitari aliquid maius te: quod fieri nequit".[20]

[20] Prooemium et nn. 1. 15: *PL* 158, 223–224.226; 235.

vocation',[18] which is without doubt as a sharer in the trinitarian life of God.[19]

14. A really novel approach to the science of philosophy is unveiled by the teachings of the two Vatican Councils. Revelation has set within the history of men and women a point of reference, from which man cannot be severed if he wishes to enter into a comprehension of the mystery of his own life; yet this knowledge has a consistent reference to the mystery of God, which the human mind clearly may not exhaust, but must in the meantime be content to perceive and grasp by faith. Meanwhile human reason has its own proper domain from where it can inquire and comprehend, being restricted by nothing else except its own finite nature before the infinite mystery of God.

Therefore Revelation introduces into our history a truth which is both universal and ultimate, and which spurs on the human mind and prevents it from coming to a standstill; instead it forces it continually to expand the limits of its knowledge until it recognizes that it has completely realized all its full potentiality. In order to appreciate this point we are helped by one of the richest and most significant minds in the history of the human race, whom both philosophy and theology regard with enormous respect – St Anselm. He was Archbishop of Canterbury and he expresses his view in his *Proslogion*: 'when I had often and seriously turned my attention to study, it even seemed to me on occasion that what I sought might be grasped, and on other occasions it totally escaped me: eventually, in despair, I wanted to cease altogether, as if in search for something which it was impossible to find. But when I wished to exclude that thought from my mind, in case by occupying my mind uselessly I had no energy left for further activity, just then increasingly that same thought came upon me with renewed vigour, despite my attempts to refuse it entrance . . . Alas! poor wretch that I am, one of the wretched sons of Eve, far from God. What had I begun? What had I achieved? Where was I going? Where had I arrived? What were my aspirations? What was I sighing for? . . . Therefore, O Lord, you are not only that which is greater than my thought can encompass. But more, you are greater than anything that can be thought. For something of that kind can be thought; if you are not that very thing, something greater than you can be thought, and that is impossible'.[20]

[18] Second Vatican Council, Pastoral Constitution on the Church *Gaudium et spes*, §22 in Flannery, (ed.), *Vatican Council II*, p. 922.

[19] Second Vatican Council, Dogmatic Constitution on Divine Revelation *Dei Verbum*, §2 in Flannery, (ed.), *Vatican Council II*, pp. 750 f.

[20] St Anselm, *Proslogion*, Preface and chapters 1 and 15. Cf. *St Anselm's Proslogion*, ed. M. J. Charlesworth (Notre Dame, IN: Notre Dame University Press, 1979).

15. Revelationis christianae veritas, quae cum Iesu Nazareno congreditur, quemlibet hominem percipere sinit propriae vitae "mysterium". Dum perinde ac suprema ipsa veritas observat illa autonomiam creaturae libertatemque eius illam etiam obstringit ut ad transcendentiam sese aperiat. Haec coniunctio libertatis ac veritatis maxima evadit planeque Domini intellegitur sermo: "Cognoscetis veritatem, et veritas liberabit vos" (*Io* 8:32).

Verum veluti astrum conductorium christiana Revelatio fit homini qui inter condiciones progreditur mentis cuiusdam immanentisticae nec non logicae technocraticae angustias; extrema est facultas quae a Deo praebetur ut pristinum amoris consilium, creatione ipsa inchoatum, denuo plene reperiatur. Hominibus verum cognoscere cupientibus, si ultra se adhuc prospicere valent et intuitum suum extra propria proposita attollere, potestas tribuitur veram necessitudinem cum sua vita recuperandi, viam persequendo veritatis. Ad hunc rerum statum bene dicta libri *Deuteronomii* adhiberi licet: "Mandatum hoc, quod ego praecipio tibi hodie, non supra te est neque procul positum nec in caelo situm, ut possis dicere: 'Quis nobis ad caelum valet ascendere, ut deferat illud ad nos, et audiamus atque opere compleamus?' Neque trans mare positum, ut causeris dicas: 'Quis nobis transfretare poterit mare et illud ad nos usque deferre, ut possimus audire et facere quod praeceptum est?' Sed iuxta te est sermo valde in ore tuo et in corde tuo, ut facias illum" (30:11–14). Quam notionem quasi vocis celebris imagine refert sententia sancti philosophi et theologi Augustini: "Noli foras ire, in te ipsum redi. In interiore homine habitat veritas".[21]

His praelucentibus deliberationibus prima iam imponitur conclusio: quam nobis Revelatio cognoscere permittit veritas non fructus est maturus neque summus alicuius cogitationis apex ratione humana enucleatae. Illa contra cum proprietatibus se exhibet gratuiti muneris, gignit notiones poscitque ut amoris tamquam declaratio suscipiatur. Haec veritas revelata locus iam anticipatus in hominum historia est illius postremae ac decretoriae Dei visionis, quae iis destinatur quotquot credunt eumque animo conquirunt sincero. Ultimus propterea singulorum hominum vitae finis tum philosophiae studium exstat tum etiam theologiae. Utraque, licet instrumentis diversis ac doctrinis, hanc "viam vitae" (cfr *Ps* 16 [15]:11) respicit quae, perinde ac praecipit nobis fides, novissimum repperit suum egressum plena in laetitia ac perpetua ex Dei Unius ac Trini contemplatione.

---

[21] *De vera religione*, XXXIX, 72: *CCL* 32, 234.

15. The truth of the Christian Revelation, which is met through Jesus of Nazareth, allows man to understand the mystery of his own life. Although this truth respects the autonomy of the creature and its freedom, at the same time it constrains him to open himself to his own self–transcendence. This union of freedom and truth is of supreme importance and finds expression in the words of the Lord: 'You will know the truth and the truth will set you free' (*Jn* 8:32).

The Christian Revelation is like a guiding star to man as he makes his way through the conditions of an immanentist mind-set and the narrow straits of a technocratic-logical approach. It is the ultimate capacity afforded by God for the recovery of the initial plan of love, ushered in by creation itself. To man in his desire to discover the truth, if he is able to look beyond himself and direct his gaze outside his own individual concerns, there is offered the possibility of restoring a full harmony with his own life, if only he will follow the way of truth. This situation is well exemplified by the words of Deuteronomy: 'This command I give you today is neither above you nor far from you, nor is its home in heaven, so that you can say: "who can ascend to heaven to bring it to us, that we may hear it and fulfil it?" Nor does it dwell beyond the seas, for you to say; "Who will cross the sea for us and bring it to us, that we may be able to hear and do what is commanded?" But the word is very near you, it is in your mouth and in your heart for you to do it' (*Deut* 30:11–14). This idea is echoed by the saying of the great philosopher and saint, Augustine: 'Do not go abroad, return into yourself. Truth dwells in the inner man'.[21]

These initial discussions yield the following conclusion. The truth Revelation allows us to know is neither the mature fruit nor the highest reach of the reflections of human reflection. On the contrary it is the expression, together with its particular characteristics, of a totally free gift; it stirs up and disturbs ideas and requires that it be accepted as a declaration of love. This revealed truth is already the anticipation in human history of the final, decisive vision of God, destined for those who believe and search for him with a sincere spirit. The ultimate purpose of the life of each person, therefore, is evident from the study of philosophy and theology. Despite their use of differing methods and ideas, both of these are concerned with the 'path of life' (cf. *Ps* 16 [15]:11), which as faith itself also tells us, at the end rediscovers its source in joyful and perpetual contemplation of the One and Triune God.

---

[21] St Augustine, *Of True Religion*, trans. J. H. S. Burleigh, (Illinois: Regnery, 1959), Book XXXIX, §72.

CAPUT II
CREDO UT INTELLEGAM

Sapientia scit omnia et intellegit (cfr *Sap* 9:11)

16. Quam sit inter fidei cognitionem ac scientiam rationis alta iunctura iam Sacris in Litteris significatur mirabilibus quibusdam perspicuitatis affirmationibus. Hoc comprobant *Libri Sapientiales* potissimum. Hoc quidem ferit oculos in hac lectione sine praeiudicatis opinationibus facta harum Scripturae paginarum, quod his in locis non sola Israelis concluditur fides, verum etiam thesaurus societatum et culturarum interea exstinctarum. Veluti ex peculiari quodam consilio Aegyptus et Mesopotamia faciunt ut sua iterum audiatur vox ac communes quaedam proprietates culturarum antiqui Orientis in his paginis revocentur ad vitam, quae nempe conceptionibus insigniter altis abundant.

Non fortuito fit ut, cum hominem describere sapientem vult auctor sacer, eum depingat ut diligentem quaerentemque veritatem: "Beatus vir, qui in sapientia morabitur et qui in iustitia sua meditabitur et in sensu cogitabit circumspectionem Dei; qui excogitat vias illius in corde suo et in absconditis suis intellegens, vadens post illam quasi investigator et in viis illius consistens; qui respicit per fenestras illius et in ianuis illius audiens; qui requiescit iuxta domum illius et in parietibus illius figens palum, statuet casulam suam ad manus illius et requiescet in deversorio bonorum per aevum. Statuet filios suos sub tegmine illius et sub ramis eius morabitur; protegetur sub tegmine illius a fervore et in gloria eius requiescet" (*Eccli* 14:22–27).

Uti patet, scriptori inspirato praebetur cognoscendi cupiditas tamquam proprietas simul omnium hominum communis. Propter intellectum cunctis, tum credentibus tum etiam non credentibus, facultas tribuitur "aquam profundam" cognitionis exhauriendi (cfr *Prv* 20:5). Procul dubio, apud antiquum Israelem orbis eiusque ostenta cognoscebantur non abstracta a rebus cogitatione, quemadmodum philosopho accidebat Ionico vel sapienti Aegyptio; tanto minus comprehendebat bonus tunc Israelita cognitionem humanam iis ipsis modis qui recentioris proprii sunt aetatis, cum magis ad scientiae partitionem tenditur. Nihilo tamen minus in latissimam provinciam totius cognoscendi rationis fecit orbis biblicus ut peculiares suae confluerent partes.

CHAPTER II
I BELIEVE THAT I MAY UNDERSTAND

Wisdom knows all and understands all (cf. *Wis* 9:11)

16. Already in Sacred Scripture the profound meeting between the knowledge of faith and the science of reason is intimated in certain wonderful affirmations of great clarity. The *Wisdom Books* are particularly clear on this point. What strikes the eyes in the reading of the pages of Scripture, if they are read without prejudicial opinion, is that they here embody not only the faith of Israel, but also the treasury of cultures and civilizations which have since vanished. As if by special design, Egypt and Mesopotamia make their voices heard once more, and certain features common to the cultures of the ancient Near East are called back into life in pages which abound in remarkably profound insights.

It is by no accident that when the sacred author wishes to describe a wise man, he should depict him as one who loves and searches for truth: 'happy is the man who meditates on wisdom and who reasons intelligently. He who reflects in his mind on her ways will also ponder her secrets. Pursue wisdom like a hunter and lie in wait on her paths. He who peers through her windows will also listen at her doors; he who encamps near her house will also fasten his tent peg to her walls; he will pitch his tent near her, and will lodge in an excellent lodging place; he will place his children under her shelter and will camp under her boughs; he will be sheltered by her from the heat and will dwell in the midst of her glory' (*Sir* 14:20–27).

As is clear to the inspired writer, the desire for knowledge is a characteristic common to all men and women. By means of intellect, everyone, believer as much as non-believer, is granted the capacity to plumb 'the deep waters' of knowledge (cf. *Prov* 20:5). Doubtless, unlike the Ionian philosopher and the sage of Egypt, ancient Israel did not arrive at its conclusions about the world on the basis of abstract thought; still less did the good Israelite of those days suppose that knowledge could be acquired in ways which are proper to our more recent time, a time which tends more often to the compartmentalization of knowledge. Even so the world of the Bible made its own peculiar contribution to the vast area of understanding the universe.

Quales denique? Proprietas ea, qua textus biblicus signatur, in eo consistit quod persuadetur altam et continuam exsistere coniunctionem inter rationis cognitionem atque fidei. Mundus eaque omnia quae in illo contingunt, perinde ac historia variique populi eventus, res quidem sunt respiciendae explorandae et iudicandae propriis rationis instrumentis, fide tamen ab hoc processu haudquaquam subtracta. Ipsa non ideo intercedit ut autonomiam rationis deiciat aut eius actionis regionem deminuat, sed tantummodo ut homini explicet his in eventibus visibilem fieri agereque Deum Israelis. Fieri itaque non potest ut funditus mundus percipiatur eventaque historiae, nisi simul fides in Deum proferatur qui in illis operatur.

Acuit interiorem intuitum fides dum mentem ipsam recludit ad operantem detegendam Providentiae praesentiam in progredientibus eventis. Libri Proverbiorum enuntiatio multum hac in re significat: "Cor hominis disponit viam suam, sed Domini est dirigere gressus eius" (16:9). Quod est: homo rationis lumine collustratus suam novit repperire viam, eam vero percurrere facile valet expediteque sine obicibus usque ad extremum, si recto animo inquisitionem suam in fidei inseruerit prospectum. Quam ob rem segregari ratio ac fides non possunt quin simul homini ipsa facultas deficiat mundum Deumque et seipsum congruo modo cognoscendi.

17. Nihil igitur causae est cur inter se ratio ac fides aemulentur: in altera enim altera invenitur et proprium utraque habet spatium sui explicandi. Proverbiorum rursus liber in hanc nos dirigit partem cum exclamat: "Gloria Dei est celare verbum, est gloria regum investigare sermonem" (25:2). Collocantur suo quisque in orbe Deus et homo quasi unica in necessitudine. Omnium rerum origo reponitur in Deo in Eoque mysterii colligitur plenitudo: quod ipsius efficit gloriam; ad hominem officium pertinet veritatem sua ratione pervestigandi, quod eius profecto constituit nobilitatem. Alia hoc ad musivum opus additur tessella a Psalmista cum precatur "mihi autem nimis pretiosae cogitationes tuae, Deus; nimis gravis summa earum. Si denumerabo eas, super arenam multiplicabuntur; si ad finem pervenerim, adhuc sum tecum (139[138]:17–18). Cognoscendi cupiditas ita magna est secumque talem infert dynamicam vim ut hominis animus, licet terminum experiatur quem praetergredi par non est, ad infinitam tamen adspiret ubertatem quae ultra iacet, quoniam in ea iam percipit responsionem custodiri consentaneam cuilibet quaestioni cui adhuc non est responsum.

What then were these contributions? Its principal characteristic, which dominates the Bible, is its conviction of the existence of a deep and perpetual connection between the knowledge offered by faith and reason. The world and all that is in it, history and the differing fortunes of peoples are indeed realities that demand the attention, examination and judgment with the aid of the instruments, without at the same time removing faith from this process. Faith does not interpose itself in order to destroy the autonomy of reason or to reduce the area of its activity, but solely to make plain to us that in these events God became manifest to the Israelites and acted among them. Hence it follows that the world itself and the events of history cannot be profoundly grasped unless faith is professed in the God who is at work in them.

Faith sharpens the inner senses, while it opens up the mind to detect the active presence of providence in the passing of events. The affirmation of the Book of Proverbs has a deep meaning in this matter: 'the human heart plans the way, but the Lord directs the steps' (*Prov* 16:9). That is to say that by the light of reason a man may discover his way, but only if he relates his understanding to the outlook provided by faith will he be able with ease and unhindered by obstacles to complete his course. It follows that faith and reason cannot be separated, without at the same time destroying the human capacity for gaining an appropriate knowledge of the world, God and itself.

17. There is no reason, therefore, for any rivalry between faith and reason. Each is to be found in the other; each has its own sphere of operation. Once again the Book of Proverbs points in the same direction, when it cries out: 'it is the glory of God to hide a word; the glory of kings, to understand and to search things out' (*Prov* 25:2). Though each belongs to its own sphere, God and man belong together in a common bond. The origin of all things is in God and in him the fullness of the mystery is gathered together, and this belongs to his glory; upon man lies the duty of searching out the truth with the aid of our own reason, and this assuredly constitutes our nobility. The psalmist adds a further piece to the mosaic, when he prays: 'your thoughts are too precious for me, O God, the sum of them is too heavy. Should I number them, they are more than the grains of sand on the sea shore; if I come to the end, you are still there with me' (cf. *Ps* 139[138]:17–18). The desire to know is so great and so dynamic that the spirit of a man, although aware of its own limits, even so aspires to an infinite richness that lies beyond, because he already perceives that there is indeed an appropriate reply to questions which as yet are without answers.

18. Quocirca adfirmari licet sua meditatione scivisse Israelem suae rationi viam ad mysterium pandere. In Dei Revelatione potuit altitudinem pertemptare, quousque ratione sua pertingere studebat non autem eo perveniens. Ex hac altiore cognitionis forma profectus, intellexit populus ille electus rationem quasdam observare oportere regulas praecipuas in quibus propriam naturam melius declararet. Prima in eo consistit regula ut ratio habeatur huius veritatis: in itinere constitutum esse hominem quod interrumpi non possit; secunda, ex conscientia nascitur neminem hanc in viam introire superbo animo eius qui omnia propriarum virium effecta esse arbitretur; consistit tertia in "timore Dei", cuius supremam agnoscere debet ratio transcendentiam simulque providum in gubernandis rebus amorem.

Quotiens ab hisce receditur regulis, periculo obicitur homo ne deficiat deveniatque in "stulti condicionem". Ad Bibliae sententiam huic stultitiae inest minatio vitae. Se enim decipit stultus plura cognoscere, verum non potest reapse animum in res necessarias intendere. Hoc etiam eum impedit quominus suam recte ordinet mentem (cfr *Prv* 1:7) rectumque affectum sumat de se deque rebus circumsistentibus. Cum adseverat deinde "non est Deus" (cfr *Ps* 14[13]:1) clarissime in posterum demonstrat quatenus sua cognitio desit et quam procul ipse a veritate rerum plena absit de rebus, de earum origine atque sorte.

19. Magni momenti loci qui plus hoc super argumentum lucis effundunt in libro Sapientiae inveniuntur. Inibi loquitur sacer auctor de Deo qui per ipsam rerum naturam sese demonstrat. Penes antiquos naturalium scientiarum studium maxima ex parte cum philosophica cognitione consonabat. Postquam asseveravit sacer textus hominem sui intellectus virtute scire posse "dispositionem orbis terrarum et virtutes elementorum, [. . .] anni cursus et stellarum dispositiones, naturas animalium et iras bestiarum" (*Sap* 7:17, 19–20), paucis verbis, philosophari eum valere, ulterius gressum facit et quidem praecipuum: repetens philosophiae Graecae notionem, ad quam hoc loco res referri videtur, affirmat auctor hominem omnino super natura ratiocinantem posse ad Deum ascendere: "A magnitudine enim et pulchritudine creaturarum cognoscibiliter potest Creator horum videri" (*Sap* 13:5). Primum ideo agnoscitur divinae Revelationis stadium quod mirabilis constituit "liber naturae", quo perlegendo homo rationis suae instrumentis ad Creatoris pertingere potest cognitionem. Si porro intellectu suo non eo usque advenit homo ut Deum omnium Conditorem cognoscat, hoc non tam deficienti instrumento est tribuendum,

18. Hence we may assert that Israel as a result of its own meditation realized that a way lay open to the mystery. By the Revelation of God Israel was enabled to arrive at the depths of all she sought to attain, but never could by the help of reason alone. On the basis of this deeper form of knowledge, the Chosen People understood the reason for observing certain rules, especially those in the keeping of which the people's proper nature would be better revealed. The first rule is that due attention must be paid to truth; man is set upon a journey which may not be interrupted; the second arises from the consciousness that no one enters upon this way with the pride of one who supposes that everything is achieved by his own power; the third consists in the 'fear of God', whose supreme transcendence reason ought to acknowledge, together with his provident love, in the governing of the world.

As often as these rules are laid aside, man runs the risk of failure and of ending up in the 'condition of the fool'. In the judgment of the Bible, in this foolishness there lies a threat to life. The fool thinks that he knows many things, but really he is incapable of directing his spirit toward the things that truly matter. Therefore he can neither rightly order his own mind (*Prov* 1:7) nor assume a right attitude about himself or the things around him. And so when he claims that 'there is no God' (cf. *Ps* 14:1), he shows with absolute clarity just in how much is his knowledge lacking and how far he is from the full truth of things, from their origin and their destiny.

19. Texts of great importance occur in the Book of Wisdom, which shed more light upon this argument. In that book the sacred author speaks of God who proves himself through the very nature of things. Among the ancients the study of natural sciences was not divorced from philosophical knowledge. After the insistence of the sacred text that man could, by the power of his intellect, know 'the structure of the world and the activity of the elements . . . the cycles of the year and the constellations of the stars, the natures of animals and the tempers of wild beasts' (*Wis* 7:17, 19–20), in a word that he can philosophize – the sacred text then takes a very significant step forward. The author repeats the Greek understanding of philosophy, to which here the text seems to refer, and insists that man in his deliberating over nature is able to rise to God: 'from the greatness and beauty of created things, their Creator may be perceived' (*Wis* 13:5). The first stage, therefore, of divine Revelation is constituted by the marvellous 'book of nature', the perusal of which by the exercise of his own reason a man may attain to the knowledge of his Creator. If a man should by his intellect fail to recognize God as the Creator of all things, it is not due to the lack of means to do so, but rather

quantum potius impedimento libera ipsius voluntate ac peccatis propriis interiecto.

20. Hoc sub prospectu bene aestimatur ratio, sed nimium non existimatur. Quidquid assequitur illa verum esse potest, at plenam suam consequitur significationem tum solum cum notiones ampliorem in rerum prospectum proiciuntur, nempe ipsius fidei: "A Domino diriguntur gressus viri; quis autem hominum intellegere potest viam suam?" (*Prv* 20:24). Apud Vetus itaque Testamentum rationem fides liberat quatenus ei congruenter attingere permittit proprium cognitionis obiectum idque in supremo reponere ordine ubi omnia suum habent sensum. Brevi: veritatem ratione consequitur homo, quoniam fide collustratus altum rerum omnium detegit sensum ac nominatim suae exsistentiae. Iure igitur ac merito auctor sacer verae cognitionis initium plane collocat in Dei timore: "Timor Domini principium scientiae" (*Prv* 1:7; cfr *Eccli* 1:14).

*Posside sapientiam, posside prudentiam (*Prv 4:5*)*

21. Non conditur, pro Veteris Testamenti hominibus, cognitio in observatione dumtaxat hominis et orbis et historiae, verum insolubilem poscit etiam coniunctionem cum fide cumque Revelationis doctrinis. Hic inveniuntur illae provocationes quibus occurrere populus electus debuit reddereque responsum. Hanc suam perpendens condicionem homo biblicus perspexit se intellegere non posse nisi "coniunctum" secum et cum populo, cum reliquo orbe ac cum Deo ipso. Haec ad mysterium patefactio, quae ex Revelatione ipsi contingebat, tandem fons illi verae cognitionis exstitit quae permisit rationi eius ut se in infinita spatia propelleret et sic comprehendere posset modis antehac omnino insperatis.

Non deerat inquisitionis impetus, pro auctore sacro, ab illo labore qui oriebatur ex conflictione cum rationis humanae limitibus. Animadvertitur illud, verbi gratia, iis in vocibus quibus Proverbiorum liber fatigationem enarrat qua quis intellegere arcana Dei consilia conatur (cfr 30:1–6). Verumtamen, quantumvis opus fatiget, credens manus non dat. Virtus illa, qua iter suum ad veritatem persequi potest, ei ex certa persuasione obtingit: Deum ipsum veluti "exploratorem" (cfr *Eccle* 1:13) creavisse eiusque munus esse nihil intemptatum relinquere, licet dubia perpetuo ei minitentur. Deo innixus, protenditur semper et ubique ille adversus ea omnia quae pulchra sunt, bona et vera.

because of the impediment placed in his way by his free will and sinfulness.

20. Seen from this point of view reason is to be highly valued, but not over much. Whatever it asserts can be true, but it only arrives at its full meaning once its basic ideas are seen in a wider perspective, namely that of faith itself: 'the steps of a man are directed by the Lord, but what man can understand his way?' (*Prov* 20:24). In the Old Testament, therefore, faith liberates reason both inasmuch as it enables it to attain its proper object of knowledge and because it is in the supreme realm, where all things have meaning. Briefly, then, man pursues truth by reason, since once he is enlightened by faith he uncovers the deep sense of everything and particularly of his own existence. With justice, therefore, and quite rightly, the sacred author identifies the fear of God as the beginning of true knowledge: 'the fear of the Lord is the beginning of wisdom' (*Prov* 1:7; cf. *Sir* 1:14).

Gain wisdom, gain prudence (Prov 4:5)

21. For those of the Old Testament, knowledge was not based solely on observation of man, the world and history. It demanded also an indissoluble connection with faith and with the doctrines of Revelation. Here are those challenges discovered which the Chosen People had to meet and give answer to. Pondering this as his situation, biblical man realized he could not understand himself except as 'a being in relation' – to himself, his own people, the rest of the world and God himself. This openness to mystery, which belongs to him as a consequence of Revelation itself, becomes in him a source of true knowledge and permits his reason to project itself into infinite spans and so to grow in understanding in ways he could not previously have hoped for.

As far as the sacred author was concerned, there was no lack of the impetus to enquiry, nor was it without that strain which arises from the struggle with the limits of reason. This is alluded to, for example, in those expressions in which the Book of Proverbs speaks of the weariness with which a man tries to understand the secret counsels of God (cf. *Prov* 30:1–6). Even so, however exhausting the work may be, the believer does not give up. The very virtue which enables him to pursue his journey to truth, belongs to him like a sort of conviction – that God himself created the believer to be an 'explorer' (cf. *Sir* 1:13) whose business it is to leave nothing unattempted, despite the continuous presence of doubts. The believer relies upon God and is ever stretching out towards whatever is lovely, true and good.

22. Primo in epistulae ad Romanos capite adiuvat nos sanctus Paulus quo melius percipiamus quam sit acuta Librorum Sapientialium deliberatio. Populari sermone argumentationem quandam philosophicam enodans Apostolus altam testificatur veritatem: per creata possunt "oculi mentis" ad Deum cognoscendum advenire. Nam ipse per creaturas facit ut ratio humana "virtutem" suam ac "divinitatem" intueatur (cfr *Rom* 1:20). Hominis rationi ergo illa adsignatur facultas quae excedere videtur ipsos eius naturae limites: non tantum intra sensuum cognitionem non circumscribitur, quoniam de iis critico iudicio meditari valet, sed de sensuum notitiis ratiocinando causam etiam tangere potest quae omnium rerum sensibilium subiacet origini. Philosophicis vocibus dici licet in pergravi loco illo Paulino potestatem hominis metaphysicam adfirmari.

In prisco creationis proposito, iudicante Apostolo, rationis humanae praevisa erat facultas facile sensuum cognitiones excedendi ut ipsa omnium origo reperiretur: Creator. Propter inoboedientiam, qua maluit homo plena et absoluta libertate sese illi opponere qui eum condiderat, defecit haec potestas ad conditorem Deum revertendi.

Figuris vivis describit Liber Genesis hanc hominis condicionem, narrans Deum eum collocavisse in hortis Eden quibus in mediis situm erat lignum "scientiae boni et mali" (cfr 2:17). Luculenta est figura: non valebat homo pervidere ex seque statuere quid bonum esset quidve malum, at superius quoddam ad principium se referre debebat. Superbiae caecitas protoparentes nostros ita fefellit ut se supremos esse crederent suique plane iuris et posse idcirco excludere cognitionem a Deo profectam. Sua prima inoboeditione viros mulieresque omnes illi implicaverunt atque rationi humanae vulnera intulerunt quae progressionem illius ad plenam veritatem erant impeditura. Facultas humana veritatis cognoscendae iam obscurata erat repudiatione Eius qui fons est veritatis atque origo. Iterum Apostolus aperit quantopere cogitationes hominum, propter peccatum, "vanae" factae sint ipsaeque eorum ratiocinationes detortae ad falsumque ordinatae (cfr *Rom* 1:21–22). Mentis oculi iam non poterant perspicue videre: paulatim facta est ratio humana sui ipsius captiva. Christi dein adventus salutis eventus fuit quo sua ex infirmitate erepta est ratio atque impedimentis liberata quibus ipsa sese omnino incluserat.

23. Postulat idcirco Christiani habitudo ad philosophiam fundamentale quoddam iudicium. In Novo Testamento, potissimum in sancti Pauli

22. In the first chapter of the Letter to the Romans, St Paul aids us to a better appreciation of the acuteness of the sapiential books. Making plain a philosophical argument in popular language, the Apostle witnesses to a profound truth: through created things 'the eyes of the mind' can arrive at the knowledge of God. For through created things, God directs human reason to discover 'power' and 'divinity' (cf. *Rom* 1:20). Human reason, therefore, is accorded the capacity which appears to exceed the limits of nature: not only is it not circumscribed by sensory knowledge, upon which it is able to pass critical judgment, but by arguing from sense data it is able to arrive at the cause which underlies the origin of all objects of the senses. In philosophical terms, it can justifiably be said that in this important Pauline text the metaphysical capacity of humanity is affirmed.

According to the judgment of the Apostle, in the primordial plan of creation the capacity of human reason had been designed to reach easily beyond sensory knowledge so that the origin of all things may be found: the Creator. Because of that disobedience, by which man preferred in its full and absolute freedom to oppose the one who had created him, this power of return to God the Creator was undone.

This is the human condition described in vivid terms by the Book of Genesis, when it tells us that God placed man in the garden of Eden, in the middle of which there stood 'the tree of knowledge of good and evil' (cf. *Gen* 2:17). The meaning shines out: man was in no position to discern and establish by his own resources what was good and what was evil, but must always relate himself to some higher principle. The blindness of pride so deceived our first parents that they believed themselves to be supreme and in control, and therefore thought they had a right to shut out the knowledge which clearly comes from God. This first disobedience implicated every man and woman and resulted in a wounding of human reason which became an impediment to progress toward the full truth. The human capacity of knowing the truth was obscured by the repudiation of him who is the source and origin of truth. Again the Apostle opens up for us how far the thoughts of man, because of sin, are made 'vain', and their very process of reasoning distorted and inclined to falsehood (cf. *Rom* 1:21–22). The eyes of the mind were no longer able to see clearly: reason became more and more a prisoner to itself. The coming of Christ was the saving event that liberated reason from its infirmity, setting it free from the shackles by which it had completely imprisoned itself.

23. The attitude, therefore, that a Christian adopts towards philosophy

epistulis, illud manifestum elucet: "huius mundi sapientia" sapientiae a Deo in Christo Iesu patefactae opponitur. Revelatae sapientiae altitudo consuetos nostros deliberationum terminos perrumpit, utpote qui consentaneo modo eam exprimere nequeant.

Funditus hanc difficultatem imponit initium Primae Epistulae ad Corinthios. Crucifixus Dei Filius ipse historicus est eventus ad quem eliditur omnis mentis conatus exstruendi defensionem de exsistentiae sensu congruam ex humanis dumtaxat ratiocinationibus. Verus enim nodus, quo omnis philosophia lacessitur, est Iesu Christi mors in cruce. Hic namque omne conamen redigendi Patris salutiferum consilium in humanam logicam puram ad interitum destinatur. "Ubi sapiens? ubi scriba? ubi conquisitor huius saeculi? Nonne stultam fecit Deus sapientiam huius mundi?", instanter percontatur Apostolus (*1 Cor* 1:20). Ad haec quae efficere cogitat Deus non amplius sola hominis sufficit prudentis sapientia, verum gressus decretorius quidam efflagitatur ad rem prorsus complectendam novam: "Quae stulta sunt mundi, elegit Deus, ut confundat sapientes [. . .] ignobilia mundi et contemptibilia elegit Deus, quae non sunt, ut ea quae sunt, destrueret" (*1 Cor* 1:27–28). Renuit hominis sapientia contueri sua in infirmitate fundamentum suae fortitudinis; at sanctus Paulus affirmare non haesitat: "Cum enim infirmor, tunc potens sum" (2 *Cor* 12:10). Non valet percipere homo quo pacto vitae fons amorisque mors esse possit, verumtamen ut sui salutis perficiendae consilii mysterium aperiret instituit Deus id quod humana ratio "stultitiam" et "scandalum" appellat. Sermone philosophorum suorum aequalium usus, sanctus Paulus attingit culmen magisterii sui atque illius paradoxi quod enuntiare cupit: "Elegit Deus, quae non sunt ut ea, quae sunt, destrueret" (*1 Cor* 1:28). Amoris demonstrati in cruce Christi gratuitam indolem ut declaret, nihil quidem dubitat Apostolus sermonem multo efficaciorem adhibere quam philosophi usurpabant ipsi suis in disceptationibus de Deo. Vacuefacere non potest ratio humana mysterium amoris quod crux exhibet, cum ex contrario eadem crux praebere potest rationi humanae responsum extremum quod ea conquirit. Non sane verborum sapientiam sed Verbum Sapientiae Paulus recenset veluti veritatis regulam simulque salutis.

Crucis sapientia igitur omnem culturae limitem transgreditur quem ei aliunde imponere nitantur atque imperat ut quisque se aperiat universali veritatis naturae quam in se ipsa gerit. Qualis rationi nostrae obicitur provocatio, qualemve inde percipit utilitatem si se dederit! Philosophia,

demands a fundamental judgment. This is particularly clear in the New Testament, above all in the letters of St Paul: 'The wisdom of this world' is contrasted with the wisdom revealed by God in Christ Jesus. The depth of revealed wisdom breaks through the accustomed limits of our normal thoughts, which are incapable of giving adequate expression to them.

The opening of the First Letter to the Corinthians gives clear expression to this difficulty. The crucified Son of God is the historic event, upon which every effort of the human mind to offer a coherent explanation of human existence based upon human rationality alone is bound to flounder. The central test upon which all philosophy is wrecked is the death of Jesus Christ upon the cross. Here above all every attempt to reduce the saving counsel of God to purely human logic is destined to total failure. So the Apostle urgently insists, 'Where is the wise man, where is the scribe, where is the disputer of this age? Has not God made foolish the wisdom of this age?' (*1 Cor* 1:20). The unaided wisdom of the prudent is incapable by itself of grasping the designs of God. What is demanded is a more decisive step toward embracing something absolutely new: 'God has chosen the foolish things of this world, in order to confound the wise . . . God has chosen the ignoble and contemptible things that are not, in order to destroy the things that are' (*1 Cor* 1:27–28). Human wisdom refused to see in its weakness the basis of its strength; yet St Paul has no hesitation in asserting: 'when I am weak, then I am strong' (2 *Cor* 12:10). Man cannot understand how death can be the fountain of life and love: even so God chose to use what human reason regards as 'foolishness' and a 'stumbling block' in order to make clear the mystery of his saving purpose. Using the language of the philosophers of his time, St Paul arrived at the very high point of his teaching and of that paradox which he was eager to declare: 'God has chosen the things that are not in order to destroy the things that are' (*1 Cor* 1:28). In order to display the total gratuity of the love of Christ displayed upon the cross, the Apostle has no hesitation in employing much more effective language than the philosophers used in their discussions about God. Human reason cannot empty of meaning the mystery of love revealed on the cross, since on the contrary the cross is able to supply reason with the ultimate answer it so earnestly seeks. St Paul sees in the Word of Wisdom and not in the wisdom of words the rule of truth and of salvation.

The wisdom of the cross, therefore, breaks through every boundary of culture which strives to contain and rule it so that each one may open himself to the universal nature which lies within truth. What a challenge this offers to our reason, or rather what advantage is gained by those who embrace it! Philosophy, which already acknowledges the everlasting

quae iam ex se agnoscere potest perpetuum hominis ascensum adversus veritatem, adiuvante fide potest se recludere ad recipiendum in "stultitia" Crucis criticum iudicium eorum qui falso arbitrantur se veritatem possidere, dum eam angustiis sui philosophici instituti involvunt. Inter fidem et philosophiam necessitudo in Christi crucifixi ac resuscitati praedicatione scopulum offendit ad quem naufragium facere potest, sed ultra quem patescere potest infinitum veritatis spatium. Hic liquido indicatur inter rationem ac fidem limes; at locus similiter clarus elucescit ubi ambae ipsae congredi possunt.

CAPUT III
INTELLEGO UT CREDAM

In via veritatem ad inquirendam

24. Lucas Evangelista in Actibus Apostolorum narrat Paulum, varia inter missionis itinera, Athenas pervenisse. Urbs illa, philosophorum sedes, simulacris affluebat, quae diversa idola ostentabant. In altare quoddam repente mentem intendit quare cito exordium sumpsit ad statuendum elementum commune unde nuntium kerigmaticum iniret: "Viri Athenienses, – ait – per omnia quasi superstitiosiores vos video; praeteriens enim et videns simulacra vestra inveni et aram, in qua scriptum erat: "Ignoto Deo". Quod ergo ignorantes colitis, hoc ego annuntio vobis" (*Act* 17:22–23).

Inde exorsus Paulus de Deo loquitur tamquam Creatore, de Eo nempe qui omnia superat et omnia vivificat. Sermonem dein ita prosequitur: "Fecitque ex uno omne genus hominum inhabitare super universam faciem terrae, definiens statuta tempora et terminos habitationis eorum, quaerere Deum si forte attrectent eum et inveniant, quamvis non longe sit ab unoquoque nostrum" (*Act* 17:26–27).

Apostolus in luce collocat veritatem quam Ecclesia uti thesaurum habere consuevit; in latebris cordis hominis flagrans Dei desiderium est seminatum. Quod vehementer recolit liturgia Feriae VI in Parasceve, cum, in precibus pro non credentibus, nos invitat ad orandum: "Omnipotens sempiterne Deus, qui cunctos homines condidisti, ut te semper desiderando quaererent et inveniendo quiescerent . . .".[22] Iter igitur quoddam exstat quod homo sua ex voluntate emetiri potest: quod

[22] "Ut te disiderando quaererent et inveniendo quiescerent": *Missale Romanum.*

ascent of man to truth, can, with the help of faith open itself up to receiving in the 'foolishness' of the cross a critical assessment of those who falsely suppose they possess the truth, despite the fact that they are imprisoned in their own narrow systems. The preaching of Christ crucified and risen is the reef upon which the reach between faith and philosophy can break up, but beyond which the infinite horizon of truth lies open. Here the difference between reason and faith can plainly be seen, but out there also shines the clear place where the two may come together.

CHAPTER III
I UNDERSTAND THAT I MAY BELIEVE

Seeking the truth on the way

24. In the Acts of the Apostles, Luke the Evangelist tells us that Paul, among his different missionary journeys, came to Athens. That city, the home of philosophers, was full of images which depicted various idols. All of a sudden his attention was directed to a particular altar which provided the impulse for establishing a common basis from which his preaching could begin: 'Athenians', he said, 'I see that in all things you are rather superstitious. As I passed along I saw your images and an altar, on which was written: 'to an unknown god'. What, therefore you worship as unknown, this I proclaim to you' (*Acts* 17:22–23).

With this beginning Paul then spoke of God as Creator, who is Lord of and bestows life on all things. This is how his speech continues: 'God made of one every nation of men to dwell on the face of the whole earth. He allotted times of their existence and places for them to dwell in, that they might search for God and might perhaps grope after him and find him, though indeed he is not far from any one of us' (*Acts* 17:26–27).

The Apostle clearly expresses a truth that the Church has always treasured, namely that in the deepest recesses of the human heart there has been sown a burning desire for God. The liturgy of Good Friday recalls this emphatically, when in the intercessions for non-believers it invites us to pray: 'Almighty, eternal God, you created mankind so that all might long to find you and have peace when you are found'.[22] There is a path, therefore, that every man and woman may freely embark

[22] Cf. *Roman Missal*, Intercessions for the Liturgy of Good Friday.

quidem initium sumit cum ratio facultate ditatur sese ultra res contingentes extollendi ut in infinitum peregrinetur.

Diversa ratione ac diversa quoque aetate homo penitum hoc desiderium exprimere scivit. Litterae, ars musica, pictura, sculptura, architectura aliique fructus eius fecundae mentis instrumenta facta sunt quibus significatur desiderium investigandi. Philosophia hunc motum peculiarem in modum in se collegit et, per sua instrumenta et secundum proprios usus scientificos, enuntiavit hoc universale hominis desiderium.

25. "Omnes homines scire volunt"[23] et huius desiderii obiectum veritas est. Ipsa vita cotidiana ostendit quantum studium inducat unumquemque nostrum ut, praeter ea quae tantum ex auditu percipiuntur, cognoscere valeat quomodo res vere se habeant. Homo solus est in universo visibili qui non solum facultate pollet sciendi, verum novit etiam se scire, atque hac de causa intendit animum authenticae veritati rerum quae illi obversantur. Nemo indifferens manere potest coram suae scientiae veritate. Si quid falsum homo invenit, eo ipso id respuit; si vero veritatem detegere potest, satiatum se sentit. Hanc doctrinam profitetur sanctus Augustinus scribens: "Multos expertus sum, qui vellent fallere, qui autem falli, neminem".[24] Persona merito dicitur adultam aetatem attigisse tantum cum, pro viribus, vera a falsis diiudicare potest, constituens ita proprium iudicium de authentica rerum veritate. In hoc consistit tot vestigationum causa, praesertim in ambitu scientiarum, quae novissimis saeculis tantos obtinuerunt exitus, ut authenticae progressioni totius humanae societatis faverent.

Non minus ponderis quam theoretica habet investigatio practica: dicimus veritatis investigationem ad bonum implendum intentam. Persona quidem, ethico more se gerens, si secundum liberum et rectum arbitrium operatur, viam beatitudinis ingreditur atque ad perfectionem intendit. Hoc quoque in casu agitur de veritate. Hanc sententiam confirmavimus in Litteris Encyclicis *Veritatis splendor*: ". . . sine libertate non datur moralitas . . . Si ius datur ut quisque observetur in itinere ad inquirendam veritatem, est tamen antea unicuique perquirendae veritatis gravis moralis obligatio eidemque cognitae adhaerescendi".[25]

---

23 Aristoteles, *Metaphysica*, I, 1.
24 *Confessiones*, X, 23, 33: *CCL* 27, 173.
25 §34: *AAS* 85 (1993), 1160–1161.

upon, a path which takes its point of departure from reason's capacity to rise beyond passing things and journey abroad into the infinite.

In various ways and at various times man has learnt how to express this desire. Literature, music, painting, sculpture, architecture and the other fruits of the creative mind have in their turn become the instruments by which the desire for enquiring has been expressed. Philosophy has in a special way made this movement its own and through its own tools and in a proper scientific fashion has given expression to this universal human desire.

25. 'All men want to know',[23] and the object of this desire is truth. Daily life shows us how seriously each one of us is able to discover the true nature of things, beyond the evidence of merely hearing. Man is alone in the visible universe as one who is not only capable of knowing, but also knows that he knows and in consequence directs his mind to the authentic truth of things that are objects of observation. No one can remain indifferent in the presence of the truth of this knowledge. If someone discovers anything false he at once rejects it; but should he discover the truth, he feels himself satisfied. St Augustine expresses this truth when he writes: 'I have come across many who want to deceive, but never across someone who wanted to be deceived'.[24] A person is deemed to have reached maturity only when, as far as she can, she is able to distinguish truth from falsehood and so able to set up her own judgment as the proper judge of the absolute truth of things. This has led to many researches, above all in scientific matters, which of recent years have met with such extraordinary success, as to be of advantage to the real progress of the whole of human society.

Practical enquiry is of no less importance than theoretical: we hold that the pursuit of truth is designed for the fulfilment of the good. A person who acts in a moral way, if she acts in accord with a free and upright judgment, enters upon the route of happiness and moves towards perfection. Here too, it is a matter of truth. We have affirmed this position in the encyclical *Veritatis splendor*: 'there is no morality without freedom. Although everyone has the right to be respected in his pursuit of the truth, there exists a prior, grave, moral obligation both of searching for the truth and of cleaving to it once it has been found'.[25]

---

[23] Aristotle, *Metaphysics*, I, 1, 980 a 22. *Πάντες ἄνθρωποι τοῦ εἰδέναι ὀρέγονται φύσει.*

[24] St Augustine, *Confessions*, trans. H. Chadwick (Oxford: Oxford University Press, 1992), Book X, Chapter 23, 33.

[25] *Veritatis splendor*, §34.

Valores igitur, selecti et propriis viribus comparati, veri sint oportet, quandoquidem dumtaxat valores veri perficere possunt personam eiusque naturam ad effectum deducere. Hanc valorum veritatem homo invenit non in se ipse se recludens sed sese aperiens ad eam accipiendam etiam in modis humanam naturam excedentibus. Haec necessaria est condicio ut quisquis ipse sit et adolescat uti adultam et sapientem decet personam.

26. Veritas ab exordiis instar interrogationis homini proponitur: *habetne vita sensum? quo illa cursum suum tendit?* Prima inspectione, exsistentia personalis ostendi posset sensu radicitus destituta. Necesse non est philosophos adire qui absurdum profitentur nec confugere ad provocatorias quaestiones quae inveniuntur in Libro Iob ut dubitetur de vitae sensu. Cotidiana doloris experientia, sive propria sive aliorum, nec non cognitio tot casuum qui sub lumine rationis inexplicabiles videntur, sufficiunt ut quaestio adeo dramatica de sensu vitae vitari nequeat.[26] Huc addendum est quod prima veritas absolute certa nostrae exsistentiae, praeter quam quod iam exsistimus, est inevitabilis mortis nostrae condicio. Hac obstupescenti re praehabita, exhaustum responsum quaeratur oportet. Unusquisque optat – immo tenetur – cognoscere veritatem de proprio fine. Scire vult utrum mors sit definitiva conclusio eius exsistentiae an sit aliquid quod mortem praetergrediatur; utrum liceat illi in vita ulteriore spem reponere necne. Non absque re mens philosophica cursum decretorium recepit inde ab obitu Socratis quo plusquam duo millennia sic est insignita. Nec casu fit ut philosophi, ob mortis eventum, hanc quaestionem simul cum quaestione de vita deque immortalitate iterum atque iterum sibi proponant.

27. Has interrogationes nemo fugere potest, nec philosophus nec homo plebeius. Ex responsis quae iisdem dantur suprema pendet investigationis pars: utrum fieri possit ut perveniatur necne ad veritatem universalem et absolutam. Ex se, quaevis veritas, etsi non integra, si est authentica, universalis exhibetur et absoluta. Quod verum est, pro omnibus et semper verum esse debet. Hanc praeter universalitatem, tamen, homo quaerit aliquid absolutum quod responsum ferre possit et sensum ad omnia quae vestigantur: ens quoddam supremum quod fundamentum exstet cuiusque rei. Ut aliis utamur verbis, homo quaerit definitivam dilucidationem, valorem quendam supremum, ultra quem nec sint nec esse possint interrogationes aut ulteriora addenda.

[26] Cfr Ioannes Paulus II, Litt. Ap. *Salvifici doloris* (11 Februarii 1984), §9: *AAS* 76 (1984), 209–210.

It is essential therefore, that the values chosen and pursued in one's own life should be true, especially seeing that true values can perfect a person and lead her nature to its true end. Man discovers these values not by locking himself up in himself, but rather by opening himself to receiving the truth in ways that exceed human nature. This is an essential condition for anyone to be himself and to grow up properly as an adult and wise person.

26. The truth comes initially to humanity as a question: *Does life have a meaning? To what does it lead in its course?* At first sight, personal existence may show itself to be radically meaningless. It is not necessary to turn to the philosophers of the absurd or to the provocative questions which emerge in the Book of Job in order to have doubts about the meaning of life. The daily experience of suffering – either one's own or that of others – and the array of facts which seem inexplicable in the light of reason are sufficient to ensure that a question as dramatic as the question of meaning cannot be evaded.[26] Here one needs to add that the first absolutely certain truth of our life, beyond the fact that we exist, is the situation of our inevitable death. Given this unsettling fact, a comprehensive answer to it needs to be sought. Each of has both the desire and the duty to know the truth of our own destiny. We want to know if death will be the definitive conclusion of our existence or if there is something which leads beyond death – if it is possible to hope for a life beyond or not. It is not insignificant that the death of Socrates gave the philosophical mind one of its decisive points of departure, no less decisive now than it was more than two thousand years ago. It is not by chance, then, that faced with the event of death, philosophers have again and again posed this question, together with the question of life and of immortality.

27. No one can avoid these questions, neither the philosopher nor the common man. The most central part of the investigation depends upon the answers given to them. Is it possible or not to arrive at universal and absolute truth? Every truth, even if it is not complete, provided it is authentic, possesses a universal and absolute character. What is true is so for everyone and always. Besides this universality, man searches for something absolute which can offer a reply and meaning to all that is being searched for: some supreme being that is the ground of all things. In other words, man seeks for a final explanation, a kind of supreme value, beyond which there can be no more questions and nothing further

[26] Cf. John Paul II, Apostolic Letter *Salvifici doloris* (11 February 1984) (London: Catholic Truth Society, 1984), §9.

Opiniones animos allicere possunt, non vero illis satisfacere. Momentum adventat pro omnibus, quo, sive admittitur sive non, necesse est ut propria exsistentia sustentetur veritate absoluta, quae certitudinem pariat nec amplius dubio subiciatur.

Similem veritatem, per saeculorum decursum, philosophi detegere et exprimere curarunt, quandam condendo doctrinam seu scholam philosophicam. Praeter doctrinas philosophicas, tamen, sunt aliae expressiones quibus homo intendit suam "philosophiam" constituere: agitur de suasionibus vel experientiis privatis, de familiae culturaeque traditionibus vel de viis exsistentiae propriis, in quibus quisque alicuius magistri auctoritati se committit. In singulis his indiciis semper flagrans permanet studium assequendi certitudinem veritatis eiusque absoluti valoris.

Diversae de homine veritatis facies

28. Veritatis investigatio non semper – quod nobis est agnoscendum! – simili ostenditur perspicuitate et congruentia. Naturalis limitatio rationis et animi iactatio investigationem cuiusque hominis obumbrant saepeque avertunt. Aliae personales diversae indolis utilitates obruere possunt veritatem. Fieri quoque potest ut homo vitet eam statim ut incipit illam cognoscere, quia eius postulationes metuit. Quo non obstante, etiam cum eam fugit, ipsa illius exsistentiam permovet. Numquam enim ille propriam vitam dubio, incertitudine vel mendacio fulcire posset; eiusmodi exsistentia metu et anxietate infestaretur. Homo igitur definiri potest *ille qui veritatem quaeritat.*

29. Cogitari nequit investigationem, tam radicitus in hominis natura confirmatam, prorsus inutilem et inanem evadere. Ipsa quaerendi veritatem facultas et interrogandi, ex se, primum iam constituit responsum. Homo quaerere non inciperet quod prorsus ignoraret aut impervium duceret. Tantummodo spes perveniendi ad quoddam responsum potest eum perducere ad primum ferendum gradum. Hoc quidem re accidit in scientifica pervestigatione: cum doctus vir, perspicientia eius quadam praehabita, cuiusdam phaenomeni explicationem logicam et probabilem quaerit, iam ab initio firmam nutrit spem responsum inveniendi, neque animo frangitur prae rebus male gestis. Inanem non considerat originalem intuitum tantummodo ex eo quod scopum non attigit; merito potius dicere poterit se aequum responsum nondum invenisse.

Idem dicendum est de perquisitione veritatis in novissimarum quaestionum contextu. Veritatis sitis ita cordi hominis est insita ut,

added. Opinions may fascinate the mind, but not satisfy it. A moment arrives for everyone, whether admitted or not, when his individual existence must be supported by absolute truth, which confers a certitude not subject to wider doubt.

With the passing of centuries it was such truth that philosophers have sought to unearth and express by establishing teachings or schools. Besides philosophical teachings there are other methods by which a man endeavours to express his own 'philosophy' – by personal convictions and private experiences, by the traditions of family and culture or in particular methods of existing, committing himself to the authority of a master. In each of these a burning desire remains to pursue certainty of truth and its absolute value.

The differing faces of the truth concerning humanity

28 The pursuit of truth – we know only too well – is not always conducted with the same clarity and coherence. The natural limits of reason and vanity of spirit may overshadow individual enquiries and not infrequently divert them. The various demands of our different personal characters can overthrow the truth. Yet, for all that they may evade it, the truth still influences life. Notwithstanding, even when fleeing from it, truth disturbs existence. Life in fact can never be grounded upon doubt, uncertainty or deceit; such an existence would be threatened constantly by fear and anxiety. Man may be defined, therefore, as *the one who seeks the truth*.

29. It cannot be supposed that this search, so deeply rooted in human nature, is useless and pointless. The very capacity to search for the truth and make enquiry about it has of itself created the initial response. Man would never embark on the search for anything he knew nothing about or which he supposed to be quite beyond his reach. Even the hope of arriving at some answer can set a man on the first stage of his journey. This is indeed what not infrequently happens in scientific enquiry. A learned man, with some sort of perception to help him, is on the look out for some logical and probable explanation and from the very beginning nourishes the hope of finding an answer. Nor is his spirit broken when things go wrong. He does not suppose his initial hunch was mistaken, simply on the grounds that he has not yet succeeded. More properly he will say that so far he has found no satisfactory answer.

The same is true of the search for truth in the context of the most immediate questions. The thirst for truth has been so firmly planted in

necessitas quaedam eam praetermittendi, propriam exsistentiam in discrimen adducat. Sufficit ut inquiratur in vitam cotidianam ut probetur quo modo demum unusquisque in seipso patiatur illam sollicitudinem quae fluit de quibusdam essentialibus quaesitis et simul quo modo in mente adumbrationem servet saltem illarum responsionum. Agitur de responsionibus, de quarum veritate conscii sumus, quoniam patet eas quoad substantiam non differre a responsionibus ad quas alii plures pervenerunt. Haud dubie quidem non quaelibet veritas quae acquiritur eodem fruitur pondere. Ex latis attamen exitibus simul sumptis confirmatur hominis facultas perveniendi, in universum, ad veritatem.

30. Nunc expedit ut hae diversae veritatum formae properato percurrantur. Numerosiores quidem sunt veritates quae immediata nituntur evidentia vel experimento confirmantur; hae veritates cotidianam vitam scientificamque pervestigationem respiciunt. Alio sub gradu inveniuntur veritates indolis philosophicae, quas homo per speculativam intellectus facultatem attingit. Sunt denique veritates religiosae, quarum fundamenta quodammodo etiam in philosophia ponuntur. Hae continentur in responsionibus, quas diversae religiones, suas secundum cuiusque traditiones, novissimis offerunt interrogationibus.[27]

Quod ad philosophicas attinet veritates, notandum est eas non circumscribi solis doctrinis, interdum evanidis, eorum qui philosophiam profitentur. Omnis homo, ut dictum est, quodam sub modo philosophus est et suas possidet philosophicas notiones, quibus vitam gubernat suam: aliter atque aliter universum quisque sibi efformat conspectum responsumque de propriae exsistentiae sensu: hoc sub lumine rem personalem interpretatur atque sese gerendi modum gubernat. Ibidem interrogandum est de habitudine quae inter veritates philosophico-religiosas intercedit et veritatem in Christo Iesu revelatam. Priusquam huic quaestioni respondeatur, ulterior philosophiae cognitio perpendatur oportet.

31. Homo creatus non est ut vitam degat solus. Ipse nascitur et crescit in familiae sinu, atque annorum decursu industria sua in societatem cooptatur. Itaque ab incunabulis variis inseritur traditionibus, ex quibus non tantum loquelam et culturae institutionem accipit, verum etiam plurimas veritates, quibus, quasi innata ratione, credit. Nihilominus adulescentia et personae maturatio efficiunt ut hae veritates in dubio

[27] Cfr Conc. Oecum. Vat. II, Declaratio de Ecclesiae habitudine ad religiones non-christianas *Nostra aetate*, §2.

the human heart that any demand to set it aside plunges existence itself into doubt. Everyday life shows well enough how each one of us is preoccupied by the presence of a few fundamental questions and how each of us has in mind at least some outline of the answers to them. One reason why the truth of these answers convinces is that they are no different in substance from the answers at which many others have arrived. Without doubt, not every truth which is acquired has the same weight. But the sum of the results achieved confirms that in general man has the faculty to arrive at the truth.

30. It may now help to turn briefly to different forms of truth. Most of them arise from immediate evidence or are confirmed by experiment; these are the truths which have to do with everyday life and scientific enquiry. At another level we find truths of a philosophical character, which man attains by means of the speculative faculty of the intellect. Finally, there are religious truths which to some degree find their foundation in philosophy. These are contained in the answers which diverse religions, according to their traditions, offer to the ultimate questions.[27]

With respect to philosophical truths, it should be said that these are not limited to the teachings, now perhaps obsolete, of professional philosophers. Every man, as has been said, is in some sense a philosopher and possesses philosophical conceptions by which he directs his life. In one way or other, he shapes a comprehensive vision and answer to the question of life's meaning; and in the light of this interprets and regulates his personal affairs and conduct. At this point, he has to pose the question of the link between, on the one hand, philosophico-religious truths and, on the other, the truth revealed in Jesus Christ. But before this question can be answered, a further area of enquiry of philosophy needs to be considered.

31. Man was not created for a solitary existence. He is born and grows up in the bosom of the family and with the passage of years in his efforts he becomes absorbed into society. This means that from the cradle he absorbs the various traditions from which he derives not only language and culture, but also many truths which, by a kind of inborn rationality, he trusts. Even so his youth and gradual maturity mean that these truths are rendered doubtful and tried out by the critical action of the mind. This does not prevent him from recovering these truths after this period

[27] Cf. Second Vatican Council, Declaration on the Relation of the Church to Non-Christian Religions *Nostra Aetate*, §2 in Flannery, (ed.), *Vatican Council II*, pp. 738 f.

collocentur et expurgentur per singularem criticam intellectus actionem. Quod non impedit quominus, post hunc transitum, hae eaedem veritates "recuperentur", sive per experientiam ex iisdem factam, sive per subsequentem ratiocinationem. Attamen, in vita hominis veritates simpliciter creditae numerosiores exstant quam illae quas ille obtinet per personalem recognitionem. Quisnam vero stricte cribrare potest innumeros scientiarum exitus, quibus hodierna nititur vita? Quis sua sponte inspicere potest cumulum notitiarum quas ex diversis orbis regionibus cotidie accepimus et quae, generaliter, uti verae habentur? Quis tandem potest iterum terere experientiae et cogitationis vias, per quas tot thesauri sapientiae et religiosi sensus humanae societatis sunt coacervati? Homo, ille nempe qui quaerit, est igitur etiam *ille qui vivit alteri fidens*.

32. Unusquisque, in credendo, fidem ponit in cognitionibus quas aliae personae sunt adeptae. Hac in re agnoscenda est quaedam significans intentio: una ex parte, cognitio ex fiducia videtur imperfecta cognitionis forma, quae paulatim per evidentiam singillatim comparatam perfici debet; alia ex parte, fiducia divitior saepe exstat quam simplex evidentia, quoniam secum fert necessitudinem interpersonalem atque in discrimen committit non tantum personales intellectus facultates, verum etiam penitiorem facultatem sese aliis personis confidendi, validiorem et intimiorem cum illis necessitudinem statuendo.

Expedit ut in luce ponatur veritates in hac interpersonali relatione adeptas ad rerum gestarum vel philosophiae ordinem non attinere. Quod potius petitur est ipsa personae veritas: nempe id quod ipsa est et quidquid intimae suae condicionis ostendit. Hominis enim perfectio non ponitur tantum in sola comparanda cognitione abstracta veritatis, verum stat etiam in vivificanti consuetudine deditionis et fidelitatis erga alterum. Hac in fidelitate, cuius vi homo se dedere novit, plenam invenit certitudinem et animi firmitatem. Eodem tamen tempore, cognitio per fiduciam, quae existimatione interpersonali nititur, non datur quin ad veritatem referatur: homo, credendo, veritati quam alter ostendit committitur.

Quot exempla proferri possunt ad illustranda quae diximus! Cogitatio autem Nostra statim vertitur ad martyrum testimonium. Martyr, enim, integerrimus testis est veritatis de exsistentia. Bene novit ille se invenisse, coram Christo Iesu, veritatem de sua vita, quam certitudinem nemo ab eo abstrahere potest. Nec dolor nec saeva mors eum seiungere poterunt a

of transition, either by means of the experience they provide or by subsequent reflection. Yet in human life truths that are simply believed are more numerous than those acquired by means of personal recognition. Who could, strictly speaking, assess the innumerable scientific discoveries which form the basis of modern life? Who could, alone, weigh the vast number of pieces of information which we receive daily from the different parts of the world and which are generally supposed to be true? Finally who is able once more to forge anew the paths of experience and thought by whose means so many treasures of wisdom and the religious sense of society have been heaped up? Man, the one who seeks, is therefore also the *one who lives trusting in others.*

32. Whenever we believe we place our confidence in the knowledge of other persons. There is a significant intention in admitting this: on the one hand knowledge derived from trust seems to be an imperfect form of knowledge. It depends on a gradual process of perfection by means of comparing evidence, yet on the other hand this trust seems richer than mere evidence. This is because it brings with it an interpersonal relationship and activates not only a person's intellectual capacities but also an even more profound capacity for trusting other persons and of establishing a stronger and more intimate relationship with them.

It is important to observe that the truths gained in this interpersonal relationship belong strictly neither to the empirical nor the philosophical realms. What is actually being looked for is the truth of the person: that is, what she is in herself, and what she displays of her own individual character. Human perfection does not solely consist in acquiring an abstract knowledge of the truth, rather it finds its place in a living habit of self-giving and fidelity towards others. In this very fidelity in which a man learns how to give himself, he discovers full certainty and firmness of spirit. But at the same time knowledge that comes through confidence and depends on interpersonal esteem is not given without reference to truth: a man, by believing, is committed to the truth which another has shown him.

How many examples can be produced to illustrate what we have said! Our reflection immediately turns to the witness of the martyrs. For a martyr is the surest witness of the truth concerning existence. He knows well before Christ Jesus that he has found the truth of his own life, a certainty of which no one can deprive him. Neither sorrow nor a savage death can separate him from the truth that he has discovered through his encounter with Christ. This is the reason why the witness of martyrs prompts our admiration even today, finds a hearing, and becomes an

veritate quam detegit cum obviam Christo occurrit. En ratio cur martyrum testimonium ad hodiernum diem admirationem moveat, auditionem inveniat et uti exemplum sumatur. Haec est causa cur eorum verbo confidatur: in illis invenitur evidentia illius amoris qui diuturnis colloquiis non indiget ad persuadendum, eo quod unicuique nostrum de eo quod penitus percepit uti verum et iam diu quaesitum loquitur. Martyr denique, altam in nobis excitat fiduciam, quoniam declarat quidquid nos percepimus et evidens reddit quod nos quoque aequa vi exprimere velimus.

33. Ita intellegere possumus diversas huius quaestionis partes paulatim perfici. Homo ex natura sua veritatem perscrutatur. Haec perscrutatio non tantum destinatur acquisitioni veritatum quarundem partium quae ex eventibus pendent vel scientiis; homo non quaerit tamtummodo verum bonum pro singulis suis consiliis. Eius perscrutatio in ulteriorem intenditur veritatem quae sensum vitae dilucidare possit; quapropter de illa agitur perscrutatione, quae exitum invenire potest tantum in absoluto.[28] Per facultates in mente insitas, homo similem veritatem et invenire et perspicere potest. Quatenus haec veritas vitalis est et essentialis ad eius exsistentiam, attingitur non tantum per viam rationis, sed etiam per fidentem relictionem in manibus eorum, qui certitudinem et authenticitatem eiusdem veritatis in tuto collocare possint. Facultas et selectio committendi semet ipsos propriamque vitam aliis constituunt sane, secundum anthropologiam, actum significantiorem et expressiorem inter plurimos.

---

[28] Haec est ratiocinatio cui iam dudum studemus quamque saepius exprimimus: "'Quid est homo, quis defectus, et quae est utilitas illius? Et quid est bonum, aut quid nequam illius?' (*Eccli* 18:7). [. . .] Queste domande sono nel cuore di ogni uomo, come ben dimostra il genio poetico di ogni tempo e di ogni popolo, che, quasi profezia dell'umanità, ripropone continuamente la *domanda seria* che rende l'uomo veramente tale. Esse esprimono l'urgenza di trovare un perché all'esistenza, ad ogni istante, alle sue tappe salienti e decisive così come ai suoi momenti più comuni. In tali questioni è testimoniata la ragionevolezza profonda dell'esistere umano, poiché l'intelligenza e la volontà dell'uomo vi sono sollecitate a cercare liberamente la soluzione capace di offrire un senso pieno alla vita. Questi interrogativi, pertanto, costituiscono l'espressione più alta della natura dell'uomo; di conseguenza la risposta ad esse misura la profondità del suo impegno con la propria esistenza. In particolare quando *il perché delle cose* viene indagato con integralità alla ricerca della risposta ultima e più esauriente, allora la ragione umana tocca il suo vertice e si apre alla religiosità. In effetti, la religiosità rappresenta l'espressione più elevata della persona umana, perché è il culmine della sua natura razionale. Essa sgorga dall'aspirazione profonda dell'uomo alla verità ed è alla base della ricerca libera e personale che egli compie del divino": Udienza Generale, 19 ottobre 1983, §§1–2: *Insegnamenti* VI, 2 (1983), 814–815.

example. This is the reason why we trust what he has to say: in him is found the evidence of that love which needs no lengthy arguments in order to be persuasive, and speaks to us of that which the martyr perceives to be true and speaks of what he has long sought. Finally a martyr stirs up within us a deep trust, declares what we already perceive and makes evident what we also would wish to express with equal force.

33. Thus, step by step, we can understand how the different aspects of this question can be gradually assembled. It is of the nature of man to pursue the truth. This search is not simply concerned with the discovery of specific truths which depend on events or on particular sciences; man is not interested in the true good solely in relation to his own individual interests. His enquiry is directed towards a higher truth which is capable of shedding light on the meaning of life: therefore we are dealing with the sort of search which culminates only in the absolute.[28] Through the capacities that exist in the mind, man is able to enter into and recognize such a truth. Because this truth is both vital and essential to human existence, it is attained not only by way of reason but also by placing trust in the hands of those who can give authenticity and certainty to the truth itself. There is no doubt that the capacity and willingness for committing oneself and one's life to another person, anthropologically speaking, are among the most significant and expressive of human acts.

---

[28] This is a deliberation which I have long pursued and which I have frequently addressed : ' "What is man, how is he flawed, and of what use is he? What is good in him and what is evil?" (*Sir* 18:8). . . . These are questions in every human heart, as the poetic genius of every time and every people has shown, posing again and again – almost as the prophetic voice of humanity – the *serious question* which makes human beings truly what they are. They are questions which express the urgency of finding a reason for existence, in every moment, at life's most important and decisive times as well as more ordinary times. These questions show the deep reasonableness of human existence, since they summon human intelligence and will to search freely for a solution which can reveal the full meaning of life. These enquiries, therefore, are the highest expression of human nature; which is why the answer to them is the gauge of the depth of man's engagement with his own existence. In particular, when *the why of things* is explored in full harmony with the search for the ultimate answer, then human reason reaches its zenith and opens to the religious impulse. The religious impulse is the highest expression of the human person, because it is the highpoint of his rational nature. It springs from the profound human aspiration for the truth and it is the basis of the human being's free and personal search for the divine.' General Audience (19 October 1983), §§1–2: *Insegnamenti*, VI, 2 (1983), pp. 814–15.

Meminisse liceat quoque rationem in sua perquisitione fidenti dialogo et authentica amicitia esse sustentandam. Suspicionis et diffidentiae aura, quae aliquando speculativam circumplectitur perquisitionem, facit ut in oblivionem detur doctrina priscorum philosophorum qui tenebant amicitiam esse inter contextus magis idoneos ad recte philosophandum.

Ex hucusque dictis colligitur hominem quodam in itinere versari perquisitionis, quae humano sensu finiri nequit: est perquisitio veritatis et cuiusdam personae cui se committere possit. Christiana fides obviam venit ut ei offerat concretam facultatem contemplandi huius inquisitionis impletionem. Postquam enim gradus simplicis fidei superatur, haec hominem inserit in ordinem gratiae ut Christi mysterium participare possit, cuius vi vera et cohaerens Dei Unius et Trini cognitio offertur illi. Ita in Christo Iesu, qui est ipsa Veritas, fides agnoscit novissimam vocationem quae vertitur ad humanam societatem, ut implere possit id quod percipit uti flagrans desiderium.

34. Haec veritas, quam Deus in Christo Iesu nobis revelat, minime opponitur veritatibus quae per philosophiam assumuntur. Immo, duo cognitionis gradus ducunt ad veritatis plenitudinem. Unitas veritatis est iam fundamentalis postulatus humanae rationis, qui principio non-contradictionis exprimitur. Revelatio offert certitudinem huius unitatis, ostendendo Deum Conditorem esse etiam Deum historiae salutis. Ipse idemque Deus, qui condit et vindicat facultatem intellegendi et ratiocinandi naturalem rerum ordinem, quo docti fidenter nituntur,[29] idem est qui revelatur Pater Domini nostri Iesu Christi. Haec unitas veritatis, naturalis et revelatae, viventem et personalem identitatem suam invenit in Christo, uti Apostolus memorat: “Veritas quae est in Iesu” (*Eph* 4:21; cfr *Col* 1:15–20). Ille est *Verbum aeternum*, in quo omnia

[29] “[Galilée] a declaré explicitement que les deux vérités, de foi et de science, ne peuvent jamais se contredire, ‘L’Ecriture sainte et la nature procédant également du Verbe divin, la première comme dictée par l’Esprit Saint, la seconde comme exécutrice très fidèle des ordres de Dieu’, comme il l’a écrit dans sa lettre au Père Benedetto Castelli le 21 décembre 1613. Le Concile Vatican II ne s’exprime pas autrement; il reprend même des expressions semblables lorsqu’il enseigne: ‘Ideo inquisitio methodica in omnibus disciplinis, si . . . iuxta normas morales procedit, numquam fidei revera adversabitur, quia res profanae et res fidei ab eodem Deo originem ducunt’ (*Gaudium et spes*, §36). Galilée ressent dans sa recherche scientifique la présence du Créateur qui le stimule, qui prévient et aide ses intuitions, en agissant au plus profond de son esprit”. Ioannes Paulus II, *Discorso alla Pontificia Accademia delle Scienze*, 10 Novembris 1979: *Insegnamenti*, II, 2 (1979), 1111–1112.

We should not fail to remember that reason should be sustained in its quest by trusting dialogue and sincere friendship. An atmosphere of suspicion and distrust which not infrequently surrounds speculative enquiries causes one to forget the teaching of the earliest philosophers, who held that friendship was among the more appropriate contexts for sound philosophizing.

From what has been said so far, it emerges that man is involved in a journey of discovery which is incapable of resolution by human means alone: it is at the same time the search for truth, and for someone to whom one may entrust oneself. Christian faith comes to our aid and provides us with the concrete capacity for realizing the fulfilment of this search. Once the step of simple faith is surmounted, this places us in the order of grace and enables us to share in the mystery of Christ, by whose strength a true and coherent knowledge of the Triune God is offered to us. Thus in Christ Jesus, who is himself the truth, faith recognizes the final appeal which is directed to human society, in order that it may come to fulfil what it experiences as its burning desire.

34. This truth, which God reveals to us in Christ Jesus is by no means opposed to the truths which are derived from philosophy. Instead both degrees of knowledge lead to the fullness of truth. The unity of truth is a basic postulate of human reason, which finds expression in the principle of non-contradiction. Revelation confirms the certainty of this unity by demonstrating that the Creator God is also the God of the history of salvation. The selfsame God who created and guarantees the faculty of understanding and reasoning about the natural order of things, upon which the learned depend,[29] is one with him who is revealed as the Father of our Lord Jesus Christ. This unity of truth, natural and revealed, finds its living and personal identity in Christ, as the Apostle reminds us: 'the truth which is in Jesus' (*Eph* 4:21; cf. *Col* 1:15–20). He is the *eternal Word*, in whom all things were created, and at the same time the

[29] '[Galileo] declared explicitly that the two truths, of faith and of science, can never contradict each other, "Sacred Scripture and the natural world proceeding equally from the divine Word, the first as dictated by the Holy Spirit, the second as a very faithful executor of the commands of God", as he wrote in his letter to Father Benedetto Castelli on 21 December 1613. The Second Vatican Council says the same thing, even adopting similar language in its teaching: "Methodical research, in all realms of knowledge, if it respects . . . moral norms, will never be genuinely opposed to faith: the reality of the world and of faith have their origin in the same God" (*Gaudium et spes*, §36). Galileo sensed in his scientific research the presence of the Creator who, stirring in the depths of his spirit, stimulated him, anticipating and assisting his intuitions.' John Paul II, *Address to the Pontifical Academy of Sciences* (10 November 1979): *Insegnamenti*, II, 2 (1979), pp. 1111–12.

creata sunt, simulque est *Verbum incarnatum*, qui in sua integra persona[30] revelat Patrem (cfr *Io* 1:14, 18). Quidquid humana ratio "ignorans" (cfr *Act* 17:23) perscrutatur, tantummodo per Christum inveniri potest: quod enim in Ipso revelatur est "plenitudo veritatis" (cfr *Io* 1:14–16) cuiusque creaturae quae in Ipso et per Ipsum creata est, et ita in Ipso constat (cfr *Col* 1:17).

35. In contextu huius summi prospectus, penitus inspiciatur oportet relatio inter veritatem revelatam et philosophiam. Haec relatio duplicem secumfert animadversionem, eo sensu quod veritas quae a Revelatione fluit, veritas est quae simul sub rationis lumine est intellegenda. Hoc duplici praehabito sensu, aequam necessitudinem revelatae veritatis cum cognitione philosophica definire licebit. Qua de re primum perpendamus relationes per saeculorum decursum habitas inter fidem et philosophiam. Hinc igitur quaedam detegi poterunt principia quae constituunt aspectus ad quos referendum est ut inter hos duos gradus cognitionis recta relatio suscipiatur.

CAPUT IV
DE HABITUDINE INTER FIDEM ET RATIONEM

Praecipui gressus in occursu fidei rationisque

36. Ut Actus Apostolorum testantur, nuntius christianus inde ab exordiis cum doctrinis philosophicis illius aetatis est collatus. Idem Liber narrat disceptationem quam Paulus Athenis habuit cum quibusdam philosophis Epicureis et Stoicis (17:18). Exegeticum examen illius sermonis ad Areopagum habiti in luce posuit usitatas mentiones de variis opinionibus populi praesertim ex origine Stoica. Hoc quidem non fortuito factum est. Primi Christiani, ut a paganis recte perciperentur, in suis sermonibus auditores dumtaxat "ad Moysen et prophetas" remittere non poterant; niti quoque tenebantur naturali Dei cognitione et voce conscientiae moralis cuiusque hominis (cfr *Rom* 1:19–21; 2:14–15; *Act* 14:16–17). Cum autem haec cognitio naturalis apud paganos in idololatriam prolapsa esset (cfr *Rom* 1:21–32), Apostolus censuit sapientius esse sermonem coniungere cum doctrina philosophorum qui ab initio fabulis et cultibus mystericis opponebant conceptus divinam transcendentiam magis reverentes.

---

[30] Cfr Conc. Oecum. Vat. II, Const. dogm. de divina Revelatione *Dei Verbum*, §4.

incarnate Word, who in his entire person[30] reveals the Father (cf. *Jn* 1:14, 18). Whatever human reason 'unknowingly' (cf. *Acts* 17:23) explores, can only be discovered through Christ. What is revealed in him is 'the fullness of truth' (cf. *Jn* 1:14–16) of every creature, which was created in him and through him and remains in him (cf. *Col* 1:17).

35. In the context offered by this broad view a more thorough exploration of the connection between revealed truth and philosophy is needed. This relationship contains within itself a double reference, in the sense that the truth which flows from revelation is one which must also be understood under the light of reason. With this double sense before us, it will be possible to define more exactly the relationship between revealed truth and philosophical knowledge. Therefore, let us first examine the relationships which have existed between faith and philosophy throughout the course of history. In this way we may be able to uncover the principles which constitute the aspects to which we need to refer in order to arrive at the right relationship between these two areas of knowledge.

CHAPTER IV
CONCERNING THE RELATIONSHIP BETWEEN FAITH AND REASON

Principal steps in the encounter of faith and reason

36. As the Acts of the Apostles testify, the Christian proclamation from the very beginning was connected with the philosophical teachings of its own age. The same book relates the discussion Paul had at Athens with Stoic and Epicurean philosophers (*Acts* 17:18). Exegesis of the speech at the Areopagus clearly exposes the usual references to various popular opinions, especially those of Stoic origin. This is by no means accidental. The first Christians, to obviate any misunderstanding by the pagans, were inhibited from simply referring them to 'Moses and the Prophets'. They were obliged to rely on the natural knowledge of God and the voice of man's moral conscience (cf. *Rom* 1:19–21; 2:14–15; *Acts* 14:16–17). But since this natural knowledge of God among the pagans lapsed into idolatry (cf. *Rom* 1:21–32), the Apostle thought it wiser to link his own speech with the teachings of the philosophers, who had from the beginning in their reverence for the divine transcendence contrasted their ideas with those of fables and of mystery religions.

[30] Second Vatican Council, Dogmatic Constitution on Divine Revelation *Dei Verbum*, §4 in Flannery, (ed.), *Vatican Council II*, pp. 751f.

Ex praecipuis propositis quae philosophi doctrinae classicae sunt amplexi, consilium exstitit expurgandi a formis mythologicis notionem quam homines de Deo profitebantur. Ut omnibus patet, etiam religio Graeca, non aliter ac pleraeque religiones cosmicae, polytheismum ita profitebatur, ut vel res et eventus naturae in deorum numerum deferret. Conatus hominis ad cognoscendam deorum originem et in eis universi originem, primam suam significationem invenerunt in arte poetica. Deorum origines primum hactenus habentur testimonium huius humanae investigationis. Munus fuit parentum philosophiae efficere ut vinculum ostenderetur inter rationem et religionem. Illi quidem contuitum dilatantes ad principia usque universalia, non amplius acquieverunt fabulis antiquis, sed voluerunt ut eorum fides de divinitate fundamento rationali sustentaretur. Ita susceptum est iter quod, relictis antiquis traditionibus particularibus, se immisit quandam in progressionem quae congruebat cum postulationibus rationis universalis. Scopus ad quem haec progressio tendebat erat criticum iudicium rerum in quas credebatur. Prima hoc in itinere utilitatem tulit divinitatis notio. Superstitiones uti tales sunt recognitae et religio, saltem partim, per rationalem recognitionem est expurgata. Hoc suffulti fundamento, Patres Ecclesiae fecundum instituerunt colloquium cum antiquis philosophis, iter aperientes ad nuntium et ad cognitionem Dei Christi Iesu.

37. Dum mentionem facimus de hoc motu quo Christiani ad philosophiam accesserunt, merito memorari decet statum circumspectionis quem apud Christianos concitabant alia culturae paganae elementa, uti, exempli gratia, doctrina "gnostica". Philosophia, tamquam sapientia practica et schola vitae, facile misceri poterat cum cognitione indolis superioris, arcanae, paucis perfectis reservatae. Absque dubio Paulus ad hoc genus speculationum arcanarum mentem vertit, cum Colossenses ita admonet: "Videte, ne quis vos depraedetur per philosophiam et inanem fallaciam secundum traditionem hominum, secundum elementa mundi et non secundum Christum" (2:8). Quam huius aetatis propria sunt Apostoli verba, si ea ad diversas arcanae doctrinae formas remittimus, quae hodie etiam mentes pervadunt quorundam fidelium qui debito critico sensu carent. Sancti Pauli vestigia sectantes, alii auctores I saeculi, praesertim s. Irenaeus et Tertullianus, vicissim exceptiones posuerunt circa excogitationem culturalem quae veritatem Revelationis interpretationi philosophorum subicere intendebat.

38. Christianismi igitur cum philosophia conventio nec immediata nec facilis exstitit. Usus philosophiae et frequentatio scholarum primis Christianis conturbatio visa sunt potius quam lucrum. Primum et urgens

One of the major concerns which preoccupied the teachings of classical philosophy was their concern to purify all mythological forms from what people professed of the notion of God. It is clear to all that even Greek religion, no less than the majority of cosmic religions, professed polytheism, with the result that things and natural events came to be treated as if from the gods. Man's attempts to discover the origin of the gods and among them of the universe found their first expression in poetry. The origins of the gods remain the first evidence of human research. The first task of the fathers of philosophy was to display the close link between reason and religion. As they broadened their view to include universal principles, they no longer acquiesced in the ancient myths, rather they desired to support their belief in divinity on rational grounds. Thus a journey began which left behind the ancient and local traditions and launched itself into a progress which was in agreement with the demands of universal reason. The end to which this progress tended was a critical assessment of the things in which they believed. The notion of divinity itself was most useful on this journey. Superstitions were recognized for what they were, and religion, at least partially, was purified through rational reflection. On this basis the Fathers of the Church carried on a fruitful dialogue with the ancient philosophers, and so opened the way to the proclamation and knowledge of God in Christ Jesus.

37. In mentioning the course by which Christians accepted philosophy, it is only fair to recall how cautiously Christians regarded other elements of pagan culture, one example of which is 'gnosticism'. Philosophy, understood as practical wisdom and a school of life, could easily be confused with knowledge of a superior kind, secret, and reserved to those few who were perfect. Without doubt Paul was concerned about this type of secret speculation when he warns the Colossians (2:8): 'see to it that no one makes a prey of you by philosophy and empty deceit, according to human tradition, according to the elemental spirits of the universe and not according to Christ'. How apt the Apostle's words are for the age we now live in – just look at the different forms of secret doctrine which poison the minds even of some of the faithful who are lacking in a critical sense. In the footsteps of St Paul other writers of the second century, above all St Irenaeus and Tertullian, in their turn made their objections to any cultural contrivance which aimed at subjecting the truth of Revelation to philosophical interpretation.

38. The encounter between Christianity and philosophy was, therefore, neither immediate nor straightforward. To the first Christians both the use of philosophy and the attendance at the schools seemed to be more distracting than profitable. Their first and most urgent business was to

eorum munus erat nuntius Christi a mortuis exsuscitati, qui singulis proponendus erat hominibus, unde illi ad mentis conversionem et ad Baptismi petitionem conducerentur. Quod tamen non significat eos munus ignoravisse perspiciendi cognitionem fidei eiusque causarum. Prorsus aliter! Iniqua ergo et simulata evadit exprobratio Celsi qui Christianum "imperitissimum quemque et rusticissimum"[31] accusare ausus est. Causa huius contemptionis initialis aliunde est perquirenda. Revera, lectio Evangelii responsum ferebat tam satisfaciens quaestioni de vitae sensu, illactenus nondum solutae, ut philosophorum frequentatio res praeterita videretur et, quodammodo, superata.

Quod quidem hodie clarius videtur, si ratio habeatur de contributione Christianismi vindicantis ius universale accedendi ad veritatem. Deiectis repagulis stirpis, ordinis socialis et sexus, Christianismus inde ab exordiis nuntiavit aequalitatem omnium hominum coram Deo. Primum huius conceptus consectarium respexit argumentum de veritate. Ita aperte superata est notio altioris societatis, cui apud antiquos perquisitio veritatis erat reservata. Quandoquidem accessus ad veritatem bonum est quod ducit ad Deum, omnibus patere debuit haec via percurrenda. Viae quae ducunt ad veritatem multiplices perstant; attamen, eo quod christiana veritas vim salvificam possidet, unaquaeque harum viarum percurri potest ea tamen condicione ut ad extremam metam conducant, videlicet ad Iesu Christi revelationem.

Inter principes viros qui positivum nexum cum doctrina philosophica fovent, etsi cauta discretio sit habenda, memorandus est sanctus Iustinus: qui, licet summam professus est existimationem erga Graecam philosophiam, vehementer ac dilucide asseruit se in Christianismo "solam certam et frugiferam philosophiam"[32] invenisse. Pariter Clemens Alexandrinus Evangelium appellavit "veram philosophiam",[33] et philosophiam interpretatus est finitimam Legi Moysis instar praeviae institutionis ad fidem christianam[34] et praeparationis ad Evangelium.[35] Quoniam "philosophia illam appetit sapientiam quae est in probitate animae et verbi atque in integritate vitae, bene praeparatur ad sapientiam et omni ope annititur ad eam assequendam. Apud nos philosophi dicuntur ii qui diligunt illam sapientiam quae omnia condit et docet, id

---

[31] Origenes, *Contra Celsum*, 3, 55: *SC* 136, 130.
[32] *Dialogus cum Tryphone Iudaeo*, 8, 1: *PG* 6, 492.
[33] *Stromata* I, 18, 90, 1: *SC* 30, 115.
[34] Cfr *Stromata*. I, 16, 80, 5: *SC* 30, 108.
[35] Cfr *Stromata* I, 5, 28, 1: *SC* 30, 65.

herald the resurrection of Christ from the dead, which was the message all needed to hear in order to lead them to conversion of mind and request for baptism. But this did not mean that they were unaware of the need to try to understand the faith and its causes. Rather the opposite. The charge made against the Christians by Celsus, namely that they were all of them 'thoroughly uncultured and uncouth',[31] turns out to have been both wicked and false. We must look for the cause of this initial contempt from another source. The real reason was that the message of the Gospel provided such a satisfying answer to the hitherto unresolved question about the meaning of life that recourse to the philosophers seemed a thing of the past and to that extent, superseded.

This is even clearer today, once we consider the contribution made by Christianity in its defence of the universal right of access to the truth. By rejecting the claims made by birth, social order and sex, from its very beginning Christianity proclaimed the equality of all men and women before God. A prime effect of this conception had to do with the argument about truth. By it the notion of social elite to whom, according to antiquity, a special access to the truth had been reserved was openly superseded. Since, however, access to the truth is a good that leads to God, this journey is one that all should be able to make. The ways that lead to truth stand out as manifold; even so, because Christian truth has the strength to save, each and every one of these paths can be entered upon with this proviso, that they lead to the final goal, namely the revelation of Jesus Christ.

Among the first of those who encouraged a positive attitude to philosophy, albeit with a certain cautious reserve, was St Justin. Despite the high regard he professed for Greek philosophy, even so he insisted with force and clarity that only in Christianity had he found 'a philosophy which combined certainty with fruitfulness'.[32] In the same way, Clement of Alexandria described the Gospel as 'true philosophy'[33] and viewed philosophy as very close to the Law of Moses in the prior instruction it offered for the Christian faith[34] and as preparatory to the Gospel.[35] Since 'philosophy yearns for the wisdom that consists in rightness of soul and

[31] Origen, *Contra Celsum*, trans. and ed. H. Chadwick (Cambridge: Cambridge University Press, 1980), III, 55.

[32] A. L. Williams, (ed.), *Justin Martyr: The Dialogue with Trypho* (London: SPCK, 1930), VIII, 1.

[33] *Les Stromates Clement d'Alexandrie* (Paris: Editions de Cerf, 1951–1999), I, 18, 90, 1.

[34] Cf. *Les Stromates Clement d'Alexandrie*, I, 16, 80, 5.

[35] Cf. *Les Stromates Clement d'Alexandrie*, I, 5, 28, 1.

est, cognitionem Filii Dei".[36] Primum philosophiae Graecae propositum, secundum auctorem Alexandrinum, non est perficere vel confirmare veritatem christianam; potius munus eius est fidem tueri: "Est quidem per se perfecta et nullius indiga Servatoris doctrina, cum sit Dei virtus et sapientia. Accedens autem Graeca philosophia veritatem non facit potentiorem; sed cum debiles efficiat sophistarum adversus eam argumentationes, et propulset dolosas adversus veritatem insidias, dicta est vineae apta sepes et vallus".[37]

39. Hac currente progressione, inspicere licet disputatores christianos cogitationem philosophicam stricto sensu sumpsisse. Prima inter exempla quae inveniri possunt, certe significantius exstat illud Origenis. Adversus impugnationes philosophi Celsi, Origenes ad argumenta responsaque eidem ferenda Platonica usus est philosophia. Memorans haud pauca doctrinae Platonicae elementa, rudimenta theologiae christianae excogitare coepit. Ipsum quidem nomen, una cum theologiae notione tamquam rationalis sermonis de Deo, ad illud tempus origini Graecae colligabatur. Verbi gratia, secundum Aristotelis philosophiam, nomen nobiliorem partem et verum culmen sermonis philosophici significabat. Sub lumine christianae Revelationis vero, id quod prius doctrinam generatim de deorum natura significabat, sensum prorsus novum assumpsit, eo quod descripsit considerationem quam fidelis faciebat ad *veram* de Deo *doctrinam* exhibendam. Haec nova christiana notio, quae iam diffundebatur, philosophia nitebatur, eodemque tamen tempore paulatim curabat ut sese ab illa secerneret. Historia docet eandem Platonicam doctrinam in theologia assumptam profundas subiisse mutationes, praesertim quod attinet ad notiones de immortalitate animae, de deificatione hominis et origine mali.

40. Hoc in processu quo doctrina Platonica et Neoplatonica paulatim christianae redduntur, peculiarem in modum memoria digni sunt Patres Cappadoces, Dionysius dictus Areopagita ac maxime sanctus Augustinus. Magnus Doctor occidentalis colloquia instituere valuit cum diversis scholis philosophicis, a quibus tamen omni spe est destitutus. Cum vero christianae fidei veritas apparuit illi, tunc fortitudine roboratus est ad absolutam explendam conversionem, ad quam philosophi, crebro ab ipso frequentati, eum inducere nequiverant. Cuius causam ipsemet narrat: "Ex hoc tamen quoque iam praeponens doctrinam catholicam, modestius ibi minimeque fallaciter sentiebam

[36] *Stromata* VI, 7, 55, 1–2: *PG* 9, 277.
[37] *Stromata* I, 20, 100, 1: *SC* 30, 124.

speech and uprightness of life, it is well prepared for that wisdom and uses every effort to achieve it. We call the philosophers among us those who love the wisdom which created all things and which teaches the knowledge of the Son of God'.[36] According to our Alexandrian author, the primary role of Greek philosophy is neither to perfect nor to confirm Christian truth; rather its role is to protect faith: 'the teaching of our Saviour, since he is the power and wisdom of God, is perfect and wants for nothing. Greek philosophy does not make truth more powerful: but when it dispels the arguments of the sophists against truth and repels their crafty deceits, then Greek philosophy is rightly called the hedge and protective wall around the vine'.[37]

39. As this process developed we may look at the defenders of Christianity who, strictly speaking, took up philosophical thinking. Easily the most significant among the first examples we can find is Origen. In order to reply to the charges of the philosopher Celsus, Origen used Platonic philosophy to furnish himself with arguments and replies. With many of the elements of Platonic teaching in his memory, he began to construct the rudiments of a Christian theology. The name theology itself, together with the conception of theology as a rational discourse, was at that time closely linked to its Greek origin. For example, according to Aristotle's philosophy, the name meant the nobler element and the true pinnacle of philosophical discourse. However, under the light of Christian Revelation, what had formerly referred to a general understanding of the nature of the gods assumed a new meaning, inasmuch as it described any understanding made by a person of faith with a view to making clear the *true doctrine* of God. As it developed, this novel Christian conception rested upon philosophy, and at the same time gradually set about distinguishing itself from it. History tells us that the same Platonic doctrine, once it had been taken up into theology, underwent certain profound changes, above all in its account of the immortality of the soul, the deification of man and the origin of evil.

40. The process whereby Platonism and Neoplatonism were gradually Christianized owes a particular debt to the Cappadocian Fathers, to Denis, called the Areopagite, and above all to St Augustine. The great Western doctor came into contact with various philosophical schools, but emerged hopeless. But when the truth of the Christian faith dawned upon him, then he was strengthened for that complete conversion toward which the philosophers whom he had often heard were unable to lead

---

[36] *Les Stromates Clement d'Alexandrie*, VI, 7, 55, 1–2.

[37] *Les Stromates Clement d'Alexandrie*, I, 20, 100, 1.

iuberi ut crederetur quod non demonstrabatur (sive esset quid, sed cui forte non esset; sive nec quid esset), quam illic temeraria pollicitatione scientiae credulitatem irrideri; et postea tam multa fabulosissima et absurdissima, quia demonstrari non poterant, credenda imperari".[38] Augustinus ipsos Platonicos, de quibus praecipuo iure mentionem facere consueverat, exprobravit, qui, quamvis scirent terminum ad quem tendere tenebantur, ignoraverant tamen viam illuc ducentem, nempe Verbum incarnatum.[39] Episcopus Hipponensis edere potuit primam summam synthesim doctrinae philosophicae et theologicae, in quam confluxerant opiniones doctrinae Graecae et Latinae. In Ipso quoque summa scientiae unitas, quae biblica doctrina fulciebatur, summitate doctrinae speculativae confirmari et sustentari potuit. Synthesis quam sanctus Augustinus ad rem perduxit, per saecula habita est altissima speculationis philosophicae et theologicae methodus apud mundum Occidentalem. Propriis vitae gestis firmatus sanctimoniaeque spiritu suffultus, inserere etiam potuit in scripta sua innumera argumenta, quae, experientiae respectu habito, futuram quarundam doctrinarum philosophicarum progressionem portendebant.

41. Diversi ergo fuerunt modi per quos Patres Orientales et Occidentales convenerunt cum scholis philosophicis. Hoc tamen non significat illos materiam nuntii eandem reddidisse ac systemata quae memorabant. Tertulliani interrogatio: "Quid ergo Athenis et Hierosolymis? Quid Academiae et Ecclesiae?",[40] evidens iudicium est conscientiae criticae, qua christiani disputatores iam ab initio quaestionem experti sunt de habitudine inter fidem et philosophiam, summatim simul aspectus considerantes sive utilitatis sive limitationis. Non erant incauti disputatores. Quoniam materiam fidei impense vivebant, altiores speculationis formas attingere sciebant. Quapropter prorsus improbum est eorum operam ad solam translationem veritatum fidei in categorias philosophicas redigere. Immo plura adhuc fecerunt! Curarunt ut in plenam lucem orirentur omnia quae adhuc manebant implicita et propedeutica in priscorum philosophorum doctrina.[41] Hi enim, uti diximus, munus habuerunt docendi methodum qua mens, externis vinculis liberata, exire poterat ab angustiis fabularum et ad modum excedentem accommodatius sese aperire. Mens igitur purgata et iusta se

---

[38] S. Augustinus, *Confessiones* VI, 5, 7: *CCL* 27, 77–78.
[39] Cfr *Confessiones*, VII, 9, 13–14: *CCL* 27, 101–102.
[40] *De praescriptione haereticorum*, VII, 9: *SC* 46, 98.
[41] Cfr Congregatio de Institutione Catholica, *Instructio de Patrum Ecclesiae studio in sacerdotali institutione* (10 Novembris 1989), §25: *AAS* 82 (1990), 617–618.

him. He himself tells us the reason; 'from this time on, however, I now gave my preference to Catholic teaching. I thought it more modest and not in the least misleading to be told by the Church to believe what could not be demonstrated – whether that was because a demonstration did exist, but could not be understood by all, or whether the matter was not one open to rational proof – rather than having a rash promise of knowledge from the Manichees with the mockery of mere belief, and then afterwards to be ordered to believe many fabulous and absurd myths impossible to prove true'.[38] Despite the fact that he frequently referred to them, Augustine even blamed the Platonists on the grounds that despite the fact that they knew the direction they were supposed to take, they did not know the way that led there, namely the incarnate Word.[39] The Bishop of Hippo was the first to produce a complete synthesis of philosophy and theology in which the teachings of Greeks and Latins alike flowed together. In him also the perfect unity of knowledge resting upon the teaching of the Bible could be supported and upheld by a crown of speculative teaching. The synthesis achieved by St Augustine was long regarded in the Western world as the supreme method of philosophical and theological speculation. It received support from his life story and was further underpinned by the holiness of his life; he was even able to introduce into his writings certain arguments which, because they rested upon his experience, heralded the future development of certain philosophical doctrines.

41. There were, therefore, many ways in which the Eastern and Western Fathers came to terms with the philosophical schools. This, however, does not mean that the content of the message they delivered was the same as the systems they employed. Tertullian's question, 'What has Athens to do with Jerusalem? The Academy with the Church?'[40] is the clear judgment of the critical mind with which from the very beginning the defenders of the Gospel confronted the question about the connection between faith and philosophy in their general consideration of the varying ways in which the latter could be either useful or a hindrance. They were certainly not careless disputants. Because they lived the matter of their faith seriously, they knew how to attain deeper forms of speculation. This means that it is grossly unfair to try to interpret their work as an attempt to reduce the truths of faith to philosophical categories. They did far more than that! They were careful to ensure that whatever was implicit and preparatory in the teaching of the early

---

[38] St Augustine, *Confessions*, trans. H. Chadwick, Book VI, Chapter 5, 7.
[39] St Augustine, *Confessions*, trans. H. Chadwick, Book VII, Chapter 9, 13–14.
[40] Tertullian, *De praescriptione haereticorum*, VII, 9.

extollere poterat ad altiores gradus meditationis, validum tribuens fundamentum ad intellegentiam creaturarum, entis transcendentis et absoluti.

Hic vere inseritur novitas a Patribus excogitata. Illi in plenitudine acceperunt rationem apertam ad absolutum atque Revelationis divitias inseverunt in eam. Coniunctio facta est non tantum in ambitu culturarum, quarum altera alterius fascinationem passa est; illa contigit in intima animorum natura et coniunctio data est inter creaturam eiusque Creatorem. Ipsum praetergrediens finem versus quem inconscie ex natura sua tendebat, ratio summum bonum et summam veritatem in persona Verbi incarnati attingere potuit. Quod attinet ad philosophias, Patres non timuerunt agnoscere sive elementa communia sive diversitates quas illae ostendebant quod ad Revelationem. Huius confluentiae conscientia recognitionem diversitatum in eis non obscuravit.

42. In theologia scholastica munus rationis ad philosophiam institutae luculentius efficitur sub impulsu Anselmianae interpretationis de intellectu fidei. Secundum sanctum Cantuariensem Archiepiscopum, primatus fidei certare non intendit cum investigatione rationis propria. Haec enim non vocatur ut iudicium ferat de materia fidei; id facere non potest, quia idoneitate caret. Potius eius munus est invenire sensum, detegere causas quae homines omnes ducere possint ad quandam fidei doctrinam intellegendam. Sanctus Anselmus lucide asserit intellectum investigare teneri quidquid diligat; quo plus diligit, eo plus cognoscere cupit. Qui pro veritate vivit protenditur ad quandam cognitionis formam quae magis magisque amore incenditur erga ea quae cognoscit, quamvis concedere teneatur se non fecisse omnia quae in suis votis fuerunt: "Ad te videndum factus sum; et nondum feci propter quod factus sum".[42] Desiderium itaque veritatis rationem impellit ad amplius progrediendum; quae, immo, quasi obruitur conscientia propriae facultatis quae in dies latior fit quam id quod attingit. Hic tamen et nunc ratio detegere potest ubinam iter suum perficiatur: "Sufficere namque debere existimo rem incomprehensibilem indaganti, si ad hoc ratiocinando pervenerit ut eam certissime esse cognoscat; etiamsi penetrare nequeat intellectu, quomodo ita sit. [. . .] Quid autem tam incomprehensibile, tam ineffabile, quam id quod supra omnia est? Quapropter si ea, quae de summa essentia hactenus disputata sunt, necessariis rationibus sunt asserta, quamvis sic intellectu penetrari non

[42] S. Anselmus, *Proslogion*, 1: *PL* 158, 226.

philosophers should come out into the full light.[41] These early philosophers, as we have said, were concerned with teaching a method by which the mind, freed from all external constraints, could emerge from the constrictions of fables and so be able to open itself up to a higher realm. The mind, therefore, purged and made righteous could rise to the higher degrees of meditation and so provide intelligent creatures with strong grounds for a transcendent and absolute being.

Here the innovation constructed by the Fathers can truly be seen. They fully accepted reason as open to the absolute, and then introduced the riches of Revelation into it. This was not simply a question of cultural cross-fertilization, where one side can be fascinated by the other; it occurred rather in the innermost nature of the spirit, where the intimate union of creature and Creator occurs. Reason, in transcending the end to which it tended by its very nature, albeit unconsciously, was able to attain to the highest good and highest truth in the person of the incarnate Word. As far as philosophies were concerned, the Fathers were not afraid of admitting either common elements or differences which pointed to Revelation. An awareness of this basic agreement did not obscure a recognition of important divergences.

42. In scholastic theology the role of philosophically trained reason was clearly explored under the impulse of St Anselm's interpretation of the understanding of faith. According to the holy Archbishop of Canterbury, the priority of faith need not enter into competition with the enquiry proper to reason. Reason is not called to pass judgment on the matter of faith; it is not able do this because it is not up to the task. Rather its task is to discover a meaning, to uncover the causes, which could lead humanity to some understanding of the contents of faith. St Anselm clearly states that the intellect is bound to explore whatever it loves. And the more it loves, so much the more does it desire to know. Whoever lives for the truth reaches out for a form of knowledge which is fired more and more with love for what is known, while having to admit that it has not yet reached what it is promised: 'To see you was I conceived, and I have yet to conceive that for which I was conceived'.[42] The want, therefore, of the truth drives reason into progressing further; and reason in its turn is overwhelmed by an awareness of its own capacity, which day by day becomes greater than that which it discovers. Yet already reason is able to work out where its journey is to be fulfilled: 'I think that whoever investigates something incomprehensible should be satisfied if, by way of

---

[41] Cf. Congregation for Catholic Education, *Instruction on the Study of the Fathers of the Church in Priestly Formation* (10 November 1989).

[42] St Anselm, *Proslogion*, chapter 1.

possint, ut et verbis valeant explicari; nullatenus tamen certitudinis eorum nutat soliditas. Nam, si superior consideratio *rationabiliter comprehendit incomprehensibile esse*, quomodo eadem summa sapientia sciat ea quae fecit, [. . .] quis explicet quomodo sciat aut dicat seipsam, de qua aut nihil, aut vix aliquid ab homine sciri possibile est?"[43]

Fundamentalis concordia inter cognitionem philosophicam et fidei cognitionem iterum confirmatur: fides postulat ut obiectum suum auxilio rationis comprehendatur; ratio, culmen investigationis attingens, necessarium ducit quidquid fides ostendit.

Perennis sancti Thomae Aquinatis sententiarum novitas

43. Locus omnino singularis hoc in longo itinere sancto Thomae reservatur, non tantum ob ea quae in eius doctrina continentur, verum etiam ob habitudinem dialogicam quam ille tunc temporis interserere scivit cum Arabica et Hebraica doctrina. Illa quidem aetate, qua christiani disputatores reperiebant veteres thesauros philosophiae, et immediatius philosophiae Aristotelicae, summum eius exstitit meritum quod eminere fecerit concordiam inter rationem et fidem. Utriusque lumen, rationis scilicet et fidei, a Deo procedit, ille ratiocinatus est, idcirco inter se opponere nequeunt.[44]

Thomas adhuc acrius denotat naturam, obiectum proprium philosophiae, ad intellegentiam divinae revelationis conferre posse. Fides igitur rationem non metuit sed eam quaerit fiduciamque in ipsa collocat. Quemadmodum gratia supponit naturam eamque perficit,[45] ita fides supponit et perficit rationem. Quae, fidei lumine illustrata, eximitur a fragilitate et a limitatione quae ex peccati commissione proveniunt, et necessariam invenit fortitudinem, qua in cognitionem mysterii Dei Unius et Trini se sublevet. Etsi in luce vehementer ponit supernaturalem fidei indolem, Doctor Angelicus non est oblitus ipsius rationabilitatis praestantiam; immo, penitus descendere scivit et sensum illius sapientiae circumscribere. Fides quidem quodam modo est "exercitium cogitationis"; ratio hominis nec abrogatur nec minuitur, cum fidei veritatibus assentit; hae tamen veritates ex libera et conscia selectione attinguntur.[46]

---

[43] S. Anselmus, *Monologion*, 64: *PL* 158, 210.

[44] Cfr *Summa Contra Gentiles* I, VII.

[45] Cfr *Summa Theologiae*, I, 1, 8 ad 2: "cum enim gratia non tollat naturam sed perficiat".

[46] Cfr Ioannes Paulus II, *Allocutio ad participes IX Congressus Thomistici Internationalis* (29 Septembris 1990): *Insegnamenti*, XIII, 2 (1990), 770–771.

reasoning, he arrives at the certainty of its existence, even if his intellect cannot penetrate its mode of being . . . But is there anything so incomprehensible, so ineffable, as that which is above all? Therefore, if that which until now has been a matter of dispute concerning the highest essence has been affirmed by necessary reasons, then this solid certainty is in no way shaken if the intellect cannot penetrate it, nor words explain it. For if the previous argument had come to the *rational conclusion that it is impossible to understand* how the highest wisdom knows what it does . . . who then will explain how this same wisdom, of which man can know nothing or next to nothing, is to be known and expressed?'[43]

The fundamental harmony between philosophical knowledge and the knowledge of faith is once again confirmed: faith demands that its object be understood with the help of reason; reason, in attaining the summit of its search, unavoidably points to what faith makes plain.

The enduring originality of the propositions of St Thomas Aquinas

43. In this long journey a particular place is reserved for St Thomas. This is not only because of the things contained in his teaching but also because of the dialogue which he undertook with the Arab and Jewish studies of his time. In an age in which Christian thinkers were discovering the ancient treasures of philosophy, and above all the philosophy of Aristotle, he had the great merit of bringing to the fore the harmony between reason and faith. He argued that the light both of reason and faith comes from God and therefore there can be no conflict between them.[44]

More sharply, however, Thomas insists that nature, which is the proper object of philosophy, can also contribute to the understanding of divine Revelation. Faith, therefore, is not afraid of reason; rather it seeks it out and places its trust in it. Even as grace both presupposes and perfects nature,[45] so, too, faith presupposes and perfects reason. Illumined by the light of faith, reason is rescued from the frailty and limitation that arise from sin and inevitably discovers the courage which it needs to lift it up to the knowledge of the mystery of the One and Triune God. Although he accords great weight to the supernatural character of faith, the Angelic Doctor never forgot the importance of its reasonableness; indeed he was

---

[43] St Anselm, *Monologion*, chapter 64. Cf. B. Davies and G. R. Evans, (eds.), *Anselm of Canterbury: The Major Works* (Oxford: Oxford University Press, 1998).

[44] Cf. St Thomas Aquinas, *Summa Contra Gentiles* (Notre Dame: University of Notre Dame Press, 1975), Book I, Chapter 7.

[45] Cf. St Thomas Aquinas, *Summa Theologiae*, (Maryland: Christian Classics, 1981), Ia, Q. 1, art. 8 ad 2: 'Since, therefore, grace does not destroy nature but perfects it.'

Hac quidem de causa iure meritoque sanctus Thomas ab Ecclesia Magister doctrinae constanter est habitus et exemplum quod ad modum theologiam tractandi. Nos iuvat in memoriam revocare ea quae Dei Servus Decessor Noster Paulus VI scripsit septimo occurrente centenario ab obitu Doctoris Angelici: "Maxima profecto fuerunt s. Thomae et audacia in veritate quaerenda, et spiritus libertas in novis tractandis quaestionibus, et illa mentis probitas, eorum propria, qui, dum nullo modo patiuntur christianam veritatem contaminari profana philosophia, hanc tamen *a priori* minime respuunt. Quare, in christianae doctrinae historia eius nomen in numerum refertur praecursorum, quibus novus philosophiae atque scientiae universalis cursus debetur. Caput autem et quasi cardo doctrinae, qua ipse, ut summa et quasi prophetica ingenii acie praeditus erat, quaestionem dissolvit de novis mutuis relationibus inter rationem et fidem, in eo positum est, quod mundi *saecularitatem* cum arduis ac severis Evangelii postulatis composuit; atque hoc modo sese subduxit ab inclinatione, naturae aliena, ad mundum eiusque bona contemnenda, neque tamen descivit a supremis et indeclinabilibus principiis supernaturalis ordinis".[47]

44. Praecipuas inter perceptiones sancti Thomae illa est quae missionem respicit quam Spiritus Sanctus explicat cum humanam scientiam maturat in sapientia. Iam a primis paginis *Summae Theologiae*[48] Aquinas Doctor primatum docere voluit illius sapientiae quae est donum Spiritus Sancti et quae ad divinarum rerum cognitionem ducit. Eius theologia nos docet sapientiae proprietatem in eius arta conglutinatione cum fide et cognitione divina. Illa cognoscit per connaturalitatem, fidem praesumit et efficit ut concipiatur rectum iudicium suum, initium sumens a veritate ipsius fidei: "... sapientia quae ponitur donum differt ab ea quae ponitur virtus intellectualis acquisita. Nam illa acquiritur studio humano: haec autem est 'de sursum descendens', ut dicitur *Iac.* 3:15. Similiter et differt a fide. Nam fides assentit veritati divinae secundum seipsam: sed iudicium quod est secundum veritatem divinam pertinet ad donum sapientiae".[49]

Primatus tamen huic sapientiae tributus non inducit Doctorem Angelicum ut duas alias additicias formas sapientiae obliviscatur:

---

[47] Litt. Ap. *Lumen Ecclesiae* (20 Novembris 1974), §8: *AAS* 66 (1974), 680.

[48] Cfr *Summa Theologiae*, I, 1, 6, ob. 3: "Praeterea, haec doctrina per studium acquiritur. Sapientia autem per infusionem habetur, unde inter septem dona Spiritus Sancti connumeratur".

[49] *Summa Theologiae*, II, II, 45, 1 ad 2; cfr etiam II, II, 45, 2.

able to plumb its depths and define the meaning of this wisdom. In some sense, indeed, faith is 'the exercise of reflection'; human reason is neither denied nor reduced when it assents to the truths of faith; these truths, however, are attained by free and conscious decision.[46]

Therefore St Thomas has always been rightly and deservedly regarded by the Church as the Master of teaching and also as an example of the way of undertaking theology. In this respect it helps us to recall what the Servant of God our predecessor Paul VI wrote on the seven hundredth anniversary of the death of the Angelic Doctor: 'St Thomas combined in himself the greatest boldness in his search for the truth, freedom of spirit in dealing with novel issues and that mental honesty which belongs to those who, though they do not allow Christian truth to be in any way contaminated by secular philosophy, do not even so reject it out of hand *a priori*. For this reason in the history of Christian doctrine his name is always to be registered among the pioneers, to which the new path of agreement between philosophy and universal knowledge owes much. The key point and almost the kernel of the solution which, with all the brilliance of his prophetic intuition, he gave to the new encounter of faith and reason was a reconciliation between the *secularity* of the world and the severest demands of the Gospel. In this way he avoided a tendency, foreign to his nature, of despising the world and its good things, while nevertheless at the same time not deserting the sublime and changeless principles of the supernatural order'.[47]

44. Among the important insights of St Thomas is that which refers to the mission of the Holy Spirit; this explains the growth of human knowledge towards wisdom. From the opening pages of the *Summa Theologiae*[48] Aquinas the Teacher desires to instruct us in the primacy of that wisdom which is the gift of the Holy Spirit, and which leads to the knowledge of things divine. His theology teaches that the peculiar characteristic of wisdom lies in the extremely close connection it has with faith and divine knowledge. This wisdom knows by means of connaturality: it presumes faith and ensures the rightness of its own judgment, taking its beginning the truth of that faith: 'the wisdom that comes as a gift differs from that which is an acquired intellectual virtue. The latter is acquired by human study: the former "comes from above" as James 3:15 states. In similar manner it differs from faith. Faith assents

[46] Cf. John Paul II, *Address to the Participants at the IX International Thomistic Congress* (29 September 1990): *Insegnamenti*, XIII, 2 (1990), pp. 770–1.

[47] Paul VI, Apostolic Letter *Lumen Ecclesiae* (20 November 1974) §8.

[48] Cf. *Summa Theologiae*, Ia, Q. 1, art. 6. obj. 3. 'Further, this doctrine is acquired by study, whereas wisdom is acquired by inspiration, that is why it is numbered among the seven gifts of the Holy Spirit.'

formam nempe *philosophicam*, quae fulcitur facultate qua intellectus, intra proprios limites, instruitur ad res investigandas; et formam *theologicam*, quae ex Revelatione pendet et fidei veritates scrutatur, ipsum Dei mysterium attingendo.

Intime persuasus de eo quod "omne verum a quocumque dicatur a Spiritu Sancto est",[50] sanctus Thomas nulla adductus utilitate, veritatem dilexit. Quaesivit eam ubicumque ea exprimi potuit, universalem eius indolem quam maxime illustrando. Magisterium Ecclesiae in ipso vidit et aestimavit ardens veritatis studium; doctrina illius, eo quod universalem, obiectivam et transcendentem veritatem semper asseruit, attigit culmina "quibus attingendis impar humana intelligentia est".[51] Merito quidem ille appellari potest "apostolus veritatis".[52] Quoniam indubitanter ad veritatem animum attendebat, revera obiectivum eius sensum agnoscere scivit. Eius vere est philosophia essendi et non apparendi dumtaxat.

Seiunctae a ratione fidei tragoedia

45. Primis conditis studiorum universitatibus, theologia propius cum aliis formis investigationis et scientificae cognitionis conferri potuit. Sanctus Albertus Magnus et sanctus Thomas, quamquam asserebant exsistentiam cuiusdam compagis inter theologiam et philosophiam, primi fuerunt viri docti qui necessariam agnoverunt autonomiam qua philosophia et scientiae indigebant, ut singulae argumentis propriae investigationis incumberent. Attamen, inde ab exeunte Medio Aevo legitima distinctio inter has duas cognitionis areas paulatim in nefastum discidium mutata est. Post nimiam animi rationalistarum cupiditatem, quorundam disputatorum propriam, sententiae talia posuerunt fundamenta, ut pervenirent ad philosophiam seiunctam et omnino autonomam quod ad fidei veritates. Varia inter consectaria huius seiunctionis diffidentia quaedam exstitit in dies validior quod attinet ad ipsam rationem. Quidam generalem, scepticam et agnosticam diffidentiam profiteri coeperunt, vel ad maius spatium fidei tribuendum, vel ad quamcumque evertendam de eadem mentionem rationalem.

---

[50] *Summa Theologiae* I, II, 109, 1 ad 1 ubi notam Ambrosiastri *In 1 Cor* 12:3 dictionem resumit: *PL* 17, 258.

[51] Leo XIII, Litt. Encycl. *Aeterni Patris* (4 Augusti 1879): *ASS* 11 (1878–1879), 109.

[52] Paulus VI, Litt. Ap. *Lumen Ecclesiae* (20 Novembris 1974), §8: *AAS* 66 (1974), 683.

to divine truth in itself; but the judgment made in accordance with divine truth belongs to the gift of wisdom'.[49]

The priority accorded by the Angelic Doctor to this wisdom does not mean that he overlooked the two other additional forms of wisdom: the *philosophical* form, which is supported by the faculty by which the intellect, within its own proper limits, is ordered to the making of enquiries; and the *theological* form, which depends on revelation and examines the truths of faith, by attaining the very mystery of God.

St Thomas loved truth, irrespective of personal advantage, being profoundly convinced that 'every truth, whatever its origin comes from the Holy Spirit'.[50] He sought truth wherever it could be expressed by illustrating as much as possible its universal character. In him, the Magisterium of the Church has seen and highly esteemed the passionate pursuit of truth; his constant teaching of universal, objective and transcendent truth reaches heights 'for the attainment of which human intelligence is by itself inadequate'.[51] He can properly be called 'the apostle of truth'.[52] Because he directed his mind without hesitation to the truth, he knew how to recognize its objective reality. His is truly a philosophy of being and not merely of appearing.

The tragedy of faith separated from reason

45. Once the first universities had been founded it became possible for theology to come into closer contact with other forms of enquiry and scientific knowledge. Although St Albert the Great and St Thomas insisted on the existence of a close link between theology and philosophy, even so they were the first learned men to admit the necessary autonomy that philosophy and the sciences needed, so that each should depend upon arguments belonging to their own sphere. Yet from the end of the Middle Ages the legitimate distinction between these two areas of knowledge gradually developed into a dangerous discord. As a result of too great a partiality of mind, some rationalists took such an entrenched position in pursuit of certain arguments that they developed a philosophy that was separate from and autonomous of the truths of faith. Among the different consequences of this separation was the gradual existence of a greater distrust of reason itself. Some came to profess a general sceptical

[49] *Summa Theologiae* IIa, IIae, Q. 45, art. 1 ad 2; cf. also IIa, IIae, Q. 45, art. 2.

[50] *Summa Theologiae*, Ia IIae, Q. 109, art. 1 ad 1, which echoes the well-known phrase of the *Ambrosiaster*, *In I Cor.* 12:3.

[51] Leo XIII, Encyclical Letter *Aeterni Patris* (4 August 1879) in J. J. Wynne SJ (ed.), *The Great Encyclicals of Pope Leo XIII: Translations from Approved Sources* (New York: Benziger, 1903).

[52] Paul VI, Apostolic Letter *Lumen Ecclesiae* (20 November 1974), §8.

Ut breviter dicamus, quidquid doctrina Patrum doctorumque Medii Aevi cogitaverat atque exsecuta erat veluti profundam unitatem, causam cognitionis accommodatae ad altissimas speculationis formas, omnino reapse deletum est ope doctrinarum faventium defensioni cognitionis rationalis a fide seiunctae eamque substituentis.

46. Extremae opinationes, quae magis valent, in occidentali praesertim historia, perbene noscuntur et videntur. Nihil est immodestiae edicere philosophicam disciplinam recentioris temporis magna ex parte esse progressam a christiana Revelatione gradatim disiunctam, eo usque opposita palam attingeret. Praeterito saeculo hic motus suum fastigium attigit. Quidam "idealismi" asseclae multifarie fidem eiusque elementa, vel Iesu Christi mortem ac resurrectionem, in dialecticas structuras ratione intellegibiles immutare contenderunt. Huic opinioni variae humanismi athei species, philosophice elucubratae, obstiterunt, quae fidem reputarunt perniciosam atque progressum plenae rationalitatis prohibentem. Haud veritae sunt ipsae ne novas religiones sese exhiberent quorundam consiliorum fulcimento utentes, quae in politica ac sociali ratione, in systemata quaedam evaserunt omnia complectentia humanitati exitiosa.

In rebus scientificis vestigandis mens positivistica adolevit, quae non modo discessit ab omni significatione opinationis christianae de mundo, verum etiam, ac potissimum, omnia indicia metaphysicae moralisque rationis prolabi sivit. Inde factum est ut quidam scientiae periti, ethica mente omnino carentes, in periculo versati sint ne amplius persona eiusque tota vita medium teneret studii locum. Immo quidam illorum, de viribus technicae artis progressus plane conscii, concedere videntur sollicitationi, praeter mercatus rationes, demiurgicae potestati in naturam ac in ipsum hominem.

Veluti consequens discriminis rationalismi tandem *nihilismus* crevit. Quatenus philosophia nullius rei, pro hominibus nostrae aetatis quandam suam habet pellicientem vim. Eius fautores inquisitionem putant in se ipsam conclusam, nulla data spe neque facultate adipiscendi veritatis metam. In nihilismi opinatione exsistentia dat tantum copiam quiddam sentiendi et experiendi, qua in re evanida primas agunt partes. Ex nihilismo illa opinio orta est de nullo officio definitive tenendo, quandoquidem fugacia et temporaria sunt omnia.

and agnostic distrust which resulted either in granting an ever wider compass to faith, or in totally removing from it any reference to reason.

To sum up briefly, whatever the teaching of the Fathers and of the learned men of the Middle Ages had constructed and achieved as a profound unity, which resulted in knowledge that reached to the highest forms of speculation, all that structure was totally destroyed through teachings that favoured the defence of a rational knowledge both separated from faith and taking its place.

46. The more influential of these extreme positions are well known and very apparent, especially in the history of the West. It is not too much to say that the discipline of philosophy of more recent years has moved further and further away and been gradually separated from Christian Revelation, so that it has attained a quite open hostility to it. In the nineteenth century this movement reached its apogee. Some 'idealists' strove in various ways to transform faith and its elements – even the death and resurrection of Jesus Christ – into dialectical structures intelligible to reason. This point of view was opposed by various kinds of atheistic humanism, philosophically embellished, who supposed faith to be dangerous and opposed to the development of full rationality. They had no fear of presenting themselves as new religions and developed ideas which served as a basis in the political and social orders for systems utterly destructive of humanity.

In scientific investigations there grew up a positivistic approach which not only ignored any Christian standpoint on the universe, but also fell away from every appeal to metaphysical or moral reason. The consequence was that certain scientists, lacking any moral sense, were in danger of failing to put the human person and her interests at the centre of their concerns. Indeed some of them, clearly conscious of the progress of the forces of technology, appear to surrender to the desire, beyond even market forces, to exercise a certain demonic power over nature and over man himself.

As a consequence of the crisis of rationalism, something akin to *nihilism* has appeared. In so far as it is a philosophy of nothing, it possesses for the men and women of our age a certain glamorous allure. Its supporters claim that it has no end beyond itself, without the hope or the capacity for arriving at the goal of truth. According to the nihilist, existence provides us only with the capacity for feeling and experiencing, in which the ephemeral takes pride of place. From nihilism the view has arisen that there should be no holding to any definitive commitment, because everything is fleeting and provisional.

47. Non est obliviscendum, ceterum, in hodierna cultura philosophiae partes esse immutatas. Ex sapientia et universali scientia, in unam quamlibet e multis scientiae provinciis redacta est; immo, quibusdam ex rationibus, partes omnino supervacanae eidem dumtaxat tribuuntur. Aliae interea rationalitatis formae magis magisque increbuerunt, quae philosophicae disciplinae leve pondus manifeste tribuerunt. Pro veritatis contemplatione atque finis ultimi sensusque vitae inquisitione, formae hae rationalitatis diriguntur – vel saltem sunt convertibiles – veluti "rationes instrumentales", quae inserviant utilitatis propositis, voluptatibus vel dominationi.

Quam lubricum sit hanc viam decurrere inde a Nostris primis Litteris Encyclicis editis ediximus, cum scripsimus: "Nostrae aetatis homo semper urgeri videtur iis ipsis rebus, quas efficit, nempe proventu operis manuum suarum et magis etiam laboris mentis et voluntatum propensionum. Fructus huius multiformis industriae humanae obnoxii sunt – nimis celeriter quidem ac saepe tali modo, qui praevideri non possit – 'alienationi', quatenus illis, qui eos protulerunt, simpliciter auferuntur: hoc non solum fieri contigit nec tanta ratione, quanta, saltem ex parte, in quodam ambitu ex eorum effectibus consequenter et oblique enato, iidem fructus contra hominem ipsum convertuntur. Haec videtur esse summa acerbissimae condicionis exsistentiae hominum nostri temporis, prout maxima et universali amplitudine patet. Quare homo maiore in dies afficitur timore. Metuit enim, ne fructus sui, non omnes quidem neque plerique, sed nonnulli et ii sane, qui singularem partem habent ingenii eius et industriae, contra se ipsum convertantur".[53]

His culturae immutationibus praepositis, nonnulli philosophi, veritatem ipsius causa inquirere desistentes, sibi hoc unum statuerunt ut obiectivam certitudinem practicamve utilitatem obtinerent. Proximum fuit ut vera rationis dignitas offunderetur, quae nempe facultatem amisit verum cognoscendi et absolutum vestigandi.

48. Quod in postrema hac historiae philosophiae parte eminet, pertinet, igitur, ad contemplatam progredientem fidei a philosophica ratione distractionem. Omnino verum est quod, res attente cogitanti, in philosophica quoque cogitatione eorum qui operam dederunt spatio inter fidem et rationem dilatando, magni pretii germina cogitationum nonnumquam ostenduntur, quae penitus excussa et recta mente cordeque exculta, efficiunt ut veritatis iter reperiatur. Haec congitationis

[53] Litt. Encycl. *Redemptor hominis* (4 Martii 1979), §15: *AAS* 71 (1979), 286.

47. It should also not be forgotten that in our modern culture the place of philosophy has been transformed. Rather than as wisdom and universal knowledge, it has been reduced to a position of one among many in the fields of knowledge. Indeed in some ways it has been consigned to a quite marginal role. Other forms of rationality have become increasingly pervasive and they have clearly contributed to the light esteem which philosophy now enjoys. Instead of the pursuit of truth and the search for the ultimate purpose and meaning of life, these forms of rationality are directed in fact or in intention as 'instrumental reason' to serve the designs of usefulness, pleasure or domination.

The danger of proceeding down this path was clearly expressed in our first Encyclical Letter, when we wrote: 'modern man seems always to be under pressure from his own achievements, whether it be the fruit of the works of his hands or even more by the labour of his mind and by the propensities of his will. The fruits of the variety of human industry often lead very quickly and quite unpredictably to "alienation" in the sense that they are simply taken away from the producer: even worse, these same fruits are turned against man himself, at least in part, through the indirect consequences of their effects turning back on themselves. In its greatest and most universal aspect this appears to be the height of the bitter situation facing the existence of the men and women of our time. As a result man is daily more and more fearful. The fear arises from the fact that a large part, if not all, of the fruits of his ability and activity may be turned against himself'.[53]

With these cultural changes in his mind, some philosophers have in consequence stopped searching for the truth and have only one objective, namely objective certitude and practical usefulness. The result has been that the true dignity of reason has been obscured and has lost the capacity for recognizing the truth and searching for the absolute.

48. What is peculiarly evident in this final part of the history of philosophy is the increasing separation of faith from philosophical reason that we have explored. Yet attentive consideration will show that, even in the thought of those who have attempted to make a total break between faith and reason, seeds of reflection of great value have from time to time appeared, which, once thoroughly examined and worked out with both a right heart and mind, have resulted in opening up the way of truth. For example these seeds of thought may be found in weighing up the explanations offered for perception and experience of the imaginary and

---

[53] John Paul II, Encyclical Letter *Redemptor hominis*, §15.

germina inveniri possunt, exempli gratia, in perpensis explicationibus de perceptione experientiaque, de specierum summa deque irrationali personalitate deque intersubiectivitate, de libertate bonisque, de tempore historiaque. Mortis quoque argumentum graviter unumquemquem philosophum compellare potest, ut in se ipse germanum suae vitae sensum reperiat. Id autem non sibi vult praesentem inter fidem et rationem necessitudinem subtilem iudicii conatum non postulare, quandoquidem tum ratio tum fides sunt extenuatae et sunt factae altera alteri debiles. Ratio, Revelatione nudata, devia itinera decucurrit, quae eandem in discrimen inferunt haud cernendi ultimam metam. Fides, ratione carens, animi sensum et experientiam extulit, atque sic in periculo versatur ne amplius sit universalis oblatio. Fallax est cogitare fidem, coram infirma ratione, plus posse; ipsa, contra, in grave periculum incidit ne in fabulam ac superstitionem evadat. Eodem modo ratio, quae fidei firmatae non obversatur, ad novitatem et radicalitatem ipsius "esse" contuendas non lacessitur.

Ne importuna igitur videatur gravis firmaque Nostra compellatio, ut fides et philosophia artam illam coniunctionem redintegrent, quae eas congruas efficiat earum naturae, autonomia vicissim servata. Fidei parrhesiae respondere debet rationis audacia.

CAPUT V
DE RE PHILOSOPHICA MAGISTERII IUDICIA

Magisterii prudens discretio uti veritati praestitum officium

49. Suam ipsius philosophiam non exhibet Ecclesia, neque quamlibet praelegit peculiarem philosophiam aliarum damno.[54] Recondita huius temperantiae causa in eo reperitur quod philosophia, etiam cum necessitudinem instituit cum theologia, secundum suam rationem suasque regulas agere debet; nullo modo alioquin cavetur ut illa ad veritatem vergat et ad eam per cursum ratione perpendendum tendat. Levis auxilii esset quaedam philosophia quae non procederet ratione gubernante secundum sua ipsius principia peculiaresque methodologias. Quod huius rei caput est, autonomiae radix, qua philosophia fruitur, in eo invenitur quod ratio natura sua ad veritatem vergit ipsaque praeterea ad eam consequendam necessaria habet instrumenta. Philosophia huius

[54] Cfr Pius XII, Litt. Encycl. *Humani generis* (12 Augusti 1950): *AAS* 42 (1950), 566.

the subconscious, the irrational side of personality, concerning intersubjectivity, freedom and goodness, and of time and history. The fact of death can also place a serious responsibility on every philosopher, to make him search for the true meaning of his life in himself. This does not mean, however that a serious attempt need not be made to achieve a subtle relationship between faith and reason, since faith and reason taken by themselves are fragile and weak. Reason, bereft of Revelation, runs into devious paths which deprive it of the ability of discovering its ultimate goal. Faith, bereft of reason, exalts the feeling and experience of the spirit, and so is in danger of being no longer a universal gift. It is a mistake to suppose that faith is more powerful when its power of reasoning is limited: on the contrary, it is then in danger of falling into myth or superstition. In a similar way reason deprived of a firm faith is not challenged to explore the newness and radical character of 'being' itself.

Our serious and weighty insistence on the need to re-establish a close connection between faith and philosophy should not therefore seem out of place. They are harmonious with each other, the autonomy of each is preserved. The boldness of reason ought to match the freedom of faith.

CHAPTER V
THE JUDGMENTS OF THE MAGISTERIUM UPON PHILOSOPHY

The prudent discretion of the Magisterium in the service of the truth

49. The Church does not have a philosophy of her own, nor does she select a particular one to the detriment of others.[54] The underlying reason for this restraint lies in this: that philosophy, even when it has a connection with theology, must act in accordance with its own character and rules: there is no other way of being sure that it tends toward the truth and makes its way forward by a course plotted by reason. Any philosophy which does not proceed under the guidance of reason in accordance with its own principles and its particular methodology would be of little assistance. The main point here is that the radical autonomy which philosophy enjoys is found in the fact that reason by its nature tends towards truth, and moreover is equipped with the necessary means to arrive at it. Any philosophy conscious of this as its 'constitutive

[54] Cf. Pius XII, Encyclical Letter *Humani generis* (12 August 1950) (London: Catholic Truth Society, 1950).

"statuti constitutivi" sibi conscia facere non potest quin servet necessitates quoque et perspicuitates veritatis revelatae proprias.

Historia tamen demonstravit declinationes et errores in quos haud semel recentiore potissimum aetate philosophicae opinationes inciderint. Munus non est Magisterii neque officium opem ferre ad lacunas philosophicae cogitationis mancae implendas. Eius est, contra, palam et strenue obsistere, cum philosophicae sententiae dubiae periculum iniciunt ne revelatio recte intellegatur nec non cum falsae factiosaeque effunduntur opiniones, quae graves errores disseminant, exturbantes Dei populi simplicitatem et fidei sinceritatem.

50. Ecclesiae ideo Magisterium, sub fidei lumine suum iudicium criticum de philosophicis opinationibus ac sententiis, quae cum doctrina christiana contendunt, ex auctoritate proferre potest ac debet.[55] Ad Magisterium in primis pertinet iudicare quae praesumptiones philosophicae et consecutiones veritati revelatae aversentur, pariterque postulata significare quae sub lumine fidei a philosophia requiruntur. In philosophicae praeterea scientiae progressu complures philosophantium scholae sunt ortae. Etiam plures hae disciplinae Magisterium compellant ad iudicium officiose enuntiandum an primigenia principia, quibus hae scholae nituntur, cum postulatis Dei verbi ac theologicae cogitationis propriis componi possint necne.

Ecclesia quippe demonstrare debet id quod fidei alienum oriri potest in quadam philosophica disciplina. Complures namque philosophicae cogitationes, ut opiniones de Deo, de homine, de eius libertate deque eius ethica agendi ratione, Ecclesiam recta compellant, quandoquidem veritatem revelatam quam ipsa tuetur contingunt. Cum hoc iudicium enuntiamus, nos Episcopi "testes veritatis" esse debemus in diaconia sustinenda humili sed tenaci, quae singulis philosophis aestimanda est, in commodum "rectae rationis", rationis videlicet quae de vero congruenter cogitat.

51. Hoc autem iudicium non quaedam infitiatio intellegi primo debet, proinde quasi Magisterium auferre vel imminuere quaslibet actiones velit. Immo eius cohortationes volunt in primis philosophicas vestigationes lacessere, promovere, incitare. Philosophi ceterum primi necessitatem percipiunt se ipsos iudicandi, errores, si qui sunt, corrigendi

---

[55] Cfr Conc. Oecum. Vat. I, Const. dogm. de Ecclesia Christi *Pastor aeternus*: *DS* 3070; Conc. Oecum. Vat. II, Const. dogm. de Ecclesia *Lumen gentium*, §25 c.

status' cannot but respect the demands and necessities proper to revealed truth.

Yet history has shown the mistakes and errors into which, above all in the recent past, philosophical opinions have fallen. It is neither the business nor the duty of the Magisterium to help fill in the gaps left by a defective philosophy. On the contrary it is its duty to make a clear and firm resistance when doubtful philosophical opinions make the correct understanding of revelation difficult, or when false and disruptive opinions are abroad that spread serious errors which disturb the people of God and upset the simplicity and sincerity of their faith.

50. Therefore the Church's teaching office in the light of faith can, and indeed should pronounce an authoritative and critical judgment upon those philosophical ideas and opinions which conflict with Christian doctrine.[55] In the first place it belongs to the Magisterium to judge what the philosophical presuppositions and consequences are that opposed revealed truth, and similarly to indicate the assumptions that, in the light of faith, are required from philosophy. With the progress of the science of philosophy many differing philosophical schools have arisen. This abundance of disciplines compels the Magisterium to take an official position to decide whether or not the principles upon which these schools rest are reconcilable with the demands of the Word of God, and what is appropriate to theological reflection.

The Church ought to show clearly what in any philosophical discipline is arising that is alien to faith. There are many philosophical ideas, as for example, opinions about God, about man, his liberty and his ethical behaviour, which affect the Church in so far as they touch upon the revealed truth which lies within her concern. When we give expression to this judgment as bishops, we ought to be 'witnesses of the truth' in a humble but determined ministry of service, which every philosopher should appreciate, as being of assistance to 'right reason', or reason which reflects congruently with truth.

51. This judgment should not in the first instance be understood as a denial, as though the Magisterium wished to eliminate or diminish certain activities. On the contrary its instructions are primarily geared to provoke, promote and encourage philosophical enquiry. Philosophers,

[55] Cf. First Vatican Council, Dogmatic Constitution on the Church of Christ *Pastor aeternus*, §4 in Tanner, (ed.) *Decrees of the Ecumenical Councils*, II, pp. 815 f.; Second Vatican Council, Dogmatic Constitution on the Church *Lumen gentium*, §25 in Flannery, (ed.), *Vatican II*, p. 926.

necnon nimis angustos fines transgrediendi in quibus eorum philosophica cogitatio gignitur. Illud praecipuum est considerandum, unam esse veritatem, quamvis eius significationes historiae vestigia exhibeant atque, insuper, e ratione humana propter peccatum sauciata et hebetata oriantur. Inde constat nullam historicam philosophiae formam legitime sibi vindicare posse facultatem totam veritatem complectendi, neque plene explanandi hominem, mundum, hominis necessitudinem cum Deo.

Hodiernis porro temporibus, cum systemata, rationes, opinationes ac argumenta philosophica saepe minutatissime digesta multiplicentur, magis magisque sub fidei lumine acumen iudicii deposcitur. Quod iudicium est arduum, quia, si quidem iam est laboriosum ingenitas ac non alienabiles facultates rationis agnoscere, finibus constitutivis et historicis additis, multo incertius interdum erit iudicium discernendi, in singulis philosophicis notionibus, id quod, sub fidei respectu, validum et frugiferum exhibent, pro eo quod praebent falsum et periculosum. Ecclesia utique scit thesauros sapientiae et scientiae in Christo abscondi (cfr *Col* 2:3); quocirca operam dat ut philosophica inquisitio evolvatur, ne via intercludatur, quae ad mysterium agnoscendum ducit.

52. Recentioribus non modo temporibus Ecclesiae Magisterium suam mentem de quibusdam philosophicis doctrinis patefecit. Ut quaedam supponamus exempla, sufficit ut memorentur saeculorum decursu declarationes de opinionibus quibusdam quae affirmabant animas praeexsistere,[56] itemque de variis idolatriae esoterismique superstitiosi obnoxiis formis quae in astrologicis enuntiationibus[57] continentur; ne obliviscamur scripta magis systematica adversus averroismi Latini sententias, quae christianae fidei aversantur.[58]

Si Magisterii verbum crebrius a superiore inde saeculo exauditum est, id accidit quod illa aetate non pauci catholici suum esse officium putarunt suam philosophiam opponere opinionibus recentiorum philosophorum. Tunc autem Ecclesiae Magisterium omnino coactum est ad vigilandum ne hae philosophicae doctrinae vicissim in formas falsas et negatorias

[56] Cfr Synodus Constantinopolitana, *DS* 403.

[57] Cfr Concilium Toletanum I, *DS* 205; Concilium Bracarense I, *DS* 459–460; Xystus V, Bulla *Coeli et terrae Creator* (5 Ianuarii 1586); *Bullarium Romanum* 4/4, Romae 1747, 176–179; Urbanus VIII, *Inscrutabilis iudiciorum* (1 Aprilis 1631): *Bullarium Romanum*, 6/1, Romae 1758, 268–270.

[58] Cfr Conc. Oecum. Viennense, Decr. *Fidei catholicae*, *DS* 902; Conc. Oecum. Laternanese V, Bulla *Apostolici regiminis*, *DS* 1440.

on the other hand are the first to appreciate the necessity of judging themselves, of correcting any errors there might be, and also of passing beyond the narrow limits from which their philosophical reflection originates. This above all should be borne in mind: that truth is one, even if its formulations both reflect historical circumstances, and further, arise from a human reason that has been wounded and weakened because of sin. As a result it follows that no historical expression of philosophy can claim for itself the power of embracing all truth, nor of offering a total explanation of man, the world, and man's relationship with God.

Today, which sees the proliferation of the most intricate systems, accounts, conjectures and philosophical arguments, there is greater and greater need for judgment made in the light of faith. Such judgment is arduous, because on the one hand it is a laborious business to recognize the natural and inalienable capacities of reason, above all when one has taken into account the restrictions imposed by nature and history upon it. On the other it is hard to distinguish in specific philosophical conceptions between what, with respect to faith, on the one hand is true and fruitful and on the other is false and dangerous. Yet the Church knows that the 'treasures of wisdom and knowledge are hidden in Christ' (cf. *Col* 2:3), and therefore insists on the development of philosophical enquiry to prevent the obstruction of the path that leads to the recognition of the mystery.

52. It is not only recently that the Magisterium of the Church has declared its mind on particular philosophical teachings. To give some examples, it is enough to recall pronouncements made in the course of time about some opinions affirming the pre-existence of souls,[56] and also about various ideas contained in astrology which are open to the danger of idolatry and esoteric superstition.[57] Nor should we forget the more systematic writings directed against the propositions of Latin Averroism, which are opposed to Christian faith.[58]

If the voice of the Magisterium was heard more frequently in the nineteenth century, it then happened that not a few Catholics thought it

---

[56] Cf. The *Synod of Constantinople* given in H. J. D. Denzinger, (ed.), *Enchiridion symbolorum definitionum et declarationum de rebus fidei et morum* (Freiburg: Herder, 1967), §403.

[57] Cf. The First Council of Toledo; The First Council of Braga, in Denzinger, (ed.), *Enchiridion symbolorum*, §205 and §459–60; Sixtus V, Papal Bull *Coeli et terrae Creator* (5 January 1586); Urban VIII, Papal Bull *Inscrutabilis iudiciorum* (1 April 1631).

[58] Cf. Ecumenical Council of Vienne, Decree *Fidei catholicae*, §1; Fifth Lateran Ecumenical Council, Bull *Apostolici regiminis* in Tanner, (ed.), *Decrees of the Ecumenical Councils*, II, pp. 360 f.; 605 f.

transgrederentur. Sunt idcirco censura aequabiliter affecti hinc *fideismus*[59] et *traditionalismus radicalis*,[60] propter eorum diffidentiam naturalium rationis facultatum, illinc *rationalismus*,[61] et *ontologismus*,[62] quandoquidem rationi naturali id tribuebant, quod solummodo fidei lumine cognosci potest. Quae valida in his disceptationibus continebantur Constitutione dogmantica *Dei filius* recepta sunt, qua primum Concilum Oecumenicum quoddam, Vaticanum scilicet I, sollemniter inter Revelationem ac fidem necessitudinem pertractavit. Doctrina quae in documento illo continetur penitus et salubriter philosophicam complurium fidelium inquisitionem affecit atque hodiernis quoque temporibus quiddam perstat praeceptivum ad quod tendere debemus ad iustam congruentemque christianam hac de re inquisitionem consequendam.

53. Potius quam de singulis philosophorum sententiis, Magisterii effata de necessitate cognitionis naturalis atque, ideo, novissime philosophicae pro fide intellegenda tractaverunt. Concilium Vaticanum I, summatim referendo et sollemniter doctrinam confirmando quam ordinarium in modum constanterque fidelibus Magisterium pontificium ministravit, lucide edixit quam inseparabiles sint simulque plane seiunctae naturalis Dei cognitio et Revelatio, ratio et fides. Concilium ex praecipua postulatione sumpsit initium, quam ipsa Revelatio praesumebat, Deum scilicet esse naturaliter cognosci posse, rerum omnium principum et finem,[63] atque sollemni illa iam memorata enuntiatione desiit: "Duplicem esse ordinem cognitionis, non solum principio, sed obiecto etiam distinctum".[64] Asseverare ideo contra omnes rationalismi species oportebat fidei mysteria a philosophicis inventis separari, illaque haec praecedere et transcendere; altera ex parte adversus proclivia ad fidem blandimenta, necesse fuit ut veritatis unitas confirmaretur ideoque etiam

---

[59] Cfr *Theses a Ludovico Eugenio Bautain iussu sui Episcopi subscriptae* (8 Septembris 1840), *DS* 2751–2756; *Theses a Ludovico Eugenio Bautain ex mandato S. Congr. Episcoporum et Religiosorum subscriptae* (26 Aprilis 1884), *DS* 2765–2769.

[60] Cfr S. Congr. Indicis, Decr. *Theses contra traditionalismum Augustini Bonnetty* (11 Iunii 1855), *DS* 2811–2814.

[61] Cfr Pius IX, Breve *Eximiam tuam* (15 Iunii 1857), *DS* 2828–2831; Breve *Gravissimas inter* (11 Decembris 1862) *DS* 2850–2861.

[62] Cfr S. Congr. S. Officii, Decr. *Errores ontologistarum* (18 Septembris 1861), *DS* 2841–2847.

[63] Cfr Conc. Oecum. Vat. I, Cost. dogm. de fide catholica *Dei Filius*, II: *DS* 3004; et can. 2,1: *DS* 3026.

[64] *Dei Filius*, IV: *DS* 3015, memoratum in Conc. Vat. II, Const. past. de Ecclesia in mundo huius temporis *Gaudium et spes*, §59.

their duty to oppose the opinions of contemporary philosophers with philosophy of their own. In those days the Church's Magisterium was compelled to make sure that these philosophical views did not in their turn assume false or negative forms. Consequently censure was imposed equally on *fideism*[59] and *radical traditionalism*[60] because of their distrust of the natural faculties of reason; on the other hand *rationalism*[61] and *ontologism*[62] were also censured because they assigned to natural reason what could only be known by the light of faith. Whatever was validly contained in these discussions was included in the decree *Dei Filius*, in which the First Vatican Council gave solemn expression to the relationship between revelation and faith. The teaching which is contained in that document had a profound and healthy effect upon the philosophical investigations of many of the faithful, and even today stands out as a point of reference for which we should aim if we wish to arrive at a fair and appropriate Christian exploration of these issues.

53. Rather than deal with the theses of individual philosophers, the pronouncements of the Magisterium have dealt with the necessity of natural and more recently of philosophical knowledge for the understanding of faith. The First Vatican Council, by summing up and solemnly confirming the doctrine which the ordinary papal Magisterium had always expressed, made it quite clear how inseparable and at the same how distinct from each other are the natural knowledge and Revelation of God, reason and faith. The Council began with a basic premise, which Revelation itself presumed, that God could naturally be known as the origin and end of all things,[63] and concluded with the solemn assertion already referred to: 'there is a double order of knowledge, distinct not only in its origin, but also in its object'.[64] Therefore it

[59] Cf. *Theses a Ludovico Eugenio Bautain iussu sui Episcopi subscriptae* (8 September 1840); *Theses a Ludovico Eugenio Bautain ex mandato S. Cong. Episcoporum et Religiosorum subscriptae* (26 April 1844), in Denzinger, (ed.), *Enchiridion symbolorum*, §§2751–6 and §§2765–9.

[60] Cf. Sacred Congregation of the Index, Decree *Theses contra tradionalismum Augustini Bonnetty* (11 June 1855), in Denzinger, (ed.), *Enchiridion symbolorum*, §§2811–14.

[61] Cf. Pius IX, Brief *Eximiam tuam* (15 June 1857); Brief *Gravissimas inter* (11 December 1862) in Denzinger, (ed.), *Enchiridion symbolorum*, §§2828–31, §§2850–61

[62] Cf. Sacred Congregation of the Holy Office Decree *Errores ontologistarum* (18 September 1861) in Denzinger, (ed.), *Enchiridion symbolorum*, §§2841–57.

[63] First Vatican Council, Dogmatic Constitution on the Catholic Faith *Dei Filius*, §2, in Tanner, (ed.), *Decrees of the Ecumenical Councils*, II, p. 806.

[64] First Vatican Council, Dogmatic Constitution on the Catholic Faith *Dei Filius*, §4, in Tanner, (ed.), *Decrees of the Ecumenical Councils*, II, p. 808, cited in Second Vatican Ecumenical Council, Pastoral Constitution on the Church in the Modern World *Gaudium et spes*, §59 in Flannery, (ed.), *Vatican Council II*, pp. 963 f.

efficax emolumentum quod rationalis cognitio tribuere potest ac debet fidei cognitioni: "Verum etsi fides sit supra rationem, nulla tamen umquam inter fidem et rationem vera dissensio esse potest: cum idem Deus, qui mysteria revelat et fidem infundit, animo humano rationis lumen indiderit, Deus autem negare se ipsum non possit, nec verum vero umquam contradicere".[65]

54. Nostro quoque saeculo, Magisterium plus quam semel hanc rem agitavit, admonens de rationalismi blanditiis. Hoc in prospectu Pii PP. X est consideranda opera, qui animadvertit modernismi fundamentum illas esse philosophicas notiones, quae phaenomenismum, agnosticismum et immanentismum redolebant.[66] Neque momentum pondusve obliviscendum catholicae detrectationis marxistarum philosophiae atque communismi athei.[67]

Pius PP. XII deinceps vocem suam intendit cum, in Litteris illis Encyclicis quarum titulus *Humani generis*, de erratis sententiis moneret, quae cum evolutionismi, exsistentialismi et historicismi opinionibus nectebantur. Idem Pontifex clarius edixit placita haec non a theologis esse elucubrata ac prolata, sed "extra ovile Christi"[68] originem traxisse; simul addidit tales errores non simpliciter eiciendos, sed iudicio critico ponderandos: "Iamvero theologis ac philosophis catholicis, quibus grave incumbit munus divinam humanamque veritatem tuendi animisque inserendi hominum, has opinationes plus minusve e recto itinere aberrantes neque ignorare neque neglegere licet. Quin immo ipsi easdem opinationes perspectas habeant oportet, tum quia morbi non apte curantur nisi rite praecogniti fuerint, tum quia nonnumquam in falsis ipsis commentis aliquid veritatis latet, tum denique quia eadem animum provocant ad quasdam veritates, sive philosophicas sive theologicas, sollertius perscrutandas ac perpendendas".[69]

Postremo etiam Congregatio pro Doctrina Fidei, peculiare suum explens officium pro universali Romani Pontificis magisterio,[70] iterum de periculo

---

[65] Conc. Oecum. Vat. I, Const. dogm. de fide catholica *Dei Filius*, IV: *DS* 3017.

[66] Cfr Litt. Encycl. *Pascendi dominici gregis* (8 Septembris 1907): *ASS* 40 (1907), 596–597.

[67] Cfr Pius XI, Litt. Encycl. *Divini Redemptoris* (19 Martii 1937): *AAS* 29 (1937), 65–106.

[68] Litt. Encycl. *Humani generis* (12 Augusti 1950): *AAS* 42 (1950), 562–563.

[69] *Humani generis*, l.m., 563–564.

[70] Cfr Ioannes Paulus II, Const. Ap. *Pastor Bonus* (28 Iunii 1988), §§48–49: *AAS* 80 (1988), 873: Congr. de Doctrina Fidei, Istructio de ecclesiali theologi vocatione *Donum veritatis* (24 Maii 1990), §18: *AAS* 82 (1990), 1558.

was necessary on the one hand, against all rationalism, to distinguish the mysteries of faith from the discoveries of philosophy, which faith must both precede and transcend; and on the other, against the seductive attractions of fideism, it was necessary to assert the unity of truth and at the same time recognize the valuable assistance that rational knowledge can and should contribute to the knowledge of faith: 'although faith is superior to reason, even so there can be no discord between the two. Since it is the same God who reveals mysteries and infuses faith who has also provided the human spirit with the light of reason, it follows that God cannot deny himself nor can truth ever contradict truth'.[65]

54. In our (twentieth) century also, on more than one occasion, the Magisterium has dealt with this subject, giving warning of rationalism's allures. In this respect we should consider the attention given it by Pius X, who realized that at the root of Modernism were certain philosophical conceptions which were redolent of phenomenology, agnosticism and immanentism.[66] Nor in this connection should we forget the Catholic condemnation of Marxist philosophy and of atheistic Communism.[67]

Later, Pope Pius XII in his Encyclical entitled *Humani generis* gave warning of certain mistaken views which were connected with evolution, existentialism and historicism. The same pope made it even clearer that these views had not been worked out and expressed by theologians, but derived their origin 'outside the flock of Christ'.[68] At the same time he added that errors such as these were not simply to be rejected, but to be weighed critically: 'Catholic theologians and philosophers, who have the serious duty, not only of protecting divine and human truth but also of introducing it into human minds, ought neither to ignore nor to neglect those opinions which more or less stray from the right path. Rather they should examine them carefully, because diseases cannot be cured unless they are correctly diagnosed, and because it not infrequently happens that in the midst of these false views there lurks something of the truth. Finally, such false views provoke the spirit to a more profound weighing up of the truths of either philosophy or theology'.[69]

---

[65] First Vatican Council, Dogmatic Constitution on the Catholic Faith *Dei Filius*, §4, in Tanner, (ed.), *Decrees of the Ecumenical Councils*, II, pp. 808 f.

[66] Cf. Pius X, Encyclical Letter *Pascendi dominici gregis* (8 September 1907) (London: Burns & Oates, 1907).

[67] Cf. Pius XI, Encyclical Letter *Divini Redemptoris* (19 March 1937) (London: Catholic Truth Society, 1946).

[68] Pius XII, Encyclical Letter *Humani generis*, §2.

[69] Pius XII, Encyclical Letter *Humani generis*, §9.

monuit in quo versari possunt quidam theologiae liberationis theologi sumendo sine iudicii acumine principia et rationes a marxismo mutuata.[71]

Superioribus igitur temporibus identidem ac diversimode de re philosophica iudicium discernendi exercuit Magisterium. Quod autem Decessores Nostri recolendae memoriae attulerunt magni pretii existimatur subsidium quod oblivione obruere haudquaquam licet.

55. Si hodiernas condiciones consideramus, animadvertimus pristinas restitui quaestiones, easdemque proprietatibus novis. Non agitur tantum de quaestionibus quae singulas personas coetusve complectuntur, sed de cogitationibus inter homines serpentibus ita ut quodammodo in mentem communem iam convertantur. Talis est, exempli gratia, radicalis de ratione diffidentia, quam recentes multarum inquisitionum philosopharum explicationes ostendunt. Hac de re compluribus ex partibus audita est vox de "interitu metaphysicae": est voluntas ut philosophia tenuioribus muneribus contenta sit, quae tantum versetur in factis intepretandis vel in vestigationibus de quibusdam certis argumentis humanae cognitionis vel eiusdem de structuris.

In ipsa theologia quaedam praeteriti temporis iterum emergunt sollicitationes. In nonnullis huius aetatis theologicis scholis, exempli gratia, quidam *rationalismus* progreditur, praesertim cum placita, quae philosophice habentur valida, praeceptiva ad theologicam inquisitionem agendam iudicantur. Id potissimum accidit cum theologus, scientiae philosophicae expers, sine iudicio sententiis iam in communem loquelam cultumque receptis, at satis rationali fundamento carentibus, temperatur.[72]

---

[71] Cfr Instr. de quibusdam aspectibus "theologiae liberationis" *Libertatis nuntius* (6 Augusti 1984), §§7–10: *AAS* 76 (1984), 890–903.

[72] Concilium Vaticanum I claris iam verbis et auctoritate hunc errorem iam condemnavit "Hanc vero fidem [. . .] Ecclesia catholica profitetur, virtutem esse supernaturalem, qua, Dei aspirante et adiuvante gratia, ab ea revelata esse credimus, non propter intrinsecam rerum veritatem naturali rationis lumine perspectam, sed propter auctoritatem ipsius Dei revelantis, qui nec falli nec fallere potest": Const. dogm. *Dei Filius*, III: *DS* 3008, et can. 3.2: *DS* 3032. Ceterum idem Concilium sic iudicat: "ratio numquam idonea redditur ad ea percipienda instar veritatum, quae proprium ipsius obiectum constituunt": *Dei Filius*, IV: *DS* 3016. Sic haec conclusio: "Quapropter omnes christiani fideles huiusmodi opiniones, quae fidei doctrinae contrariae esse cognoscuntur, maxime si ab Ecclesia reprobatae fuerint, non solum prohibentur tamquam legitimas scientiae conclusiones defendere, sed pro erroribus potius, qui fallacem veritatis speciem prae se ferant, habere tenentur omnino": *Dei Filius*, IV: *DS* 3018.

Finally the Congregation for the Doctrine of the Faith, in fulfilling its particular work for the universal Magisterium of the Roman Pontiff,[70] has also given warning of the danger of some liberation theologians who uncritically adopt principles and reasons borrowed from Marxism.[71]

In the past, then, on different occasions and in different ways the Magisterium has exercised its discerning judgment in the area of philosophy. Our revered Predecessors have thus made an invaluable contribution which ought not to be forgotten.

55. When we take a look at the modern situation, we recognize the return of the same original questions, but with new features. We are not, however, dealing here with questions that concern particular individuals or groups, but with reflections which have such currency for humanity that they can be seen as forming a sort of common mind. One such example is the rooted distrust of reason, which many recent philosophical enquiries demonstrate. In this matter we hear not infrequently the expression 'the end of metaphysics': the desire is that philosophy should rest content with lighter duties, restricted to the interpretation of facts, or making enquiries into particular matters concerning human knowledge or its structures.

In theology itself particular concerns from an earlier age again emerge. For example in some modern theological faculties a certain *rationalism* arises, above all when principles accepted to be philosophically well-founded are judged normative for the advance of theological research. This especially occurs when a theologian, neglectful of the discipline of philosophy, is influenced injudiciously by ideas which, though they have been accepted in the realm of normal speech and ideas, still lack sufficiently rational grounds.[72]

---

[70] Cf. John Paul II, Apostolic Constitution *Pastor Bonus* (28 June 1988), §§48–49: Congregation for the Doctrine of the Faith, Instruction on the Ecclesial Vocation of the Theologian *Donum veritatis* (24 May 1990) (London: Catholic Truth Society, 1990), §18.

[71] Cf. Congregation for the Doctrine of the Faith, Instruction on Certain Aspects of the 'Theology of Liberation' *Libertatis nuntius* (6 August 1984), §§7–10.

[72] In language as clear as it is authoritative, the First Vatican Council condemned this error, affirming on the one hand that 'as regards this faith . . . the Catholic Church professes that it is a supernatural virtue by means of which, under divine inspiration and with the help of grace, we believe to be true the things revealed by God, not because of the intrinsic truth of the things perceived by the natural light of reason, but because of the authority of God himself, who reveals them and who can neither deceive nor be deceived': Dogmatic Constitution *Dei Filius*, III: and Canon 3, §3 in Tanner, (ed.), *Decrees of the Ecumenical Councils*, II, p. 807. On the other hand, the Council declared that reason is never 'able to penetrate [these mysteries] as

Neque desunt qui in *fideismum* periculose regrediantur, quippe qui rationalis cognitionis philosophicaeque scientiae pondus ad fidem intellegendam, immo ad ipsam facultatem possidendam in Deum credendi, non agnoscat. Hodie pervagata opinio huius fideisticae propensionis est "bliblicismus", qui Sacrarum Litterarum lectionem earumque explicationem unicum arbitratur veridicae congruentiae caput. Sic evenit ut Dei verbum cum sola Sacra Scriptura aequetur, hoc modo Ecclesiae doctrinam perimendo, quam Concilium Oecumenicum Vaticanum II palam confirmavit. Constitutio *Dei Verbum* postquam commonefecit simul in Sacris Libris simul in Traditione[73] inesse Dei verbum, graviter edicit: "Sacra Traditio et Sacra Scriptura unum verbi Dei sacrum depositum constituunt Ecclesiae commissum, cui inhaerens tota plebs sancta cum Pastoribus suis adunata, in doctrina Apostolorum et communione, fractione panis et orationibus iugiter perseverat (cfr *Act* 2:42)".[74] Non ad Sacram Scripturam dumtaxat igitur sese refert Ecclesia. Etenim "suprema fidei eius regula"[75] ex unitate oritur quam inter Sacram Traditionem, Sacram Scripturam et Ecclesiae Magisterium posuit Spiritus, quae sic mutuo implicantur, ut haec tria seiunctim nullo modo esse possint.[76]

Non est porro subaestimandum periculum quod inest in proposito quodam Sacrae Scripturae veritatem eruendi ex una tantum adhibita methodologia, necessitate neglecta latioris exegesis, quae una cum tota Ecclesia ad textus plene intellegendos accedere sinat. Quotquot in Sacrae Scripturae studium incumbunt prae se usque ferre debent varias methodologias explanatorias in aliqua ipsas etiam inniti opinatione philosophica: est illa acumine pensitanda antequam sacris scriptis aptetur.

Aliae absconditi fideismi formae agnosci possunt eo quod theologia speculativa parvi aestimatur ac pariter philosophia classica despicatui habetur, ex cuius notionibus sive fidei intellectus sive dogmaticae ipsae formulae verba exceperunt. Pius PP. XII, felicis recordationis, de hac traditionis philosophicae oblivione necnon de desertis translaticiis locutionibus monuit.[77]

---

[73] Cfr *Dei Verbum* §§9–10.
[74] *Dei Filius*, §10.
[75] *Dei Filius*, §21.
[76] Cfr *Dei Filius*, §10.
[77] Cfr Litt. Encycl. *Humani generis* (12 Augusti 1950): *AAS* 42 (1950), 565–567: 571–573.

There are some who dangerously revert to *fideism*, simply because they fail to recognize the value of rational knowledge and of the discipline of philosophy both for the understanding of faith and even for the capacity for believing in God in the first place. Today a widespread expression of this fideistic tendency is to be found in 'biblicism', which holds that the reading and explication of Scripture is the only criterion of truth. Thus it occurs that the Word of God is equated solely with Holy Scripture, which results in eliminating the teaching of the Church, a teaching clearly confirmed by the Second Vatican Council. The constitution *Dei Verbum*, having insisted that the Word of God was to be found both in Sacred Scripture and in Tradition,[73] made the following solemn pronouncement: 'Sacred Tradition and Sacred Scripture together make up the one sacred deposit entrusted to the Church. By adhering to this the entire holy people of God together with their pastors continually persevere in the teaching and fellowship of the Apostles, in the breaking of bread and prayers' (cf. *Acts* 2:42).[74] The Church, therefore, does not appeal only to Scripture by itself. On the contrary, the 'supreme rule of her faith'[75] arises from the unity created by the Spirit between Sacred Tradition, Sacred Scripture and the Magisterium of the Church, and these three all imply one another and cannot be separated from each other.[76]

One should not underestimate the danger that lurks in attempting to extract the truth of Scripture by the use of one methodology only, in danger of neglecting a wider exegesis, which, united with the whole Church, allows for fully understanding the texts. Those who devote themselves to a study of Scripture should remember that the various explanatory methodologies are themselves dependent on a particular philosophical approach. This must be subjected to a sharp scrutiny before it is applied to the sacred writings.

Other forms of hidden fideism can be recognized from the scant

---

it does the truths which are its proper object': First Vatican Council, Dogmatic Constitution *Dei Filius*, §4, p. 810. It then drew a practical conclusion: 'the Christian faithful not only have no right to defend as legitimate scientific conclusions opinions which are contrary to the doctrine of the faith, particularly if condemned by the Church, but they are strictly obliged to regard them as errors which have no more than a fraudulent semblance of truth': *Dei Filius*, §4, p. 809.

[73] Cf. Second Vatican Council, Dogmatic Constitution on Divine Revelation *Dei Verbum* §§9–10 in Flannery, (ed.), *Vatican Council II*, pp. 755 f.

[74] Second Vatican Council II, Dogmatic Constitution on Divine Revelation *Dei Verbum* §10 in Flannery, (ed.), *Vatican Council II*, pp. 755 f.

[75] Second Vatican Council, Dogmatic Constitution on Divine Revelation *Dei Verbum* §21 in Flannery, (ed.), *Vatican Council II*, p. 762.

[76] Second Vatican Council II, Dogmatic Constitution on Divine Revelation *Dei Verbum* §10 in Flannery, (ed.), *Vatican Council II*, pp. 755 f.

56. Aliquo modo, postremo, effatis omnia complectentibus et absolutis diffidunt, ii potissimum qui arbitrantur ex consensu, non ex intellectu obiectivae realitati obnoxio depromi veritatem. Certe illud intellegi potest, in mundo qui in multas peculiaresque partes dispertitur, eum complexivum ultimumque vitae sensum difficulter agnosci, quem translaticia philosophia quaesivit. Verumtamen sub lumine fidei quae in Christo Iesu hunc ultimum sensum agnoscit, facere non possumus quin philosophos, christianos vel non christianos, incitemus ut rationis humanae facultati confidant neque metas in philosophandi arte nimis mediocres prae se ferant. Huius iam ad finem vergentis millenni historica lectio testatur hanc esse calcandam viam: oportet veritatis ultimae cupido vestigationisque desiderium non amittantur, quae cum audacia novos cursus detegendi coniunguntur. Fides ipsa rationem lacessit ad omnem secessionem deserendam et ad omnia periclitanda, ut persequatur quae pulchra, bona veraque sunt. Fides sic rationis fit certus atque suadens advocatus.

Ecclesia philosophiae studiosa

57. Magisterium, utcumque, in erroribus notandis doctrinisque philosophorum aberrantibus non se continuit. Pari cura praecipua principia ad germanam philosophicae cogitationis renovationem assequendam confirmavit, definita demonstrando etiam curricula, quae sunt tenenda. Hac in re, Leo PP. XIII, Litteris suis Encyclicis *Aeterni Patris*, vere historicae significationis fecit illam pro Ecclesiae vita progressionem. Id scriptum ad hoc usque tempus unum exstat documentum pontificium illius gradus, quod philosophiae totum dicatur. Concilii Vaticani I eximius ille Pontifex doctrinam de necessitudine inter fidem et rationem repetiit atque amplificavit, idemque philosophicas cogitationes fidei ac theologicae scientiae summo esse auxilio demonstravit.[78] Uno plus post saeculo complura illius scripti indicia sive re sive paedagogico usu nihil amiserunt utilitatis; primum ex omnibus est id quod ad incomparabilem sancti Thomae philosophiae praestantiam spectat. Doctoris Angelici doctrina restituta Leoni PP. XIII optima videbatur semita ad illum philosophiae usum recuperandum, quem postulabat fides. Sanctus Thoma – scripsit ille – "rationem, ut par est, a fide apprime distinguens, utramque tamen amice consocians, utriusque tum iura conservavit, tum dignitati consuluit".[79]

---

[78] Cfr Leo XIII, Litt. Encycl. *Aeterni Patris* (4 Augusti 1879): *ASS* 11 (1878–1879), 97–115.

[79] *Aeterni Patris*, *ASS* 11, 109.

consideration accorded to speculative theology and similarly in the disdain for classical philosophy, from which the terms of both the understanding of faith and the language of dogmatic formulations were drawn. Pope Pius XII, of happy memory, warned of the dangers both of neglect of the philosophical tradition and of a desertion of traditional terminology.[77]

56. Finally, in another way, there are those who distrust every proposition that claims any absoluteness or universality and prefer to suppose that truth is arrived at by general agreement and not derived from the intellect's exposure to objective reality. Certainly it is not hard to understand that in a world which is divided into so many distinct areas, an all embracing and ultimate understanding of life is hard to recognize, especially of the kind traditionally sought by philosophy. Even so, in the light of faith which recognizes ultimate meaning in Christ Jesus, we cannot help but encourage all philosophers, Christian or non-Christian, to trust to the capacity of human reason and not to impose goals which are too modest in their philosophizing. The lesson of history in this millennium – now drawing to its close – shows that this is the path to follow: it is vital not to abandon the desire for ultimate truth, the eagerness to search for it or the audacity for discovering new paths in the search. Faith itself provokes reason to avoiding all isolation and to take bold steps in seeking out whatever is beautiful, true and good. In this way faith becomes the certain and persuasive advocate of reason.

The Church as the student of philosophy

57. The Magisterium does not confine itself to noting the errors and false teachings of the philosophers. With equal care it insisted on the importance of certain principles necessary for the correct renewal of philosophical thinking, even to the extent of laying down definite pathways which were to be held to. In this matter Pope Leo XIII in his Encyclical *Aeterni Patris* made progress of truly historic importance for the life of the Church, since it remains to this day the one papal document of such authority devoted entirely to philosophy. This extraordinary pope repeated and amplified the teaching contained in the First Vatican Council about the close connection between faith and reason. He also showed that the reflections of philosophy were of enormous assistance for faith and theological discipline.[78] A century later many insights of that writing have lost nothing of their usefulness either in practice or from the point of view of teaching: first above all things is the stress laid on the

---

[77] Cf. Pius XII, Encyclical Letter *Humani generis*, §§ 14–17, 29–31.

[78] Cf. Leo XIII, Encyclical Letter *Aeterni Patris* translated as *The Study of Scholastic Philosophy* in Wynne, (ed.), *The Great Encyclicals of Pope Leo XIII*, pp. 34–57.

58. Quae feliciter consecuta sit haec Pontificis invitatio omnes noverunt. Sancti Thomae de doctrina inquisitiones nec non aliorum scholasticorum auctorum novum impetum habuerunt. Historica studia valde excitata sunt et hanc ob rem mediaevalium philosophorum iterum sunt repertae divitiae, quae tunc temporis fere ignorabantur, atque novae Thomisticae scholae ortae sunt. Historica adhibita methodologia, sancti Thomae operum cognitio admodum progressa est atque innumeri fuerunt vestigatores qui animose in rerum philosophicarum theologicarumque disputationes illius aetatis thomisticam traditionem induxerunt. Catholici theologi huius saeculi auctoritate praestantiores, quorum cogitationibus et vestigationibus multum debet Concilium Oecumenicum Vaticanum II, huius renovationis philosophiae Thomisticae filii sunt. Ecclesia, saeculo vertente XX, valida philosophorum turma uti sic potuit, qui Angelici Doctoris in schola sunt instituti.

59. Thomistica utcumque et neothomistica renovatio, philosophicae repetitae cogitationis in cultura christianae indolis non fuit solum signum. Iam antea, atque una cum Leoniana invitatione, non pauci catholici philosophi exstiterant, qui recentioribus philosophantium cogitationibus innitentes, propria utentes methodologia, magnae auctoritatis duraturique momenti opera philosophica ediderant. Fuerunt qui sic altas summas composuerunt ut nihil ab his esset invidendum maximis idealismi commentis; alii porro ad fidem nova ratione tractandam, lumine praefulgente renovati intellectus conscientiae moralis, epistemologica fundamenta iecerunt; alii quandam induxerunt philosophiam quae, ab immanentia vestiganda sumpto initio, ad transcendentiam aditum reseravit; alii tandem in phaenomenologicae provinciam methodologiae fidei postulata inserere contenderunt. Diversis denique rationibus formae philosophicarum cogitationum sunt effectae, quae praeclaram christianae doctrinae traditionem in fidei rationisque unitate vitalem servaverunt.

60. Concilium Oecumenicum Vaticanum II autem pro parte sua de philosophia locupletissimam ac fertilissimam exhibet doctrinam. Oblivisci non possumus, his potissimum consideratis Litteris Encyclicis, Constitutionis *Gaudium et spes* integrum quoddam caput anthropologiae biblicae esse quasi compendium, idemque exstare pro philosophia quoque consilii fontem. Illis in paginis de humanae personae valore agitur, quae ad imaginem Dei creata est, eius dignitatis et praestantiae prae ceteris creaturis ratio affertur atque eius rationis transcendens

incomparable importance of the philosophy of St Thomas. Pope Leo XIII thought that bringing back the teaching of the Angelic Doctor was the best way of recovering the use of philosophy which faith requires. St Thomas – he wrote – 'correctly distinguished reason from faith, yet he also united them in friendship, and he protected the rights and respected the dignity of both'.[79]

58. The positive results of the papal summons are well known. Doctrinal researches into St Thomas and those of other scholastic authors received a new impetus. Historical studies were mightily encouraged and as a result the riches of the Mediaeval philosophers which at that time were quite unknown were rediscovered; new Thomistic schools also arose. By the use of the historical method knowledge of the writings of St Thomas greatly increased, and innumerable researchers have enthusiastically brought the Thomistic tradition into contact with modern philosophical and theological discussions. The more distinguished of the Catholic theologians of this century, to whose reflections and researches Vatican II owes so much, are children of the restoration of the philosophy of St Thomas. The Church in the course of the twentieth century has been served by a powerful collection of philosophers brought up in the school of the Angelic Doctor.

59. This Thomist and Neo-Thomist revival was not the only indication of a renewal of philosophical thought in Christian culture. Even earlier, and together with the Leonine summons, there were not a few Catholic philosophers who, by relying on the reflections of contemporary philosophers and employing their own methodology, produced philosophical works of great authority and lasting importance. Some produced such profound treatises that they had no reason to fear comparison with the greatest efforts of idealism; others established the epistemological foundations for a new consideration of faith in the light of a renewed understanding of the moral conscience. Others, too, introduced a philosophy which, though it began as a form of immanentism, opened up an approach to transcendence. Others again tried to introduce the postulates of faith into a phenomenological methodology. From different quarters, then, modes of philosophical reflections resulted which all served to protect the noble and vital tradition of Christian doctrine in the unity of faith and reason.

60. The Second Vatican Council for its part displays a very rich and fertile teaching on the subject of philosophy. We cannot forget as we write this Encyclical, that the constitution *Gaudium et spes* contains in effect a compendium of biblical anthropology and at the same time, as

[79] Cf. Leo XIII, Encyclical Letter *The Study of Scholastic Philosophy*, p. 49.

facultas ostenditur.[80] Atheismi quoque quaestionem *Gaudium et spes* considerat et illius philosophicae opinationis errorum apposite afferuntur causae, non alienabili praesertim personae spectata dignitate ac libertate.[81] Procul dubio altam philosophicam significationem habent illarum paginarum sententiae, quas Nos in Nostras primas Litteras Encyclicas *Redemptor hominis* rettulimus, quaeque veluti firmum quoddam constituunt ad quod Nostra doctrina costanter convertitur: "Reapse nonnisi in mysterio Verbi incarnati mysterium hominis vere clarescit. Adam enim, primus homo, erat figura futuri (*Rom* 5:14), scilicet Christi Domini. Christus, novissimus Adam, in ipsa revelatione mysterii Patris eiusque anoris, hominem ipsi homini plene manifestat eidemque altissimam eius vocationem patefacit".[82]

Concilium de philosophia quoque discenda tractavit, cui ad sacerdotium candidati operam dare debent; quae cohortationes in universum sunt ad christianam totam institutionem convertendae. Affirmat enim Concilium: "Philosophicae disciplinae ita tradantur ut alumni imprimis ad solidam et cohaerentem hominis, mundi et Dei cognitionem acquirendam manuducantur, innixi patrimonio philosophico perenniter valido, ratione quoque habita philosophicarum investigationum progredientis aetatis".[83]

Haec praecepta etiam atque etiam sunt confirmata nec non in aliis Magisterii documentis explicata, ut solida philosophica institutio praestetur, iis praesertim qui ad theologicas disciplinas se comparant. Ipsi autem saepenumero huius institutionis pondus ostentavimus iis qui, in pastorali vita, aliquando cum hodierni mundi necessitatibus contendere et causas aliquorum morum intellegere debebunt, prompta responsa daturi.[84]

---

[80] Cfr *Gaudium et spes* §§14–15.

[81] Cfr *Gaudium et spes*, §§20–21.

[82] *Gaudium et spes*, §22; cfr Ioannes Paulus II, Litt. Encycl. *Redemptor hominis* (4 Martii 1979), §8: *AAS* 71 (1979), 271–272.

[83] Decr. de institutione sacerdotali *Optatam totius*, §15.

[84] Cfr Ioannes Paulus II, Const. Ap. *Sapientia christiana* (15 Aprilis 1979), §§79–80: *AAS* 71 (1979), 495–496; Adhort. Ap. postsynodalis *Pastores dabo vobis* (25 Martii 1992), §52: *AAS* 84 (1979), 750–751. Cfr quoque quaedam S. Thomae de philosophia commenta: *Discorso al Pontificio Ateneo Internazionale Angelicum* (17 Novembris 1979): *Insegnamenti* II, 2 (1979), 1177–1189; *Discorso ai partecipanti dell'VIII Congresso Tomistico Internazionale* (13 Septembris 1980): *Insegnamenti* III, 2 (1980), 604–615; *Discorso ai partecipanti al Congresso Internazionale della Società "San Tommaso" sulla dottrina dell'anima in S. Tommaso* (4 Ianuarii 1986): *Insegnamenti* IX, 1 (1986), 18–24. Praeterea S. Congr. pro Educatione Catholica, *Ratio fundamentalis institutionis sacerdotalis* (6 Ianuarii 1970), 70–75: *ASS* 62 (1970), 366–368; Decr. *Sacra Theologia* (20 Ianuarii 1972): *AAS* 64 (1972), 583–586.

far as philosophy is concerned, acts as a source of counsel. In its pages much is said concerning the dignity of the human person created in the image of God, and reasons are advanced for assigning her a dignity and importance above all other creatures, whilst at the same time the transcendent capacity of reason is demonstrated in her.[80] *Gaudium et spes* also examines the subject of atheism, and the causes of the basic flaw in that philosophical outlook are exposed, especially in relation to the inalienable dignity and freedom of the human person.[81] Without doubt that chapter is profoundly significant for philosophy; and it was this thesis which I took up in my first Encyclical Letter *Redemptor hominis* and to which our teaching constantly reverts: 'it is only in the mystery of the Incarnate Word that the mystery of humanity becomes clear. For Adam, the first man, was a type of the one to come, that is Christ the Lord (*Rom* 5:14). Christ, the new Adam, in the very revelation of the mystery of the Father and of his love for us, at the same time reveals humanity fully to itself and uncovers his deepest vocation in so doing'.[82]

The Council also discussed the study of philosophy which is required of candidates for the priesthood, though its advice should be listened to more generally in so far as it applies to the Christian education of all. The council affirms that 'the disciplines of philosophy should be so handed on that students at the very beginning should be led to acquire a solid and coherent knowledge of man, of the world and of God. They should depend in this on a perennially valid philosophical heritage, while at the same time taking account of the progress of philosophical enquiries'.[83]

These instructions have been reinforced over and over again and have been expounded in other documents of the Magisterium, with the intention that a solid philosophical education may be offered above all to those who are preparing themselves for theological studies. We have frequently stressed the importance of this education for those in the pastoral ministry who have to give prompt replies on occasions when

---

[80] Cf. Second Vatican Council, Dogmatic Constitution on the Church in the Modern World *Gaudium et spes*, §§14–15 in Flannery, (ed.), *Vatican Council II*, pp. 914–16.

[81] Cf. Cf. Second Vatican Council, Dogmatic Constitution on the Church in the Modern World *Gaudium et spes*, §§20–21 in Flannery, (ed.), *Vatican Council II*, pp. 919–22.

[82] Cf. Second Vatican Council, Dogmatic Constitution on the Church in the Modern World *Gaudium et spes*, §22 in Flannery, (ed.), *Vatican Council II*, pp. 922–4; cf. John Paul II, Encyclical Letter *Redemptor hominis*, §8.

[83] Second Vatican Council, Decree on Priestly Formation *Optatam totius*, §15 in Flannery, (ed.), *Vatican Council II*, p. 718.

61. Si quidem compluribus temporibus necesse habuimus hanc questionem iterum attingere, cogitationum Doctoris Angelici vim confirmavimus atque ut eius philosophia comprehenderetur institimus, id ex eo ortum est quod Magisterii praescripta haud semper optanda animi promptitudine servata sunt. In catholicis scholis multis, annis post Concilium Oecumenicum Vaticanum II finitum, huius rei quaedam visa est hebetatio propterea quod minoris aestimata est non modo philosophia scholastica, verum etiam in universum tota philosophica disciplina. Mirantes ac dolentes animadvertimus haud paucos theologos esse participes huius neglegentiae philosophicae disciplinae.

Diversae numerantur rationes quae alienae huic voluntati subsunt. Diffidentia de ratione apprime est referenda, quam huius aetatis philosophia magnam partem ostendit, quippe quae metaphysicam de ultimis hominis quaestionibus inquisitionem late deserat, ut proprium studium in peculiaria regionaliaque negotiaconvertatur, quae nonnumquam mere sunt formalia. Huic rei praeterea accedit erratum iudicium quod circa praesertim "scientias humanas" exstitit. Concilium Oecumenicum Vaticanum II saepe probandum pondus scientificae inquisitionis confirmavit, ut hominis mysterium altius intellegeretur.[85] Si quidem theologi ad has scientias cognoscendas easdemque recte in suis inquisitionibus adhibendas invitantur, id tamen intellegi non debet ipsis implicite dari potestatem philosophiam segregandi vel amovendi in pastorali institutione ac "fidei praeparatione". Oblivisci denique non potest in fidei inculturationem reciperatum studium. Vita praesertim novensilium Ecclesiarum effecit ut, una cum praeclaris cogitationis formis, intellegeretur compluras inesse popularis sapientiae manifestationes, quae verum patrimonum culturae et traditionum constituunt. Harum tamen consuetudinum inquisitio una cum philosophiae vestigatione procedere debet. Haec ipsa sinet ut probanda popularis sapientiae lineamenta exsistant, dum necessario illa cum Evangelio enuntiando coniungit.[86]

62. Firmiter confirmare placet philosophiae disciplinam praecipuum habere momentum quod abstrahi non potest in studiorum theologicorum ratione et in alumnorum apud Seminaria institutione. Haud igitur inconsiderate studiorum theologicorum *curriculum* antecedat

---

[85] Cfr Const. past. de Ecclesia in mundo huius temporis *Gaudium et spes*, §57; §62.

[86] Cfr *Gaudium et spes*, §44.

they have to deal with the necessities of today's world and need to understand the causes of certain behaviours.[84]

61. The principal reason why we have found it necessary on so many occasions to touch on this problem, and to reaffirm the strength of the reflections of the Angelic Doctor, and have stressed the importance of comprehending his philosophy, is because the requirements of the Magisterium have not always been followed with the readiness of spirit desired. In many Catholic institutions in the years after the end of the Second Vatican Council a certain weakness in this matter has been evident, not only in the diminished respect accorded to scholastic philosophy, but in general to the whole philosophical discipline. It is with both surprise and sorrow that we have observed this neglect also to be shared by not a few theologians.

Several reasons account for this lack of interest. Above all there is a lack of trust in reason itself displayed to a large extent by modern philosophy itself, in that it gives a wide berth to the metaphysical search for man's ultimate questions in order to concentrate attention upon matters which are of particular and localized interest and are perhaps even merely formal. This is reinforced by a mistaken judgment which exists concerning the 'human sciences'. The Second Vatican Council frequently insisted on the importance of scientific enquiry with the aim that the mystery of man might be more profoundly understood.[85] But if theologians are encouraged to understand these sciences and to use them correctly in their own explorations, this does not give them leave to separate off philosophy or to remove it from pastoral instruction or in 'preparation for faith'. Finally the care demanded for the inculturation of faith should not be forgotten. The life of the young churches above all demands that, together with clear forms of knowledge, there be an understanding of the many expressions of popular wisdom which make up the valuable

[84] Cf. John Paul II, Apostolic Constitution *Sapientia christiana* (15 April 1979) (London: Catholic Truth Society, 1979), §§79–80; Post-Synodal Apostolic Exhortation *Pastores dabo vobis* (25 March 1992) (London: Catholic Truth Society, 1992) §52: Cf. also various remarks on the philosophy of Saint Thomas: *Address to the International Pontifical Athenaeum 'Angelicum'* (17 November 1979): *Insegnamenti* II, 2 (1979), pp. 1177–89; *Address to the Participants of the Eighth International Thomistic Congress* (13 September 1980): *Insegnamenti* III, 2 (1980), pp. 604–15; *Address to the Participants at the International Congress of the Saint Thomas Society on the Doctrine of the Soul in Saint Thomas* (4 January 1986): *Insegnamenti* IX, 1 (1986), pp. 18–24. Also the Sacred Congregation for Catholic Education, *Ratio fundamentalis institutionis sacerdotalis* (6 January 1970), §§70–75; Decree *Sacra theologia* (20 January 1972).

[85] Cf. Vatican Council II, Pastoral Constitution on the Church in the Modern World *Gaudium et spes*, §§57, 62, in Flannery, (ed.), *Vatican Council II*, pp. 961 f., 966–8.

temporis quoddam spatium, quo peculiare philosophiae ediscendae praevideatur opus. Electio haec, quam Concilium Lateranense V confirmavit,[87] in experientia radices agit quam Media Aetas est adepta, cum convenientia inter philosophicam et theologicam disciplinam conspicuum obtinuit locum et momentum. Haec studiorum ratio affecit, iuvit et curavit, quamvis oblique, maximam partem promotionis recentioris philosophiae. Conspicuum exemplum exhibet beneficium, quod contulerunt Francisci Suárez *Disputationes metaphysicae*, quae etiam in Studiorum Universitatibus Germaniae Luteranis reperiebantur. Haec autem methologia relicta sive in sacerdotali institutione sive in theologica inquisitione grave detrimentum attulit. Conspiciatur, exempli gratia, cogitationis et hodiernae culturae indiligentia, quae effecit ut omnes dialogi formae tollerentur vel omnes philosophiae sine iudicio susciperentur.

Magna Nos tenet spes has difficultates sublatum iri, prudenti intercedente philosophica et theologica institutione, quae numquam in Ecclesia desinere debet.

63. Has propter rationes, Nobis visum est instantem esse rem, his Nostris Litteris Encyclicis, acre studium confirmare, quod philosophiae tribuit Ecclesia; immo artam coniunctionem, qua theologicum opus et philosophica inquisitio nenctuntur. Inde Magisterii officium oritur philosophicam scientiam discernendi et concitandi, quae fidei minime aversetur. Nostrum est quaedam principia et indicia exhibere, quae necessaria arbitramur, ut ordinata necessitudo et efficax inter theologiam et philosophiam instituatur. Eorum sub lumine clarius iudicari poterit an qualemve necessitudinem cum diversis philosophicis scholis opinationibusque instituere debeat theologia, quas hodiernus mundus exhibet.

---

[87] Cfr Conc. Oecum. Lateranense V, Bulla *Apostolici regiminis sollicitudo*, Sessio VIII: Conc. Oecum. Decreta, 1991, 605–606.

patrimony of culture and traditions. Investigation of these traditions ought to go hand in hand with philosophical enquiry. This will allow for the outlines of popular wisdom to become clear and at the same time make the necessary connection with the proclamation of the Gospel.[86]

62. It must be clearly understood that the discipline of philosophy has great importance, which must not be removed from any programme of theological studies or the training of students in seminaries. For this very good reason, before the study of the theological *curriculum* begins, a period of time must be allotted to the special study of philosophy. This decision, confirmed by the Fifth Council of the Lateran,[87] has its roots in the experience of the Middle Ages, when the coherence of philosophical and theological discipline had both place and importance. This ordering of studies influenced, promoted and enabled much of the development of modern philosophy, albeit indirectly. A notable example of this is the blessing conferred, even in the Lutheran universities of Germany, by the *Metaphysical Disputations* of Francis Suárez. But the abandoning of this methodology has brought grave consequences, whether it be in priestly training or in theological research. Consider, for example, the neglect of contemporary reflectiveness and culture which has resulted in the disappearance of any form of dialogue and an indiscriminate acceptance of all kinds of philosophies.

It is our great hope that these difficulties will be removed, with the prudent help of philosophical and theological formation, which must never be lacking in the Church.

63. For these reasons it has seemed important to us in this Encyclical to reaffirm the intense interest the Church has in philosophy, and to insist upon the close connection between theological work and philosophical enquiry. From this comes the duty of the Magisterium to discern and promote philosophical knowledge which is not at odds with faith. It is our business to set forth certain principles and criteria which we suppose to be necessary, if an ordered and helpful relationship is to be established between theology and philosophy. In the light of these principles it will be possible to determine what, if any, sort of relationship theology ought to embark on with the variety of philosophical schools of today.

---

[86] Cf. Second Vatican Council Pastoral Constitution on the Church in the Modern World *Gaudium et spes*, §44, in Flannery, (ed.), *Vatican Council II*, pp. 946 f.

[87] Cf. The Fifth Ecumenical Council of the Lateran, Bull *Apostolici regiminis sollicitudo*, Session VIII, in Tanner, (ed.), *Decrees of the Ecumenical Councils*, II, p. 606.

CAPUT VI
MUTUA INTER THEOLOGIAM ET PHILOSOPHIAM ACTIO

Fidei scientia atque philosophicae rationis postulata

64. Dei verbum singulis hominibus omni tempore et in omnibus terrarum orbis locis destinatur; et homo est naturaliter philosophus. Theologia autem, quatenus repercussa et scientifica elaboratio intellectus huius verbi sub fidei lumine, seu quasdam suas propter rationes seu ad peculiaria munia obeunda facere non potest quin necessitudinem cum philosophicis scholis instituat, quae reapse annorum decursu invaluerunt. Peculiaribus methodologiis theologis haud significatis, quod quidem ad Magisterium non pertinet, quaedam munia theologiae propria memorare potius volumus, in quibus ad philosophicas cogitationes ipsam propter naturam revelati Verbi est decurrendum.

65. Theologia veluti scientia fidei ordinatur duobus statutis principiis methodologicis, quae sunt: *auditus fidei* et *intellectus fidei*. Altero principio ipsa Revelationis depositum obtinet, quemadmodum id pedetemptim collustraverunt Sacra Traditio, Sacrae Litterae et vivum Ecclesiae Magisterium.[88] Altero, theologia cogitationis postulatis respondere vult per speculativam ratiocinationem.

De congrua *auditus fidei* comparatione, philosophia theologiae suam peculiarem affert opem cum cognitionis personalisque communicationis structuram considerat atque nominatim varias species et officia loquelae. Aequum pariter est pondus quod confert philosophia ut ecclesialis Traditio, Magisterii effata nec non eximiorum theologiae magistrorum sententiae aptius intellegantur: hi enim mentem suam patefaciunt saepe per cogitata formasque cogitationis, quae a certa quadam philosophica traditione mutuo suscipiuntur. Hac in re theologus rogatur ut non modo significet notiones vocabulaque, quibus Ecclesia cogitat suamque docrinam definit, verum etiam ut penitus philosophicas opinationes intellegat quae forte tam notiones quam nomina affecerint, ut ad rectas congruasque significationes perveniatur.

---

[88] Cfr Conc. Oecum. Vat. II, Const. dogm. de Divina Revelatione *Dei Verbum*, 10.

CHAPTER VI
THE INTERACTION BETWEEN THEOLOGY AND PHILOSOPHY

The knowledge of faith and the demands of philosophical reason

64. The Word of God is destined for every single person, in every age and every place in the whole world; man is naturally a philosopher. Theology, however, in so far as it is a reflective and scientific development of the understanding of this Word in the light of faith, either according of its own structure or because of the special functions it must perform, cannot help but establish a relationship with the philosophical schools which have actually gathered strength over the years. Without paying attention to the methodologies peculiar to theology, which is not pertinent to the Magisterium, we wish instead to recall some specific tasks of theology, which, by the very nature of the revealed Word, demand recourse to philosophical reflections.

65. Theology, in so far as it is the science of faith, is ordered by two established methodological principles, which are *the hearing of faith* and the *understanding of faith*. With one principle it makes its own the content of Revelation, illustrated in the progress of time by Sacred Tradition, Holy Scripture and the living Magisterium of the Church.[88] With the other theology wishes to reply to the demands of reason by means of speculative reasoning.

In preparation for the proper *hearing of faith*, philosophy supplies its own unique contribution to theology, above all in its understanding of the structure of knowing and of interpersonal communication and specifically of the different types and functions of speech. A service of equal weight is provided by philosophy in rendering more easily intelligible ecclesial tradition, the pronouncements of the Magisterium, and the opinions of the distinguished masters of theology: for these latter often express themselves by means of thoughts and forms of thinking, which derive in their turn from a particular philosophical tradition. In this area the theologian is often asked not only to explain the concepts and vocabulary with which the Church reflects on and defines her teaching, but also to have a deep understanding of the various philosophical tenets which have perhaps created the ideas and expressions in order to find correct and appropriate meanings for them.

---

[88] Cf. Second Vatican Council, Dogmatic Constitution on Divine Revelation *Dei Verbum*, §10, in Flannery, (ed.), *Vatican Council II*, pp. 755 f.

66. Si vero *intellectus fidei* ponderatur, animadvertendum est apprime divinam Veritatem "propositam nobis in Scripturis Sacris secundum doctrinam Ecclesiae intellectis"[89] propria fruere intellegibilitate tam logice congruenti ut proponatur veluti germana sapientia. *Intellectus fidei* hanc veritatem clarius recludit, non modo logicas intellectivasque structuras percipiens enuntiationum quibus Ecclesiae doctrina componitur, verum etiam, et in primis, salutis sensum extollens quam tales enuntiationes pro singulis et pro humanitate continent. Per has nimirum enuntiationes simul sumptas fidelis ad salutis historiam cognoscendam pervenit, cuius fastigium in persona Christi eiusdemque paschali mysterio reperitur. Fidei assentiendo fit ipse huius mysterii particeps.

Theologia dogmatica, ex parte sua, facultatem possidere debet adipiscendi universalem sensum mysterii Dei Unius et Trini atque oeconomiae salutis simul per rationem narrationis, simul, potissimum per formam ratiocinationis. Id efficere debet, profecto, intellectivis adhibitis notionibus quae critico iudicio effinguntur cum omnibus communicabili. Etenim absque philosophiae adiumento res theologicae illustrari non possunt, quales exempli gratia, sermo de Deo, personales intra Trinitatem relationes, actio Dei in mundo creantis, necessitudo inter Deum et hominem, Christi identitas qui est verus Deus et verus homo. Idem in diversis theologiae moralis argumentis viget, ubi quaedam notiones immediate usurpantur, veluti lex moralis, conscientia, libertas, personalis responsalitas, culpa, et similia, quae ad philosophicae ethicae rationem definiuntur.

Necesse est ideo ut fidelis ratio naturalem habeat, veram congruentemque cognitionem de rebus creatis, de mundo et de homine, quas res etiam revelatio divina tractat; magis etiam, ipsa facultatem habere debet moderandi hanc cognitionem per modum intellectionis et argumentationis. Quapropter theologia dogmatica speculativa praesumit et complectitur philosophiam hominis, mundi atque, altius, ipsius "esse", quae quidem in obiectiva veritate innititur.

67. *Theologia fundamentalis*, suam propter disciplinae indolem quae officium sustinet rationem fidei reddendi (cfr *1 Pt* 3:15), munus in se recipere debebit comprobandi et enodandi necessitudinem inter fidem et philosophicam scientiam. Concilium iam Vaticanum I, doctrinam

---

[89] S. Thomas Aquinas, *Summa Theologiae* II–II, 5, 3 ad 2.

66. If, however, we devote our attention to the *understanding of faith* we ought above all to remember that the divine Truth 'which is proposed to us in Holy Scripture understood in accordance with the teaching of the Church'[89] enjoys its own natural intelligibility, which is so logically coherent that it stands as an authentic wisdom. The *understanding of faith* opens up this truth more clearly, both by perceiving the logical and intellectual structures of the propositions which make up Christian doctrine, and above all by making quite clear the salvific meaning contained by these propositions for the good of individuals and of humanity. From the sum of these propositions taken together the faithful undoubtedly come to a knowledge of the history of salvation, the summit of which is found in Christ and in his Paschal Mystery. By their assent of faith they then share in this mystery.

Dogmatic theology for its part ought to possess the ability of arriving at an understanding of the mystery of the One and Triune God, and of the economy of salvation, whether through the structure of narrative, or preferably through the form of reasoning. It ought to achieve this above all by the use of those intellectual conceptions which are formed with critical judgment, in a way communicable to all. Indeed without the help of philosophy theological issues cannot be clarified, as, for example, language concerning God, the personal relations within the Trinity, God's creative activity in the world, the relationship between God and man, and the identity of Christ as true God and true man. The same applies in various assertions of moral theology, in which certain concepts recur, like the moral law, conscience, freedom, personal responsibility, guilt, and so forth, all of which are defined with reference to philosophical ethics.

It is therefore necessary that faithful reason should possess a natural true and appropriate knowledge of created things, the world and of man, things which are also treated by divine revelation; even more than this, it should have the capacity for defining this knowledge through the form of understanding and argument. For this reason speculative dogmatic theology presumes and embraces the philosophy of man and of the world, and more profoundly of 'being' itself, which rests on objective truth.

67. *Fundamental theology*, because of its nature as a discipline which informs the task of producing an account of faith (cf. *1 Pet* 3:15) ought to assume the responsibility of affirming and explaining the relationship between faith and philosophical knowledge. The First Vatican Council, following the teaching of St Paul (cf. *Rom* 1:19–20) has already turned

[89] St Thomas Aquinas, *Summa Theologiae*, IIa IIae, Q. 5 Art. 3 ad 2.

resumens Pauli (cfr *Rom* 1:19–20), in id iam animos converterat, quasdam scilicet exstare veritates quae naturaliter, ideoque philosophice, cognosci possunt. Earum cognitio necessario anteponitur ad Dei revelationem suscipiendam. In revelatione eiusque credibilitate vestiganda una cum consentaneo fidei actu, theologia fundamentalis demonstrare debet, sub cognitionis per fidem lumine, quasdam eminere veritates, quas iam ratio suo in autonomo vestigationis itinere percipit. Iisdem plenitudinis sensum tribuit Revelatio, dum eas ad divitias dirigit mysterii revelati, in quo ultimum finem reperiunt. Cogitetur, exempli gratia, de naturali Dei cognitione, de facultate divinam revelationem ab aliis phaenomenis secernendi vel de eius credibilitate agnoscenda, de humana loquela habili, facta ad loquendum significanti veroque modo de illis etiam rebus, quae humanam experientiam praegrediuntur. Omnibus ex his veritatibus mens ducitur ad exsistentiam agnoscendam cuiusdam viae quae est fidei reapse praeparatoria, quae in revelationem accipiendam recidere potest, propriis principiis propriaque autononia haud declinatis.[90]

Simili modo theologia fundamentalis intimam convenientiam ostendere debebit inter fidem eiusque praecipuam necessitatem sese explicandi per rationem, quae maxima cum libertate consentire potest. Fides poterit hoc modo "iter plene demonstrare rationi illi, quae sincere veritatem requirit. Sic fides, Dei donum, quamvis ratione haudquaquam innitatur, nullo pacto ea carere potest; similiter exstat necessitas, ut ratio ex fide vim sumat, novosque fines consequatur, ad quos sola pervenire non potest".[91]

68. *Theologia moralis* fortasse etiam maiore indiget philosophiae auxilio. In Novo Foedere enim humana vita multo minus temperatur quam in Vetere Testamento. Vita in Spiritu fideles ducit ad libertatem responsalitatemque quae ipsam Legem transgrediuntur. Evangelium utcumque et apostolica scripta sive universalia christiane agendi principia ministrant sive doctrinam praeceptaque singularia. Ut eadem peculiaribus vitae individualis et socialis condicionibus accommodentur,

---

[90] "Eo quod condiciones perquiruntur in quibus homo per se ipse praecipuas quaestiones de vitae sensu, de fine ad eam tribuendo atque de ea re quae post mortem erit, interrogat, id pro theologia fundamentali constituit necessarium exordium, ut hodiernis quoque temporibus fides plene iter ipsi rationi ostendat, quae sincere veritatem requirit." Ioannes Paulus PP. II, *Lettera ai partecipanti al Congresso internazionale di Teologia Fondamentale a 125 anni dalla "Dei Filius"* (30 Septembris 1995), 4: *L'Osservatore Romano* (3 Octobris 1995), p. 8.

[91] Ioannes Paulus PP. II, *Lettera ai partecipanti al Congresso internazionale di Teologia Fondamentale a 125 anni dalla "Dei Filius"* (30 Septembris 1995), 4: *L'Osservatore Romano* (3 Octobris 1995), p. 8.

our minds to the existence of truths which can be known naturally, and thus philosophically. Knowledge of these is a necessary prerequisite for receiving divine revelation. In investigating revelation and its credibility together with the corresponding act of faith, fundamental theology should show how, in the light of the knowledge of faith, some truths emerge which reason in its independent journey of truth already perceives. Revelation endows these truths with their fullest meaning, directing them towards the richness of the revealed mystery in which they find their ultimate purpose. Consider, for example, the natural knowledge of God, of the ability of distinguishing divine revelation from other phenomena, or of the recognizing of its believability, of the faculty of human language, designed for discoursing in a true and meaningful fashion upon the very things which pave the way for human experience. From all these truths the mind is led to recognize the existence of a particular path truly preparatory for faith, which itself leads to the accepting of revelation, without in any way denying either its own principles or its own autonomy.[90]

In the same way fundamental theology ought to be able to show the close connection between faith and the important need of explaining itself by way of human reason fully free to give its assent. In this way faith will be able to 'indicate the path to reason which sincerely seeks the truth. Thus faith, the gift of God, though it in no sense rests upon reason, can never proceed without it; a similar need exists for reason to derive its strength from faith and thus pursue new ends which it could not arrive at by itself'.[91]

68. *Moral theology* needs perhaps even more support from philosophy. In the New Covenant human life is much less burdened than in the Old Testament. Life in the Spirit leads the faithful to a freedom and responsibility which passes beyond the Law. The Gospels and Apostolic writings provide either for universal principles of Christian activity or doctrine as well as specific precepts. In order to apply these to the particular circumstances of individual and communal life, Christians must be able to have a profound mastery of their own conscience and power of reasoning. In

---

[90] 'The search for the conditions in which man on his own initiative asks the first basic questions about the meaning of life, the purpose he wishes to give it, and what awaits him after death, constitutes the necessary preamble to fundamental theology, so that today too, faith can fully show the way to reason in a sincere search for the truth': John Paul II, *Letter to Participants at the International Congress of Fundamental Theology on the 125th Anniversary of 'Dei Filius'* (30 September 1995), §4: reported in *L'Osservatore Romano* (3 October 1995), p. 8.

[91] John Paul II, *Letter to Participants at the International Congress of Fundamental Theology on the 125th Anniversary of 'Dei Filius'*, §4.

oportet Christianus suam conscientiam funditus obstringere possit suique ratiocinii vim. Aliis verbis, id requirit ut theologia moralis recto philosophico prospectu utatur sive quod ad naturam humanam societatemque spectat sive quod ad ethicae deliberationis principia universalia.

69. Quispiam fortasse obiciat in praesenti condicione theologo esse deveniendum ut opem recipiat, potius quam a philosophia, ab aliis humanae scientiae formis quae sunt historia ac potissimum scientiae, quarum omnes homines singulares mirantur recentiores progressus. Alii autem, post auctum de necessitudine inter fidem et culturam sensum, affirmant theologiam esse convertendam potius ad translaticias sapientias quam ad philosophiam quae ex Graecia orta est quaeque Eurocentrica dicitur. Alii denique, initium ex falsa culturarum pluralismi opinatione sumentes, universale plane respuunt patrimonii philosophici bonum, quod recepit Ecclesia.

Hae aestimationes, quae ceterum in conciliari doctrina reperiuntur,[92] aliquam veritatem prae se ferunt. Eo quod ratio fit ad scientias, quae ratio compluribus in casibus utilis est quandoquidem pleniorem de obiecto vestigando cognitionem praebet, necessaria tamen non est obliviscenda pars quam agit cogitatio proprie philosophica, critica et in universalem rem vergens, quae ceterum a feraci culturarum permutatione requiritur. Illud proprie confirmare cupimus in uno certoque casu non esse consistendum, princeps munus neglegendo, ostendendi videlicet universalem indolem obiecti fidei. Hoc praeterea non est obliviscendum: quod philosophica cogitatio peculiariter confert, intellegere sinit tum in diversis vitae opinationibus tum in culturis, "non quid homines senserint, sed qualiter se habeat veritas rerum".[93] Non variae hominum opiniones, sed veritas dumtaxat theologiae opitulari potest.

70. Peculiariter autem est ponderandum argumentum, quod convenientiam tangit inter culturas, etiamsi necessario de ea re penitus non edisseratur, propter implicationes quae inde sive in re philosophica sive in re theologica oriuntur. Quod Ecclesia convenit culturas et cum iisdem contendit, id usque ab Evangelii praedicati initio experta est Ecclesia. Christi praeceptum discipulis datum lustrandi omnia loca, "usque ad

[92] Cfr Conc. Oecum. Vat. II, Const. past. de Ecclesia in mundo huius temporis *Gaudium et spes*, §15; Decr. de activitate missionali Ecclesiae *Ad gentes*, §22.

[93] S. Thomas Aquinas, *De Caelo*, 1, 22.

other words this means that moral theology must employ a correct philosophical standpoint, with regard either to human nature and society or to the universal principles of ethical discourse.

69. Someone might perhaps object in the present situation that the theologian should be depending for help more on other forms of human knowledge than philosophy, such as history and the natural sciences, whose recent advances have stirred such singular admiration among men and women. There are others who have developed a profound sense of the relationship between faith and culture and who as a result maintain that theology should be translated into a form of so called 'common wisdom' rather than into a philosophy which arose in Greece and is therefore Eurocentric. Finally there are those who take their starting-point from a mistaken notion of the pluralism of cultures, and in consequence reject the universal good of a philosophical patrimony, which the Church accepts.

These assessments, which also appear in the documents of the council, contain some truth.[92] But the fact that reference is often made to the sciences, which in many cases are useful in so far as they provide a fuller knowledge of the object under investigation, must not imply that the role of philosophy proper should be forgotten, a philosophy which is both critical and universal in intention and which is required if there is to be a fruitful exchange among cultures. What we wish to emphasize is the duty to go beyond the particular and concrete, lest the prime task of demonstrating the universality of the content of faith be abandoned. Nor must we forget that philosophical reflection has this peculiarity: it allows us to understand both in the diversity of opinions about life and in cultures, that what matters is 'not what people think, but the very nature of truth in itself'.[93] It is not the various opinions of men and women, but rather truth itself that can be of assistance to theology.

70. Special attention must be given to the argument which touches upon the relationship between cultures, even if of necessity it is not fully treated here, because of the implications which arise for philosophy or in theology. From the very beginning of the preaching of the Gospel the Church has contended with meeting and facing differing cultures. Christ gave his disciples the command to go out to all places, 'even to the ends of the earth' (*Acts* 1:8) in order that the Truth revealed by Him be passed

[92] Cf. The Second Vatican Council, Pastoral Constitution on the Church in the Modern World *Gaudium et spes*, §15; Decree on the Church's Missionary Activity *Ad gentes*, §22, in Flannery, (ed.) *Vatican Council II*, pp. 915 f., 839 f.

[93] St Thomas Aquinas, *De Caelo*, Book I, Lect. 22, No. 8.

ultimum terrae" (*Act* 1:8), ut ab Eo revelata Veritas transmitteretur, copiam communitati christianae dedit probandi continuo nuntii universalitatem atque impedimenta ex culturarum diversitate inducta. Locus epistulae sancti Pauli ad Ephesios efficacem opem fert, ut intellegatur quemadmodum primaeva christiana communitas hoc negotium egerit. Apostolus scribit: "Nunc autem in Christo Iesu vos, qui aliquando eratis longe, facti estis prope in sanguine Christi. Ipse est enim pax nostra, qui fecit utraque unum et medium parietem maceriae solvit" (2:13–14).

Eiusmodi scripto ob oculos habito, nostra cogitatio latius panditur et mutationem attingit quae facta est postquam Gentiles ad fidem pervenerunt. Pro divitiis salutis, quam Christus attulit, decidunt impedimenta quae varias culturas dissociant. Dei repromissio in Christo fit nunc donatio universalis: non amplius circumscripta cuiusdam populi proprietatibus, eius sermone et moribus, sed cunctis destinatur ut patrimonium ex quo quisque haurire libere potest. Locis ex diversis ac consuetudinibus omnes in Christo ad unitatem participandam familiae filiorum Dei vocantur. Christus ipse sinit ut duo populi "unum" sint. Qui erant "longinqui", novitatis beneficio quam paschale mysterium attulit "proximi" fiunt. Iesus divisionis parietes diruit et peculiari consummatoque modo per participationem sui mysterii unitatem efficit. Haec unitas tam est alta ut cum sancto Paolo effari possit Ecclesia: "Ergo iam non estis extranei et advenae, sed estis concives sanctorum et domestici Dei" (*Eph* 2:19).

Hac tam simplici enuntiatione luculenta veritas significatur: fidei concursus cum diversis culturis reapse effecit novam rem. Culturae, cum altius radices in natura humana agunt, testimonium secum ferunt illius apertionis ad universalitatem et transcendentiam quae propria est hominis. Ipsae ideo exhibent diversas ad veritatem accessiones, quae perutiles sunt homini, cui valores praebent qui magis magisque humanam reddere valent eius exsistentiam.[94] Eo quod culturae antiquarum consuetudinum repetunt valores, ipsae secum ferunt – etiamsi implicite, sed hanc propter rationem haud minus vere – indicium, quod remittit ad Deum in natura sese manifestantem, sicut antea demonstratum est cum de sapientialibus scriptis et de sancti Pauli doctrina sermo factus est.

---

[94] Cfr Conc. Oecum. Vat. II, Const. past. de Ecclesia in mundo huius temporis *Gaudium et spes*, §§53–59.

on; he gave the means simultaneously for the Christian community to recognize the universality of the message and the obstacles arising from the diversity of cultures. A passage from the Letter of St Paul to the Ephesians offers useful help for understanding how the early Christian community performed this task. The Apostle writes: 'but now in Christ Jesus, you who once were far off have been brought near in the blood of Christ. For he is our peace, who has made both one and broken down the wall of hostility' (*Eph* 2:13–14).

With a text like that before our eyes, our reflection is broadened to touch on the transformation which occurred after the Gentiles came to the faith. In response to the riches of salvation attained by Christ, the hindrances created by differing cultures collapse. In Christ the promise of God becomes a universal gift: no longer circumscribed with the particular characteristics of one nation with its own language and customs, but destined for all, as a birthright from which each may freely draw. From the diversity of places and customs, in Christ all are called to participating in the unity of the family of the children of God. Christ himself allows that the two peoples should be 'one'. Those who were once 'afar off' have become 'near' thanks to the newness achieved by the Paschal Mystery. Jesus breaks down the walls of division and in a unique and perfect manner creates a unity through participation in his mystery. This unity is so profound that the Church is able to say with St Paul: 'therefore you are no longer strangers and sojourners, but you are fellow citizens with the saints and members of the household of God' (*Eph* 2:19).

In this simple expression a profound truth is contained: the meeting of faith with the diversity of cultures truly creates something new. Cultures, which make their roots deep in human nature, carry with themselves proof of an openness to universality and transcendence which is proper to humanity. Therefore they express the diverse approaches to the truth, which are of great use to us inasmuch as they provide values which are capable of rendering our existence more and more human.[94] In so far as cultures appeal to the values of older traditions, they carry with them, albeit implicitly but none the less really for all that, a sign that returns them to the God who reveals himself in nature, as was dealt with earlier when we were considering the Wisdom literature and the teaching of St Paul.

---

[94] Cf. The Second Vatican Council, Pastoral Constitution on the Church in the Modern World *Gaudium et spes*, §§53–9 in Flannery, (ed.) *Vatican Council II*, pp. 958–64.

71. Culturae, quippe quae cum hominibus eorumque historia arte coniungantur, eosdem communicant cursus ad quos humanum tempus manifestatur. Immutationes ideo progressionesque recensentur, inductae a congressionibus quas homines inter se convenientes effecerunt quasque mutuae communicationes eorum vitae exemplarium pepererunt. Culturae aluntur bonorum communicatione, earumque vis vitalis ac diuturnitas pendent ex facultate patendi novitatibus suscipiendis. Quomodo hi motus explicantur? Quisque homo in quadam cultura illigatur, ex ea pendet, eandemque magnopere afficit. Ipse est simul filius perinde ac pater culturae in qua defigitur. In omnibus vitae significationibus, is aliquid secum comportat quod eum inter creaturas denotat: id est, duratura ad mysterium apertio eiusque inexplebile cognitionis desiderium. Quapropter unaquaeque cultura habet in se et patefacit inustam intentionem in aliquam consummationem. Itaque dici potest culturam habere in se facultatem suscipiendi divinam revelationem.

Ratio ipsa, secundum quam Christiani suam fidem experiuntur, cultura imbuitur illius loci qui proximus est et efficit vicissim ut eiusdem natura procedente tempore effingatur. Unicuique culturae Christiani immutabilem Dei veritatem praebent, quam Ipse in populi historia et cultura revelavit. Saeculorum sic decursu ille repetitur eventus cuius testes fuerunt peregrini qui die illo Pentecostes Hierosolymis adstabant. Cum Apostolos audivissent, rogaverunt: "Nonne ecce omnes isti, qui loquuntur, Galilaei sunt? Et quomodo nos audimus unusquisque propria lingua nostra, in qua nati sumus? Parthi et Medi et Elamitae, et qui habitant Mesopotamiam, Iudaeam quoque et Cappadociam, Pontum et Asiam, Phrygiam quoque et Pamphyliam, Aegyptum et partes Libyae, quae est circa Cyrenem, et advenae Romani, Iudaei quoque et proselyti, Cretes et Arabes, audimus loquentes eos nostris linguis magnalia Dei" (*Act* 2:7–11). Evangelium diversis in culturis enuntiatum, dum a singulis quibus destinatur fidei adhaesionem requirit, non impedit quominus ii suam culturalem proprietatem retineant. Id nullam discretionem gignit, quandoquidem baptizatorum populus illa universalitate distinguitur, quae omnes humanos cultus recipit, progressum iuvando illius rei quae in ea implicatur, ad plenam in veritate explicationem consequendam.

Quapropter id quod est cultura numquam fieri potest iudicandi norma, minus ac minus norma veritatis novissima pro Dei revelatione. Huic illive culturae non aversatur Evangelium, proinde quasi, eam conveniens, id quod ad eam pertinet eripere velit eandemque cogat extrarias formas et

71. These cultures, simply because they are yoked to men and women and their history, share the same tendencies which are manifested in the human condition. These transformations and advances are accounted for from the communality which men in their convergences produce when they meet and share amongst themselves their ways of life. Cultures are nourished by the exchange of goods, and their vital force and continuation depend on the ability to remain open to accepting new ideas. How are these dynamics to be explained? Every man is bound to some culture, depends upon it and in some measure moulds it. He is at the same time both child and parent of the culture he finds himself in. In all important things of life, he always bears with him what marks him out from all other creatures; that is an enduring openness to mystery and the insatiable desire for knowledge. This means that every culture contains within itself and displays an indestructible urge for some sort of fulfilment. We can therefore say that culture contains within itself the capacity for receiving divine revelation.

Reason itself, in accord with which Christians experience their faith, is soaked in the culture of the place nearest to it, and in its turn ensures that with the progress of time its own nature is bit by bit transformed. To every culture Christians offer the immutable truth of God, which he himself has revealed in the history and culture of a people. Time and again, therefore, in the course of the centuries we have seen the event repeated whose witnesses were the strangers that gathered in Jerusalem for the feast of Pentecost. When they had heard the Apostles they asked: 'are not all these who are speaking Galileans? And how is it that we each of us hear, in our own native language? Parthians, Medes, Elamites, and the inhabitants of Mesopotamia, Judaea and Cappadocia, Pontus, and Asia, Phrygia and Pamphilia, Egypt and the parts of Libya belonging to Cyrene, and visitors from Rome, both Jews and proselytes, Cretans and Arabs, in our own tongues we have heard them speaking about the mighty works of God' (*Acts* 2:7–11). While the Gospel has been proclaimed in many different cultures, and although it requires from those for whom it is meant the adherence of faith, this does not mean that they should not each retain their cultural distinctiveness. This does not produce any division, since the company of the baptized is marked out by that universality which embraces all human cultures by fostering the growth of whatever lies within them that will lead to a full unfolding of the truth.

The consequence is that a culture can never become the norm, and much less the ultimate criterion of truth, for judging the divine revelation. The Gospel is not opposed to this or that culture, nor, when it comes into contact with a culture does it attempt to tear from it what belongs to it

alienas sumere. Nuntius contra, quem in mundum atque in culturas defert fidelis, vera est liberationis forma ab omni perturbatione a peccato effecta, itemque est vocatio ad plenam veritatem. Hac in conspiratione, non modo culturae nulla re exuuntur, sed concitantur potius ut sese ad veritatem evangelicam aperiant, unde incitamenta ad alios progressus assequendos nanciscantur.

72. Eo quod evangelizationis missio suo in cursu philosophiam Graecam primam convenit, id haudquaquam significat ceteros aditus excludi. Hodie, quotiescumque Evangelium culturae ambitus attingit ad quos christiana doctrina antea non accessit, nova exsurgunt inculturationis opera. Eaedem fere quaestiones, quas primaeva aetate enodare debuit Ecclesia, hodiernis hominibus afferuntur.

Cogitationes Nostrae sua sponte ad orientales plagas convertuntur, quae perantiquis pietatis philosophiaeque traditionibus locupletantur. Inter eas India conspicuum obtinet locum. Grandis spiritalis impetus Indianam impellit mentem ad eam experientiam adipiscendam, quae, temporis spatiique impedimentis animo expedito, absolutum bonum attingat. In huius liberationis exquirendae processu, praecipuae metaphysicae scholae ponuntur.

Huius temporis Christianorum est, praesertim Indianorum, locupleti ex eiusmodi patrimonio elementa illa depromere quae cum illorum fide coniungi possunt, ita ut christiana doctrina ditior fiat. Hac in discretione agenda, quae ex conciliari Declaratione *Nostrae aetate* sumit consilium, quasdam iudicandi normas ii ob oculos habebunt. Prima norma est humani spiritus universalitas cuius postulata in diversissimis culturis eadem reperiuntur. Altera, quae ex prima oritur, haec est: cum Ecclesia maioris momenti convenit culturas antea haud attactas, id, quod per inculturationem Graecae et Latinae disciplinae adepta est, posthabere non potest. Talis si repudiaretur hereditas, providum Dei consilium oppugnaretur, qui per temporis historiaeque semitam suam ducit Ecclesiam. Haec, ceteroqui, iudicandi lex propria est Ecclesiae omnium aetatum, etiam subsequentis, quae se persentiet divitem factam iis ex rebus quas adepta erit per orientalium culturarum hodiernum accessum, et in hac hereditate nova indicia reperiet, ut frugifer instituatur dialogus cum culturis illis, quas humanitas iuvabit ut prosperent in suo ad futuram aetatem itinere. Tertio, cavebitur ne legitima proprietatis singularitatisque Indianae philosophiae expostulatio cum sententia illa confundetur, culturalem scilicet traditionem sua in diversitate concludi

and force it to adopt external and alien expressions. On the contrary the message which the faithful carry into cultures is the true form of liberation, freed from the disturbance created by sin, and at the same time a call to full truth. In this common vision, far from cultures being in any sense rejected, on the contrary they are encouraged to open themselves to the truth of the Gospel and from this find the incentive to further developments.

72. Simply because the mission of preaching the Gospel came first upon Greek philosophy in its journey, this is not taken to mean that other approaches are excluded. Today, as often as the Gospel meets an area of culture as yet untouched by Christian teaching, so new efforts of inculturation arise. Exactly the same questions face contemporary men and women as the Church had to face in her earliest times.

Our thoughts naturally turn to Eastern shores, which have been enriched from of old with ancient traditions of religion and philosophy. Amongst them India takes a prominent place. An immense spiritual impulse compels the Indian mind to an acquiring of that experience which would, with a spirit freed from the distractions of time and space, attain to the absolute good. It is in this process of seeking for liberation that the great metaphysical schools are constructed.

This is the time, above all for Indian Christians, to unlock these treasures from their inheritance which can be joined to their faith and so enhance the richness of Christian teaching. In this work of discernment, which finds its inspiration in the conciliar declaration *Nostra aetate*, they will keep before their eyes certain norms of judgment. The first norm is the universality of the human spirit, whose requirements in the most widely diverging cultures can be seen to be in agreement. The second, which derives from the first, is: when the Church deals for the first time with cultures of great importance, but previously unexamined, it must even so never place them before the Greek and Latin inculturation already acquired. Were this inheritance to be repudiated the providential plan of God would be opposed, who guides his Church down the paths of time and history. This is a law appropriate to the Church of all the ages, even of that which is to come. She will perceive herself enriched from the daily access of treasures acquired from oriental cultures and in this new inheritance she will discover indicators for showing how a fruitful dialogue with these cultures may be entered upon and which will help humanity in its journey to a new future. Thirdly, care must be taken to avoid confusing the rightful demands of the distinctiveness and peculiar character of Indian philosophy with the viewpoint that allows every

debere eamque per dissidentiam cum ceteris traditionibus emergere, quod quidem naturae humani spiritus ipsi est contrarium.

Quod de India dictum est, adscribitur patrimonio praestantium culturarum Sinensium et Iaponensium aliarumque Asiae Nationum itemque refertur thesauro culturarum Africae translaticiarum, quae verbis potissimum sunt transmissae.

73. His rebus consideratis, necessitudo quae inter theologiam et philosophiam opportune institui debet notam habebit cuiusdam circularis progressionis. Theologiae initium atque primigenius fons est Dei verbum in historia revelatum, dum ultimum propositum necessario erit ipsius intellectio quae sensim est perspecta succedentibus aetatibus. Quandoquidem autem Dei verbum est Veritas (cfr *Io* 17:17), fieri non potest quin ad eiusdem aptiorem intellectum opem conferat humanae veritatis inquisitio, philosophans scilicet mens, quae suis servatis legibus explicatur. Non agitur de hac vel illa notione vel parte cuiusdam systematis philosophici in theologico sermone simpliciter adhibenda; decretorium est quod fidelis ratio suae cogitationis facultatem exerceat ad verum reperiendum quendam intra motum, qui, initium ex Dei verbo sumens, consequi conatur pleniorem eiusdem comprehensionem. Omnino porro liquet, agendo has intra duas res – Dei verbum scilicet altioremque eius cognitionem – rationem paene percipi et quodammodo gubernari, ut semitas illas vitet quae extra Veritatem revelatam eandem perducant ac, tandem, simpliciter extra ipsam veritatem; immo ea incitatur ad explorandas semitas, quas sola ne suspicatur quidem se illas decurrere posse. Hoc ex circulari motu cum Dei verbo philosophia locupletior evadit, quia novos et inexspectatos attingit fines.

74. Ubertatis comprobatio huius necessitudinis exhibetur personalibus eventibus clarorum theologorum christianorum, qui ut philosophi etiam eximii enituerunt, qui scripta sic altae speculativae praestantiae reliquerunt, ut iure antiquae philosophiae aequarentur doctoribus. Id tum de Ecclesiae Patribus dici potest, inter quos saltem sanctus Gregorius Nazianzenus atque sanctus Augustinus annumerantur, tum de Doctoribus mediaevalibus, inter quos trias illa elucet quam constituunt sancti Anselmus, Bonaventura et Thomas Aquinas. Fecunda illa philosophiae verbique Dei consociatio etiam ex magnanima emergit investigatione a recentioribus doctis provecta, in quibus memorare placet ex orbe occidentali homines veluti Ioannem Henricum Newman, Antonium Rosmini, Iacobum Maritain, Stephanum Gilson, Edith Stein

cultural tradition to be enclosed in its own diversity such that it should be allowed to persist despite its disagreement with other traditions. This would be in direct contradiction to the nature of the human spirit.

What has been said of India applies also to the inheritance of the distinguished cultures of China and Japan and of the other nations of Asia, and the same may be said of the riches of African culture, which have for the most part been handed down orally.

73. With these things before us, the relationship between philosophy and theology is marked by a kind of circular progress. The beginning and the primal source of theology is the Word of God revealed in history, while its ultimate purpose is necessarily the understanding of that Word, which grows gradually with the progress of time. But since the Word of God is Truth (cf. *Jn* 17:17) the human search for truth – the philosophical mind observing its own laws– can only help God's Word to be better explained. We are not dealing here with the simple adoption of this or that concept or element of a philosophical system in theological discourse; what is important above all is that the reason of the believer should employ her own capacity for reflection in the discovery of truth, in the course of the movement which, beginning by taking up the Word of God, tries to gain a fuller comprehension of it. It is very evident that, moving between these two poles – that is between the Word of God and its deeper comprehension – reason is offered guidance and is warned against paths which would lead it to stray from revealed truth and to stray in the end from the truth pure and simple: rather reason is in this way spurred on to exploring new paths which, left to itself, it could hardly imagine that it could find. From this circular movement philosophy emerges the richer from its contact with the Word of God in its attainment of new and unexpected ends.

74. Clear proof of the fruitfulness of this relationship can be discovered in the personal lives of distinguished Christian theologians who also shone out as remarkable philosophers. They left behind them writings of such astounding speculative profundity that they were rightly judged to be on a level with the masters of ancient philosophy. This is true both of the Fathers of the Church, especially Gregory of Nazianzus and Augustine, and of the Mediaeval Doctors, above all Sts Anselm, Bonaventure and Thomas Aquinas. The fruitful relationship between philosophy and the Word of God can also be glimpsed in the generous researches of more recent thinkers. In the West we find John Henry Newman, Anthony Rosmini, Jacques Maritain, Etienne Gilson and Edith Stein and in the East Vladimir Soloviev, Paul A. Florensky, Peter K.

simulque ex orientali orbe studiosos ut Vladimirum S. Solov'ev, Paulum A. Florenskij, Petrum K. Čaadaev, Vladimirum N. Lossky. Uti paret, hi cum memorantur auctores, quibuscum alia pariter proferri possunt nomina, non omnem eorum doctrinae aestimationem prodere cupimus, verum exempla quaedam praestantiora illius efferre itineris investigationum philosophicarum ad quod beneficia singularia comparatio attulit cum fidei doctrinis. De hoc autem non est ambigendum: horum doctorum spiritalis itineris contemplatio non poterit quin progredienti veritatis inquisitioni proficiat atque usui consectariorum in hominum utilitatem. Sperari oportet hanc eximiam philosophicam-theologicam traditionem nunc et futuro de tempore suos successores necnon pro Ecclesiae humanitatisque bono cultores esse inventuram.

De diversis philosophiae statibus

75. Quemadmodum patet ex historia necessitudinum inter fidem et philosophiam sicut supra paucis dictum est, diversi philosophiae status prae fide christiana distingui possunt. Primus status *philosophiam a Revelatione evangelica penitus distractam* complectitur: philosophiae est condicio quae aetatibus illis ante Redemptorem natum historice exstitit atque post Eum in regionibus nondum ab Evangelio contactis. Hac in condicione philosophia legitime affectat se *sui iuris* esse inceptum, quae videlicet secundum suas ipsius leges agit, quae suis unis viribus innititur. Quamvis de gravibus limationibus conscii simus, quae ingenitae humanae debilitati adscribuntur, haec affectatio est sustentanda et roboranda. Philosophicum namque studium, prout ad veritatem intra naturalem provinciam perquirendam tendit, saltem implicite rei supernaturali patens est.

Immo magis: etiam cum theologicus ipse sermo philosophicis notionibus et argumentationibus utitur, cogitationis rectae autonomiae necessitas est servanda. Etenim argumentatio, quae secundum strictas normas rationales evolvitur, effecta quaedam universaliter valida consequitur et praestat. Etiam hic viget principium, secundum quod gratia non destruit, sed perficit naturam: fidei assensus, qui tum intellectum tum voluntatem obstringit, liberum arbitrium cuiusque fidelis rem revelatam suscipientis haud dissolvit sed perficit.

Ex hoc congruo postulato penitus opinio illa digreditur sic dictae philosophiae "seiunctae", quam complures philosophi recentiores persequuntur. Potius quam ut aequam philosophandi autonomiam

Chaadaev and Vladimir N. Lossky. The mention of these names, and others not referred to here, should not be interpreted as suggesting acceptance of all that they taught: rather they are to be understood as outstanding examples of a journey of philosophical enquiries in which an engagement with the doctrines of faith brought singular benefits. There is no room for doubting that an understanding of the spiritual pilgrimage of these teachers cannot but be of great profit for the progress of truth and its application to the needs of society. It is to be hoped that this marvellous philosophical and theological tradition, both now and in the future, will find successors for the good of both the Church and humanity.

On the differing stances of philosophy

75. As is clear from the history of the connections between faith and philosophy that we have briefly indicated, one can distinguish different stances of philosophy with regard to Christian faith. First, there is a *philosophy completely independent of the Gospel's Revelation*: this is the condition of philosophy as it took shape in history before the birth of the Redeemer and later in regions as yet untouched by the Gospel. In this condition philosophy rightly *assumes its autonomy*, acts according to its own laws, and depends upon its own strengths. Aware though we are of the grave limitations which are innate to the natural feebleness of humanity, even so this effort is to be encouraged and strengthened. The study of philosophy, in so far as it leads to searching for truth within the natural order, is at least implicitly open to the supernatural.

Moreover, even when a theological argument employs philosophical concepts and argumentation, respect must be had for a valid autonomy of thought. Argumentation itself, which is worked out in accordance with strict norms of reason, arrives at and exhibits results which are universally valid. This also confirms the principle that grace does not destroy nature, but perfects it: the assent of faith which binds both intellect and will, does not destroy but perfects the free will of the believer who accepts the things that have been revealed.

This coherent premise is at variance with the viewpoint that speaks of a 'separate' philosophy, which is pursued by many modern philosophers. Rather than simply affirming the perfectly acceptable autonomy of philosophizing, it arrogates to itself the right of deliberating in its own province, and this is quite illegitimate: to reject the aids to truth which have arisen from divine revelation is effectively the same as cutting off a deeper knowledge of the truth, to the detriment of philosophy itself.

affirmet, ipsa sibi arrogat ius quidlibet sua in provincia excogitandi, quod quidem, ut patet, illegitimum est: veritatis adiumenta respuere, quae ex divina revelatione oriuntur, idem est ac aditum intercludere ad altiorem veritatem cognoscendam, ipsius philosophiae detrimento contingente.

76. Alter philosophiae status locutione *philosophiae christianae* a multis designatur. Haec appellatio legitima est, dummodo ipsa in ambiguum ne detrahatur: id enim non significat Ecclesiam philosophiam publicam suam habere, quandoquidem fides qua talis non est philosophia. Hac locutione ars designatur christiane philosophandi, meditatio scilicet philosophica quae vitaliter cum fide coniungitur. Non agitur ideo simpliciter de philosophia quadam a christianis philosophis confecta, qui suis in inquisitionibus aliquid contra fidem dicere noluerunt. Cum de philosophia christiana sermo fit, omnes comprehendi debent praestantes illi progressus philosophicae disciplinae, qui numquam contigissent nisi opem directe vel oblique christiana fides attulisset.

Duae ergo sunt christianae philosophiae species, quarum altera est subiectiva, secundum quam fides purificat rationem. Ut theologalis virtus, ipsa rationem a nimia confidentia exsolvit, ad quam illecebram facile philosophi inclinant. Iam sanctus Paulus Ecclesiaeque Patres, atque nobis proximi philosophi veluti Pascal et Kierkegaard, censura quadam id notarunt. Humiliter animum colligit philosophus ut quasdam quaestiones tractet, quas difficulter explicare valet haud consideratis Revelationis elementis. Puta, exempli gratia, mali dolorisque quaestiones, personalem Dei identitatem atque interrogationem de vitae sensu vel, strictius, quaestionem metaphysicam radicalem: "Cur est aliquid?".

Pars exinde adest obiectiva, quae ad ipsam materiam spectat: lucide quasdam exhibet veritates Revelatio, quas tametsi attingere potest ratio, nunquam tamen easdem repperisset si suis unis viribus innixa esset. Hoc in rerum prospectu quaestiones ponuntur, veluti notio Dei personalis, liberi et creatoris, quae ad philosophicae cogitationis progressum tantum pondus habuit, potissimum quod spectat ad philosophiam respicientem "esse". Ad hanc provinciam ipsa peccati realitas quoque pertinet, quemadmodum ipsa fidei lumine manifestatur, quae quidem operam dat ut quaestio de malo congruenti ratione philosophice ponatur. Persona quoque, quae veluti spiritale quiddam consideratur, est peculiaris fidei proprietas: dignitatis christianus nuntius, aequalitatis ac libertatis hominum procul dubio vim habuit in philosophica cogitata, quae

76. Another approach to the subject of philosophy is designated *Christian philosophy* by many people. This is appropriate terminology, provided it is freed of ambiguity: it must not be seen to imply that the Church has her own public philosophy, since faith as such is not a philosophy. By it is meant the art of philosophizing in a Christian manner; namely a philosophical reflection that is vitally conjoined to faith. It is not therefore simply a question of a philosophy created by Christian philosophers, who in their researches are unwilling to say anything against faith. When we speak of Christian philosophy, we understand thereby all those varied advances in the discipline of philosophy, which would never have occurred without the direct or indirect help of Christian faith.

There are, therefore, two types of Christian philosophy, of which one is subjective, inasmuch as faith purifies reason. As a theological virtue it rescues reason from over self-confidence, a danger into which philosophers easily fall. Already St Paul and the Fathers of the Church as well as philosophers closer to us in time, like Pascal and Kierkegaard, have laid up censure against this. With humility the philosopher might devote himself to addressing questions which he can hardly manage without considering the data of Revelation. Take for example questions about evil and sorrow, about the personal identity of God, about the investigation of the meaning of life, or more strictly the root metaphysical question: 'Why is there anything at all?'

There is also an objective type dealing with the material itself: Revelation brings into clear focus certain truths, which, though available to reason, would never have been discovered by it were it left to its own resources. In this general area certain questions are asked about the concept of a personal God who is both free and creator, which have had a profound influence on the progress of philosophical thought, above all with respect to the philosophy of 'being'. To this area also belongs the reality of sin in so far as it is manifested in the light of faith; faith itself regards it as her concern that the discussion of evil should take place philosophically with appropriate use of reason. The person also, who is considered as something spiritual, is herself a particular aspect of faith; the Christian proclamation of the dignity, equality and freedom of humanity has doubtless exerted a generative force on philosophical reflection for modern philosophers. Closer to our own day we must recall that the importance for philosophy of historical occurrence has been acknowledged, for this is the apex of Christian Revelation. It is no accident that this has become pivotal for a philosophy of history which stakes its claim as a new chapter in the human search for truth.

recentiores philosophi pepererunt. Ad propiora tempora accedentes, id memorare debemus quod agnitum est momentum quod induit etiam pro philosophia historicus eventus, christianae Revelationis culmen. Non casu ille cuiusdam historiae philosophiae factus est cardo, qui veluti novum veritatis humanae inquisitionis caput exhibetur.

Inter obiectiva philosophiae christianae elementa necessitas quoque adnumeratur perquirendi rationalitatem nonnullarum veritatum, quae in Sacris Scripturis significantur, veluti supernaturalis vocationis hominis possibilitas atque peccatum ipsum originale. Haec munia rationem lacessunt ad agnoscendum quiddam inibi inesse veri rationalisque, longe multumque ultra illos angustos fines quibus ipsa se conclusura erat. Argumenta haec reddunt re rationis provinciam laxiorem.

Has agitantes rationes, philosophi haud facti sunt theologi, propterea quod fidei veritatem intellegere et collustrare non studuerunt sumpto initio a Revelatione. Sua in ipsorum provincia, via meraque ratione sua usi agere perrexerunt, sed suam inquisitionem ad novos veri ambitus explicaverunt. Asseverare licet quod sine hac Dei verbi acri opera, philosophiae recentioris ac recentissimae magna pars haud exsisteret. Res suum praecipuum habet momentum, quamvis christianam orthodoxiam a compluribus novissimorum horum saeculorum philosophis deseri observetur.

77. Alius philosophiae significans status habetur cum *ipsa theologia ad philosophiam provocat*. Theologia reapse semper philosophico indiguit adiumento atque indiget. Cum sub fidei lumine rationis criticae sit opera, theologica inquisitio rationem cognitionibus et argumentationibus excultam et figuratam tota in sua vestigatione praesumit atque deposcit. Theologia porro philosophia indiget quacum paene dialogum instituat, ut comprobet intellegibilitatem universalemque principiorum suorum veritatem. Non casu accidit ut philosophiae non christianae susciperentur ab Ecclesiae Patribus et mediaevalibus theologis explicandi causa. Haec historica res praestantiam demonstrat *autononiae* quam etiam hoc in suo tertio statu servat philosophia, sed necessarias praecipuasque immutationes pariter ostendit, quas ipsa pati debet.

Hoc ipsum propter necessarium insigneque adiumentum a Patrum usque aetate *ancilla theologiae* vocitata est philosophia. Nomen istud minime usurpatum est ad subiectionem servitutemque quandam significandam vel munus demonstrandum merae functionis philosophiae in theologiam

Among the objective elements of Christian philosophy must be mentioned the necessity of examining the rational character of certain truths mentioned in Holy Scripture, such as the possibility of man's supernatural vocation, and original sin itself. These are tasks which challenge reason to recognize that there is something true and rational lying far beyond the narrow bounds within which it would of itself be confined. These matters render much wider the domain of reason.

In rehearsing matters such as these, philosophers have not become theologians, precisely because their aim was not to understand and illustrate the truth of faith by beginning with Revelation. In their own province they proceeded to act by using the powers of reason alone, but they broadened their enquiry to include new areas of truth. It is possible to affirm that, deprived of the sharp goad of the Word of God, a large part of more and very recent philosophy would hardly exist. This conclusion retains all its relevance despite the fact that it is clear that Christian orthodoxy has been abandoned by a large number of recent philosophers.

77. We find another significant situation for philosophy, when *theology itself calls upon it.* Theology has always needed and still depends upon the help of philosophy. Seeing that in the light of faith there is need of critical reason, theological enquiry, throughout the whole of its own investigation both assumes and demands a reason that is both educated and formed by reflection and by argument. Moreover, theology also needs a philosophy with which it can conduct a dialogue, in order that it may confirm the intelligibility and universal truth of its own principles. It is no accident that non-Christian philosophers were taken up by the Fathers of the Church and the Mediaeval theologians for explaining matters. This historical fact points to the importance of the *autonomy* which philosophy deserves even in this third situation, but it shows as well the necessary and important transformations which philosophy itself must undergo.

It is as a result of this distinguished and useful assistance that from the age of the Fathers philosophy has been termed the '*handmaid of theology*'. This title was certainly not employed in order to indicate its subjection or servitude, or to suggest that its sole purpose consisted in its functional relationship to theology. The expression was adopted to imply what Aristotle meant when he spoke of the experimental sciences as 'handmaids of first philosophy'. As we stated above, an expression of this type can only be employed with reserve these days because of the

collatum. Locutio potius significatione adhibita est qua usus est Aristoteles, cum de scientiis experimentalibus quasi de "ancillis primae philosophiae" dissereret. Eiusmodi locutio, quae difficulter hodie propter autonomiae principia, quemadmodum supra dictum est, adhibetur, saeculorum decursu iuvit ut necessaria inter duas scientias necessitudo significaretur earumque dissociationis impossibilitas.

Si autem theologus recusaret philosophia uti, periculum esset ne ipse inscius philosopharetur seque concluderet structuris cogitationis fidei intellegendae parum aptis. Philosophus, ex parte sua, si quodlibet excludendum esse cogitaret cum theologia commercium, per se fidei christianae principia capessere suum esse sentiret, sicut nonnullis recentioribus philosophis contigit. In utroque casu periculum exstaret ne delerentur primaria autonomiae principia, quae omnis scientia servare vult.

Hic philosophiae status quem consideravimus, quandoquidem in Revelatione intellegenda implicatur, una cum theologia sub Magisterii eiusque iudicii auctoritate strictius ponitur, sicut antea demonstravimus. Ex fidei namque veritatibus quaedam necessitates derivant, quas philosophia servare debet cum necessitudinem instituit cum theologia.

78. His praepositis cogitationibus, probe intellegitur cur subinde laudaverit Magisterium sancti Thomae philosophiae merita eundemque putaverit ductorem atque theologicae disciplinae exemplar. Nihil intererat philosophicas quasdam quaestiones complecti, neque imperare peculiares opinationes ut tenerentur. Magisterii propositum erat, atque est, significare quemadmodum sanctus Thomas germanum sit exemplar illorum qui veritatem perquirunt. Eius enim in meditatione rationis postulata et fidei vis altissimam invenerunt summam ex iis quae humana cogitatio unquam attigit, quippe qui Revelationis proprietatem radicitus tuitus sit, proprium rationis cursum numquam deprimendo.

79. Clarius quae antea edixit Magisterium ostendentes, novissima hac in parte quaedam postulata enuntiare volumus, quae theologia – immo, antehac Dei verbum – philosophicae cogitationi ac recentioribus philosophicis hodie exhibet. Quemadmodum supra dictum est, ad suas regulas agere suisque principiis inniti debet philosophus; nisi una tamen esse non potest veritas. Revelatio, et quae in ea continentur, rationis inventa eiusque legitimam autonomiam numquam comprimere possunt; at ratio, ex parte sua, sese interrogandi et percontandi facultatem

principle of autonomy; yet in the past it has served to indicate the necessary connection between the two disciplines and the impossibility of separating them.

Should theologians, however, decline to use philosophy there would be a danger of their philosophizing ignorantly and confining themselves to structures poorly adapted to the understanding and knowledge of faith. Should philosophers on their part seek to reflect by excluding any relationship with theology, they might well suppose that they were capable of grasping the principles of Christian faith by themselves, as several recent philosophers have supposed. But in both cases the basic principles of autonomy which every science rightly wants guaranteed would be seriously endangered.

The situation of philosophy which we have considered, in so far as it is implied in the understanding of Revelation, is, as we have previously indicated, placed together with theology under the authority of the Magisterium and its discernment. The truths of faith make certain demands which philosophy must respect whenever it engages theology.

78. With these thoughts before us, we rightly understand why it is that the Magisterium has praised the merits of St Thomas and put him forward as both leader and exemplar of the discipline of theology. It was not in order to embrace certain philosophical positions, nor to require particular views to be held. The design of the Magisterium was, and is, to indicate how St Thomas is an authentic exemplar for those who seek truth. In his reflections the demands of reason and the vigour of faith found the most profound unity of any that human thought has ever yet attained. This was precisely because he radically protected the particularity of Revelation, without at the same time diminishing the proper course of reason.

79. We wish to show more clearly what the Magisterium has already taught, and so in this final part we intend to point out certain requirements which theology, or rather more than this, the Word of God, makes today of philosophical knowledge and contemporary philosophers. As was said above, philosophers ought to act according to their own rules and follow their own principles; nevertheless truth can only be one. Revelation and what is contained within it can never repress the discoveries and legitimate autonomy of reason. But reason on her part should never lose the faculty of self-questioning and of being challenged, conscious as she is that she is not absolute and cannot be her own mistress. Revealed truth, which begins from the splendour created by

numquam amittere debet, sibi omnino conscia se absolutum quiddam propriumque non esse. Veritas revelata, clare id quod est collustrando sumens initium ex splendore quem efficit id quod per se Est, philosophicae cogitationis iter illuminabit. Revelatio christiana verus fit, itaque, locus ubi philosophica et theologica disciplina, mutuam necessitudinem instituentes, coniunguntur et reciprocantur. Optandum igitur est ut theologi ac philosophi a sola veritatis auctoritate temperentur ita ut philosophia cum Dei verbo congruens contexatur. Philosophia haec locus erit ubi humani cultus et christiana fides convenient, consensionis erit sedes inter fideles et non fideles. Opem feret ut fideles sibi sint altius conscii altitudinem sinceritatemque fidei iuvari dum nectitur cum cogitatione dumque eam non recusat. Patrum rursus doctrina in hanc nos persuasionem perducit: "Et ipsum credere, nihil aliud est, quam cum assensione cogitare [. . .] Omnis qui credit, et credendo cogitat, et cogitando credit [. . .] quoniam fide si non cogitatur nulla est".[95] Et etiam: "Si tollatur assensio fides tollitur, quia sine assensione nihil creditur".[96]

CAPUT VII
POSTULATA HODIERNA ET OFFICIA

Verbi Dei postulationes haud renuntiandae

80. Continent Sacrae Litterae, tam explicito quam modo implicito, complura elementa ex quibus haurire licet claram cuiusdam philosophicae crassitudinis aestimationem hominis orbisque. Gradatim conscii facti sunt Christiani iis in paginis sacris divitem concludi thesaurum. Inde quidem elucet id quod experimur non esse absolutum, non esse increatum neque ex se ipso generatum. Deus est Absolutus unus. De Bibliorum paginis praeterea manifesto apparet species hominis veluti *Dei imaginis*, quae certa prae se fert indicia de eius essentia ac libertate nec non animae immortalitate. Quandoquidem orbis creatus non sibi solus sufficit, omnis deceptio autonomiae, quae creaturas omnes a Deo suapte natura pendere proindeque hominem etiam negaverit, ad calamitates perducit quae rationabilem harmoniae inquisitionem sensusque humanae vitae delent.

---

[95] S. Augustinus, *De praedestinatione sanctorum*, 2, 5: *PL* 44, 963.
[96] S. Augustinus, *De fide, spe et caritate*, 7: *CCL* 46, 61.

that which IS, clearly shines upon all that exists and will enlighten the journey of philosophical reflection. Christian Revelation therefore becomes the true place where the philosophical and theological disciplines in their mutual relationships, are yoked together and interact. It is to be desired, therefore, that theologians and philosophers should be so guided by the authority of truth alone that there exists a mutual connection between philosophy and the Word of God. Philosophy will be the place where human culture and Christian faith come together, and will provide the place of agreement between believers and non-believers. It will help the faithful to become more profoundly conscious that the depth and sincerity of their faith is aided when it is united with reflective thought and does not refuse it. The teaching of the Fathers assures me of this: 'belief itself is nothing other than thinking with assent . . . whoever believes, thinks by believing and believes by thinking . . . for unthinking faith is nothing'.[95] And again, 'take away assent and you take away faith, because without assent nothing is believed'.[96]

CHAPTER VII
MODERN DEMANDS AND DUTIES

The requirements of the Word of God that may never be neglected

80. Holy Scripture contains both explicitly and implicitly many elements which are the source of a clear appreciation of great philosophical depth concerning man and the world. Gradually Christians have become aware that a rich treasure is to be found in these sacred pages. From here it becomes clear that what we experience is neither absolute nor uncreated nor self-generated. God alone is the Absolute. Besides, from the pages of the Bible it is very clear that the species of man is as it were *in the image of God*, and bears upon himself signs of his being, and freedom, and not least the immortality of the soul. Since the created world is not self-sufficient, all deception of autonomy – which denies that every creature, man included, naturally depends upon God – leads to disasters, which threaten the search for rational harmony and for the meaning of human life.

---

[95] St Augustine, *On the Predestination of the Saints*, trans. R. G. Wallis, chapter 5, in W. J. Oates, (ed.), *Basic Writings of Saint Augustine* (New York: Random House, 1948), p. 780.

[96] St Augustine, *The Augustine Catechism: The Enchiridion on Faith, Hope and Love*, trans. J. F. Shaw, chapter 20, in Oates, (ed.), *Basic Writings of Saint Augustine*, p. 670.

Mali pariter moralis quaestio, quod omnium est tristissimum, in Bibliis agitatur, ubi illud dicitur haud posse ad aliquod vitium materiae debitum redigi, verum vulnus potius esse quod ex inordinata libertatis humanae affirmatione proficiscitur. Verbum Dei, denique, quaestionem providet de ipsius vitae sensu suumque praebet responsum dum ad Christum Iesum, incarnatum Dei Filium, dirigit hominem qui vitam humanam plenissime complet. Aliae similiter rationes enucleari possunt ex textus sacri lectione; attamen repudiatio inde elucet cuiuslibet formae relativismi, materialismi, pantheismi.

Primaria huius "philosophiae" in Bibliis repositae persuasio haec est: humana vita et mundus ipse aliquid significant et ordinantur ad sui perfectionem quam in Christo Iesu eveniunt. Incarnationis mysterium manebit semper veluti medium punctum ad quod quis referatur ut comprehendere possit arcanum vitae humanae, orbis conditi et Dei ipsius. Hoc in mysterio extremae fiunt philosophiae provocationes, quoniam incitatur ratio humana ut suam efficiat logicam viam ad deruendos muros quibus periculum est ne ipsa circumdetur. Hic, vero, tantummodo vitae humanae sensus in summum evadit. Intima enim Dei hominisque essentia intellegibilis redditur: in Verbi Incarnati mysterio, divina natura atque humana cum suis cuiusque proprietatibus servantur simulque declaratur necessitudo singularis qua colligantur in coniunctione mutua sine permixtione.[97]

81. Animadverti oportet inter significantiora hodiernae nostrae condicionis elementa esse "discrimen significationis". Iudicia, saepe indolis scientificae, de vita et mundo eatenus sunt multiplicata ut praebeatur nobis re vera species aliqua divisarum notitiarum. Istud efficit ut difficulter ac nonnumquam frustra sensus sive significatio rerum conquiratur. Immo vero – id quod magis animum obturbat – in hac datorum factorumque congerie quibus hodie vivitur et quae videntur condere ipsius vitae viam, sunt qui interrogent utrum adhuc interrogare attineat de ipso rerum sensu. Opinationum multitudo inter quas disputatur cui sit respondendum, aut etiam variae rationes interpretandi et contemplandi mundum hominisque vitam, nihil aliud perficiunt nisi ut exsecutam efficiant intimam hanc dubitationem quae facile in scepticismi atque indifferentiae affectionem transit vel etiam varias in nihilismi indicationes.

Hinc autem consequitur ut hominum animus quadam forma ambiguae

[97] Cfr Conc. Oecum. Chalcedonense, *Symbolum, Definitio*: *DS* 302.

Equal with this the question of moral evil, of all forms the saddest, is dealt with in the Bible, where it is said that it cannot be reduced to some defect of matter, but is rather a wound which issues from a disordered affirmation of human freedom. Finally the Word of God poses a question about the meaning of life and provides an answer by directing us to Christ Jesus, the Incarnate Son of God, who most completely fulfils human life. Other reasons can be also worked out from the reading of the sacred text; even so what remains quite clear is the rejection of every form of relativism, materialism and pantheism.

The basic conviction of this biblical 'philosophy' is as follows: human life and the world itself signify something and are ordered to their fulfilment, which occurs in Christ Jesus. The mystery of the Incarnation remains like a fixed point to which everyone should be referred in order to comprehend the secret of human life, the created universe and God himself. It is in this mystery that philosophy experiences its most profound challenges, since human reason is provoked to create its own logical route for destroying the walls by which it might be in danger of being encircled. Yet only here does the meaning of human life appear in full clarity. The intimate essence of God and man is rendered intelligible: in the mystery of the Word Incarnate, divine and human nature are both preserved, each with its own individual characteristics, and at the same the particular connection is made manifest that yokes both together in a mutual union which avoids all confusion.[97]

81. Among the more significant elements of our present situation, it should be noted, is the 'crisis of meaning'. Perspectives on life and the world, often of a scientific stamp, have been so multiplied that we are in truth presented with an increasing fragmentation of knowledge. In consequence this even frustrates or makes it difficult to discover the sense and meaning of things. Further still – and more unsettling to the spirit – in that the mass of data and facts that we live with seem to make up the very stuff of life, there are some who question whether we should still seek to attain the meaning of things in themselves. The immense variety of standpoints each claiming a reply, or even the variety of ways of interpreting and looking at the world and human life, results in nothing other than inducing a profound doubtfulness, which easily leads into scepticism and indifference or even various expressions of nihilism.

As a result, the human spirit is overwhelmed by a form of ambiguous

[97] Cf. Ecumenical Council of Chalcedon, *Symbolum, Definitio* in Tanner, (ed.), *The Decrees of the Ecumenical Councils*, I, pp. 83–7.

cogitationis occupetur, quae eo illos permovet ut magis etiam in se concludantur intra propriae immanentiae fines, nulla habita transcendentis ratione. Philosophia quae caret omni interrogatione de vitae humanae significatione magno obicitur periculo ne humana ratio in usum dumtaxat alicuius instrumenti reducatur, omni vero veritatis inquirendae studio sublato.

Ut autem verbo Dei conveniat necesse in primis est philosophia suam reperiat *sapientialem amplitudinem* quaerendi novissimum ac omnia complectentem sensum vitae. Haec prima necessitas, si res bene ponderantur, ipsi philosophiae addit perutile incitamentum ut suae ipsius naturae accomodetur. Id agens, enim, non erit dumtaxat decretoria quaedam et critica postulatio quae diversis scientiae partibus earum fundamentum ac limitem designat, verum proponetur etiam veluti extrema facultas colligandi totam scientiam actionemque hominum, dum ad unum finem eos concurrere cogit adque sensum ultimum. Haec sapientialis amplitudo eo magis hodie poscitur quia amplior technicae humani generis potentiae auctus renovatam peracutamque petit bonorum supremorum conscientiam. Si technica haec instrumenta forma alicuius ordinationis ad finem non solum utilitatis deficiant, cito videri illa possint inhumana, immo in generis humani potentiales eversores aliquando se convertere.[98]

Ultimum hominis finem patefacit verbum Dei universalemque addit sensum ipsius actionibus in terris. Hanc ob causam philosophiam illud hortatur ut se dedat reperiendo naturali sensus huius fundamento, qui nempe religiosa cuiusque hominis constitutio est. Quaecumque philosophia negare voluerit hunc ultimum et universalem sensum reperiri posse, erit non modo impar verum etiam erronea.

82. Ceterum hoc sapientiae munus non potest aliqua philosophia explere quae ipsa vicissim non est vera solidaque scientia, quae scilicet non tantum dirigitur ad elementa peculiaria et relativa – sive functiones tangunt sive formas vel utilitates – rerum ipsarum, sed ad totam ultimamque earum veritatem, id est ad essentiam ipsam obiectorum cognitionis. Ecce itaque secunda postulatio: ut hominis comprobetur facultas adipiscendae *veritatis cognitionis*; quae, ceterum, cognitio obiectivam attingat veritatem, per illam *adaequationem rei et intellectus*

---

[98] Cfr Ioannes Paulus II, Litt. Encycl. *Redemptor hominis* (4 Martii 1979), 15: *AAS* 71 (1979), 286–289.

thinking, so that people are ever more self-enclosed in the limits of their own immanence, with no account of transcendence. Any philosophy which lacks all discussion of the meaning of human life is exposed to the great danger of reducing human reason to the status of a mere instrument, without any real concern for the pursuit of truth.

To be consonant with the Word of God, philosophy must rediscover its *fullness of wisdom* in searching for the final and most all-embracing meaning of life. This first requirement, if the matter is well considered, gives philosophy a useful spur to bring itself into its own genius. By doing so, not only will it be the decisive critical factor which determines the foundations and limits of the different fields of knowledge, but it will also take up its place as the ultimate faculty for the gathering together of human knowledge and action, leading all to converge towards a final purpose and meaning. This fullness of wisdom is all the more needed today because the immense expansion of humanity's technical capability demands a renewed and sharpened awareness of the ultimate goods. If these technical instruments lack any sense of being ordered to something greater than a merely utilitarian end, they could appear to be inhuman, and turn themselves into potential destroyers of the human race.[98]

The Word of God lays bare the final purpose of man and adds meaning to his actions upon earth. For this reason it exhorts philosophy to give itself to recovering the natural basis of that sense, which is part of the religious make up of each of us. If any philosophy wishes to deny the possibility of recovering this ultimate and universal sense, it will be not only inadequate but false.

82. Yet this sapiential task could not be performed by any philosophy which is not in its turn a true and solid knowledge, that is to say one which is not merely interested in the particular or relative origins – functional, formal or utilitarian – of things in themselves, but is concerned rather with their complete and ultimate truth, that is, with the essence itself of the objects of knowledge. This is the second requirement: the capacity of man to arrive at the *knowledge of truth* must be admitted; this relates to the first, that knowledge attain to objective truth, by the means named by the teachers of Scholasticism the *correspondence between thing and intellect*.[99] This requirement, fully proper to faith, was

---

[98] Cf. John Paul II, Encyclical Letter *Redemptor hominis*, §15.

[99] Cf., for example, St Thomas Aquinas, *Summa Theologiae*, Ia, Q. 16, Art. 1; Bonaventure, *Collationes in Hexameron*, Collatio III, Q. 8, Art. 1 in R. Wood, *A Transcription of the Collatio III of the Hexameron* (*Franciscan Studies* 53, 1993).

quam Scholasticae disciplinae doctores appellaverunt.[99] Haec postulatio, fidei plane propria, explicatis verbis in Concilio Oecumenico Vaticano II est rursus inculcata: "Intellegentia enim non ad sola phaenomena coarctatur, sed realitatem intellegibilem cum vera certitudine adipisci valet, etiamsi, ex sequela peccati, ex parte obscuratur et debilitatur".[100]

Philosophia prorsus phaenomenorum aut rerum aequivocarum haud idonea erit quae hoc suppeditet auxilium divitiis verbi Dei altius perscrutandis. Etenim, pro concesso semper Sacra Scriptura habet hominem, licet falsitatis sit reus fallaciaeque, cognoscere tamen posse et comprehendere perlucidam semplicemque veritatem. Libris Sacris ac praesertim Novo Testamento, insunt loci et adfirmationes indolis omnino ontologicae. Veras enim declarationes potuerunt proferre auctores inspirati, quae nempe res denotarent obiectivas. Dici non potest Traditionem catholicam ullo modo erravisse cum dicta quaedam sancti Ioannis ac sancti Pauli accepit velut sententias de ipsa Christi essentia. Cum his affirmationibus et intelligendis et exponendis dat operam, theologia subsidio proinde indiget alicuius philosophiae quae facultatem cognitionis obiective verae non neget, quantumvis perfici illa possit. Hoc pariter de conscientiae moralis valet iudiciis, quae Sacrae Litterae concedunt esse posse obiective vera.[101]

83. Priores hae postulationes tertiam secum important: opus est philosophia naturae *vere metaphysicae*, quae excedere nempe valeat empirica indicia ut, veritatem conquirens, ad aliquid absolutum ultimum, fundamentale pertingat. Haec postulatio iam implicita reperitur in cognitionibus indolis sapientialis tum etiam analyticae; est necessitas praesertim cognitionum de bono morali cuius extremum fundamentum est Bonum supremum, Deus ipse. Nolumus hic loqui de metaphysica re tamquam de peculiari schola aut particulari consuetudine historica. Adfirmare id dumtaxat interest realitatem ac veritatem transcendere facta et elementa empirica; refert etiam defendere hominis potestatem cuius vi hanc rationem transcendentem ac metaphysicam percipiat modo vero certoque, licet imperfecto et analogico. Ita quidem metaphysica disciplina non respicienda est tamquam anthropologiae opposita, quandoquidem metaphysica ipsa sinit solide stabiliri dignitatis personae conceptum ex eius spiritali natura. Persona, nominatim, locum

[99] Cfr verbi causa S. Thomas Aquinas, *Summa Theologiae*, I, 16, 1; S. Bonaventura, *Coll. in Hex.*, 3, 8, 1.

[100] Const. past. de Ecclesia in mundo huius temporis *Gaudium et spes*, §15.

[101] Cfr Ioannes Paulus II, Litt. Encycl. *Veritatis splendor* (6 Augusti 1993), §§57–61: *AAS* 85 (1993), 1179–1182.

explicitly reaffirmed by the Second Vatican Council: 'the intelligence is not restricted to appearances alone, but is strong enough to attain with real certainty intelligible reality, even though as a result of sin it is partly obscured and weakened'.[100]

A philosophy restricted to phenomena or the provisionality of things will be quite unsuitable to assist a deeper exploring of the riches of the Word of God. Holy Scripture always insists that man, however prone he may be to falsity and deception, can always reflect on and comprehend clear and simple truth. In the sacred writings, above all in the New Testament, we can find passages and affirmations of genuinely ontological content. The sacred authors were capable of producing statements of a truly objective character. It cannot be said that the Catholic tradition was in any way in error in treating the words of St John and St Paul as opinions about the very being of Christ. When theology applies itself to the understanding and exposition of these statements, she relies upon the aid of a philosophy which does not deny the capacity for truly objective knowledge, even though that knowledge can be further perfected. This applies equally to judgments of the moral conscience, which Holy Scripture treats as capable of being objectively true.[101]

83. These two requirements involve a third. There is need of a *truly metaphysical* philosophy of nature, able to go beyond empirical evidence in such a way that, seeking the truth, it arrives at something absolute, ultimate and grounded. This assumption is implicit in sapiential and analytical knowledge alike; it is a necessity above all for the knowledge of moral good, whose ultimate basis is the supreme Good, God himself. We are not speaking here about metaphysics as about some particular school or historical tradition. What is important to stress is that reality and truth transcend empirical facts and origins. It is vital to defend man's power of arriving in a true and certain way at this transcendent and metaphysical reason, even though that way may be imperfect and analogical. We must not therefore think of metaphysics as in some way opposed to anthropology, rather it is metaphysics itself that permits the conception of the dignity of the human person, based on her spiritual nature, to be solidly grounded. The person, specifically, constitutes the place for the encounter with the very activity of being, and therefore with metaphysical reflection.

---

[100] Vatican Council II, Pastoral Constitution on the Church in the Modern World *Gaudium et spes*, §15 in Flannery, (ed.), *Vatican Council II*, p. 916.

[101] Cf. John Paul II, Encyclical Letter *Veritatis splendor* (London: Catholic Truth Society, 1993), §§57–61.

constituit praecipuum ut quis congrediatur cum actu essendi ac, propterea, cum meditatione metaphysica.

Ubicumque praesentem quandam appellationem ad absolutum et transcendens detegit homo, inibi ei aperitur indicatio metaphysicae rerum interpretationis: in veritate ac pulchritudine, in bonis moralibus ac personis ceteris, in esse ac in Deo. Magna manet nos provocatio hoc exeunte millennio, ut nempe transitum facere sciamus tam necessarium quam urgentem *a phaenomeno ad fundamentum*. Non ideo licet in sola experientia consistere; etiam quotiens haec exprimit et ostendit interiorem hominis naturam eiusque spiritalitatem, necesse est speculativa ponderatio spiritalem substantiam attingat nec non fundamentum cui innititur. Philosophica notio ideo quae omne metaphysicum spatium negaverit ex se prorsus inepta erit nec idonea ut officium congruum expleat mediationis ad Revelationem comprehendendam.

Perpetuo se verbum Dei ad ea refert quae experientiam praetergrediuntur atque etiam hominum cogitationem; at hoc "mysterium" patefieri non posset neque theologia illud quadamtenus intelligibile efficere valeret,[102] si humana cognitio artis experientiae sensuum limitibus circumscriberetur. Quocirca metaphysica exsistit tamquam quaedam intercessio praestans in theologica inquisitione. Theologia quidem, prospectu metaphysico destituta, ultra experientiae religiosae investigationem progredi non poterit neque permittere ut *intellectus fidei* congruenter universalem veritatis revelatae transcendentemque vim significet.

Si metaphysicae partes tantopere extollimus, hoc ideo accidit quod persuasum Nobis habemus necessariam hanc esse viam ad statum discriminis superandum, in quo hodie philosophia magna ex parte omnino versatur, et ad quosdam improbos nostra in societate diffusos emendandos mores.

84. Manifestius etiam elucet metaphysici operis pondus si progressus expenduntur quos hodie scientiae hermeneuticae iam efficiunt nec non variae sermonis humani pervestigationes. Consectaria quae his effluxerunt ex studiis utilissima esse possunt ad fidei intellectum, quatenus structuram cogitationis humanae sermocinationisque patefaciunt atque omnem sensum in sermone inclusum. Verumtamen earundem disciplinarum cultores sunt qui suis inquisitionibus eo

[102] Cfr Conc. Oecum. Vat. I, Const. dogm. de fide catholica *Dei Filius*, IV: *DS* 3016.

Wherever man detects a summons to the absolute and transcendent, there is opened up for him some indication of the metaphysical interpretation of things: in truth and beauty, in moral good, and in other people, in being, and in God. There is a great demand upon us as the present millennium draws to a close that we be able to make a transition, both necessary and urgent, *from appearance to foundation*. Experience by itself is inadequate: even if it does reveal man's interior nature and his spiritual character, it is vital that some speculative consideration arrive at the spiritual substance and ground upon which it rests. A philosophical position, therefore, which rejects every form of metaphysics will be quite incapable and unfit to perform its mediating role for comprehending Revelation.

The Word of God always deals with those things that go beyond both human experience and thought; but, if human knowledge were circumscribed within the narrow limits of sensory experience this 'mystery' would remain incapable of being revealed, nor would theology be able to render it intelligible.[102] Metaphysics, therefore, exercises an important mediating role in theological research. Theology, however, destitute of a metaphysical outlook, will be incapable of going beyond the investigation of religious experience and will not be therefore the *understanding of faith* to give appropriate expression to the universal and transcendent force of revealed truth.

Our reason for laying so much stress on the importance of metaphysics is simply the fact that we are convinced that this is a necessary way of dealing with the difficult situation now faced for the most part by philosophy, and at the same time of correcting certain deplorable practices that prevail in society.

84. An even clearer proof of the importance of metaphysics arises from the awareness of the progress made in the discipline of hermeneutics and in the various explorations of the nature of human language. The results of these researches can greatly contribute to the understanding of faith because they lay bare the structure of human thought and expression and all the meaning enclosed in language. However, experts in these areas, despite their intention in their investigations of arriving at a means and agreement by which the universe of things is explained and understood, fail to go further and explore the capacity of reason in order to lay bare the essence of things. How could we fail to see in such an attitude

---

[102] Cf. First Vatican Council, Dogmatic Constitution on the Catholic Faith *Dei Filius*, §4 in Tanner, (ed.), *The Decrees of the Ecumenical Councils*, II, pp. 808 f.

dumtaxat adveniunt ut explicent quo pacto intellegatur et quo modo exprimatur rerum universitas, non tamen rationis humanae facultatem probant ut rerum essentia detegatur. Quomodo non dispici potest hoc in affectu confirmatio illius discriminis fiduciae, quod aetas nostra patitur, de rationis humanae potestate? Cum vero, ex praemissis quibusdam gratuitis, hae sententiae iam fidei doctrinam obscurant eiusve universalem denegant virtutem, tunc non modo rationem demittunt, verum sese ipsas omnino excludunt. Fides etenim luculenter postulat ut hominum sermo via quadam universali – etiam vocibus analogicis tamen non ideo minus significantibus – realitatem divinam ac transcendentem.[103] Res nisi ita se haberent, Dei verbum, quod semper divinum est licet lingua humana contineatur, nihil de Deo significare posset. Huius Verbi interpretatio non huc illuc ab explicatione alia in aliam explicationem conicere nos potest, ad nullam nos adducens affirmationem simpliciter veram; alioquin nulla esset Dei revelatio, sed tantummodo significatio humanarum notionum de Deo et de iis quae existimatur ille de nobis cogitare.

85. Probe novimus postulata haec, a philosophia ipsi Dei verbo iniuncta, videri posse ardua multis qui hodiernam investigationis philosophicae experiuntur condicionem. Hanc omnino ob causam, ea omnia Nostra facientes quae iam complures annos Summi Pontifices docere non desistunt quaeque rursus inculcavit Concilium Oecumenicum Vaticanum II, vehementer confitemur Nobis esse persuasum hominem visionem unicam et ordinatam scientiae assequi posse. Hoc unum officiorum est quod christiana cogitatio proximo quidem christianae aetatis millennio in se recipere debebit. Multiplex scientiae humanae partitio, quatenus partim tantum ad veritatem accedere sinit ideoque etiam sensum ipsum perfringit, interiorem hominis hodierni impedit unitatem. Quare de his omnibus non potest sollicitari Ecclesia? Hoc sapientiae munus in eius pastores recta via ex Evangelio defluit neque ipsi se subducere possunt officio illius muneris explendi.

Quotquot hodie veluti philosophi respondere cupiant illis postulationibus quas cogitationi humanae Dei verbum imponit, eos credimus omnino suum debere explicare sermonem secundum easdem postulationes nec non continuam cohaerentiam cum diuturna illa traditione quae, ab antiquis profecta, transit per Ecclesiae Patres atque scholasticae disciplinae magistros, ut tandem ad intellegendos cogitationis recentioris atque huius aequalis temporis praecipuos fructus adveniat. Philosophus si hanc traditionem usurpare noverit seque ex ea dirigere, certe non

[103] Cfr Conc. Oecum. Lateranense IV, *De errore abbatis Ioachim*, II: *DS* 806.

confirmation of the current crisis of confidence in the powers of reason from which we suffer? When, on the basis of preconceived assumptions, these positions tend to obscure the contents of faith or to deny their universal validity, then not only do they abase reason but in so doing they also disqualify themselves. For faith clearly requires that human speech should in some universal way give expression – even though voiced analogically, but no less meaningfully – to divine, transcendent reality.[103] Deprived of this assumption, the Word of God, which despite its use of human language remains divine, could signify nothing of God. The interpretation of this Word cannot merely keep tossing us from one interpretation to another, never directing us to a statement that is simple and true: were that the case there could be no revelation of God, but instead only the expression of human concepts about God and of the things it is presumed he thinks about us.

85. We are well aware that these requirements which the Word of God imposes upon philosophy may seem daunting to many people involved in philosophical research today. It is for this very reason that we endorse what previous popes have taught for many years and what the Second Vatican Council also stressed; we therefore wholeheartedly declare ourselves convinced that man can reach a single, ordered vision of knowledge. This is one of the duties to which in the coming millennium Christian thought must apply itself. The interior unity of modern man is severely frustrated by the fragmentation of human knowledge, which impedes an overall approach to truth and splits up its meaning. How could the Church not be concerned about this? The gift of wisdom descends upon her pastors directly from the Gospel and they cannot shrink from the obligations their position gives them.

Whoever today wishes to respond, like philosophers, to the demands which the Word of God imposes upon human reflection should, we believe, work out their ideas in accordance with these demands, and should also point out their coherence with the great tradition, beginning with the ancients, passing through the Fathers of the Church and the masters of Scholasticism and coming at last to an understanding of the particular fruits of more recent and even contemporary reflection. Philosophers who know how to apply this tradition and allow themselves to be directed by it certainly will not be unfaithful to the demand for the autonomy of philosophical research.

---

[103] Cf. Fourth Lateran Ecumenical Council, *Concerning the Error of Abbot Joachim*, in Tanner, (ed.), *The Decrees of the Ecumenical Councils*, II, pp. 231–3.

poterit ipse fidelem se non demonstrare ipsi necessitati autonomiae philosophicarum investigationum.

Hoc sensu plurimum id significat, quod nempe quidam philosophi hodiernis in adiunctis se exhibeant fautores iterum detecti pergravis ponderis traditionum ad rectam cognitionis formam. Appellatio enim ad traditionem non sola praeteriti temporis recordatio est; agnoscit potius illa patrimonium culturae quod pertinet omnes ad homines. Par immo est dicere nos ad traditionem pertinere neque licere statuere de ea uti velimus. Hinc plane, quod radices in ipsam traditionem aguntur, permittitur nobis hodie ut cogitationem aliquam primam et novam et de futuro tempore providam enuntiemus. Eadem haec appellatio magis etiam pertinet ad theologiam. Non solum quia vivam Ecclesiae Traditionem ipsa possidet tamquam primigenum rerum fontem,[104] verum etiam quod idcirco theologia posse debet tum revocare altam traditionem theologicam quae priora saecula signavit, tum perennem illius philosophiae traditionem quae novit spatii temporisque fines excedere suam ob sapientiam.

86. Inculcata haec necessitas solidi vinculi continuationis deliberationum philosophicarum cum inquisitionibus traditionis christianae illuc spectat ut praevertatur periculo quod quibusdam hodie latius diffusis sententiis subest. Quamquam breviter, opportunum censemus immorari iis in sententiis quarum ostendantur errores indeque pericula philosophicae industriae intenta.

Eorum quidem primum (periculum) voce *eclecticismi* nuncupatur, quo nomine illius hominis describitur affectio qui, in investigando, in docendo et in argumentatione theologica, singulas notiones accipere solet diversis perceptas ex philosophiis, nulla earum habita ratione cohaerentiae neque ordinatae coniunctionis nec historicae collocationis. Hoc pacto ita se praebet ut veritatis partem in aliqua notione distinguere ab aliis erratis vel imperfectis rebus nequeat. Extrema eclecticismi dispici potest forma etiam rhetorico in abusu vocabulorum philosophicorum quae aliqui theologi interdum usurpant. Non utilis est similis abusus inquisitioni veritatis neque mentem sive theologicam sive philosophicam instituit ut modo serio doctoque argumentetur. Grave et altum doctrinarum philosophicarum studium tum etiam proprii earum sermonis et contextus ex quo sunt enatae, multum adiuvat ut eclecticismi

[104] Cfr Conc. Oecum. Vat. II, Const. dogm. de divina Revelatione *Dei Verbum*, §24; Decr. de institutione sacerdotali *Optatam totius*, §16.

In this connection it is very significant that in the present day some philosophers have shown themselves, in their search for an appropriate form of knowledge, enthusiastic for the rediscovery of the importance of tradition. This appeal to tradition is not simply a remembrance of time past, rather it recognizes the cultural inheritance which is proper to all men and women. Indeed it may be said that it is we who belong to the tradition and that it is not ours to dispose of as we wish. Precisely because our roots lie in the tradition itself, are we today able to develop for the future new and original reflections. What is named here applies even more to theology. This is not only because theology possesses as its primary source of knowledge the living Tradition of the Church,[104] but also because theology ought to be able to call upon the deep theological tradition that has marked earlier ages, and further may call upon that enduring tradition of philosophy which knows how in its search for wisdom to exceed the limits imposed by time and place.

86. Our insistence on the necessity for a strong link between philosophical deliberation and research into the Christian tradition is intended to avert the danger which lies within many widely held philosophical opinions. We think it appropriate to dwell for a moment, however briefly, on these positions in order both to expose their errors and also the dangers they present to philosophical endeavour.

The first of these (dangers) is called *eclecticism*, by which name is described that attitude of mind which in researching, in teaching, and in theological argument, lifts individual concepts from different philosophies, without attending either to their coherence, their connection with other ideas or their historical context. They therefore run the risk of being unable to distinguish the part of truth of a given doctrine from elements of it which may be erroneous or ill-suited to the task at hand. An extreme form of this eclecticism can be seen in the rhetorical abuse of philosophical terminology, which some theologians employ on occasion. Such an abuse is quite useless when it comes to the search for truth, nor does it prepare the theological or philosophical mind for serious and learned discussion. A serious and deep study of philosophical teachings, both of the language they employ and of the contexts from which they are born is of great help for avoiding the dangers of eclecticism and also provides a suitable preparation for theological arguments.

---

[104] Cf. Second Vatican Council, Dogmatic Constitution on Divine Revelation *Dei Verbum*, §24; Decree on the Training of Priests *Optatam totius*, §16 in Flannery, (ed.), *Vatican Council II*, pp. 763 f.; 718 f.

pericula vincantur permittitque aptam in earum argumentationes theologicas ingressionem.

87. Error ipsius methodi est eclecticismus, qui tamen in se opinationes etiam *historicismi* contegere potest. Recte ut praeteriti temporis comprehendatur doctrina, ea necesse est sua in historiae atque culturae inseratur adiuncta. Primaria historicismi sententia, ex contrario, ea est ut philosophiae cuiusdam veritas sustineatur natura propria sua ad aliquod certum tempus aptata aut ad definitum historicum munus. Ita quidem, saltem implicite, perennis veri virtus negatur. Id quod aliqua aetate valebat ut verum, potest cessare id esse alio tempore, uti defendet historicista. Notionum humanarum historia, demum, ad eius iudicium paulo plus est quam archeologicum inventum ex quo haurire licet ut sententiae prioris temporis demonstrentur iam maximam partem praetermissae et in praesentia omni significatione carentes. Contra, potius reminiscendum est, etiamsi ipsa veritatis formula temporibus quadamtenus et culturae formis vinciatur, veritates vel errores inibi repertos posse nihilominus agnosci et uti tales aestimari, quantumvis spatio temporeve distent.

Intra theologicam meditationem plerumque se praebet historicismus quadam sub ratione "modernismi". Dum enim quis merito studet sermonem theologicum accommodum et pervium reddere aequalibus suis, affirmationibus et dictionibus philosophicis tantummodo recentioribus utitur, criticis neglectis iudiciis quae ad traditionis lumen tandem aliquando proferenda sunt. Haec modernismi via, quoniam veritatem praesenti pro utilitate permutat, haud idonea reperitur ad veritatis satisfaciendum postulatis quibus respondeat theologia oportet.

88. Aliud expendendum est periculum, nempe *scientismus*. Haec philosophiae notio respuit tamquam validas omnes cognitionis formas alienas iis quae sunt scientiarum positivarum propriae atque in provinciam solorum phantasmatum reicit tum religiosam et theologicam cognitionem tum ethicam et aestheticam scientiam. Praeteritis temporibus eadem notio intra positivismum et neo-positivismum declarabatur, qui sensu destitutas iudicabant affirmationes metaphysicae indolis. Censura epistemologica omnem huic sententiae abstulit fidem, sed ecce novo renascitur sub scientismi vestitu. Hoc sub prospectu, bona ad animi motuum dumtaxat effecta rediguntur atque "essendi" notio praeteritur ut aliquid spatii nudis et simplicibus tribuatur factis. Sese igitur scientia praeparat ut per technologicos progressus omnibus

87. Eclecticism is an error of method itself, and it can at the same time conceal within itself the suppositions of *historicism*. For the correct understanding of the teaching of a past age it is necessary that it be located in historical and cultural context. The primary precept of historicism, however, is that the truth of a particular philosophy is limited in its relevance to a particular time and only for a particular historical purpose. In this way, at least by implication, the persisting value of truth is denied. Thus historicism claims that what in one age was held to be true can cease to be so at another period. Thus for it the history of thought becomes little more than an archaeological resource useful for illustrating positions once held, but for the most part outmoded and meaningless now. We on the contrary ought to remember that, even though the formulation of truth is up to a point determined by previous ages and cultural forms, yet the truths and errors discovered there can invariably be acknowledged and judged for what they are, despite the distance in space and time.

Within the general area of theological reflection historicism often appears in the shape of 'modernism'. In the praiseworthy effort to adapt theological language to the demands of the present and so make it accessible to our contemporaries it employs only the affirmations and philosophical expressions which are current, while neglecting the critical judgments which the light of tradition from time to time demands. This modernist approach, since it exchanges truth for usefulness, is inadequate to satisfying the requirements of truth to which theology should respond.

88. A further danger to be aware of is *scientism*. This concept of philosophy rejects as invalid all those forms of knowledge which are alien to the positive sciences and therefore relegates to the area of pure imagination both religious and theological knowledge, as well as ethical and aesthetic knowledge. In time past the same idea was expressed within positivism and neo-positivism, which judged metaphysical statements to be devoid of meaning. Epistemology deprived this idea of its viability, but behold it, reborn in the dress of scientism. In its view values are reduced to products of the emotions, the concept of 'being' is passed over, to clear the way for bare simple facts. So it is that science proposes to dominate all parts of life through technological progress. The undeniable and happy triumphs of scientific enquiry and modern technology have helped disseminate this scientistic frame of mind, which appears to know no circumscriptive limits, seeing that it has made its way into a variety of cultural forms and also produced fundamental transformations in them.

dominetur vitae humanae partibus. Felices qui nullo modo possunt negari successus scientificae investigationes nec non horum temporum technologiae plurimum adiuverunt ut mens scientistica disseminaretur quae nullis iam videtur finibus circumscribi, cum in varias iam intraverit culturae formas et mutationes fundamentales ibi quoque effecerit.

Pro dolor, quod ad interrogationem pertinet de vitae sensu, notandum est a fautoribus scientismi eandem haberi quaestionem tamquam propriam orbis irrationalis aut omnino ficti. Non minus autem deludit huius mentis tractatio magnis de aliis philosophiae quaesitis quae, si iam non omnino praetermittuntur, aliqua deliberatione agitantur quae similitudinibus apparentibus fulcitur, fundamento carentibus omnino rationali. Hoc humanam rerum ponderationem reddit pauperiorem, cui fundamentales quaestiones illae subtrahuntur quas *rationale animal*, inde suis ab initiis in terra, perpetuo sibi proposuit. Postquam, hanc secundum sententiam, criticum iudicium ex ethica aestimatione est omissum, scientistarum doctrina efficere valuit ut plures sibi persuaderent id quod technica ratione fieri possit hanc ipsam ob causam morali ratione accipi posse.

89. Haud minorum periculorum praenuntius est ipse *pragmatismus*, qui animi affectus ad eum maxime pertinet qui, suis in electionibus, usum recusat deliberationum theoreticarum vel existimationum ethicis principiis innitentium. Insignia sunt practica consectaria quae ab eiusmodi mentis opinatione profluxerunt. Nominatim vero eo deventum est ut popularis regiminis opinatio proferretur quae nullo modo ad fundamenta ordinis officiorum et debitorum referretur ac propterea immutabilia: honestas vel inhonestas quorundam morum secundum maioris partis suffragia in senatibus statuitur.[105] Patent autem huiusmodi iudicationis consectaria: praecipuae morales sententiae sive pronuntiationes paulatim disputationibus subduntur quorundam institutorum. Praeterea: ipsa anthropologica disciplina graviter afficitur, proposita una dumtaxat hominis visione, a qua longe absunt ethicae dubitationes nec non vitales explicationes de sensu doloris ac sacrificii, vitae et mortis.

90. Hucusque recensitae opinationes perducunt vicissim ad latiorem quandam notionem quae hodie efficere videtur communem multarum philosophiarum prospectum quae iam a sensu essendi recesserunt. Loquimur enim de interpretatione nihilista quae simul omnis fundamenti

---

[105] Cfr Ioannes Paulus II, Litt. Encycl. *Evangelium vitae* (25 Martii 1995), §69: *AAS* 87 (1995), 481.

Sadly, that which relates to the question of the meaning of life has to be branded by promoters of scientism as belonging to the realm of the irrational or altogether fictitious. No less disappointing is the way in which it approaches the other great problems of philosophy which, if they are not ignored, are subjected to analyses based on superficial analogies, lacking all rational foundation. All this renders the human consideration of matters the poorer by depriving it of those fundamental questions which the *rational animal* from its very origins on earth has always asked itself. According to this view, by depriving the critical judgment of all ethical dimensions, the teaching of scientism has had the effect of persuading many that what is technically possible is therefore morally admissible.

89. No less dangerous is *pragmatism*, an attitude of mind which, in making its choices, precludes theoretical considerations or judgments based on ethical principles. The practical consequences that result from such a habit of mind are distinctive. In particular there is growing support for a concept of democracy without any reference to the changeless bases of rights and duties: the honesty or dishonesty of certain moral practices is decided by reference solely to the view of the parliamentary majority.[105] The consequences of this method of decision are quite clear: bit by bit moral decisions and pronouncements are made dependent upon the discussions of particular institutions. Moreover: the discipline of anthropology itself is severely affected, seeing that only one understanding of humanity is envisaged, which excludes ethical dilemmas and vital discussions of the meaning of sorrow and sacrifice, life and death.

90. The opinions so far discussed lead to a broader concept that today seems to dominate the shared view of many philosophies, which have deserted the meaning of being. We are speaking, indeed, of the nihilist interpretation which implies at the same time both a rejection of all foundations and the negation of all objective truth. *Nihilism* is the denial of the humanity and the very identity of man, even before it opposes all the demands and doctrines that belong particularly to the Word of God. We should not forget that the neglect of 'being' itself involves also a self-distancing from objective truth and further from that foundation that supports human dignity. It can also happen that the face of man may be deprived of those very elements and ideas which reveal his likeness to God, which little by little leads in its turn either to the destructive desire

[105] Cf John Paul II, Encyclical Letter *Evangelium vitae* (25 March 1995) (London: Catholic Truth Society, 1995), §69.

repudiationem continet omnisque veritatis obiectivae negationem. *Nihilismus* est humanitatis hominis ipsius negatio et eius proprietatis, prius quam adversetur postulationibus et doctrinis verbi Dei propriis. Etenim haud oblivisci licet neglectum ipsius "esse" necessario secum etiam longinquitatem adferre ab obiectiva veritate ac, proinde, ab ipso fundamento illo quod hominis sustinet dignitatem. Fieri sic potest ut de vultu hominis illae submoveantur partes et species quae similitudinem Dei patefaciunt, unde paulatim aut ad destructivam potentiae cupiditatem adducitur aut solitudinis ad desperationem. Amota enim semel hominis veritate, omnino quis decipitur se liberum illum facere contendens. Nam veritas atque libertas aut coniunguntur simul aut simul misere amittuntur.[106]

91. Explanantes principia sententiarum modo propositarum noluimus integram praebere descriptionem hodiernae philosophiae condicionis: ceterum difficulter redigi illa potest unicam ad aestimationem. Adseverare Nostra potius interest haereditatem scientiae ac sapientiae revera pluribus locupletari in regionibus. Satis memorare est logicam, sermonis philosophiam, epistemologiam, naturae philosophiam, anthropologiam, altiorem investigationem affectuum cognitionis, existentialem accessum ad libertatis explicationem. E contrario, principii immanentiae affirmatio, quae veluti media subiacet postulatis rationalistis, iam a priore saeculo responsiones excitavit quibus altissima dubitatio inducta est de aliis postulatis de quibus eo usque disputatum non erat. Enatae ita sunt sententiae irrationales, simulque criticum iudicium aperuit manifesto vacuam omnino postulationem absoluti dominii rationis.

A quibusdam subtilioribus auctoribus aetas nostra uti tempus "post-modernum" est designata. Vocabulum istud, saepius quidem adhibitum de rebus inter se dissidentibus, indicat emergentem quandam elementorum novorum summam quae sua amplitudine et efficacitate

---

[106] Eandem in sententiam primis Nostris in Litteris Encyclicis, cum Evangelii sancti Ioannis exponeremus dictionem "cognoscetis veritatem, et veritas liberabit vos" (8:32), sic elocuti sumus: "Haec verba principalem in se necessitatem continent simulque admonitionem: necessitatem videlicet animi honesti erga veritatem uti condicionis verae libertatis; admonitionem pariter, ut declinetur quaevis simulata tantum libertas, quaelibet levis unique tantum parti favens libertas, omnis demum libertas, quae totam veritatem de homine ac mundo non permeet. Etiam hodie, duobus annorum milibus post, Christus nobis comparet tamquam ille, qui homini libertatem in veritate innixam affert, ille, qui hominem ab omnibus liberat, quae istam libertatem coarctant, minuunt et quasi perfringunt ipsis in eius radicibus, nempe in hominis anima, corde, conscientia": Litt. Encycl. *Redemptor hominis* (4 Martii 1979), §12: *AAS* 71 (1979), 280–281.

for power or to the despair of isolation. Once the truth about man has been removed he is often deluded in supposing he can make himself free, for truth and freedom are either joined together or together they perish miserably.[106]

91. In discussing these currents of thought it was not our intention to offer a total description of the condition of modern philosophy: indeed it would be hard to reduce it to a unified definition. We would far rather stress that the inheritance of knowledge and wisdom has in many areas been greatly enriched. It is enough to recall logic, the philosophy of language, epistemology, the philosophy of nature, anthropology, a more profound investigation of the affective character of knowledge and an existential approach to the analysis of freedom. However since the nineteenth century the affirmation of the principle of immanence, which is a sort of basis to the claims of rationalism, has provoked the profoundest doubting of claims once thought indisputable. In response, currents of irrationalism have arisen, while at the same time critical judgment clearly showed the emptiness of the claims of the absolute domination of reason.

Some more subtle writers have labelled the age in which we live 'post-modern'. This expression, frequently employed in vastly differing fields, indicates the emergence of an assembly of new features which, while widespread and successful, have produced serious and lasting changes. The word was first employed in order to indicate ideas in the aesthetic, social and technological orders. Thence it made its way into the philosophical arena, though it is always marked by a certain ambiguity, partly because the judgments it made about things designated as 'post-modern' were sometime favourable, sometimes not so, partly because no consensus has been arrived at on the difficult question as to the actual boundaries of various historical ages. Even so one thing has been discovered which admits of no doubt: the reasons and reflections which refer to the area of post-modernity always merit serious consideration.

---

[106] In the same sense we commented in our first Encyclical Letter on the expression in the Gospel of St John, 'you will know the truth, and the truth will set you free' (*Jn* 8:32): 'these words contain both a fundamental requirement and a warning: the requirement of an honest relationship with regard to truth as a condition for authentic freedom, and the warning to avoid every kind of illusory freedom, every superficial unilateral freedom, every freedom that fails to enter into the whole truth about humanity and the world. Today also, even after two thousand years, we see Christ as the one who brings humanity a freedom based on truth, frees humanity from what curtails, diminishes and as it were breaks off this freedom at its root, in the human soul, heart and conscience.' (John Paul II, Encyclical Letter *Redemptor hominis*, §12.)

graves manentesque perficere potuerunt mutationes. Ita verbum idem primum omnium adhibitum est de notionibus ordinis aesthetici et socialis et technologici. In provinciam deinde philosophiae est translatum, at certa semper ambiguitate signatum, tum quia iudicium de iis quae uti "post-moderna" appellantur nunc affirmans nunc negans esse potest, tum quia nulla est consensio in perdifficili quaestione de variarum aetatum historicarum terminis. Verumtamen unum illud extra omnem dubitationem invenitur: rationes et cogitationes quae ad spatium post-modernum referuntur congruam merentur ponderationem. Secundum enim quasdam earum opinationes certitudinum tempus dicitur iam sine remedio transiisse et homini ipsi iam discendum esse in rerum quodam prospectu vivere ubi nullus reperiatur sensus, sub nomine nempe rerum fugientium ac temporariarum. Omnem certitudinem iudicio suo delentes, complures auctores, necessariis neglectis distinctionibus, in dubium etiam fidei certitudines deducunt.

Quadamtenus confirmatur hic nihilismus in terrifica malorum experientia quibus aetas nostra est distincta. Ante calamitosum huius experimenti casum, optimismus rationalista, qui in historia deprehendebat victricem rationis progressionem, felicitatis libertatisque fontem, haud restitit ita ut iam ex maximis periculis et minis huius exeuntis saeculi invitatio sit ad desperationem.

Verum nihilominus est certam quandam mentem positivistam etiam nunc fidem tribuere deceptioni, cuius vi, propter reperta scientifica et technica, homo veluti demiurgus assequi ex se solo possit sibique obtinere plenum suam in fortunam dominatum.

Hodierna theologiae officia

92. Quatenus est Revelationis intellegentia, variis in historiae aetatibus theologia semper cognovit sibi diversarum culturarum postulationes esse suscipiendas ut intra eas, consentanea cum doctrinae explicatione, fidei elementa tradere posset. Hodie quoque duplex ad eam pertinet munus. Altera ex parte opus explicet illa oportet quod Concilium Oecumenicum Vaticanum II suo tempore ei commisit: suas ut proprias renovaret docendi rationes quo evangelizationi efficacius inserviret. Hac in re quis recordari non potest de verbis a Summo Pontifice Ioanne XXIII prolatis dum aperiret Concilium? Dixit enim tunc: "Oportet ut, quemadmodum cuncti sinceri rei christianae, catholicae, apostolicae fautores vehementer exoptant, eadem doctrina amplius et altius cognoscatur eaque plenius animi imbuantur atque formentur; oportet ut haec doctrina certa et

According to some points of view the time of certainties is said to have passed beyond recall and man must learn to live in a world where no meaning may be found, because everything is fleeting and transitory. By a judgment such as this many authors do away with certainty altogether and by disregarding certain vital distinctions lead even the certitudes of faith into doubt.

To some extent this nihilism finds confirmation in the appalling awareness of evils by which our age has been distinguished. Before the disastrous arrival of this experience a rationalist optimism reigned, which viewed history as the triumphant progress of reason and the source of happiness and freedom, and yet it has been unable to prevent the temptation to despair after the terrible dangers and menaces of the outgoing century.

Even so, it remains true that a certain positivist cast of mind continues to nurture the illusion that, thanks to scientific and technical progress, man may live as a demiurge, single-handedly and completely taking charge of his destiny.

The contemporary duties of theology

92. As an understanding of Revelation, theology has always had to respond in different historical periods to the demands of the diversity of cultures, in order to communicate the content of faith to those cultures with the appropriate formulation of doctrine. On the other hand she must explore the task committed to her by the Second Vatican Council: the task of renewing her own structures of teaching for the better service of evangelization. On this subject who does not recall the words with which Blessed Pope John XXIII opened the Council? He said then: 'it is imperative, as many sincere members of the Christian Catholic and Apostolic faith earnestly desire, that this teaching should be more widely and deeply known and that minds should be more imbued with and formed by it. It is vital that the same certain and changeless teaching to which we owe faithful obedience should also be explored and presented in a way which meets the needs of our time'.[107]

On the other hand theology must direct its attention to that ultimate truth that Revelation commits to it, never content to stop short of that

[107] John XXIII, *Address at the Opening of the Second Vatican Council* (11 October 1962), in F. Anderson, (ed.), *Council Daybook: Vatican II: Sessions 1 and 2* (Washington: National Catholic Welfare Conference, 1965), p. 25.

immutabilis, cui fidele obsequium est praestandum, ea ratione pervestigetur et exponatur quam tempora postulant nostra".[107]

Ex altera vero parte oculos theologia intendat necesse est ultimam in veritatem quam ei commendat Revelatio ipsa neque sibi satis esse existimet in mediis consistere intervallis. Decet enim reminisci theologum opus suum respondere "ad vim dynamicam, quae in ipsa fide inest" suaeque inquisitionis argumentum id esse: "Veritas, Deus vivus eiusque salutis consilium per Iesum Christum revelatum".[108] Hoc munus, quod ante omnia afficit theologiam, simul quidem philosophiam provocat. Quaestionum enim multitudo, quae hodie premunt, communem poscit operam etiamsi multiplicibus rationibus illa expletur, ut cognoscatur denuo veritas atque exprimatur. Veritas, quae Christus est, ubique auctoritate universali se imponit quae gubernat, incitat et prosperat tum theologiam tum etiam philosophiam.

Quod creditur veritatem ubique validam cognosci posse, haud prorsus inde oritur intollerantia; condicio contra necessaria est ad verum sincerumque inter homines dialogum. Hac sola condicione fieri potest ut discidia vincantur et iter ad unam integram veritatem percurratur secundum eas semitas quas solus Domini resuscitati Spiritus cognoscit.[109] Nunc ipsum cupimus explicare quo pacto unitatis necessitas hodie in re conformetur, inspectis praesentibus theologiae officiis.

93. Propositum princeps quod explere vult theologia in eo consistit, ut *Revelationis intellectus praebeatur fideique doctrina.* Media propterea ipsius pars ac veluti centrum eius deliberationum erit mysterii ipsius Dei Unius et Trini contemplatio. Huc per mysterii Incarnationis Filii Dei

---

[107] *Allocutio qua Concilium est inchoatum* (11 Octobris 1962): *AAS* 54 (1962), 792.

[108] Congr. pro Doctrina Fidei, Instr. de vocatione ecclesiali theologi *Donum veritatis* (24 Maii 1990), §§7–8: *AAS* 82 (1990), 1552–1553.

[109] In Litteris Encyclicis *Dominum et vivificantem* explicantes locum *Io* 16:12–13 scripsimus: "Iesus Paraclitum, Spiritum veritatis, exhibet ut eum qui 'docebit et suggeret', ut eum qui ei 'testimonium perhibebit'; nunc vero ait 'deducet vos in omnem veritatem'. Locutio 'deducet vos in omnem veritatem', prout ad ea refertur, quae Apostoli 'non possunt portare modo', imprimis necessario coniungitur *cum exinanitione Christi*, passione et Cruce peracta, quae eo tempore, quo has protulit voces, iam impendebat. Postea tamen patefit illud 'deducere in omnem veritatem' necti non solum cum scandalo Crucis, sed etiam cum iis omnibus, quae Christus 'fecit et docuit' (*Act* 1:1). Re enim vera mysterium Christi, ut totum, postulat fidem, cum haec hominem in mysterii revelati 'realitatem' opportune inducat. Illud ergo 'deducere in omnem veritatem' in fide et per fidem ad effectum adducitur: quod Spiritus veritatis operatur, idque ex eius actione in homine promanat. Hac in re Spiritus Sanctus est hominis summus magister, est lux spiritus humani", §6: *AAS* 78 (1986), 815–816.

goal. Theologians should remember that their work is a response to the 'dynamic force which exists in faith itself' and that the proper quest of its argument is to be: 'Truth, the living God, and his plan for salvation revealed through Jesus Christ'.[108] This task, which above all concerns theology, challenges philosophy as well. The vast number of questions which press upon us today demand a joint reply, even though it be worked out with differing methods, in order that truth be known and expressed anew. The Truth, which is Christ, imposes itself with a universal authority, which rules, encourages and gives success to theology and philosophy alike.

That truth is held to be universally known and valid need not lead to intolerance: on the contrary it is the precondition for a true and sincere dialogue among men and women. Solely on this condition can disagreements be overcome and a journey be made to the one integral truth along those paths that the Spirit of the risen Lord alone knows.[109] We now wish to examine how today the necessity of this unity may be achieved by exploring the present tasks of theology.

93. The principal task of theology consists in this, *to provide both an understanding of Revelation and the teaching of faith*. The central part, therefore, of theology and as it were the heart of its deliberations will be the contemplation of the mystery of the One and Triune God himself. This is to be approached through pondering the mystery of the Incarnation of the Son of God: his being made man, that he suffered and died, the subsequent mystery of his glorious resurrection and ascension to the right hand of the Father, and finally the sending of the Spirit of truth for establishing and enlivening the Church. In this general conspectus the central

---

[108] Congregation for the Doctrine of the Faith, Instruction on the Ecclesial Vocation of the Theologian *Donum veritatis*, §§7–8.

[109] In the Encyclical Letter *Dominum et vivificantem*, commenting on *Jn* 16:12–13, we wrote: 'Jesus presents the Paraclete, the Spirit of truth, as the one who "will teach" and "bring to remembrance", as the one who "will bear witness" to him. Now he says: "he will guide you into all truth". This "guiding into all truth", referring to what the Apostles "cannot bear now", is necessarily connected *with Christ's self-emptying* through his Passion and Death on the Cross, which, when he spoke these words, was just about to happen. Later however it becomes clear that this "guiding into all truth" is connected not only with the scandal of the Cross, but also with everything that Christ "did and taught" (*Acts* 1:1). For the sign of Christ, taken as a whole, demands faith, since it is faith that adequately introduces humanity into the "reality" of the revealed mystery. The "guiding into all truth" is therefore achieved in faith and through faith: and this is the work of the Spirit of truth and the result of his action in humanity. Here the Holy Spirit is to be our supreme guide and the light of the human spirit.' (John Paul II, Encyclical Letter *Dominum et vivificantem* [18 May 1986] (London: Catholic Truth Society, 1986), §6.)

ponderationem acceditur: eo quod ipse factus est homo ac deinde occuccurrit passioni et morti, quod mysterium in gloriosam eius resurrectionem atque ascensionem ad dexteram Patris evasit, unde veritatis Spiritum misit suam ad constituendam et animandam Ecclesiam. Hoc in rerum prospectu principale theologiae munus fit Dei *kenosis* intellectus, quod magnum humanae menti restat mysterium quae vix credibile opinatur dolorem mortemque posse amorem illum declarare qui nihil vicissim expetens sese dono concedit. Hac autem in re primaria quaedam necessitas iniungitur urgensque simul locorum ipsorum intenta pervestigatio: in primis Sacrarum Litterarum, deinde eorum quibus viva Ecclesiae Traditio profertur. Hic autem hodie nonnullae emergunt quaestiones, ex parte dumtaxat novae, quibus addi non potest solutio neglectis philosophiae officiis.

94. Respicit prima difficilis quaestio necessitudinem inter significationem et veritatem. Quemadmodum omnibus aliis in textibus accidit, ita etiam fontes, quos interpretatur theologus, ante omnia aliquam transmittunt significationem quae illuminanda est atque explananda. Nunc vero se exhibet haec significatio tamquam de Deo veritatem, quae a Deo ipso sacrum per textum traditur. Quocirca hominum in sermone incorporatur Dei sermo, qui suam veritatem communicat, ea admirabili "indulgentia" quae logicam Incarnationis rationem refert.[110] Revelationis ideo interpretans fontes oportet theologus se ipse interroget quae alta et germana sit veritas quam Scripturarum loci aperire volunt etiam intra sermonis limites.

Ad Bibliorum quod attinet locos ac praesertim Evangeliorum, minime quidem redigitur eorum veritas in eventuum dumtaxat historicorum narrationem vel in factorum nudorum patefactionem, perinde ac positivismus historicista contendit.[111] Hi ex contrario loci proponunt eventus quorum veritas ponitur ultra simplicem historiae casum: in eorum significatione *in* et *pro* salutis historia reperitur. Plene haec explicatur veritas illo ex perenni usu quem Ecclesia fecit illorum textuum saeculorum decursu, pristinam eorundem servando significationem. Pernecessarium itaque est ut etiam philosophice de necessitudinis ratione interrogetur quae inter factum eiusque significatum intercedit; haec necessitudo proprium historiae efficit sensum.

95. Non uni populo neque aetati uni destinatur Dei verbum.

[110] Cfr Conc. Oecum. Vat. II, Const. dogm. de divina Revelatione *Dei Verbum*, 13.

[111] Cfr Pontificia Commissio Biblica, *Instr. de historica Evangeliorum veritate* (21 Aprilis 1964): *AAS* 56 (1964), 713.

business of theology is the understanding of the *kenosis* of God, which remains a great mystery for the human mind, hardly able to believe that sorrow and death can reveal a love which seeks nothing in return and gives of itself freely. Truly in this a first and urgent necessity is imposed upon us of carefully exploring the texts: above all of Holy Scripture, and subsequently those in which the living Tradition of the Church is expressed. But here today several questions arise, some quite new, which are incapable of solution without using the help of philosophy.

94. The first difficult question concerns the connection between meaning and truth. As occurs in every other text, so also the sources with which the theologian deals, before anything else communicate a meaning which needs to be illuminated and explained. Furthermore, this meaning displays itself as a truth about God, which is given to the sacred text by God himself. This means that the Word of God which communicates this truth is expressed in human language, by means of that amazing 'condescension' which reflects the logical reason of the Incarnation.[110] Therefore in interpreting the sources of Revelation theologians must remind themselves of the depth and appropriateness of the truth that the passages of Scripture desire to open up, even within the limits imposed by human language.

Concerning the passages of the Bible and above all of the Gospels, their truth can in no way be reduced to a mere historical narrative or to the laying out of bare facts, as historical positivism supposes.[111] On the contrary these texts deal with events which lie beyond the realm of mere history: their truth is to be found in the meaning they have *in* and *for* the history of salvation. This truth is fully expressed in the use the Church has made through the centuries of these texts, by preserving their original meaning. It is therefore imperative that we should examine philosophically the structure of the relationship that exists between fact and meaning: this relationship constitutes the proper sense of history.

95. The Word of God is destined neither for one people nor for one age. In the same way dogmatic pronouncements, despite the fact that they reflect the culture of the age from where they come, even so produce truth which is at once constant and decisive. The question therefore arises as to how the absolute and universal nature of truth can be reconciled with

---

[110] Cf. The Second Vatican Council, Dogmatic Constitution on Divine Revelation *Dei Verbum*, §13 in Flannery, (ed.), *Vatican Council II*, p. 758.

[111] Cf. Pontifical Biblical Commission, *Instruction on the Historical Truth of the Gospels* (21 April 1964).

Dogmaticae similiter pronuntiationes, quantumvis temporis illius culturam referant quo eduntur, constantem tamen et decretoriam efferunt veritatem. Hinc ergo quaestio exsistit quomodo inter se concilientur absoluta universalisque veritatis indoles atque inevitabiles historiae culturaeque condiciones earum formularum quibus eadem significatur veritas. Uti superius iam diximus, historicismi opinationes haud possunt defendi. Usus autem disciplinae hermeneuticae, quae ad metaphysicae scientiae patet postulata, demonstrare valet quo pacto ex adiunctis historicis et incertis, in quibus textus sacri maturuerunt, ad veritatem transitus fiat ibidem patefactam, quae easdem illas praetergreditur condiciones.

Suo historico circumscriptoque sermone licet homini veritates expromere quae linguarum transcendunt usum. Etenim numquam potest nec tempore nec aliqua culturae forma coarctari veritas; intra historiam cognoscitur at historiam ipsam egreditur.

96. Sinit, haec consideratio, nos alterius iam difficultatis providere solutionem: de perpetua agitur auctoritate et vi sermonum conceptuumque adhibitorum in conciliorum definitionibus. Venerabilis iam Noster Decessor Pius XII hanc eandem quaestionem suis Encyclicis Litteris *Humani generis* pertractavit.[112]

Hoc de argumento non facile disceptatur, quandoquidem serio animo ratio habeatur oportet ipsius significationis quam variis in culturae regionibus temporumque aetatibus verba sibi sumpserunt. Cogitationis humanae historia utcumque luculenter comprobat per progressionem varietatemque culturarum quasdam principales notiones universalem suam adservare cognoscendi vim proindeque veritatem earum affirmationum quam recludunt.[113] Res ita si non sese haberent, philosophia

[112] "Liquet etiam Ecclesiam non cuilibet systemati philosophico, brevi temporis spatio vigenti, devinciri posse: sed ea quae communi consensu a catholicis doctoribus composita per plura saecula fuere ad aliquam dogmatis intellegentiam attingendam, tam caduco fundamento procul dubio non nituntur. Nituntur enim principiis ac notionibus ex vera rerum creatarum cognitione deductis; in quibus quidem deducendis cognitionibus humanae menti veritas divinitus revelata, quasi stella, per Ecclesiam illuxit. Quare mirum non est aliquas huiusmodi notiones a Conciliis Oecumenicis non solum adhibitas, sed etiam sancitas esse, ita ut ab eis discedere nefas sit": Litt. Encycl. *Humani generis* (12 Augusti 1950): *AAS* 42 (1950), 566–567; cfr Commissio Theologica Internationalis, docum. *Interpretationis problema* (Octobre 1989): *Ench. Vat.* 11, §§2717–2811.

[113] "Ipse autem *sensus* formularum dogmaticarum semper verus ac secum constans in Ecclesia manet, etiam cum magis dilucidatur et plenius intellegitur.

unavoidable historical and cultural conditioning of the formulae in which truth finds expression. As I said above the views of historicism cannot be defended. However the use of the discipline of hermeneutics, which is not closed to metaphysics, is capable of showing how out of the historical and contingent circumstances in which the sacred texts matured one can pass to a clearly demonstrated truth, that advances beyond these particular conditions.

Man is able to express truths that transcend the normal use of words in language that is both historical and circumscribed. Even so truth cannot be confined in one time or cultural form: it is known within history, but also goes beyond history.

96. This consideration allows us to provide a solution to a further difficulty: the permanent authority and force to be accorded to the language and concepts employed in conciliar definitions. Our venerable predecessor Pius XII treated the same question in his Encyclical *Humani generis*.[112]

It is no easy matter dealing with this argument since we must reckon seriously with the varied meanings the words have been accorded in differing ranges of cultures and periods of time. Even so the history of human reflection clearly demonstrates that in and through the progress and variety of cultures certain basic concepts have preserved both their universal validity for knowledge and the truth of the propositions they express.[113] Were it otherwise, philosophy and the sciences would be unable to engage in mutual interchange nor could they be understood

---

[112] 'It is clear that the Church cannot be tied to any and every passing philosophical system. Nevertheless, those notions and terms which have been developed though common effort by Catholic teachers over the course of the centuries to bring about some understanding of dogma are certainly not based on any such weak foundation. They are based on principles and concepts deduced from a true knowledge of created things. In the process of deduction, this knowledge, like a star, gave enlightenment to the human mind through the Church. Hence it is not astonishing that some of these concepts have not only been employed by the Ecumenical Councils, but even sanctioned by them, so that it is wrong to depart from them.' Pius XII, Encyclical Letter *Humani generis* (12 August 1950): §16; Cf. International Theological Commission, Document *Interpretationis problema* (October 1989).

[113] 'As for the meaning of dogmatic formulas, this remains ever true and constant in the Church, even when it is expressed with greater clarity or more developed. The faithful therefore must shun the opinion, first, that dogmatic formulas (or some category of them) cannot signify the truth in a determinate way, but can only offer changeable approximations to it, which to a certain extent distort or alter it.' Sacred Congregation for the Doctrine of the Faith, Declaration in Defence of the Catholic Doctrine on the Church *Mysterium Ecclesiae* (24 June 1973).

atque scientiae inter se haud quidquam communicare valerent neque percipi apud culturas diversas ab iis a quibus excogitatae sunt et elaboratae. Restat propterea hermeneutica quaestio, at solvi potest. Ceterum multarum notionum vera vis non prohibet quin imperfecta sit earum significatio; qua in re philosophica disceptatio multum efficere potest. Optatur, incirco, ut peculiari studio coniunctio pervestigetur inter sermonem intellectivum et veritatem, atque etiam proponantur apta itinera ad rectam eius intellegentiam.

97. Si grave theologiae officium est fontium interpretatio, aliud etiam et maioris prudentiae necessitatisque est *revelatae veritatis perceptio* sive *intellectus fidei* explicatio. Sicut iam superius innuimus, *intellectus fidei* postulat ut philosophia essendi partes quae in primis sinant ut *theologia dogmatica* consentaneo modo expleat sua munia. Dogmaticus primorum annorum huius saeculi pragmatismus, ad quem fidei veritates nihil aliud quam morum normae esse dicuntur, iam redargutus est atque reiectus;[114] nihilominus semper quis allicitur ut has intellegat veritates modo plane functionali. Tunc enim res recidet in rationem quandam prorsus inopportunam, reductivam ac necessaria gravitate speculativa destitutam. Verbi causa, Christologia, quae "de basi" dumtaxat proficiscatur, quemadmodum hodie dicere consueverunt, vel ecclesiologia ad societatis civilis exemplum solummodo composita, talis reductionis periculum declinare non possent.

Si traditionis theologicae universos complecti vult *intellectus fidei* thesauros, ad philosophiam essendi decurrere debet. Haec enim necessario quaestionem essendi rursus proponet secundum postulationes atque totius traditionis philosophicae etiam recentioris utilitates adlatas, omni omissa opportunitate in superatas iam philosophicas rationes futiliter recidendi. Intra metaphysicae christianae traditionis prospectum philosophia essendi est philosophia actuosa seu dynamica quae ipsis in suis ontologicis, causalibus et communicativis structuris praebet veritatem. Impetum suum ac perennem impulsum in eo reperit quod actu ipso "essendi" sustentatur, unde plena et generalis permittitur ad solidam rerum universitatem patefactio, omnibus excessis terminis ut Ille

Christifideles ergo se avertant oportet ab opinione secundum quam [. . .] formulae dogmaticae (aut quaedam earum genera) non possint significare determinate veritatem, sed tantum eius commutabiles approximationes, ipsam quodammodo deformantes seu alterantes". S. Congr. Pro Doctrina Fidei, Decl. circa Catholicam Doctrinam de Ecclesia contra nonnullos errores hodiernos tuendam *Mysterium Ecclesiae* (24 Iunii 1973), §5: *AAS* 65 (1973), 403.

[114] Cfr Congr. S. Officii, Decr. *Lamentabili* (3 Iulii 1907), §26: *ASS* 40 (1907), 473.

outside the cultures where they were first conceived and worked out. There remains, therefore the hermeneutic question, but it can be solved. Even so the true force of many concepts does not mean that their meaning is perfect, and in this area philosophical discussion can have great effect. It is to be wished, therefore, that an examination be set on foot with great seriousness to explore the relationship between conceptual language and truth, and that appropriate paths be suggested for its correct understanding.

97. A serious duty of theology is the interpretation of sources; but there is another of even greater prudence and necessity and that is the *perception of revealed truth* and the explanation of the *understanding of faith*. As we have already previously suggested, *the understanding of faith* demands the assistance of a philosophy of being, which allows *dogmatic theology* to perform its task in an appropriate fashion. The dogmatic pragmatism of the first years of the previous century, for which truths of faith were little more than norms of behaviour, has already been refuted and rejected;[114] even so people are still lured into wanting to understand these truths in a purely functional way. As a result things fall into an unhappy condition, which is reductive and devoid of all speculative seriousness. For example, a Christology which begins as many claim today 'from below', or an ecclesiology which uses civil society alone as a model, are alike exposed to the danger of reductionism.

If the *understanding of faith* wishes to enfold within itself all the treasures of the theological tradition, it must have recourse to a philosophy of being. This necessity of the question of being will in its turn advance all the requirements and insights of the whole philosophical tradition, including the more recent, while at the same time without lapsing into the sterile repetition of antiquated formulas. Within the compass of the Christian metaphysical tradition the philosophy of being is an active or dynamic philosophy, which presents truth by means of structures which are at the same time ontological, causal, and capable of being shared with others. It discovers its impetus and continual impulse in the very fact that it is upheld by the act of 'being', and as a result it possesses a complete and general access to a solid universe of things and goes beyond every limit to arrive at Him in whom the consummation of all things is attained.[115] In theology, which draws its principles from

---

[114] Cf. Congregation of the Holy Office, Decree *Lamentabili* (3 July 1907), §26 at http://www.memorare.com/reform/lamentabili.html

[115] Cf. John Paul II, *Address to the Pontifical Athenaeum 'Angelicum'* (17 November 1979), §6: *Insegnamenti,* II, 2 (1979), pp. 1183–85.

qui rebus omnibus consumationem tribuit attingatur.[115] Ea in theologia, quae sua ex Revelatione desumit principia tamquam a novo cognitionis fonte, haec omnino confirmatur indicandi ratio intimum secundum illud vinculum inter fidem et metaphysicam rationalitatem.

98. Explicari similes possunt deliberationes etiam ratione habita *moralis theologiae*. Philosophiae redintegratio postulatur etiam ut intellegatur fides ad credentium vitam actionemque spectans. Ante oculos constitutis provocationibus hodiernis in re sociali, oeconomica, in re politica ac scientifica, ethica hominis conscientia confunditur. In Litteris Encyclicis *Veritatis splendor* docuimus Nos complures in orbe nostro exsistentes difficultates inde oriri quod est "crisis circa veritatem. Amissa notione veritatis universalis de bono quod ab humana mente percipi potest, necessario de conscientia opinio est immutata, quae iam suo in primigenio statu non consideratur, tamquam scilicet actus intellectus personae cuius est adhibere universalem cognitionem boni in peculiari quadam condicione et iudicium facere de honesto eligendo hic et nunc; eo tenditur ut personae conscientiae privilegium tribuatur statuendi autonoma ratione normam boni malique, indeque agendi. Mens haec arte coniungitur cum individualistica ethica, secundum quam quisque cum sua confertur veritate, quae ab aliorum veritate differt".[116]

Totas per easdem Encyclicas Litteras praecipuas extulimus partes attinentes ad veritatem morali in provincia. Veritas haec de plerisque ethicis quaestionibus, quae magis hodie premunt, a theologia morali intentam exposcit meditationem quae eius in Dei verbo radices illuminet. Suum ut expleat hoc munus, debet ideo moralis theologia uti ethica philosophiae disciplina, quae bonorum veritatem respicit; ethica videlicet utatur oportet disciplina quae neque subiectiva sit neque utilitati soli serviat. Haec postulata ethica ratio importat atque ante flagitat philosophicam anthropologiam nec non metaphysicam bonorum tractationem. Hanc unicam rerum iudicationem adhibens, quae cum christiana vitae sanctitate virtutumque humanarum et supernaturalium exercitatione cohaeret, moralis theologia diversas sua in regione quaestiones agitare poterit – cuius generis sunt pax socialisque iustitia, familia, vitae defensio locorumque naturae custodia – multo quidem efficacius et plenius.

---

[115] Cfr Ioannes Paulus II, *Allocutio apud Pontificium Athenaeum "Angelicum"* (17 Novembris 1979), 6: *Insegnamenti*, II, 2 (1979), 1183–1185.

[116] §32: *AAS* 85 (1993), 1159–1160.

Revelation as a new source of knowledge, this perspective is confirmed by the intimate relationship which exists between faith and metaphysical reasoning.

98. Likewise, the deliberations of *moral theology* can also be clarified according to reason. Again, a restoration of philosophy is required, so that the faith which concerns the life and action of believers may be understood. Today the ethical conscience of man is confused, as he sees the challenges offered by social, economic, political and scientific matters confronting him. In the Encyclical *Veritatis splendor* we suggested that many difficulties arise because of 'the crisis about truth. Once the concept of a universal truth of the good that can be grasped by the human mind is lost our view of conscience is necessarily altered, in that it is no longer considered for its primordial role as the intellectual act of a person who applies a universal knowledge of the good to a particular situation, and then makes a judgment about the good to be chosen here and now: instead, there is a tendency of giving to personal conscience the privilege of establishing by virtue of its own independent reason the norms of good and bad, and of acting accordingly. Such a frame of mind is closely connected with an individualistic ethic, according to which each person is presented with her own truth, which differs from the truth of others'.[116]

Throughout this Encyclical I have laid great stress on those elements which have to do with truth in the area of morality. The truth in many contemporary and pressing ethical questions demands from moral theology serious consideration, illuminated with the brilliance of the Word of God. In order to fulfil this task it must employ the discipline of ethical philosophy, which looks to the truth of the good: it must be served by a discipline of ethics which is neither subjective nor utilitarian. Ethical reason of this kind requires and looks to philosophical anthropology and at the same time a metaphysical treatment of the good. Moral theology, keeping to a singular determination of matters which accords with a Christian holiness of life and with the practice of human and supernatural virtues, will be able to deal more effectively and fully in its own field with a diversity of questions such as peace, social justice, the family, the defence of life and the protection of the natural environment.

[131] John Paul II, Encyclical Letter *Veritatis splendor*, §32.

99. Theologicum Ecclesiae opus ad fidem et catechesim in primis nuntiandam deputatur.[117] Nuntiatio sive "kerygma" ad conversionem vocat, Christi proponendo veritatem quae eius consummatur paschali in Mysterio: in Christo, enim, uno veritatis agnosci potest plenitudo quae homines salvat (cfr *Act* 4:12; *1 Tim* 2:4–6).

Hinc probe pariter intellegitur cur praeter theologiam sibi etiam *catechesis* adsumat maius quoddam pondus: in se enim haec complectitur philosophica aliqua consectaria fidei sub lumine vestiganda. Doctrina intra catechesim tradita aliquid certe ad instituendam personam humanam confert. Debet catechesis, quae etiam communicatio est facta per verba, Ecclesiae Magisterium tota ex ipsius integritate praebere,[118] coniunctionem illius etiam cum credentium vita demonstrans.[119] Unicum ita efficitur doctrinam inter et vitam vinculum quod aliter attingi non potest. Non sane veritatum intellectivarum corpus in catechesi traditur, verum viventis Dei mysterium.[120]

Plurimum aequabiliter philosophica disputatio confert ad necessitudinem collustrandam inter veritatem et vitam, inter eventum et doctrinalem veritatem ac, praesertim, rationem inter transcendentem veritatem et sermonem qui humanitus intellegi potest.[121] Mutua consociatio inter disciplinas theologicas et exitus variis ex opinationibus philosophicis perceptos exprimet, itaque, veram fecunditatem in fide communicanda altiusque in ea comprehendenda.

CONCLUSIO

100. Quandoquidem iam transierunt plus quam centum anni cum Leonis XIII Litterae Encyclicae *Aeterni Patris* prodierunt, quas saepenumero hoc in Nostro scripto commemoravimus, necessarium Nobis visum est de necessitudine inter fidem et philosophiam distinctius sermonem repetere. Omnino manifestum est momentum quod habet philosophica cogitatio in cultura explicanda et in personalibus

---

[117] Cfr Ioannes Paulus II, Adhort. Ap. *Catechesi tradendae* (16 Octobris 1979), §30: *AAS* 71 (1979), 1302–1303; Congr. pro Doctrina Fidei, Instr. de vocatione ecclesiali theologi *Donum veritatis* (24 Maii 1990), §7: *AAS* 82 (1990), 1552–1553.

[118] Cfr Ioannes Paulus II, Adhort. Ap. *Catechesi tradendae* (16 Octobris 1979), §30: *AAS* 71 (1979), 1302–1303.

[119] Cfr *Catechesi tradendae*, §22, 1295–1296.

[120] Cfr *Catechesi tradendae* , §7, 1282.

[121] Cfr *Catechesi tradendae* , §59, 1325.

99. The theological work of the Church is assigned as its first priority the proclaiming of faith and catechesis.[117] Proclamation, or 'kerygma', is a summons to conversion, setting out the truth of Christ which is fully realized in the Paschal mystery: for in Christ alone can the fullness of truth that saves men and women be recognized (cf. *Acts* 4:12; *1 Tim* 2:4–6).

Hence it is easy to understand why it is that in addition to theology, *catechesis* enjoys a great importance: since it contains within itself certain philosophical consequences to be explored in the light of faith. The teaching communicated in the course of catechesis confers something which helps towards the developing of the human person. Catechesis, as a communication by means of speech, must present the teaching of the Church's Magisterium in its integrity,[118] demonstrating its connection with the lives of believers.[119] The result is a unique bond between teaching and living which is otherwise unattainable. It is not a body of intellectual truths that is communicated in catechesis, but the mystery of the living God.[120]

Philosophical discussion offers much to illustrate the connection between truth and life, between event and doctrinal truth and above all between reason, transcendent truth and language which is humanly intelligible.[121] A mutual relationship between the theological disciplines and the insights drawn from the various suppositions of philosophy thus produces a great fruitfulness in the handing on of faith and the deeper comprehending of it.

CONCLUSION

100. Despite the fact that more than a hundred years have passed since the appearance of Leo XIII's Encyclical *Aeterni Patris*, a work frequently cited in this Encyclical, even so we think it imperative to insist more clearly on the close link between faith and philosophy. The importance of philosophical reflection both in explaining culture and in moderating personal and social morality is absolutely clear. It can also

[117] Cf. John Paul II, Apostolic Exhortation *Catechesi tradendae* (16 October 1979) (Slough: St Paul, 1979), §30; Congregation for the Doctrine of the Faith, Instruction on the Ecclesial Vocation of the Theologian *Donum veritatis* (24 May 1990), §7.

[118] Cf. John Paul II, Apostolic Exhortation *Catechesi tradendae*, §30.

[119] Cf. John Paul II, Apostolic Exhortation *Catechesi tradendae*, §22.

[120] Cf. John Paul II, Apostolic Exhortation *Catechesi tradendae*, §7.

[121] Cf. John Paul II, Apostolic Exhortation *Catechesi tradendae*, §59.

socialibusque moribus temperandis. Ipsa multum potest, quod haud semper clare percipitur, etiam circa theologiam eiusdemque diversas disciplinas. Has propter causas consentaneum necessariumque esse iudicavimus vim confirmare quam philosophia pro fidei intellectu finibusque habet, quibus ipsa occurrit cum obliviscitur vel Revelationis veritates denegat. Ecclesia enim persuasissimum habet fidem et rationem "opem sibi mutuam" ferre,[122] dum utraque simul iudicium criticum et purificatorium exercet, simul stimulum admovet ad inquisitionem producendam et altius perscrutandas res.

101. Si autem opinationum historiam respicimus, in occidentali potissimum parte, commode percipiuntur divitiae quae ad hominum progressum a philosophiae et theologiae occursu atque ab earum ipsarum acquisitionum permutationibus manarunt. Theologia, quae dono apertionem recepit proprietatemque quarum vi tamquae fidei scientia exsistere valet, rationem certe lacessivit ut radicali novitati pateret, quam Dei revelatio secum fert. Hoc sine dubio philosophiae fuit utilitati, quae hoc modo novos prospectus in alias significationes comparere vidit, quae rationi altius sunt perscrutandae.

His quidem consideratis rebus, quemadmodum confirmavimus theologiae esse sinceram cum philosophia necessitudinem redintegrare, ita similiter iterare debemus philosophiae pro cogitationis bono et progressu recuperandam esse cum theologia necessitudinem. Reperiet in ea non singulorum hominum cogitationem, quae, quamvis alta locuplesque sit, unius personae tamen limitibus et lineamentis circumscribitur, sed communis cogitationis divitias. Theologia namque in veritate perquirenda, sua natura, nota *ecclesialitatis*[123] sustentatur itemque Dei Populi traditione cum multiformitate sapientiae et culturarum in fidei unitate.

102. In momento et philosophicae cogitationis vera magnitudine hoc modo innitens, Ecclesia tum hominis dignitatem tum evangelicum nuntium tuetur. Nihil hodie plus quam haec praeparatio instat, perducendi scilicet homines ad eorum detegendam facultatem

---

[122] Conc. Oecum. Vat. I, Const. dogm. de fide catholica *Dei Filius*, IV: *DS* 3019.

[123] "Nemini idcirco licet theologiam tractare, quasi de quibusdam agatur notionum eius collectaneis: sed quivis sciat oportet se arcte coniunctum esse debere cum hoc munere docendi, cum hoc munere veritatem docendi, quod Ecclesiae ipsi incumbat". Ioannes Paulus II, Litt. Encycl. *Redemptor hominis* (4 Martii 1979), §19: *AAS* 71 (1979), 308.

achieve much in the realm of theology and its differing disciplines though this is not always clearly perceived. For these reasons we have judged it both appropriate and necessary to underline the importance of philosophy for the understanding of faith, as well as the limits philosophy faces when it forgets or denies the truths of Revelation. The Church is utterly persuaded that faith and reason 'contribute to each other',[122] since both at the same time exercise a critical and purifying critique, while also providing a stimulus for further enquiry and deeper understanding.

101. If we cast our eye back over the history of standpoints, above all in the West, a clear perspective of the riches derived from the meeting of philosophy and theology can be gained, and of the advantages deriving from their mutual interchange, both of which have contributed to human progress. Theology has received as a gift an entry into and possession of things by whose vigour the science of faith is able to exist, and has certainly challenged reason to be open to the radical newness which the revelation of God brings with it. Without doubt this has been greatly useful for philosophy, which in this way has witnessed the appearance of new openings and other meanings for reason to explore more deeply.

With these things in mind, as we have insisted upon the need of re–establishing a true relationship of theology with philosophy, so too we wish to insist also upon the need philosophy has both for the good of thought and for its progress to restore a close connection with theology. Philosophy will discover thereby, not the thinking of individuals, which however deep and rich it may be is still circumscribed by the limitations and features of one person, but the riches of a common reflection. For theology, in its searching for truth, by its very nature enjoys the mark of *ecclesiality*[123] as the tradition of the people of God, together with the pluriformity of wisdom and cultures in the unity of faith.

102. Relying in this way upon the importance and vastness of philosophical reflection, the Church protects both the dignity of man and the proclamation of the Gospel. There is today no more urgent preparation for the performance of these tasks than this: to lead people to discover

---

[122] First Vatican Ecumenical Council, Dogmatic Constitution on the Catholic Faith *Dei Filius*, §4 in Tanner, (ed.), *The Decrees of the Ecumenical Councils*, II, p. 809.

[123] 'Nobody can make of theology a kind of collection of his own personal ideas, but everybody must be aware of being in close union with the mission of teaching truth for which the Church is responsible': John Paul II, Encyclical Letter *Redemptor hominis*, §19.

cognoscendi verum[124] inveniendique anhelitum versus summam consummatamque exsistentiae significationen. Harum altarum rationum in prospectu, quas Deus in hominum natura inscripsit, liquidius humana apparet significatio Dei verbi, quod humaniores reddit homines. Philosophiae beneficio, quae etiam vera facta est sapientia, huius temporis homo sic agnoscet se tanto esse humaniorem quanto plus, Evangelio confidendo, Christo pateat.

103. Philosophia, praeterea, est tamquam speculum in quod populorum cultus repercutitur. Philosophia, quae, theologicis necessitatibus impellentibus, una cum fide concorditer progreditur, particeps est illius "culturae evangelizationis", quam Paulus VI inter praecipua evengelizationis proposita annumeravit.[125] Dum autem *novae evangelizationis* necessitatem iterare numquam intermittimus, philosophos compellamus, qui altius veri, boni et pulchri granditatem vestigent, quibus Dei verbum aditum patere sinit. Id magis instat, si provocationes expenduntur, quas novum millennium secum ferre videtur: ipsae peculiari ratione regiones antiquaeque traditionis christianae culturas afficiunt. Haec quoque consideratio veluti praecipuum originaleque ad novam evangelizationem persequendam habendum est adiumentum.

104. Philosophica in disciplina saepe solummodo invenitur consensus et dialogus instituitur cum illis qui nostram fidem haud communicant. Hodiernus philosophicus motus postulat ut philosophi attente periteque fideles agant partes facultatibusque polleant ea percipiendi quae hodiernis temporibus exspectantur, recluduntur et agitantur. Dum secundum rationem eiusque regulas argumentatur, christianus philosophus, qui illo semper intellectu dirigitur quem Dei verbum subministrat, quandam ratiocinationem agere potest quae etiam ab illis, qui nondum omnem veritatem capiunt quam divina Revelatio ostendit, intellegi et sensu percipi potest. Provincia haec in qua consensus ac dialogus reperiuntur eo plus habet momenti propterea quod quaestiones quae impensius humanitati opponuntur – puta quaestionem oecologicam, pacis quaestionem vel convictum stirpium et culturarum – communi opera eaque perspicua et sincera Christianorum et asseclarum aliarum religionum expediri possunt necnon illorum quibus, quamvis

---

[124] Cfr. Conc. Oecum. Vat. II, Declaratio de libertate religiosa *Dignitatis humanae*, §§1–3.

[125] Cfr Adhort. Ap. *Evangelii nuntiandi* (8 Decembris 1975), §20: *AAS* 68 (1976), 18–19.

both their capacity to know the truth,[124] and their yearning for the ultimate and definitive meaning of life. With these profound needs before us, which God has inscribed within human nature, the human meaning of the Word of God becomes even more obvious, in that it makes us more human. As a result of the good offices of a philosophy which is also a true wisdom, modern man will, by trusting the Gospel, come to recognize himself as all the more human, the more open he is to Christ.

103. In addition philosophy acts as a sort of mirror in which the culture of differing peoples is reflected. The philosophy, which under the pressure of theological demands, proceeds in harmony with faith, shares in that 'culture of evangelization' which Paul VI numbered among the most important tasks of evangelization.[125] But though we never cease insisting upon the necessity of this *new evangelization*, we also exhort philosophers to explore in greater depth the majesty of the true, the good, and the beautiful, to which the Word of God gives access. This is all the more pressing if we consider the challenges the new millennium brings along with it, and which particularly affect those places and cultures where the Christian tradition is very ancient. This attention to philosophy should also be thought of as a special and original contribution to implementing the new evangelization.

104. It is often the case that only in the discipline of philosophy do we find mutual understanding and dialogue with those who do not share our faith. The current ferment in philosophy demands of believing philosophers an attentive and competent commitment, while at the same time that they excel in qualities which enable them to discern the points of openness and the key issues of the contemporary situation. Although discoursing according to reason and its rules, the Christian philosopher is at the same time always guided by the understanding supplied by the divine Word, and so is able to conduct a rational discussion which can be understood and appreciated even by those who as yet have not grasped all the truth offered by divine Revelation. The discovery of an area of mutual understanding and dialogue is all the more important, since the pressing questions which face humanity – ecology, peace, and the co-existence of differing races and cultures – can be discussed by the joint, honest and sincere co-operation of Christians, of followers of other religions and even of those who despite their lack of any religion have the renewal of the human race at heart. The Second Vatican Council

---

[124] Cf. Second Vatican Council, Declaration on Religious Freedom *Dignitatis humanae*, §§1–3 in Flannery, (ed.), *Vatican Council II*, pp. 799–802.

[125] Cf. Paul VI, Apostolic Exhortation *Evangelii nuntiandi* (8 December 1975) (London: Catholic Truth Society, 1975), §20.

nullius sint religionis, cordi est hominum renovatio. Id quidem confirmavit Concilium Oecumenicum Vaticanum II: "Desiderium talis colloquii, quod sola caritate erga veritatem ducatur, servata utique congrua prudentia, ex nostra parte neminem excludit, neque illos qui praeclara animi humani bona colunt, eorum vero Auctorem nondum agnoscunt, neque illos qui Ecclesiae opponuntur eamque variis modis persequuntur".[126] Philosophia illa, in qua aliquid Christi veritatis splendet, qui est humanarum quaestionum una ac postrema responsio,[127] fulcimentum erit illius ethicae verae simulque omnem orbem complectentis, qua hodiernus homo indiget.

105. His Litteris encyclicis finem imponentibus, Nobis placet cumprimis ad theologos mentem Nostram postremo convertere, qui peculiari animi intentione philosophicas Dei verbi implicationes observent ac cogitationes in illa re defigant, unde speculativa ac practica scientiae theologicae granditas emergat. De ecclesiali opera iis gratias agere cupio. Artus inter sapientiam philosophicam et theologicam disciplinam nexus in singularissimis christianae traditionis divitiis de revelata veritate vestiganda ponitur. Quapropter eosdem cohortamur ut recipiant et veritatis metaphysicam rationem clarius extollant ad criticum et impellentem dialogum instituendum sive cum nostrae aetatis philosophia sive cum omni philosophica traditione, quae cum Dei verbo concinat aut dissonet. Ob oculos continenter habeant sententiam praeclari cogitationis spiritalitatisque magistri, sancti Bonaventurae scilicet, qui legentem suum in *Itinerarium mentis in Deum* introducens, eundem monet "ne forte credat, quod sibi sufficiat lectio sine unctione, speculatio sine devotione, investigatio sine admiratione, circumspectio sine exultatione, industria sine pietate, scientia sine caritate, intelligentia sine humilitate, studium absque divina gratia, speculum absque sapientia divinitus inspirata".[128]

Mens quoque Nostra ad eos dirigitur *quorum est sacerdotibus institutionem tradere*, tam academicam quam pastoralem, ut peculiari studio philosophicam praeparationem curent illorum qui hodiernis hominibus Evangelium enuntiare debebunt, ac magis illorum qui theologiae perquirendae et docendae operam dabunt. Ad Concilii Oecumenici Vaticani II praescripta[129] et subsequentia praecepta operari

[126] Const. past. de Ecclesia in mundo huius temporis *Gaudium et spes*, §92.
[127] Cfr *Gaudium et spes*, §10.
[128] *Prologus*, §4: Opera omnia, Firenze 1891, t. V, 296.
[129] Cfr Decr. de institutione sacerdotali *Optatum totius*, §15.

confirmed this when it wrote: 'the desire for such a discussion – provided it be conducted in charity – leads to truth and preserves the appropriate prudence, in our view excludes no one, even those who despite their possession of outstanding mental gifts disregard their author or those who oppose and persecute the Church in different ways'.[126] Such philosophy, in which something of the truth of the Christ who is the one and final response to all human questions shines out,[127] will be the basis for the true global ethics which modern man so much needs.

105. In conclusion we wish to direct our attention above all to the theologians, that they may pay serious attention to the philosophical implications of the Word of God, and root their reflections in that which is the source of the speculative and practical majesty of the discipline of theology. We wish to express our thanks for their work within the Church. In the exploration of revealed truth the close connection between the wisdom of the philosophical and theological disciplines is one of the particular riches of the Christian tradition. Therefore we exhort theologians to accept and make much of the metaphysical understanding of truth, that they may begin a critical and demanding dialogue either with modern philosophy or with the whole philosophical tradition, whether in agreement or at odds with the Word of God. They should have constantly before their eyes the thesis of that distinguished master of thought and spirituality, St Bonaventure, who, in introducing the reader to his *Itinerarium mentis in Deum* warns: 'be on guard against supposing that reading is enough without fervour, speculation without devotion, research without wonder, carefulness without any delight, labour without piety, knowledge without charity, understanding without humility, study without divine grace, clarity without divinely inspired wisdom'.[128]

Our mind is also directed towards *those who are involved* in the academic and pastoral *education of priests*, that they may devote special attention to the philosophical preparation of those who are concerned with preaching the Gospel today, and above all to those who will later have to research and teach theology. They should endeavour to act in accordance with the directives of the Second Vatican Council,[129] and sub-

---

126 Second Vatican Council, Pastoral Constitution on the Church in the Modern World *Gaudium et spes*, §92 in Flannery, (ed.), *Vatican Council II*, p. 1000.

127 Cf. Second Vatican Council, Pastoral Constitution on the Church in the Modern World *Gaudium et spes*, §10 in Flannery, (ed.), *Vatican Council II*, p. 910 f.

128 St Bonaventure, *The Soul's Journey into God*, Prologue, in E. Cousins, (ed. and trans.), *The Soul's Journey into God; The Tree of Life; The Life of Francis* (London: SPCK, 1978).

129 Cf. Second Vatican Council, Decree on the Training of Priests *Optatam totius*, §15 in Flannery, (ed.), *Vatican Council II*, pp. 718 f.

contendant, ex quibus instans officium oritur, quod a nemine posthaberi potest, quodque nos omnes alligat, ut opem sincere profundeque feramus ad fidei veritatem communicandam. Grave porro officium non est obliviscendum magistrorum antea convenienterque instituendorum, qui in Seminariis et ecclesiasticis Institutis philosophiam tradant.[130] Necesse est hoc docendi opus congruentem scientificam institutionem secum ferat, ordinatam rationem exhibeat, magnum traditionis christianae suppeditando patrimonium efficiaturque denique debito iudicio, hodiernis spectatis Ecclesiae mundique necessitatibus.

106. Ad *philosophos* praeterea Nos convertimus et *eos qui philosophiam docent*, ut, ob oculos philosophica traditione usque probabili habita, animose repetant sincerae sapientiae veritatisque, metaphysicae etiam, philosophicae disciplinae rationes. Se illis interrogari patiantur postulationibus, quae e Dei verbo effluunt ac strenue suam ratiocinationem et argumentationem agant ut ei interrogationi respondeatur. Ad veritatem usque tendant atque ad bonum quod verum continet sint intenti. Hoc modo sinceram illam ethicam effingere poterunt, qua homines, his potissimum annis, omnino indigent. Ecclesia attente et amabiliter eorum inquisitiones spectat; pro certo ideo habeant eam iustam eorum scientiae autonomiam colere. Credentibus praesertim animum addere volumus, qui in philosophica provincia agunt, ut varios ambitus humanae industriae per rationem illam collustrent quae securior acriorque fit propter adiumentum quod fides ministrat.

Facere denique non possumus quin *scientiae peritos* alloquamur, qui suis inquisitionibus de mundo in universum plus plusque cognitionum praebent deque incredibili varietate ipsius elementorum, tum animalium tum inanimorum, quae multiplices structuras atomicas et moleculares exhibent. Hoc potissimum saeculo ii tam progressi sunt ac tales attigerunt metas, ut admiratione nos subinde afficiamur. Dum admiramur ac simul incitamus hos scientificae inquisitionis vestigatores principes, quibus multum praesentis prosperitatis debet humanitas, eos cohortemur oportet ut suos labores usque persequantur, semper in illa *sapientiae* provincia manentes, in qua cum scientiae technicaeque artis fructibus bona philosophica et ethica coniunguntur, quibus peculiariter et artissimo vinculo persona humana significatur. Scientiae cultor prorsus sibi est conscius veritatis vestigationem numquam desinere, etiam cum ad quandam finitam mundi hominisve partem spectat; ad

[130] Cfr Ioannes Paulus II, Const. Ap. *Sapientia christiana* (15 Aprilis 1979), artt. §§67–68: *AAS* 71 (1979), 491–492.

sequent legislation, which speak clearly of the urgent and binding obligation, which can be neglected by no one, that we devote a sincere and deep attention to communicating the truth of faith. Nor should we forget the important and serious duty of giving an appropriate training to the teachers who are to hand on philosophy in seminaries and ecclesiastical institutes.[130] Teaching in this field necessarily entails a suitable scholarly preparation, a clearly ordered system for understanding the great inheritance of the Christian tradition and finally due discernment within the light of the present needs of the Church and the world.

106. We turn our attention now to *philosophers* and to *those who teach philosophy*, asking that they should keep in their sight a philosophical tradition worthy of approbation, and also have the courage to recover the grounds of a sincere wisdom and – even metaphysical – truth of the philosophical discipline. They should be open to the impelling questions which proceed from the Word of God, and must strenuously use their own efforts of reasoning and argument to respond to this questioning. Let them strive toward the truth and be intent upon the good that embraces the truth. In this way will they be able to create the genuine ethics which, especially these days, men and women so badly need. The Church looks upon their researches with interest and affection: and they should rest assured of her respect for the rightful autonomy of their discipline. We should like also to encourage believers working in the area of philosophy to illuminate the various ranges of human activity through the exercise of a reason which grows more penetrating and assured because of the support it receives from faith.

Finally, we cannot fail to address a word to *scientists*, whose research offers an ever greater knowledge of the universe as a whole and of the incredibly rich array of its component parts, animate and inanimate, with their complex atomic and molecular structures. So far has science come, especially in this century, that its achievements never cease to amaze us. In expressing our admiration and in offering encouragement to these brave pioneers of scientific research, to whom humanity owes so much of its current prosperity, we would urge them to continue their efforts without ever abandoning the horizon of *wisdom* within which scientific and technological achievements are wedded to the philosophical and ethical values that are the distinctive and indelible mark of the human person. Scientists are well aware that the search for truth, even when it concerns a finite reality of the world or of man, is

---

[130] Cf. John Paul II, Apostolic Constitution *Sapientia christiana* (15 April 1979), §§67–8.

quiddam reicit enim quod locatur supra proxima studiorum obiecta, ad interrogationes scilicet quae Mysterii aditum recludunt.[131]

107. Omnes rogamus ut penetralia contueantur hominis, quem Christus suo in amoris mysterio servavit, quique usque veritatem sensumque perquirit. Complures philosophicae scholae, eum fallentes, ei persuaserunt ipsum absolutum esse sui dominum, qui de fortuna sua deque eventura sorte per se decernere possit, sibimet ipsi suisque dumtaxat fidens viribus. Numqua haec erit hominis praestantia. Illud tantum eum efficiet quod in veritatem se inseri eligit, sub Sapientiae umbra suum struens domicilium ibique inhabitans. Hoc solummodo in veritatis prospectu intelleget plane exprimi suam libertatem ac suam ad dilectionem Deique congnitionem vocationem, veluti summam sui explicationem.

108. Postremam Nostram cogitationem ad Eam convertimus, quae Ecclesiae deprecatione *Sedes Sapientiae* invocatur. Ipsius vita vera est parabola quae collustrare poterit quae antea a Nobis dicta sunt. Etenim inter vocationem Beatae Virginis et verae philosophiae strictam consonantiam prospicere licet. Quemadmodum namque ad suam humanitatem et femininam naturam tradendam ipsa vocata est, unde Dei Verbum carnem sumere posset fieretque unus ex nobis, sic ad operam sustinendam, rationalem videlicet et criticam, vocatur philosophia, ut theologia, veluti fidei intellectio, fecunda sit et efficax. Atque sicut Maria, Gabrielis nuntio assentiendo, nihil suae verae humanitatis ac libertatis amisit, sic philosophica disciplina, in his accipiendis quae Evangelii veritas suppeditat, nihil suae autonomiae amittit, sed omnes suas inquisitiones ad summam perfectionem propelli experitur. Hanc quidem veritatem plane intellexerunt sancti antiquitatis christianae monachi, a quibus Maria "fidei mensa intellectualis"[132] appellabatur. Ipsam congruentem verae philosophiae effigiem respiciebant sibique erant conscii se debere *cum Maria philosophari.*

Sedes Sapientiae iis qui sapientiae vestigandae dependunt vitam portus sit tutus. Ad sapientiam iter, quod est postremum sincerumque omnis scientiae propositum, ab omnibus impedimentis expediat intercedendo Ea quae, Veritatem parturiens eandemque in corde servans, in sempiternum tota cum humanitate ipsam communicavit.

---

131 Ioannes Paulus II, *Discorso all'Università di Cracovia per 600° anniversario dell'Alma Mater Jagellonica* (8 Iunii 1997), 4: *L'Osservatore Romano*, 9–10 Iunii 1997, p. 12.

132 *ἕ νοηρὰ τὲς πὶστεος τρὰπεζα*: S.P.N. Epiphanius, *Homilia in laudes Sanctae Mariae Deiparae*: *PG* 43, 493.

never-ending, but always points beyond to something higher than the immediate object of study, to the questions which give access to Mystery.[131]

107. I ask everyone to contemplate the inner nature of man, whom Christ has saved in the mystery of his love and who is always searching for truth and meaning. Many philosophical schools deceive us by persuading us that we are the absolute lords of ourselves, that we are able by ourselves to decide our destiny and ultimate lot, provided we trust in ourselves and our own efforts. Such will never be the true nobility of man. We can find fulfilment only in choosing to enter the truth, to make a home under the shade of Wisdom and dwell there. Only within this horizon of truth will we understand our freedom in its fullness and our vocation to know and love God as our highest self-explanation.

108. Our final thought is directed towards Her whom the prayer of the Church invokes as *Seat of Wisdom*. Her life is a true parable which can shed light upon all that I have said here. We can perceive a close connection between the vocation of Our Lady and what is strictly called philosophy. Even as she was called to offer up both her humanity and her feminine nature so that the Word of God might take flesh and become one of us, so also philosophy is called to carry out its rational and critical task in order to enable the fruitfulness and efficacy of theology considered as the understanding of faith. And as Mary, consenting to the message of Gabriel, lost nothing of her humanity and freedom, so too the discipline of philosophy in its accepting the superabundant truth of the Gospel loses nothing of its autonomy, but discovers that all its researches are propelled towards the highest perfection. This truth was clearly perceived by the holy monks of Christian antiquity, by whom Mary was called 'the table of intellectual faith'.[132] In her they saw a suitable image of true philosophy and realized that they must *be philosophizing with Mary*.

May Mary, Seat of Wisdom, be a sure haven for all who devote their lives to the search for wisdom. May their journey into wisdom, sure and final goal of all true knowing, be freed of every impediment by the interceding of her who, in giving birth to the Truth and treasuring it in her heart, has forever shared it with the whole of humanity.

---

[131] John Paul II, *Address to the University of Krakow for the 600th Anniversary of the Jagiellonian University* (8 June 1997), §4 in *L'Osservatore Romano*, 9–10 June 1997, p. 12.

[132] *ἑ νοηρὰ τêσ πὶστεος τρὰπεζα*: Pseudo-Epiphanius, *Homily in Praise of Holy Mary Mother of God*: *Patrologia Graeca*, 43, §493.

Datum Romae, apud S. Petrum, die XIV mensis Septembris, in festo Exaltationis Sanctae Crucis, anno MCMXCVIII, Pontificatus Nostri vicesimo.

IOANNES PAULUS PP. II

Given at Rome in Saint Peter's on September 14th, the feast of the Exaltation of the Holy Cross 1998, in the twentieth year of Our Pontificate,

JOHN PAUL II.

Commentary

JAMES McEVOY

Introduction

The commentary makes a number of distinct but complementary approaches to the letter in an effort to bring out its major themes and to highlight its importance, and so this commentary should be read in conjunction with the Encyclical, and not in place of it. This is not a summary of the letter: paraphrase will be kept to a minimum.[1] The approach is in this regard selective, and makes no claim to be comprehensive. The commentary is based on the Latin text together with the English translation contained in this volume.

It is over a hundred and twenty years since Leo XIII issued the Encyclical Letter *Aeterni Patris* recommending Thomistic thought to the Church.[2] *Fides et ratio* is a successor document to that statement. A commentary is in the nature of things a compilation – many books and articles have been read with profit in the course of the preparation of this one. Not all of these can be cited in the footnotes, which are reserved to the principal sources. I acknowledge with thanks the help I have received from many quarters, both through discussion and by way of the printed word.

The structure of the Encyclical

Fides et ratio may conveniently be divided into two parts, as follows:

I. Laying the foundations (Introduction and chapters I–III; sections

---

[1] See the summary of *Fides et ratio* by Richard John Neuhaus: 'A Passion for Truth: The Way of Faith and Reason', in *First Things* 88 (Dec. 1998), pp. 65–73. André-Mutien Léonard, Bishop of Namur, has published a more detailed thematic summary under the title 'Un guide de lecture pour l'encyclique *Fides et ratio*', in L.-M. Billé et al., (eds.), *Foi et raison: Lectures de l'encyclique Fides et ratio* (Paris: CERP, 1998), pp. 31–73.

[2] Leo XIII, Encyclical Letter *Aeterni Patris* in *Acta Sanctae Sedis*, Vol. XII (Rome: Sacra Congregatio de Propaganda Fide, 1879), pp. 97–115. ET J. J. Wynne SJ (ed.), *The Great Encyclicals of Pope Leo XIII: Translations from Approved Sources* (New York: Benziger, 1903).

§§1–35), or the relationship of human beings to truth in its various dimensions.

Divine revelation (chapter I: *The Disclosure of Divine Wisdom*);
Wisdom and understanding (chapter II: *I Believe that I May Understand*);
Seeking the truth (chapter III: *I Understand that I May Believe*).

II. The relationship between faith and reason, especially philosophy (chapters IV to VII, or sections §§36–108).

The historical meeting of faith and reason, their interrelationship, and separation (chapter IV: *Concerning the Relationship between Faith and Reason*);
The Church's interest in philosophy (chapter V: *The Judgments of the Magisterium upon Philosophy*);
The intrinsic relationship between theology and philosophy (chapter VI: *The Interaction Between Theology and Philosophy*);
Philosophical implications of Christianity, and current theological requirements (chapter VII: *Modern Demands and Duties*).

Chapter VI may be regarded as the culmination of the document – it is there that lessons are drawn from the series of surveys that fill the earlier chapters, lessons that are subsequently (chapter VII) distilled into a set of challenges to Catholic theologians and to philosophers regarding their professional practice. The sixth chapter has been carefully prepared from the beginning of the document. The chapters and subheadings throughout are organically articulated and the argument unfolds according to an inner logic.

Motivation

To the question why this Encyclical was prepared, one clear answer is given in §§62–63 in terms of a practical requirement: 'I wish to repeat clearly that the study of philosophy is fundamental and indispensable to the structure of theological studies and to the formation of candidates for the priesthood' (§62). The document identifies six areas of difficulty for theology in its relationship with philosophy:

(i) A serious problem in theology is the uncritical modishness of some of its practitioners, whose neglect of philosophy leads to the undiscriminating adoption of all kinds of ideas (§62). The aim of the Letter is to propose the restoration of a harmonious and creative relationship

between theology and philosophy. The theme which lends unity to the entire Letter is that of *truth*: the search for truth is described as the very definition of what it means to be human (§28). The '*Diakonia* of the truth' is a responsibility of the Church (§2).

Some commentators have understood §§55–56 to be the core of the entire document's argument. In these sections the Pope identifies intellectual tendencies which have definite repercussions on Catholic thought. First comes the current cultural phenomenon of the deep-seated distrust of reason. This, he claims, has surfaced in much recent philosophical research, to the point where 'we hear not infrequently the expression "the end of metaphysics"'. This is a clear allusion to the way in which a particular phrase of Heidegger's has been taken up, and to those 'post-modernists' who claim a certain reading of Heidegger and Nietzsche as their inspiration, a reading often inspired by the influence of Heidegger and Nietzsche in post-war French philosophical thought. In recent years some Catholics have felt attracted to French post-modernism as a possible vehicle for Christian thought.[3] Emmanuel Lévinas also developed a critical relation to metaphysics (save in so far as ethics becomes first philosophy for him); he has had considerable influence on contemporary theological thought.

(ii) Philosophy has restricted itself to modest tasks. This remark seems to be aimed at the dominant 'analytic' tradition in Anglo-American philosophy. Perhaps there is in general less consciousness in Rome of what goes on in English-speaking philosophy; positivism excepted, the latter must seem (and on the whole it undoubtedly is) much less ideological than were some prominent currents of continental European philosophy in the course of the twentieth century.

(iii) Rationalism is a risk, especially for those theologians who may too easily accept the conventional views making up the *Zeitgeist*.

(iv) Fideism is re-appearing (this is noticed at various points in the document). Sometimes it refers to the neglect of speculative theology and disdain for philosophy; however, it can also take the form of

(v) 'biblicism' which tends to make exegesis the only theological discipline. In the Catholic outlook the Scriptures cannot be interpreted properly without reference to tradition and the magisterium of the Church.

---

[3] See Kenneth L. Schmitz, 'Postmodernism and the Catholic Tradition' in *American Catholic Philosophical Quarterly* 73 (1999), pp. 233–52. Schmitz is very critical of this recent trend. The object of some of his criticism, John Caputo, replies in the same issue, pp. 253–60. This volume of the *American Catholic Philosophical Quarterly* was devoted largely to this question, and has given rise to the publication of a new journal, *Catholic Horizons*, founded in 2001. A quarterly journal of Catholic philosophy, theology, and social theory, it is in critical dialogue with the thought of modernity and postmodernity.

(vi) Finally, the exclusive use of the historical-critical method of biblical exegesis is questioned as reductive, fragmenting as it does, the sense, and the text, of the biblical writings; the truth in Scripture is not adequately captured by this method.[4]

In the context of the prevailing mistrust of rationality and statements having a universal reference, 'non-foundationalist' or 'anti-foundationalist' appeals are often made to consensus as providing a basis for 'truth' (Jürgen Habermas or Richard Rorty represent examples of these kinds of thinker).[5] Besides, increasing specialization threatens the unity and depth of the philosophical enterprise in its noblest aim at 'the full and ultimate meaning of life'.[6] Faith is capable, where it is not rejected, of spurring and challenging reason to more audacious undertakings – faith is reason's advocate.

These are bold words to use in the face of the prevailing secularism affecting Western lands, and also of the marked degree of secularization that has developed in Catholic teaching institutions.

The recovery of a truly *sapiential* dimension in philosophical inquiry is urged upon us, and the means to it is suggested: listening to the religious message of the Christian faith. It would not be unreasonable to claim that no notable philosophical movement has been able to develop or sustain itself entirely apart from the well-springs of religious belief, either in Ancient Greece or Rome, in India, in the European Middle Ages or out of German Idealism. The document therefore poses the question: has a philosophical style or milieu which meets the deepest questions of life only with sceptical resignation not abdicated from the role of reason and withdrawn from the most human claims of truth?[7]

Sources

The document has drawn together thoughts and themes from the entire tradition of the Catholic Church, from the single viewpoint of the interrelationship of faith and reason. The sources are multiple and play a very

[4] Cf. the document of the Pontifical Biblical Commission published in English as *The Interpretation of the Bible in the Church* (Rome: Libreria Editrice Vaticana, 1993).

[5] Cf. *Fides et ratio*, §56.

[6] Cf. *The Interpretation of the Bible in the Church*.

[7] John Haldane regards the advocacy of a 'sapiential dimension' as the most original thrust of *Fides et ratio*. Perhaps Haldane, a proponent of analytic Thomism, is particularly conscious of the absence of that dimension in Anglo-Saxon professional philosophy. See his reflections, 'Thomism and Renewal' in J. McEvoy and M. Dunne, (eds.), *Thomas Aquinas: Approaches to Truth*, The 2000 Aquinas Lectures at Maynooth (Dublin: Four Courts Press, 2001).

fundamental role in the elaboration of the message of the Letter, which amounts to a *status quaestionis* of the whole problematic, when studied both in its historical unfolding over the centuries, and also in its structural elements and form. I seek here to draw attention to the most significant of them and to the way in which they are deployed.

The biblical foundation of the Christian faith must be considered in the very first place. It occupies the first two chapters and lays the basis for the rest to build upon. Chapter I, *The Disclosure of the Divine Wisdom*, concentrates upon Jesus Christ, the revealer of the Father and the giver of the message of salvation to his Church. *I Believe that I May Understand*, is based upon the Wisdom literature (Wisdom, Proverbs), together with St Paul's teaching on the capacity of the mind to rise to knowledge of the Creator,[8] and the wisdom of the cross which contradicts human speculation.[9] St Paul is called upon to remind us that God chose to reveal his saving truth through his Son; this truth did not originate in human speculation. The Church's tradition has constantly sought to understand the faith (*intellectus fidei*): reference is made to the continuously developing teaching about faith and reason in the councils of Trent, Vatican I (especially in the Dogmatic Constitution on Revelation of that Council, *Dei Filius*) and Vatican II (the Dogmatic Constitution on Divine Revelation, *Dei Verbum*). References to *Dei Verbum* recur, and are joined at appropriate points by allusions to other documents of Vatican II, such as the Declaration on the Relation of the Church to Other Religions (*Nostra aetate*), The Pastoral Constitution on the Church in the Modern World (*Gaudium et spes,* particularly in its consideration of the spiritual needs of the contemporary situation), and the Decree on Priestly Formation, *Optatam totius,* regarding the employment of the teaching of St Thomas in seminaries.[10] Naturally, in Chapter V, dealing with the interventions of the Magisterium in philosophical matters, the entire range of relevant councils is cited, together with papal pronouncements such as *Aeterni Patris* (Leo XIII, 1879), *Pascendi dominici gregis* (Pius X, 1907), *Divini redemptoris* (Pius XI, 1937), and *Humani generis* (Pius XII, 1950). To these are added a wide selection of the encyclicals of the present pontificate, and in particular, *Redemptor hominis* (1979) in its consideration of the principle that 'it is only in the mystery of the Incarnate Word that the mystery of humanity becomes clear',[11] as well as its other publications.[12]

---

[8] Rom 1:20.

[9] 1 and 2 Corinthians.

[10] *Fides et ratio*, §87.

[11] *Fides et ratio,* §60; cf. also *Veritatis splendor*, §25.

[12] Cf., *Pastores dabo vobis*, on the importance of the philosophical formation of future pastors, §60.

Reference to councils and to publications of the popes is of course a standard feature of official Vatican documents. It is meant to make explicit the continuity in teaching, even as each new encyclical thematizes, develops, or updates, the inherited stock of ideas. Very early on the Pope describes his task by saying that he is 'following upon similar initiatives by my Predecessors'.[13] Throughout the document the references to Vatican II in particular convey a deliberate message: the most recent general council of the Church is normative, and an inspiration of the highest authority in the apostolic life of the Papacy. The Holy Father was present as a bishop at all the sessions and took a prominent part in its commissions; he is entitled by experience as well as by office to regard himself as an accredited judge of its meaning.

The documents of the present pontificate have been so numerous and weighty that in some ways Pope John Paul II has become a source in his own right, drawing upon a large number of letters, exhortations, allocutions and occasional addresses of all kinds. Such references, where they abound in a particular theme or topic, serve to point up the significance of these themes. A good example is where the invocation of *Sapientiae christianae* and *Pastores dabo vobis* is followed by references to three papal addresses underlining the value of the philosophy of St Thomas, together with two publications of the Congregation for Catholic Education making the same recommendation. The personal message about the value of St Thomas's philosophy and the Pontiff's commitment to it is unmistakable. The references to St Thomas do not exclude even rival traditions of interpretation: one of the lengthiest quotations made in the text of the Letter from a thinker of the Christian past comes from the prologue of the *Itinerarium mentis in Deum* of St Bonaventure, which the document describes as 'that great master of thought and spirituality'.[14]

Self-knowledge and the love of wisdom

A number of the major themes of the Letter are announced in the first six introductory sections, which is headed by the Delphic adage, 'Know thyself!' The image of faith and reason with which the Letter opens ('like two wings. . .') suggests their common finality, that of helping the spirit 'to rise to the contemplation of truth'. The words 'contemplation of the truth' place truth and its appreciation beyond pragmatic or reductivist notions, as the very object of the human spirit. The desire for truth comes from the Creator who has placed it in 'the human heart'. This desire, like the desire for God with which it is ultimately one, is universal, and to be

[13] *Fides et ratio*, §5.
[14] *Fides et ratio*, §105.

found in all men and women. It is a *concrete* universal, present at every point in human history and in each person's life. For the philosophy lecturer at Lublin, Karol Wojtyła, philosophical anthropology was the privileged scene of the battle against Communism; for the Pope, the experience of being human is still where the fundamental questions arise. He remarks that 'modern philosophy is often praised because it focuses our minds upon man himself':[15] the summary which elucidates this remark weighs positive results against one-sided subjectivism and anthropocentrism. Each of us has access to the depth of his or her own existence, through the great questions which come to us simply because we are human.

These opening affirmations are of fundamental importance for the Encyclical, and they give rise to the claim which follows them: through coming to know and love God human beings come to the full truth about themselves. In other words, it is not in faith that human alienation is to be located but on the contrary in atheism and in ignorance of God. Thus knowledge of God and knowledge of the self are implied by each other; St Augustine's *noverim te, noverim me* – if I knew myself I would know you – can be validly reversed by the creature: *noverim te, noverim me* – inasmuch as I know you, I know myself.

All cultures and times, and every individual human being, are journeying. The Church is part of that questing, journeying humanity – a pilgrim in history. On the other hand, a journey only becomes a pilgrimage through consciousness of the goal that gives meaning to the way. The Church has the task of preaching the one who is the way,[16] and of witnessing to that complete truth which lies at the end, when we shall at last understand fully. A breadth of perspective characterizes *Fides et ratio* as a whole: historical and biblical perspectives in Chapter II, anthropological and cultural ones in the Introduction. From all of these, fundamental anthropological questions arise which unsettle people and initiate their quest for meaning: 'Who am I? Where do I come from? Where am I going? Why do evils appear? What remains to us after this life?' These could be amplified still more: 'What can I do to become more human? Why do the innocent suffer, the rich and powerful seem to thrive? Can one love another as oneself? How can genuine happiness be found?'[17]

These questions lie at the origin and at the heart of philosophy. Of

---

15 *Fides et ratio*, §5.

16 Jn 14:6.

17 See the questions mentioned in Chapter 1 of the Declaration on the Relation of the Church to Non-Christian Religions, *Nostra aetate*, in A. Flannery OP, (ed.), *Vatican Council II: The Conciliar and Post-Conciliar Documents* (Grand Rapids, MI: Eerdmans, 1992) pp. 738–42.

course, 'philosophy' has more than one meaning.[18] It may be taken in a general sense to mean the love of wisdom (*philo-sophia*). *Fides et ratio* notes that every people on earth has been and is possessed of a cultural treasure of native wisdom, and every human being is by nature a philosopher.[19] 'Philosophy' may also refer to the various systems or strands of thought, for instance, what goes under the name of Platonism, Aristotelianism, Thomism, idealism, empiricism, that have been proposed by Western thinkers; or, when understood in a more restricted, technical sense, philosophy may mean the category of activity currently carried out in departments of philosophy in universities and colleges. *Fides et ratio* has some critical things to say about academic philosophy and some suggestions to make for its deepening. Part of the argument of the letter is to move deliberately from the narrow sense of 'philosophy' to a more primordial meaning, in order to open up a renewed direction for professional philosophers to consider. The academic discipline of philosophy is thus returned to its historical origins in the love of wisdom and the search for truth. Much philosophical thinking has tended to neglect or reject metaphysics during the past two or three centuries. When it has done so, it has lost its guiding role in culture generally. Even in academic life, philosophy has become one discipline among many, losing any guiding or integrating function that it had regarding the direction of the mind for the sake of engaging in other disciplines, and so becoming marginal – simply one subject to be found among the various arts and humanities courses. Philosophy is frequently pursued as a technical art or discipline dedicated to conceptual differentiation and analysis, but omitting much of reality from its investigation. The sacrifice of what the Encyclical calls 'the sapiential dimension of philosophy' is held largely responsible for the narrowing and specialization of academic philosophy, and for its particularization as one discipline among others. The academic philosopher, like every man and woman, is touched by general and existential questions that arise within experience and that lie at the origin of philosophizing, of wondering, of seeking truth, and of pursuing self-knowledge in the Socratic vein – in short, the quest for self-knowledge.

To be faced with these questions, in the manner indicated above, is fundamental to being human.[20] The sapiential urge which issued in philosophical investigation among the Greeks should still have priority over the technical development of the discipline that has come to dominate its contemporary expression. Academic philosophy is not an end in itself. Philosophy should draw its vital energy, and even part of its content,

---

[18] Cf. *Fides et ratio*, §4.

[19] Cf. *Fides et ratio*, §§4, 30, 64.

[20] Cf. *Fides et ratio*, §§5–6.

from the natural philosopher, deeply embedded in every person, and who is revealed by the universal capacity for a deep questioning which goes beyond limited interests and appraisals. The philosopher, in the more specialized, professional, sense of the word, owes it to humanity (both in the philosopher's own self and in the human race at large) to aim at truth in a broader and deeper sense than is frequently met with. Philosophy should be able to inform and guide the very culture in which it is practised.

This plea is not to be confused with the conventional demand for academic interdisciplinarity; in some ways it is the opposite of this academic concern, being instead a reminder of the dimension of universality that lies at the heart of the philosophical enterprise. Although critical of both major streams of academic philosophy in the secular world, *Fides et ratio* does not issue any condemnations, but adopts an encouraging tone, repeatedly advocating confidence in the capacities of human reason: 'Have confidence in the work of the mind; go further; raise your sights, aim higher!' These imperatives would aptly express the sense of the work.

Some readers may find the Letter too optimistic or uncritical, preferring to draw attention to the illusory promise of any Pure Reason, or to post-modern deconstruction of the 'pretensions' of reason, or to fideist suspicion regarding the pervasive destruction of human capacities through sin. In resisting these tendencies, and in its defence of realism and of metaphysics, the Encyclical develops a recognizably Catholic position concerning the relations between faith and reason, especially that noblest fruit of reason, philosophy.

Karol Wojtyła, Pope John Paul II and philosophy

To regard any papal encyclical as being a personal work of the Pope would be too simple by far, for in the process of writing many experts are consulted and several of the constituent offices of the Vatican – the Curial Congregations and Pontifical Commissions – take an active interest in its preparation (the Congregation for the Doctrine of the Faith in particular). Nevertheless it is generally agreed that the initiative which gave rise to *Fides et ratio* is the expression of a deeply personal, lifelong study of philosophy and theology on the part of Karol Wojtyła, who has on occasion been called the philosopher-Pope.[21] Although it

[21] Some of his writings before becoming Pope have been translated into English (with, it has to be said, varying degrees of felicity). Among them are the following (all under his name, Karol Wojtyła): *Faith According to Saint John of the Cross,* trans. Jordan Aumann (San Francisco, CA: Ignatius Press, 1981) [Doctrina de fide apud S. Joannem a cruce, Pontifical University of St Thomas Aquinas, 1948]; *Love*

appeared only in 1998, the preparation of *Fides et ratio* began in the mid-1980s.[22]

Why did *Fides et ratio* follow *Veritatis splendor* (1993) and other recent, weighty encyclicals – *Evangelium vitae* (1995), for instance – rather than preceding them? Surely the Letter dealing with the interplay of faith and reason, and their mutual dependence, should have come first in logical order? Is *Fides et ratio* not, after all, meant to elucidate the Catholic method of access to truth? Is it not a key, perhaps even *the* key, to Catholic intellectual culture? We can only suggest that its long gestation speaks of a thorough thought-preparation, not the fitful attention that might be accorded to an afterthought.

The philosophical purpose and worth of the Letter have been underlined by the philosopher, Alasdair MacIntyre. His high regard for the Encyclical is as a contribution to philosophy, in particular because it advocates epistemological realism in the wake of St Thomas: '*Fides et ratio* not only is an encyclical about philosophy, as was *Aeterni Patris,* but is also, as *Aeterni Patris* was not, itself a contribution to philosophy, inviting philosophical scrutiny of its arguments and assertions in a way that is rare, perhaps unique, among encyclicals. It does so just because the questions which are central to it are in part philosophical questions and the Encyclical insists that in pursuing them "philosophy must remain faithful to its own principles and methods".'[23]

---

and Responsibility, trans. H. T. Willetts (London: Collins, 1981) [*Miłość i odpowiedzialność*], (San Francisco, CA: Ignatius Press, 1993 (1961)); *The Acting Person*, trans. Andrzej Potocki and Anna-Teresa Tymieniecka, in *Analecta Husserliana*, Vol. 10 (Dordrecht: Reidel, 1979) [Osoba i Czyn, Krakow]; a collection of his personalist essays dating from his Lublin days has been published: *Person and Community* (New York: Peter Lang, 1993). An isolated philosophical article appeared under his name: 'The Person: Subject and Community', in *Review of Metaphysics* 33 (1979), pp. 273–308. For a representative list of his publications during his professorate and also his pontificate see George Weigel, *Witness to Hope* (London: HarperCollins, 1999), pp. 947–9.

[22] In the early 1980s Castel Gandolfo, the Pope's residence on Lake Albano, was the scene, each summer for several years, of a week or so of philosophical reflection organized by the Pope. He addressed his invitation to philosophers from various backgrounds to take part in the discussion of topics he himself proposed. On holiday, he attended the evening sessions (to which he invited some young compatriots), and listened without commenting or intervening. He was there to observe, to learn, to evaluate – and also, perhaps, to make a distant preparation for *Fides et ratio.*

[23] A. MacIntyre, 'Truth as a Good', in *Thomas Aquinas: Approaches to Truth*, quoting *Fides et ratio* §49. Like MacIntyre but independently, Laurence Hemming argues that the view of reason and of truth upon which *Fides et ratio* reposes comes from St Thomas: cf. 'Unreasonable Faith', in *New Blackfriars* 81 (September 2000) pp. 389–99. This entire issue of *New Blackfriars* was given over to considerations of *Fides et ratio.* The article by John Haldane referred to below (cf. note 34) also discusses philosophical realism in relation to *Fides et ratio.* The dimensions of the notion of truth in *Fides et ratio* are mapped by Thomas Kelly, '*Intelligo ut Credam*:

What role has philosophy played in the life and thought of the man who became Pope in 1978? Only the most general characterization of the philosophy and theology of John Paul II is possible here.[24]

The shape taken by the early studies of Karol Wojtyła as a seminarian was dictated by the circumstances of war and occupation in his native Poland.[25] War conditions reduced his seminary studies to only the four years 1942–46. His reading of philosophy was done privately while working in a chemical plant, and was based on neo-scholastic textbooks of logic, ethics, metaphysics, philosophical psychology and the like, of the kind that was current in the seminary curriculum of the period. Following ordination he was sent to Rome and in the years 1946–48 he studied theology at the Angelicum University under the supervision of Fr Garrigou-Lagrange OP. His doctoral dissertation was written in Latin: *Doctrina de fide apud S. Ioannem a Cruce*,[26] his interest in Carmelite spirituality dating from very early years. In September 1951 he began to prepare his Habilitation thesis, a post-doctoral period of study required to qualify him to teach at University level in the European system. He studied the value ethics of Max Scheler (1874–1928), and in due course submitted a thesis: 'An Evaluation of the Possibility of Constructing a Christian Ethics on the Basis of the System of Max Scheler'.[27] It must be stressed that in philosophy Karol Wojtyła was and remains essentially what might be termed an Aristotelian Thomist; his application to phenomenology had a deep impact on him, without unsettling this fundamental commitment in philosophy.[28] He came to regard phenomenology

---

Reason and Philosophy in Relation to Faith', in *The Diakonia of Truth*, ed. J. McEvoy (forthcoming).

24 Specialist monographs have been written, concentrating on his philosophy. See: Kenneth L. Schmitz, *At the Centre of the Human Drama: The Philosophical Anthropology of Karol Wojtyła/John Paul II* (Washington, DC: Catholic University of America Press, 1993); Kevin Doran, *Solidarity: A Synthesis of Personalism and Communalism in the Thought of Karol Wojtyła* (New York: Peter Lang, 1996); Rocco Buttiglione, *La pensée de Karol Wojtyła* (Paris: Fayard, 1984). Four recent studies are published as chapters in a collective work, *The Diakonia of Truth: The Challenges of Fides et ratio,* ed. James McEvoy (forthcoming); these are, James McEvoy, 'The Singular Shape of Karol Wojtyła's Studies'; Patrick Gorevan, 'Karol Wojtyła in Philosophical Dialogue with Max Scheler'; Mette Lebech, 'John Paul II and Edith Stein: His Reasons for Referring to Her in *Fides et ratio*'; Kevin Doran, 'Faith and Freedom in the Personalism of Karol Wojtyła'. I wish to acknowledge my indebtedness to these studies in writing this commentary.

25 This is recounted in detail by George Weigel in *Witness to Hope*.

26 The Doctrine of Faith According to St John of the Cross. See note 21 above.

27 An Italian version has been published as: Karol Wojtyła, *Valutazioni sulla possibilità di costruire l'etica cristiana sulle basi del sistema di Max Scheler*, trans. S. Bucciarelli (Rome: Logos, 1980).

28 In seminars over many years he is said to have studied the entire *Summa Theologiae* of St Thomas Aquinas.

as being more of a pedagogy than a philosophy in itself. From Scheler's phenomenology he learned sensitivity to the human subject and the personal activity (or *efficacy*, Wojtyła's preferred term) of the moral agent. Much of his effort as a moralist went in the direction of extending Thomist categories in an experiential and personalist direction. While professor of ethics at Lublin, he wrote of Aquinas, rather revealingly, that 'he shows us the particular faculties, both spiritual and sensory, thanks to which the whole of human consciousness and self-consciousness . . . takes shape, but that is also where he stops. Thus St Thomas gives us an excellent view of the objective existence and activity of the person, but it would be difficult to speak in his view of the lived experience of the person'.[29]

Through the experience of efficacy (or being oneself the cause of action), the person experiences himself as self-possessing, self-determining and self-governing. Within the experience of 'the acting person' there lies the transcendence of the person, who goes beyond the boundaries of his fixed nature. This is the immanent profile of human action, the very core of which is a decision reached in the presence of attraction or motivation. The act of deciding may have effects and consequences of an objective kind (i.e. lying outside the subject or agent) but its principal efficacy regards the acting person himself: in a free act I move myself towards the object of my motivation, and in that sense I am the object of the action, and my every action consequently possesses personalistic value.

Though Wojtyła's hopes of finding in Scheler's personalism a grounding for Christian ethics were disappointed, still his absorption in Scheler's phenomenology undoubtedly helped him to develop a personalist approach to ethics and left a lasting mark on his thinking.[30] The influence crystallized in three areas which Scheler had developed with originality: the notions of resentment, of shame, and of the personal human subject who cannot be made into an object. When Wojtyła wrote on love and

[29] K. Wojtyła, 'Thomistic Personalism' in *Person and Community: Selected Essays*, Catholic Thought from Lublin, Vol. 4, trans. T. Sandok (New York: Peter Lang, 1993), pp. 170–1.

[30] The Pope has referred to the genesis of his personalism in these terms: 'In *Love and Responsibility*, I formulated the concept of a personalist principle. This principle is an attempt to translate the commandment of love into the language of philosophical ethics. *The person is a being for whom the only suitable dimension is love.* We are just to a person if we love him. This is as true for God as it is for man. Love for a person *excludes the possibility of treating him as an object of pleasure.*' John Paul II, *Crossing the Threshold of Hope*, trans. J. McPhee and M. McPhee (London: Jonathan Cape, 1994), pp. 200–1. This principle recalls Scheler's claim that knowledge of the person is not 'objective' but must always pass through love – indeed it also recalls St Augustine: 'nemo cognoscitur nisi per amicitiam', nothing is known except through loving friendship.

responsibility, for instance, his analyses of resentment and of shame underpinned his retrieval of the virtue of chastity.[31] He was also a supporter of the critique Scheler developed of Kantian formal ethics, and he has echoed Scheler's rebuttal of the anthropomorphic critique of religion: justice can be done to human beings only by regarding them in a 'theomorphic' light, as the image and likeness of God. He parted ways with Scheler, however, in formulating the criticism that Scheler makes his value-ethics depend upon the hierarchy of importance given to particular things (an emotional criterion of worth, therefore).[32] Wojtyła, in contrast, has insisted upon a direct relationship between truth and freedom: morally good action makes a person better and more truly what the person as such should be.[33] He concluded that Scheler did not exploit the phenomenological method to the full when examining moral experience: specifically he did not ask 'what is given in experience?', but rather 'what *can* be given in experience?'

In summary, the Lublin professor developed his own, very contemporary, form of Thomism: personalist ethics founded upon a metaphysical anthropology and a realist philosophy of being.[34] He saw in phenomenology the complement of the great tradition of metaphysics, not its replacement – a method for exploring subjectivity in a modern way, an implement for personalist developments in ethics, but not the abandonment either of realism or of the normativity of truly personal existence. A largely invisible dimension of his philosophy is the presence within it of his life-long, interior, resistance to totalitarianism (to National Socialism and to Communism): to that situation where the person is reduced by an all-powerful state to simply a productive member of a collectivity so that the *dignity of the human person*, that great principle so often invoked in the Pope's writings, is violated.[35] This conviction is frequently expressed by John Paul II in terms of the mutual

---

[31] See the Chapter 'The Metaphysics of Shame', in K. Wojtyła, *Love and Responsibility*, pp. 141–73.

[32] In his lectures Scheler asked the rhetorical question, 'How is reality given?', and answered, 'through value-feelings' (*Wertgefühle*).

[33] Scheler's was not the only contemporary influence on Wojtyła's philosophy, for Gabriel Marcel and Emmanuel Mounier have left a mark, and perhaps also Maurice Blondel and authors like Maritain and Gilson, who are mentioned in *Fides et ratio*. De Lubac would also appear to have marked his theology.

[34] Professor John Haldane has described Wojtyła's philosophy, aptly enough, in terms of Thomistic anti-Cartesian personalism, Christian Aristotelianism filtered through phenomenology; see his article 'The Diversity of Philosophy and the Unity of its Vocation: Some Philosophical Reflections on *Fides et ratio*', in *Faith and Reason*, (ed.), Timothy L. Smith (Chicago: St Augustine's Press, 2001). This collective work is devoted to the themes of *Fides et ratio*.

[35] This is the perspective out of which the Encyclical Letter on justice and human work, *Laborem exercens* (1981) was written.

implication of truth and freedom. Solidarity, as he thinks of it (and he has largely defined the current sense of this term derived from Scheler), belongs with the moral virtues: it is the commitment of the will to the pursuit of the common good rather than individual interest. It is a moral principle of international development, of peoples and of the living conditions befitting their dignity and equality.[36]

It should be borne in mind that in the course of his teaching career Wojtyła interrelated philosophy and theology, as a teacher of ethics especially. He practised the integration of both disciplines and the articulation of Christian wisdom in reliance upon both. His emphasis on the methodological autonomy of philosophy vis-à-vis theology is a reflection of his own practice in this regard: he had a clear sense of the danger of confusing the two methods, and is for that reason not embarrassed about their interrelationship.[37]

Many cultures, one truth of salvation

Fides et ratio contains much more than the teaching on faith and reason which is indeed its central message, and on philosophy and theology which belong to the reflection on reason and faith. Culture is referred to in seventeen sections and thematized in §§70–71 of the Encyclical. Culture is placed in relationship to other realities, such as tradition and language, religions and philosophy, revelation, faith and the mission of the Church. The rich nature of the term, its interrelatedness with others, and the significance assigned to it in *Fides et ratio*, make it worthwhile to examine the document from the perspective of culture.

The theme of culture is introduced as part of a contemporary challenge to the message the Encyclical would like to renew and impart. The traditional Catholic appeal to philosophy as the uniquely privileged partner of theology in the elaboration of a Christian wisdom does not go

[36] See also *Sollicitudo rei socialis* (1987), §33.

[37] Cf. esp. *Fides et ratio*, §49. Anthony Kenny has criticized *Fides et ratio* for not allowing philosophers complete autonomy in regard to approach and conclusions (*The Tablet*, 26 June 1999, pp. 874–6). John Paul II's integration of faith and reason may be illustrated here by his message for the celebration of the World Day of Peace on 1 January 2002. In the wake of the terrorist attacks on New York in September 2001, the Pope appeals for forgiveness as the deliverer of justice and the condition of peace: 'Forgiveness therefore has a divine source and criterion. This does not mean that its significance cannot also be grasped in the light of human reasoning; and this, in the first place, on the basis of what people experience when they do wrong. They experience their human weakness, and they want others to deal leniently with them. Why not therefore do towards others what we want them to do towards us? All human beings cherish the hope of being able to start all over again, and not remain for ever shut up in their own mistakes and guilt. They all want to raise their eyes to the future and to discover new possibilities of trust and commitment.'

unquestioned at the present time. Why canonize an élite practice of philosophy at the expense of, for instance, ethnic, traditional, or local wisdom? Could not faith inculturate itself better in any of these than in philosophy, which is, after all, Greek in origin and largely European in its development, and thus the product of a particular historical culture? Why should the entire Church, from Africa to Asia and beyond, be tied to particularities of a European tradition and past?

In what follows, *Fides et ratio* undertakes a dialectical discernment, of a particularly Catholic kind. This operation begins from a *No!* – the role of philosophy must not be forgotten! – but enjoins a larger *Yes!* – philosophy is required if the different cultures are to talk to each other and bear fruit in their exchange.[38] The Catholic dialectic at work in this approach is nothing other than the methodological translation of the Catholicity of the Church, in which universality and particularity are both present, while neither excludes the other, each requires the presence of the other, and the one Church subsists in the whole multitude of races, peoples, tongues and traditions, wherever it appears in its particularity: this is the event of Pentecost ever renewed in history.

Culture, and the diversity of peoples, are not new and unheralded experiences for the Church, for ever since the Gospel was first preached she has been meeting different cultures and contending with them.[39] The meeting of Christian faith with the diversity of cultures brings a new reality into being. In each culture the deepest impulses of human nature find expression – the universal in the particular. Yet the particular way in which the human is expressed is unique to each. Taken together, therefore, the cultures of the world are a variety of approaches to the truth of what we are as human beings. *Fides et ratio* argues that every 'culture contains within itself the capacity for recognizing the divine revelation'.[40]

The decades following the Second Vatican Council have witnessed numerous efforts on the part of Catholics in various parts of the world (notably in Asian and African countries) to realize the expression of their faith in the context of their specific culture and tradition. The faith and culture movement in the Church, which has developed rapidly under the encouragement of the Pontifical Council for Faith and Culture, is in part a product of these efforts toward a deeper inculturation of faith and a more receptive attitude to the particularity of cultures in all their density of meaning and tradition.

Fides et ratio extends positive support to this search, noting, for instance, those in India who seek to 'unlock the treasures from their

---

[38] Cf. *Fides et ratio*, §69.
[39] Cf. *Fides et ratio*, §70.
[40] *Fides et ratio*, §71.

inheritance which can be joined to their faith and so enhance the richness of Christian teaching'.[41] In this instance, the Encyclical proposes three norms or guidelines regarding culture which are not seen as restrictive, but as giving shape to the act of discernment. The *first* of these concerns the universality of the human spirit, which is essentially the same in all cultures. The *third* concerns the distinctiveness of Indian thought (which is not in question) and counsels against regarding every cultural tradition as being purely and simply enclosed in its own particularity, for to do so would run counter to the first. It is with the *second* that the question of Eurocentrism should be raised: 'When the Church deals for the first time with cultures of great importance, but previously unexamined, it must even so never place them before the Greek and Latin inculturation already acquired. Were this inheritance to be repudiated the providential plan of God would be opposed, who guides his Church down the paths of time and history'.[42]

The insistence that the philosophical heritage which the Church received early in its history cannot be renounced is probably aimed critically at the 'de-Hellenization of Dogma/Christianity' movement, which, originating in German liberal protestantism (with Adolf von Harnack) around 1900, has found some Catholic defenders ever since the 1960s. The question can be put in these terms: can truth speak beyond the limits of the cultural form(s) from which it has sprung; can it speak in such a way as to engage all, and to be for each human being a truth which concerns that person, irrespective of the latter's cultural setting? Cultural loss, or the loss of values (including religious ones) inculturated and inherited from the past, is a feature of life in Europe that has prompted Pope John Paul II to appeal to Europeans: 'We must never tire of saying and repeating to Europe: rediscover yourself! Rediscover your soul!'[43] But that is a quite different thing from urging cultural colonialism.

A similar spiritual dynamic governed the encounter of the Fathers of the Church with Greek philosophy. They were far from taking over Hellenistic culture for its own sake, for the inner meaning it had for itself was not the concern of these Christian thinkers. What interested them was neither Greek religion, nor the syncretistic cults of Isis or Serapis, nor the mystery religions. The philosophical impulse of Greece and its

---

[41] *Fides et ratio*, §72.

[42] *Fides et ratio*, §72. The Letter continues: 'This is a law appropriate to the Church of all the ages, even of that which is to come. She will perceive herself enriched from the daily access of treasures acquired from oriental cultures and in this new inheritance she will discover indicators for showing how a fruitful dialogue with these cultures may be entered upon, one which will help humanity in its journey to a new future.'

[43] Pope John Paul II to the *Council of Bishops' Conferences of Europe* (CCEE), 11 October 1997.

achievements through Plato, Aristotle, the Stoics, and Plotinus, on the contrary, exercised the Fathers repeatedly. They appreciated philosophy's purifying critique of polytheism. They saw that the philosophical standpoint had made possible for its adepts a critical distance regarding their own Greek or Latin culture. They realized that this standpoint resulted from the philosophical search for the transcendent, unique divinity, or Logos, or One. The Christian mind met Greek and Hellenistic culture, not in the purely particular features of the latter but at the point where it was moving beyond itself in the direction of universality. This culture was never canonized by the Church, but the most universal results of philosophical thought were sifted through and integrated into what was from the start, and what remained from then on, a Christian theology and anthropology.

Courage for the truth is what the Pope wishes to restore to people. He does so in the evangelical conviction that (only) the truth can and shall make us free.[44] He shares also his conviction that there can be a communion of cultures in the truth that unites them. The divine revelation, he insists, is not an alien and alienating force; far from being foreign to the cultures of the world it answers an inner expectation that is present within every one of them, since each culture expresses what is deepest in the human person, including the desire for self-knowledge, the longing for healing and forgiveness, and the hope for the overcoming of injustice, and for life beyond death.

Names and their significance

Chapter IV of the Encyclical, *Concerning the Relationship between Faith and Reason*, depicts with scope and precision the most important and historic moments in the encounter between Christian faith and the human mind. The survey reflects the patristic and mediaevalist scholarship of the past century. Its narrative character may make it easier to follow than other chapters, and the whole argument of *Fides et ratio* is present here under the historical form of exemplary figures and developments over time. Some interest attaches to the names mentioned and the relative value accorded to them.

Many of the names occasion little surprise: Justin Martyr was a philosopher before his conversion and saw in the Christian faith 'a philosophy which combined certainty with fruitfulness', as did Clement of Alexandria.[45] Origen countered the attacks of the pagan philosopher Celsus, and produced a reasoned 'theology', adopting the word coined

---

[44] Jn 8:32.
[45] Cf. *Fides et ratio*, §38.

by Plato and taken up by Aristotle.[46] Platonic thought was Christianized by the Cappadocian Fathers and the writer known now as Pseudo-Dionysius. St Augustine was of major importance in the exercise of the critical discernment of Neoplatonic thinking, and his expansive mind, together with the exemplary character of his personal story and his saintliness, won him a dominant place for centuries after his time.[47] Tertullian's question, 'What does Athens have in common with Jerusalem?', is a reminder that early Christian thinkers were critically minded and not at all syncretistic in their attitude to pagan intellectual achievements.[48]

Augustine, Anselm of Canterbury, and Aquinas win most notice in this narrative. Anselm is mentioned in Chapter I to illustrate (through a quotation from the *Proslogion* – the longest quotation in *Fides et ratio*) the kind of focussing and stretching of the reason which faith in the divine mystery alone is capable of bringing about. He figures as a great exponent of the *intellectus fidei* – 'faith seeking understanding'.[49] His exemplarity is drawn out over two pages; in what is certainly the most striking tribute paid to that brilliant and saintly mind in any official document of the Church.

'A quite special place' is accorded to St Thomas Aquinas, 'who gave pride of place to the harmony which exists between faith and reason.' His is the only name to receive a particular section-heading: 'The enduring originality of the propositions of St Thomas Aquinas'.[50] An exegesis is offered of Aquinas's threefold distinction regarding wisdom: philosophical wisdom, which is based on the capacity of the intellect, for all its limitations, to understand reality; theological wisdom, which explores the content of faith on the basis of Revelation; and infused wisdom which, as the direct gift of the Holy Spirit, enables judgment to be formed according to divine truth. The tribute to St Thomas concludes: 'In him, the Church's Magisterium has seen and recognized the passion for truth; and, precisely because it stays consistently within the horizon of universal, objective and transcendent truth, his thought scales "heights unthinkable to human intelligence". Rightly, then, he may be called an "apostle of the truth". Looking unreservedly to truth, the realism of Thomas could recognize the objectivity of truth and produce not merely a philosophy of "what seems to be" but a philosophy of "what is".'[51]

[46] Cf. *Fides et ratio*, §39.
[47] Cf. *Fides et ratio*, §40.
[48] Cf. *Fides et ratio*, §41.
[49] Cf. *Fides et ratio*, §42.
[50] 'Perennis sancti Thomae Aquinatis sententiarum novitas'. In §45, Albert the Great is associated with Aquinas as early defenders in the university of the autonomy of philosophy and the sciences, but also of their organic link with theology.
[51] Cf. *Fides et ratio*, §44.

This invocation of the realism of the Thomistic philosophy of being resonates with the very core of what *Fides et ratio* has to say in promotion of philosophy within Catholic circles in §§80–83: such philosophy should have a sapiential dimension, it should be realistic (not concerned simply with phenomena, nor relativist) and it should be genuinely metaphysical, and thus capable of grounding the concept of personal dignity. The incorporation into this section of quotations from Pope Leo XIII from the encylical *Aeterni Patris* and Pope Paul VI's encyclical *Lumen ecclesiae* (1974) in praise of St Thomas emphasizes the continuous advocacy of his method and thought on the part of the papacy.

Aquinas is proposed as a model to theologians, in a way that has disconcerted, even distressed, some Catholic philosophers.[52] On the other hand, the context of §§43–44 is Christian wisdom, and the recommendation to Catholic theologians to take up Aquinas is quite appropriate here. His philosophy, however, is not forgotten in *Fides et ratio*. The name of Aquinas is repeated in ways that are instructive – in §61, 'surprise and sorrow' is the reaction of the Pope to the neglect of Aquinas's thought, and also of 'scholastic philosophy and in general the whole philosophical discipline', which has affected many Catholic institutions 'since the end of Vatican II', and which extends to theologians;[53] in this regard 'the requirements of the Magisterium' have frequently not been followed and curricula have been watered down, philosophy being marginalized in favour of 'the human sciences'. The papal Magisterium's consistent support for Thomistic thought is footnoted, for emphasis. In §57, *Aeterni Patris* is recalled, and Leo XIII's insistence on the 'incomparable importance' (the Latin here emphasizes pre-eminence: *incomparabilis S. Thomae philosophiae praestantiam*) of the *philosophy* of St Thomas is reaffirmed. In §78, Aquinas is recommended as a model for theologians, not for the sake of imposing particular opinions or views or philosophical positions of his, but precisely because of his philosophical gifts and the respect he showed for the order of reason even as he upheld the irreducible originality of revealed truth.

The value of St Thomas's philosophical thought has in recent decades come to be widely acknowledged and appreciated in university circles very little touched by direct Catholic influence, and in particular by some philosophers working in the analytic tradition – the dominant voice of Anglo-American philosophy. It is somewhat paradoxical that he goes to some extent unrecognized in his own country, being largely replaced by

[52] Cf. *Fides et ratio*, §43.

[53] A scholarly, positive evaluation of Scholasticism has been written by Paul Gilbert SJ, 'The Richness of Scholasticism', in *L'Osservatore Romano* (English edition) (12–24 March 1999), pp. 8–10.

authors who are thought to be more relevant. The decline of Latin has no doubt something to do with this.

The name of Francisco Suárez appears at §62: he is credited, justly enough, with passing on 'the constructive harmony of faith and reason' to early modern times, and to Lutheran universities as well as Catholic ones. Blaise Pascal is the only thinker of his age to be named, and Kierkegaard is associated with him: both reproached the presumption of rationalists.

The other set of exemplary names at §74 groups notable Christian theologians who were also distinguished philosophers: Gregory of Nazianzen and Augustine; 'the great triad' of Mediaeval Doctors, Anselm, Bonaventure, and Aquinas; and then thinkers of the nineteenth and early twentieth centuries. John Henry Newman is the first of these, not unsurprisingly. Antonio Rosmini is rehabilitated, somewhat unexpectedly, given that a list of forty propositions from his writings was condemned by Leo XIII in 1887. The Thomists Maritain and Gilson follow, and then Edith Stein, whom the Pope has called 'a paradigmatic figure'[54] and 'a symbol embodying the deepest tragedy and the deepest hopes of Europe'.[55] The Pope has much in common with her, both in the personal matter of their shared philosophical concerns, and also more widely in their understanding of phenomenology, Thomism, anthropology and ontology. He holds her up as the latest in the long line of distinguished philosophers who have integrated their faith and their science.

The four Russian names mentioned in *Fides et ratio* are not very well known outside Slavic circles. Perhaps they were put there by the Pope to remind Westerners that Slavic Christian thought is to be taken seriously; himself a Slav, the Pope is conscious of bridging a gulf (both cultural and ecumenical) of experience between West and East. A brief word may be said here about each of these figures.[56]

Piotr Yakovlevich Chaadaev (1794–1856) initiated the 'Destiny of Russia' reflection, asking – can it be that Russia will become the saviour

[54] Speaking to George Weigel; see *Witness to Hope*, p. 540.

[55] Cf. the Apostolic Letter proclaiming St Brigid of Sweden, St Catherine of Siena and St Teresa Benedicta a Cruce (Edith Stein) co-patronesses of Europe, 1 October 1999. See also the Pope's *Homily at the Beatification of Edith Stein*, in John Paul II, *Spiritual Pilgrimage: Texts on Jews and Judaism 1979–1995*, ed. E. J. Fisher and L. Klenicki (New York: Crossroad, 1995).

[56] Robert G. Slesinski has given a panoramic view of these thinkers and their contribution in 'Believing Thought as a Category in Russian Religious Philosophy', *Communio: International Catholic Review* (Fall 1999), pp. 571–82. He is a North American Byzantine Catholic priest, and professor of philosophy at the Catholic Seminary in St Petersburg. His article is well documented with references to primary sources in translation.

of the West and restore the moral and religious values sacrificed by the Enlightenment? At first rather negative regarding Russian culture, he later tended towards a positive appreciation: its relative isolation had spared it the decadence induced by modern philosophy. His successors deepened and focussed his criticism of Western empiricism and rationalism, retaining the sense of a providential, spiritual destiny attaching to the Slavic peoples. Khomiakov and Kireevsky are not mentioned in *Fides et ratio*, despite their historical significance – perhaps for the reason that Vladimir Soloviev (1853–1900) mastered their themes and surpassed all previous Russian thinkers in systematic power. He was heir to the Slavophile tradition. He contrasted and confronted the power of living, 'integral', mystical-religious and metaphysical consciousness with the abstract formalism of Western rationalists, and was a critic of the reductivism of positivism. He argues that the fragmentation of the philosophical discipline induced by specialization, and secularization of thought, can only be countered from the higher vantage point of realist Christian belief, otherwise thinking will end in scepticism and nihilism. Fr Pavel A. Florensky (1882–1937) developed similar themes. For his principal work, *The Pillar and the Ground of the Truth*,[57] he chose the epigraph 'Knowledge becomes love' – taken from the *Soul and Resurrection* of St Gregory of Nyssa. The ultimate ground of truth is the Trinity of divine persons, or absolute love. Vladimir N. Lossky is somewhat better known in Western lands than the other three names, for he wrote extensively on the Cappadocians and the apophaticism through which they sought to preserve the transcendent mystery of God.

What kind of philosophy – and what kind of theology?

Fides et ratio is neither a textbook of philosophy or of theology, nor does it prescribe future researches. It is more like a framework document for the pursuit of Christian and Catholic wisdom in both present and future. It gives some clear, general orientations, regarding at once the directions to be avoided (such as rationalism and fideism) and the approaches to be favoured (metaphysics and realism). No programme is to be found in it for some new and unheralded Christian philosophy. The document may be said to foresee that future developments in what we may loosely term 'Christian philosophy' will come about as organic extensions of its rich and multiform past. The nature of these cannot be forecast, any more than the contributions made over the past century could have been foreseen at the time when Leo XIII issued *Aeterni Patris*. The expected and

[57] Translated by Boris Jakim and published under this title in English (Princeton, NJ: Princeton University Press, 1997). It was first published in Moscow in 1914.

hoped-for developments will contain new things, yet they will manifest at the same time some continuity with the names cited in *Fides et ratio* itself, from Origen to Edith Stein.[58]

The traditional description of philosophy as the handmaiden of theology, which was meant to express the interlinking of the two disciplines is repudiated, because it is irreconcilable with the due autonomy of philosophical method;[59] which is not to deny that philosophy should continue to be invoked as an indispensable aid to the *intellectus fidei*[60] but only to recognize that this instrumental role does not exhaust the value of philosophy.[61] The same consideration precludes the Church from having an official philosophy. Despite the unparalleled position which *Fides et ratio* accords to St Thomas Aquinas, it does not 'officalize' his philosophy in the way that *Aeterni Patris* did. Instead we find the following positive recommendation regarding philosophy: 'Whoever today wishes to respond as philosophers to the demands which the word of God imposes upon human reflection should, we believe, work out their ideas in accordance with these demands, and should also point out their coherence with the great tradition, beginning with the ancients, passing through the Fathers of the Church and the masters of Scholasticism and coming at last to an understanding of the particular fruits of more recent and even contemporary reflection. Philosophers who know how to apply this tradition and allow themselves to be directed by it certainly will not be unfaithful to the demand for the autonomy of philosophical research'.[62] There can be no doubt that the Pope is advocating an approach to faith and reason, and to the place of philosophy in Catholic

---

[58] Writing on *Fides et ratio* and its challenge to Catholic thinkers, Thomas Kelly has said: 'Here, then, is a task to be performed both by philosophers and theologians, working in harmony. The vindication of faith in a non-fideistic way must show that the nature of the rational life which philosophy both is and uncovers, the truth of the person, is not only preserved by faith but that it is deepened and extended by faith. Such a vindication, in short, must show that reason is not lost or derailed in faith, but that in faith reason becomes even more itself than it could ever have hoped to be without faith. This is what it means to say that faith is the fulfilment of reason. Indeed, this completion is only a particular instance of what grace always achieves – we become more ourselves by loving God, not less. We become more ourselves in accepting the love of God than we ever could hope to have seen otherwise. Losing our lives is, we are assured, saving our lives'. Thomas Kelly, '*Intelligo ut Credam*: Reason and Philosophy in Relation to Faith', in *The Diakonia of Truth*, ed. J. McEvoy (forthcoming).

[59] *Fides et ratio*, §77; see also §§49, 73, 75, 78.

[60] *Fides et ratio*, §5.

[61] *Fides et ratio*, §3. For a lively comment see J. L. A. Garcia, 'Death of the (Hand)maiden: Contemporary Philosophy in Faith and Reason', *Logos: A Journal of Catholic Thought and Culture* 2 (1999), pp. 11–19.

[62] *Fides et ratio*, §85. The reflection on the importance of tradition which immediately follows the above is doubtless made with Hans-Georg Gadamer in mind.

education, which is identical to one the Second Vatican Council intended the Church to take.

To whom is *Fides et ratio* addressed?

Every encyclical letter is addressed in the first place to the Pope's 'venerable brother bishops', 'with whom I share the mission of "proclaiming the truth openly" '.[63] Some bishops will carry direct responsibility for teaching or research institutions located in their dioceses and provinces. Unusually, the Letter makes a direct address also to 'philosophers and theologians whose vocation it is to explore different aspects of the truth, and finally [to] all of those who are still seeking it'.[64] Similar categories recur towards its close: to theologians a plea is made in favour of breadth of approach, together with consciousness of the philosophical heritage, of the philosophical implications of Christianity, and of the need for critical dialogue with contemporary thought. Those responsible for priestly formation, and for the teaching of theology and philosophy in ecclesiastical faculties, are also addressed directly.[65] The Encyclical turns then to philosophers and teachers of philosophy, repeating the plea of the document for extension of intellectual range and the pursuit of wisdom.[66] Scientists are next: they are challenged to remember that their research takes place within a horizon, and that truth attained to always leaves more to discover, as it points beyond itself towards something higher.[67] Finally, to everyone there is addressed an appeal to true wisdom as the deepest calling and realization of self.[68]

These widening circles of addressees, unusual in encyclicals, reflect fittingly the subject matter of the Letter, which is a defence of truth in the widest and strongest sense – a challenge which embraces all of humanity. Much as *Gaudium et spes* (Vatican II's Pastoral Constitution on the Church in the Modern World) in virtue of its message addressed 'not only the children of the Church but all humanity' (Preface, 2), and before then Pope John XXIII spoke to 'all men of good will', so *Fides et ratio* hopes to speak to the humanity of all, in all cultures and conditions of life.

[63] *Fides et ratio*, §6, citing 2 Cor 4:2.
[64] *Fides et ratio*, §6.
[65] *Fides et ratio*, §105.
[66] *Fides et ratio*, §106.
[67] *Fides et ratio*, §106.
[68] *Fides et ratio*, §107.

Petrine diakonia

Rome exercises a presiding, primatial function within the Communion of the Catholic Bishops. By history and culture it is administratively adapted to studying wider issues that concern the entire Church, and doing so in a way that local conferences of bishops cannot always manage to do. The Petrine See calls to the attention of local bishops underlying or overarching questions that concern the whole Church. It might, I think, be said that the Holy Father exemplifies his own thesis about philosophy and theology, and that he does so with considerable distinction: both disciplines, philosophy and theology, make their best contribution to wisdom when they are integrated in the mind of the Christian believer. There they are not schizophrenically separated – each retains its specific character. Neither obscures the other, neither borrows the other's clothes, each is what it is. Neither ever replaces faith, which is beyond rational discovery, and imparted through the gift of God's self-revelation. Provided that the two disciplines are integrated (and not simply mixed) in such a mind, then they cease to be simply two unrelated disciplines and two methods. They become dynamically-interacting partners in the search for truth, and also in its exploration and expression.

Writing about this Encyclical, W. Norris Clarke, SJ, has described it as a 'remarkable one in many ways. Athough he never talks about himself in it, it is actually the distillation, worked out over some eight to ten years, of his own personal experience of what it means to be a fully alive Catholic intellectual, reflecting at the same time the authentic Catholic tradition of what it means to be a fully developed *Christian mind*, with its two complementary dimensions, faith and *reason*.'[69]

Avery Dulles draws the following striking analogy, with which we bring this commentary to a close: 'Faith and reason, as described by John Paul II, are united like the two natures of Christ, which coexisted without confusion or alteration in a single person. Christian wisdom, similarly, involves a synthesis of theology and philosophy, each supporting and benefiting the other . . . The entire Encyclical is an inspiring summons to the pursuit of a wisdom in which theology and philosophy are harmoniously integrated to the advantage of both and the detriment of neither.'[70]

---

[69] W. Norris Clarke SJ, 'John Paul II: The Complementarity of Faith and Philosophy in the Search for Truth', *Communio: International Catholic Review* (Fall 1999), pp.557–70. This entire issue was dedicated to the Encyclical.

[70] Avery Cardinal Dulles SJ, 'Can Philosophy be Christian?', *First Things* 102 (2000), p. 27.

Practical Considerations about Teaching Philosophy and Theology Now[1]

WAYNE J. HANKEY

Theology and metaphysics (or first philosophy) are theoretical disciplines anticipating and preparing us for contemplative union. Subordinating them to ends beneath this highest good diminishes their proper freedom. This liberty derives from their relation to the end in itself, by nature elevated beyond being used. The destruction of this freedom is, and ultimately proves itself to be, both impossible and ruinous for those who attempt to manipulate truth. Such subordinations and manipulations are the special temptations of the Church generally, from top to bottom, as well as of those who are particularly called to tell the truth in her. Theologians and philosophers who have surrendered *theoria* to *praxis* and *poiēsis*, and who need a severe *metanoia* may be willing to listen to the plea in *Fides et ratio* to respect the integrity of truth in so far as it comes from the same Pope who used the turn of the millennium for ecclesial repentance.

It is impossible to come to *Fides et ratio* without drawing back at the recollection of the Encyclical *Aeterni Patris* of Leo XIII, the centenary of which occurred in the reign of John Paul II. Leo's Encyclicals of a hundred years ago have greatly influenced the present Pontiff. Though the subject of the two letters is the same – faith and reason looked at largely in terms of theology and philosophy – their differences are crucially important. The present Encyclical is more narrowly concerned with the state of the Church's intellectual life, does not impose a particular philosophy – even if certain directions are lamented and criticized, while others are proposed and hoped for. *Fides et ratio* may perhaps be an act of reparation in so far as it recommends thinkers condemned or dismissed in the nineteenth century turn to neo-Thomism. In that vain attempt to remedy her political and social situation, as well as

[1] Begun while I was a Visiting Fellow at Clare Hall in Cambridge University and completed when I was a Visiting Scholar at Boston College and Harvard University, this essay owes much to my hosts, whom I thank.

to resist modernity, the Church was guilty of fabricating a philosophy, falsely projected on to St Thomas, for purposes alien to his own. Though I suggest below that its results were not all bad, in the Church we are still troubled everywhere and everyday by the wreckage remaining from the collapse of that impossible and typically modern experiment in exploiting the philosophical past. The revolutionary iconoclasms of the necessary reaction against it leave us impoverished. We have also the sad recollection of the miserable abuse of the mediaevals, whose thought was colonized. Real, fruitful and distinctive intellectual Catholic engagement with modern philosophy was condemned, while Thomas was reconstructed as a modern rationalist in the war against modern rationalism. Only since Vatican II liberated him from servitude, has Aquinas been able to make his particular contribution authentically. Freed from having to bless every enterprise of philosophical theology which sought ecclesiastical approbation, his own proper thought now enjoys the revival which its excellence merits and excites.

In any new attempt to enter the middle ground between philosophy and theology, the Church now, in so far as it has an organized practical will, must respect the freedom of the philosophical and theological spirit. The nature of the things themselves requires it. And because it is essential to her own endeavour to restore *theoria*, and because of her terrible experience with the alternative, she must let 'the wind blow where it wills' trusting in the Spirit of truth. How, then, can there be practical considerations about teaching philosophy and theology now?

Fides et ratio identifies grave problems in present philosophy, in the relations of philosophy and theology, and consequently in theology. These cannot be rectified by the creation of philosophies or theologies to order, or by the anachronistic retrieval and manipulation of past intellectual forms as if they were ours immediately. However, the provision of the right circumstances for the study and teaching of philosophy and theology is of necessity a practical matter – for this we have colleges, universities, seminaries, institutes, and *studia*, professors and deans, credentials, degrees, certificates and the like. Here there is much which urgently needs doing.

Philosophia ancilla theologiae

One of the most lamentable recent developments in the Anglo-American world is the more and more general possibility of studying theology as a first degree. I distinguish this from the availability or even prescription of a limited number of classes in theology as a supplement to other arts and sciences, including philosophy, provisions which may be appropriate. Students, often nearly illiterate even at the greatest universities, are

encouraged to make theology their primary study. By illiterate I mean that very many of them cannot write or speak grammatically, let alone in a decent literary or rhetorical style. Even worse, these same students cannot read, that is, they cannot get beyond 'word-bites' to the logical structure of a sentence, a paragraph or an essay. They think, speak and write in clichés. Most of them have no language except English (and that barbarically). If another language has been acquired, it will rarely be Greek, Latin or Hebrew, and it will usually have been taught in the present conversational mode, which excludes analysis of grammatical structure. Such students will have virtually no philosophy beyond the sentimental, ideological or doxological treatments schools sometimes provide. The result is a student who has little capacity to read texts (and almost certainly no discipline of reading), who knows nothing of the history of philosophy or of culture generally, and who has no training in discerning or critically examining arguments. Such students can be told almost anything – and they are!

Theological movements now sweeping the Anglo-American world feed upon these kinds of illiteracy, upon ignorance of history, literature and philosophy, and upon the absence of a disciplined critical faculty. What passes for theology are, in fact, ideological fantasies or fables about our origins and cultural history. Their authors, supposing that they write in a poetic ecstasy, instead produce yet another form of the past pre-packaged for touristic consumption. We have another 'colonization' of the philosophical and theological tradition, but this time with a sophisticated post-modern 'strategy of deception'.[2] Representations of that history, set out by teachers without the tools or disciplines to write it, commit the most elementary errors.[3] These are accepted by students without knowledge of the texts being manipulated and without the capacities needed to judge what they are being taught. Philosophy has been absorbed within this pseudo-theology. The proper distance between the two disciplines and their proper autonomy are denied. Though such movements are praised (with some justice if the circumstances in which they have arisen are considered) for opening theology to its wider tradition and resources, in fact, students are deprived of truth about the tradition at the same moment that they suppose they have gained access to it. Their state is a dangerous union of ignorance and arrogance. Those who have respect for the dignity and

---

[2] J. Hanvey, 'Conclusion: Continuing the Conversation', in L. P. Hemming, (ed.), *Radical Orthodoxy? – A Catholic Inquiry* (Aldershot: Ashgate, 2000), pp. 155 and 164.

[3] See N. Lash, 'Where does Holy Teaching Leave Philosophy? Questions on Milbank's Aquinas', *Modern Theology* 15 (1999), pp. 433–4; W. J. Hankey, 'Why Philosophy Abides for Aquinas', *The Heythrop Journal* 42 (2001), pp. 329–48.

needs of theology – and this is surely a place for ecumenical co-operation – will seek the required educational reforms. In the broadest sense, this entails the restoration of philosophical study – as *Fides et ratio* maintains. Here the Catholic Church, in part because of what was positive in her experience in the neo-Thomist revival, has something particular to contribute.

Some of Pope John Paul's hopes and prescriptions for philosophy in *Fides et ratio* may seem too determined by his own intellectual experience, horizons and history, and may appear too much the habitual repetition of typical Catholic judgments, to recommend themselves outside a narrow circle. What, however, in them seems altogether necessary to correct the present distortions of our minds, is the call to a deeper wonder and awe, to genuine openness and receptivity, to *theoria* and contemplation as both necessary to the beginning, and also subsisting at the heart, of philosophy.

The lack of these in most of Anglo-American 'Analytic' philosophy has driven theologians, especially in England, where little else is available at the centres which establish the norms, to the absorption of philosophy within theology. Their good purposes are both to challenge the arrogance of secular reason and to provide the Christian mind, imagination, memory and love with what is broader, deeper and richer than the 'Analytic' tradition usually provides. These theologians rightly aim to restore to philosophy herself the millennium and a half largely missing from the normative Anglo-American philosophical memory. The universities at the imperial centres, whose certified 'philosophers' prescribe what counts as reason in our world, normally exclude from 'Philosophy' what falls between Ancient Scepticism and Descartes. Eliminated from 'Philosophy' are those Platonisms, ancient and mediaeval, which were essential to the formation of Christian doctrine and in which philosophy, theology and religion recognized and embraced their mutual dependence. By this exclusion, these universities and their 'philosophers' serve and subordinately determine the structures of the secularized Protestant world.

Philosophy in the Catholic colleges and universities of the Anglo-American world – which substantially means North America, the place of almost all of these – has a different history and character from that in England, or in the state or private, but definitively secularized Protestant universities of America. This Catholic difference is the result of the reign of neo-Thomism.[4] In Catholic institutions, the reaction against the

[4] See W. J. Hankey, 'From Metaphysics to History, from Exodus to Neoplatonism, from Scholasticism to Pluralism: the fate of Gilsonian Thomism in English-speaking North America', *Dionysius* 16 (1998), pp. 157–88.

narrow, sharply ideological, and exclusive rationalism of this Thomism – ironically comparable in this regard to 'Analytic' philosophy – turned enough toward 'Continental' philosophy to produce a pluralism not found at Oxbridge and scarcely in the Protestant Ivy League.[5] During and after Vatican II, Catholic philosophers and theologians discovered much of what they had sought in Thomism in various renditions of Heidegger. His engagement with the sweep of Western history entailed, sometimes paradoxically, that Catholic philosophy included or even privileged what Protestant secular philosophy excluded. Ironically, the Platonic tradition, and its 'negative theology', were retrieved as a substitute for or way of saving mediaeval philosophy from Heidegger's critique.[6] Now, however, as Catholics move into the centres of power and prestige, and as 'Continental' philosophy enters new stages of post-modern deconstruction, the temptation is to 'up-grade' to the imperial centre, to increase power and respectability by accepting its defining exclusions. To do this would be not only to conform our minds to the ruling secular culture, but also to throw away part of what has been so painfully gained in the last two centuries of struggle about philosophy within the Church.

Fidelity to that experience requires that, after freedom, the first characteristic of philosophy, as it is cultivated among us, must be openness to its full history and to the full range of its schools, traditions and methods. The freedom which is essential to philosophy and to the academy means that, in principle, providing for this should be left to the philosophers themselves, but intervention from above will be required when the *odium philosophicum* reaches as far as its periodically ascendant desire to win the argument by purging the adversaries.

Learning to read

I have treated the necessity for the study of philosophy as distinct from and preliminary to theology under the traditional (and also Thomistic, though not exclusively)[7] tag *philosophia ancilla theologiae*. This is in

---

[5] See J. D. Caputo, 'Philosophy and Prophetic Postmodernism: Toward a Catholic Postmodernity,' *American Catholic Philosophical Quarterly* 74 (2001), pp. 549–67, especially pp. 550–5.

[6] See Caputo, 'Philosophy and Prophetic Postmodernism', pp. 555–67; J.-M. Narbonne, *Hénologie, ontologie et Ereignis: Plotin, Proclus, Heidegger*, L'ane d'or 15 (Paris: Les Belles Lettres, 2001) and W. J. Hankey, 'Denys and Aquinas: Antimodern Cold and Postmodern Hot', *Christian Origins: Theology, Rhetoric and Community*, ed. Lewis Ayres and Gareth Jones, Studies in Christian Origins (London: Routledge, 1998), pp. 139–84.

[7] See *Summa Theologiae* 1.5 ad 2, and R. D. Crouse, 'St. Thomas, St. Albert, Aristotle: *Philosophia Ancilla Theologiae*', *Atti del Congresso Internazionale Tommaso nel suo settimo centenario*, i (Naples: Edizioni Domenicane Italiane, 1975), pp. 181–5.

part to prevent the assumption that philosophy is preliminary in the sense that its study (and especially those parts of it most necessary for theology) can be completed some time before taking up the disciplines of theology. Neither Plato nor Aristotle supposed that the young were capable of the highest philosophical work. Aquinas follows them, Moses Maimonides, and others in this. The abstractness of philosophy generally, and of metaphysics particularly, the weakness of our minds which must be strengthened by mathematical and other studies, the extent of the ground which must be covered to reach it, the length of time traversing this takes, the need for developed moral virtues and the proper temperament, are all reasons why we require the gift of faith.[8] Faith gives a knowledge necessary for salvation which philosophy cannot by itself attain. Nonetheless, philosophy, acquired with such difficulty, remains subordinately necessary not only because one of its parts is theology, but also for the sake of that theology which is Sacred Doctrine.

Formally reading (*lectio*), that is expositing and commenting on the works of Aristotle, an activity by which Aquinas carried forward the philosophical tradition as it had come down to him from the Arabs and late antiquity, was not a preliminary exercise belonging to Thomas's early years. Almost all of his twelve commentaries on the works of The Philosopher were undertaken in the last six years of his writing and, like the *Summa Theologiae*, five were left unfinished.[9] Since this reading continued along with the writing of his own proper *Summa*, Aquinas clearly found engaging the philosophical tradition to be necessary to his work as a Christian theologian. In our circumstances, were the study of philosophy to be completed as a temporal preliminary to the study of Sacred Doctrine, it would have been reduced either to a contentless lexicon, or to a sceptical sophistic, or to the dogmatic repetition of a 'science'. It would again have lost the freedom which belongs to its anticipatory participation in the absolute cosmic goal.

The kind of philosophical study which is temporally prior to proper theological thinking, and which is suitable for the young, is pointed to by reading (*lectio*), as Aquinas and his contemporaries practised it. This reading was an act of critical reception. For Aquinas and his predecessors, *lectio* is not passive receptivity. It involves both philo-

[8] *Sententia Libri Ethicorum*, 6.7 (Leonine 47/2, pp. 358–9); *Super Boetium de Trinitate*, 3.1 (Leonine 50, p. 108); *Quaestiones Disputatae de Veritate*, 14.10 (Leonine 22/2, p. 467); *Summa Theologiae*, 1a.1.1; *Super Librum de Causis Expositio*, prooemium (Saffrey p. 2).

[9] I. Aertsen, 'Aquinas's Philosophy in its Historical Setting', *The Cambridge Companion to Aquinas*, ed. N. Kretzmann and E. Stump (Cambridge: Cambridge University Press, 1993), p. 20; M. D. Jordan, *The Alleged Aristotelianism of Thomas Aquinas*, The Etienne Gilson Series 15 (Toronto: Pontifical Institute of Mediaeval Studies, 1992), pp. 9–10.

sophical and historical judgment. Historical investigation, dialectical inquiry and rational demonstration are all part of philosophy as textual commentary. The commentator determines the subject and nature of the work, and to what philosophical tradition it belongs. The commentary shows how the text stands to that tradition, sorting out what in the work is genuinely within the philosophical school, what is inauthentic, what has been distorted, and where the author, moved perhaps by a better authority or reason, has taken another path. Aquinas distinguishes conclusions from the arguments which are supposed to support them. He seeks to identify the fundamental principles and the particular kinds of reasoning which distinguish schools from one another. He sorts out the contributions, oppositions, concords and complementarities of the philosophical traditions. We need to imitate his patient and careful reading.

Nonetheless, to bring mediaeval *lectio* into the present, we must correct Aquinas' approach to compensate for the systematization, simplifications and reductions of philosophy to which its neo-Thomistic form showed it to be subject. We must broaden his history of philosophy both forwards and backwards – Aquinas probably never read a dialogue of Plato! The study of philosophy proper must be supplemented with, and even grounded in, the linguistic, literary, and historical knowledge and appreciation he lacked – in short with what the Renaissance Humanists added to education. And recollecting that philosophy once included these, we must add what of modern mathematics, natural and social science is necessary to appreciate the modern construction of the human world. In short, the preliminary to theological study is an option within the Liberal Arts and Science undergraduate curriculum as it has been developed in North America. The traditional forms of that curriculum must be modified to match the present 'illiterate' students as I have defined them above. This modification involves facing frankly the point from which education now begins for most students, but not relenting on the linguistic, literary, historical, mathematical, scientific and philosophical requirements which theological study makes.

I have already named some of the characteristics of the study which is preliminary to sacred doctrine: freedom, openness to the full history of philosophy and to the full range of its schools, traditions and methods, actively receptive reading which is careful, patient and critical. To these must be added the breadth and depth of a humanistic and modern liberal education. The alternatives are either a return to the Scylla of philosophy as neo-scholastic dogmatism or the disintegration of history and philosophy in the Charybdis of theology as post-modern mythopoiesis. The Holy Father is right to set us a task which begins by rejecting both of these.

Objective Truth: Relations between Truth and Revelation in the Encyclical *Fides et ratio*

EILERT HERMS

The Encyclical contains what for a Lutheran is a fascinating message. It runs as follows: only when the universal authority of the truth is the sole factor guiding human life, do human beings, as persons, become aware of their destiny and dignity, and thereby also of their inner unity, fullness and freedom. Only then, also, does the communal life of human beings find an appropriate form.[1]

This message needs to be understood accurately, and we therefore need to ask the right sort of questions. The most important one concerns this very issue of how the Encyclical understands truth. What is it referring to when it talks about truth? It becomes clear that it means objective truth, in particular the objective truth of the Absolute – the transcendent ground and goal of all things. This objective truth of Being – and ultimately the Absolute – can only be appropriately understood if it is seen not only as the objective truth *about* the Absolute, but also and at the same time as the objective truth *of* the Absolute itself, enabling all this objective truth about itself. This shows that Absolute Being in itself includes the fact of its being there, truly, for the likes of us to understand and to symbolize. This leads thus to a second question: what does the Encyclical say about how the Absolute is of its very nature accessible to our understanding in this way? Does it develop its fundamental insight about the objective character of truth consistently? These two questions – that of truth and that of its accessibility to us – guide this response to the Encyclical.

How *Fides et ratio* uses the word 'truth'

The Encyclical often talks about 'truths' in the plural, denoting either individual truths or classes of truth.[2] However, the predominant usage of

[1] *Fides et ratio*, §§79, 85, 92.

[2] See e.g. *Fides et ratio*, §§5, 30–3, passim.

'truth' is in the singular. Sometimes it has a specifying attribute; sometimes it is without one; sometimes there are explicit references to unity, totality, universality or the Absolute.[3] 'Truth' without any attribute often refers to the goal towards which each and every instance of human knowledge naturally tends, the aim of all natural human recognitions.[4] Even the loss of eagerness for the truth, of 'concern for the pursuit of truth', can only be recognized as such against the background of a natural orderedness of the human person to truth.[5] Perhaps this fundamental vision of the human as a being-for-truth (*Wahrheitswesen*) is also why the different human cultures can be understood as 'diverse approaches to the truth'.[6] This orientation to truth in human nature implies that there are 'requirements of truth' that need to be satisfied.[7]

Objective truth

What is being referred to here? To start with – those qualities which have to be present for various insights, recognitions, expressions, or systems of expressions to be 'true', something which is proper to all individual, particular 'truths'; in other words, their correspondence with a reality given prior to knowledge and speech. Recognition attains truth 'by the means named by the teachers of Scholasticism the *correspondence between thing and intellect*'. Abstracting from particular content, the truth attained by knowledge is thus, for the Encyclical, always in itself objective truth. At the same time, statements are only true when they are 'objectively true', as in those 'sacred authors' who 'were capable of producing statements of a truly objective character'.[8]

There is a complexity here that already indicates how the phrase 'objective truth' has a diversified – in fact threefold – meaning. Firstly it describes the quality of acts of recognition, or of statements, whereby they appropriately designate their object. But the text also uses it in a second way, albeit related to the first. Philosophy striving for 'objective truth' can only be a 'Philosophy of Being', that is, a knowledge aimed at the very reality of its object. In so far as reason is aiming for 'objective truth', it is aiming at the same time for what is real, for the 'truth of being', for the knowledge of what things truly are, for the recognition of the 'truth of human life', and the truth of the absolute ground of all

---

[3] As in *Fides et ratio*, §2. The usage in the singular with a specifying attribute, *veritas ex philosophica deliberatione percepta* (§9), has the same kind of referent as 'truths' referring to classes of truth, just mentioned. It can be left aside here.

[4] See e.g. *Fides et ratio*, §§3, 22, 33, 82.

[5] *Fides et ratio*, §81.

[6] *Fides et ratio*, §70.

[7] See e.g. *Fides et ratio*, §87.

[8] *Fides et ratio*, §82.

being, in other words the truth of God. The purely formal sense of the phrase 'objective truth', then, exists only alongside a particular reference to an external reality: the truth of objects, the truth of how things are.[9]

Perhaps we can also add a third meaning of 'objective truth'. Truth, however we arrive at it, can itself be an object which knowers or speakers recognize. The Encyclical can talk of truth as an object, which is to be discovered or recognized, and by which we can differentiate between true and false.[10] It can also talk of truth as a reality that grounds certainty, as something which is present, leading us authoritatively on.[11]

There are passages which can only be fully understood if one has all three meanings of 'objective truth' in mind. Thus: 'We should not forget that the neglect of "being" itself involves also a self distancing from objective truth and further from that foundation that supports human dignity'.[12] Such a complex phrase brings out the intrinsic connections between the three meanings of 'objective truth', but does not alter the fact that we are dealing with three irreducibly different realities: truth denoting the rightness of our epistemic dealings with a reality given prior to our knowledge; truth as a characteristic of this reality; and truth as a reality (truth in both the previous senses) confronting *us*. The Encyclical does not differentiate between these three meanings, or consider the distinctive nature of each one. One referent of 'objective truth' is the object *in itself*; another is a *relationship to* that reality. The Encyclical deals with both of these without taking full cognisance of the differentiation, so there are issues here about how reality is present to us which the Encyclical thus elides.

The Encyclical protests the limitation of reality to what can be experienced by one's senses. It insists on the acknowledgment of the realm of reality which surpasses this, calling this the 'metaphysical'. But this still leaves the question open of how to distinguish this pre-existence from the sensual existence within the 'metaphysical' – a matter that requires discussion of the reflexivity of experience. There is another gap too. There is no explicit reflection on the relationship between objectively true knowledge in general and its appropriate expression. The Encyclical does make the claim that true knowledge of reality can be reflected in true linguistic expression, but it does not show us why this should be regarded as more than a mere claim, as something which is already given and available to us.

[9] *Fides et ratio*, §5.
[10] *Fides et ratio*, §25.
[11] *Fides et ratio*, §79.
[12] *Fides et ratio*, §90.

Unity of Truth

With this observation we can leave this discussion of 'objective truth' used without qualification, and pass on to another usage: 'truth' in conjunction with such words as 'unity', 'totality', 'universality', and 'absoluteness'. The 'unity of truth' is often explicitly mentioned, a unity that embraces both truths deriving from natural reason and truths deriving from revelation in Christ.[13] Thus there is a unity of truth both formally and materially. All truths, whether of reason or revelation, share the same formal quality – 'the correspondence between thing and intellect' – and this formal commonality between truths of reason and revelation extends materially to the whole range of possible truths.

The implication of this unity is drawn out in the word 'totality', which seems to refer both to the permanent characteristics of reality, and therein to their transcendent ground, as well as to the transcendent goal of all levels of reality. Only that truth which is 'all-embracing', which is not claimed by any one 'historical expression of philosophy', but rises beyond these 'narrow limits' can offer 'a total explanation of man, the world, and man's relationship to God'.[14] An aspect of this totality is made explicit by the use of the term 'universal', used of truth derived from revelation of Christ, of truth derived from reason, and of truth in general – no matter what its source.

This claim about the universality of truth is only making explicit something already implied: the material totality of truth includes the truth about the transcendent ground and the transcendent goal of all that occurs. This truth transcends all inner-worldly truths, as a truth of another kind, grounding, encompassing and preserving them. It is thus permanently true – true, therefore, for all possible realities or persons participating in truth, true for all times and places within the world. Thus one must hold fast to the idea of the 'persisting value of truth', against a historicist claim 'that what in one age was held to be true can cease to be so at another period'.[15] One must also be clear that '. . . truth can never be limited by time or culture'; on the contrary, though it is recognized in history, it in itself 'goes beyond history'.[16] 'Every truth, even if it is not complete, provided it is authentic, possesses a universal and absolute character. What is true is so for everyone and always.'[17] If truth is 'total', it is 'universal', and therefore permanently valid.

---

13 *Fides et ratio*, §§34, 53, 79.
14 *Fides et ratio*, §51.
15 *Fides et ratio*, §87.
16 *Fides et ratio*, §95.
17 *Fides et ratio*, §27.

The consequence of this is then the relationship between the totality of truth and the Absolute, which is the transcendent ground and goal of all being, and so with what in the biblical and the Greek philosophical tradition is called 'God'.[18] The Encyclical speaks of this Absolute in four ways:

> as Being which is the transcendent, ultimate ground of things and so the source and origin of truth;[19]
> as that goal towards which humanity's natural striving is directed, an ultimate truth which is disclosed in revelation;[20]
> as that which is in the beyond (*jenseitig*) and so which is found by transcending sensual, empirical facts;[21]
> as that which is of absolute value and of itself excludes any kind of doubt.[22]

The Encyclical does not explicitly make an identification of truth with the Absolute; the Absolute, rather, is explicitly identified only with God, and exclusively so – 'God alone is the Absolute'.[23] Obviously this does not exclude the identification of the Absolute *as* truth, given an assumption that God is (absolute) truth – a move which the Encyclical may not make, but which it also does not exclude. Indeed, it is saying something very like this when it says that the search for absolute truth is the search for the Absolute itself, and that every human being's search for truth surpasses all empirical truth and therefore can find fulfilment only in the Absolute.

Quite apart from such implicit hints, however, there is one line of substantive reflection that must compel us to attribute to the Encyclical an understanding of absolute truth not only as the truth *about* the Absolute, but also as the truth *of* the Absolute, that is, the truth identical with the Absolute. The argument goes like this: even the absolute truth is 'objective truth', and absolute truth can only be objective truth if it refers to the truth proper to the Absolute, and this in an appropriate, adequate way. For the Encyclical, objective truth consists in our understanding and speaking being rightly measured against the true and distinctive reality of what is given to us. This being given to us cannot in any sense be something we initiate or ground: it can only be the object itself that does this.

---

18 See *Fides et ratio*, §80.
19 *Fides et ratio*, §22.
20 *Fides et ratio*, §§56, 81.
21 *Fides et ratio*, §5, 83.
22 *Fides et ratio*, §27.
23 *Fides et ratio*, §80.

Therefore, truth about the Absolute can only be objective truth to the extent that the Absolute itself is truly real, and truly real *as* something for us to understand and express. Thus the Absolute – God – can only be the source and origin of objective truth, if it truly exists. But then, and therefore, the Absolute – the transcendent ground of all things – is also the source and origin of all objective truth – even of those truths that are merely truths *about* the world, humanity and individual events, truths which are referred to in the plural because of the plurality of their objects. Ultimately then, the proper revelation of the Absolute to us can be the only foundation for this kind of objective truth. This revelation to us is the ultimate ground of our ability to understand objects and so to know the objective truth about things for ourselves.

How the truth of the Absolute shows itself to people like us

On terminology

Fundamental to the Encyclical's concept of objective truth is the idea of the truth of the Absolute, in the sense of its essential true *Dasein* for us, as something we can appropriately understand. This truth for us is primordially initiated by the Absolute itself, and sustained right through to completion. What follows can only be clear if this reality is clearly expressed. We need a brief formula, but one that makes unmistakably clear this implication of the Encyclical's concept, and also one that does not give occasion to oversimplifications or misunderstandings.

One might at first think that we could use the term 'revelation' for this purpose. This, however, is not appropriate, above all because the Encyclical itself uses the term 'revelation' in a narrower and quite specific sense. Following high scholasticism, it reserves 'revelation' for God's supernatural communication, culminating in Christ; it is continuing the teaching of Trent and of the two Vatican Councils in this regard. We need a term covering a broader reality.

The Encyclical itself offers no term for this purpose. An interpreter has to make a choice. In what follows, I am going to use 'the foundational givenness of the Absolute by itself as something to be understood by us and the likes of us' – or, more briefly, 'the foundational givenness of the Absolute as a reality to be understood by us (*das ursprüngliche Uns-zu-verstehen-Gegebensein des Absoluten*). Implicit in this expression are the following points:

(i) We are dealing with an existence of the Absolute for me, but which does not stand or fall with my existence, but rather has its own identity, preceding and outlasting my existence, and there for me and all possible individuals like me. This applies to human beings collectively as well. We

can participate in proper identity of this being-for (*Seins-für*) thanks to its own initiative, in a way that is for us freely chosen.

(ii) This existence of the Absolute for me and those like me is foundational in two ways. It constitutes our being – both *that* we are and *what* we are; it constitutes our capacities and thus grounds all the acts proper to us or to the likes of us. But there is a second sense of 'foundational' at work here too: the reality of the Absolute for individual finite persons is foundational also for the Absolute itself. This reality-for-us is the free manifestation of its *essence,* of how it specifies itself. This is the reason why this manifestation is the true reality in itself of the Absolute for us. In being-for us, the Absolute is not making a kind of mask for itself, but being its proper self-grounding essence and activity.

(iii) This being-for, foundational in two senses, is for me and such as me, and therefore it also grounds collective life for the likes of us.

(iv) This being-for is given to us as something to be *understood;* it is not arbitrary, but something of its own initiative given for our understanding in an appropriate way.

(v) This being-for is given for *us* as something to understand. We are not simply beings derived from the Absolute: we are individuals who freely and responsibly understand whatever is given us to understand.

(vi) The formula also contains a gerundive construction: '*to be* understood'. We do not simply have a choice in the matter; it is somehow incumbent on our freedom and responsibility.

(vii) Finally the formula points to how this Absolute necessitates us to form our selves, and so to our freedom, our responsibility. We cannot but *in some fashion* respond with our understanding to given reality, but the *how* is not necessitated, in particular not whether this how is appropriate or not. The appropriateness of our understanding of this foundational givenness of the Absolute is a task unavoidably laid upon us, but not something guaranteed.

The substantive question

How, then, does the Encyclical understand and present this fundamental, complex concept? The Encyclical sees itself as continuing the teaching of the First Vatican Council regarding the two orders of knowledge: natural reason, and supernatural revelation in Christ.[24] We need therefore to consider each of these in turn, and then also the disruptive effects of sin. The question is whether it is consistent in its presentation of absolute truth's unity, totality, universality and absoluteness.

---

[24] This happens in connection with the reminder of the continuity of Roman Catholic teachings about the revelation from the Tridentine to the First and Second Vatican Councils, *Fides et ratio*, §§8–9.

Natural reason

Through many expressions, the Encyclical speaks of human longing, striving and seeking for the ultimate objective truth, as we have seen. This yearning is not in vain, because human nature includes an ability to go beyond the merely empirically factual, the world of humanity, and reach the 'truth about being'. We need to ask then four questions:

(i) What constitutes this capacity?
(ii) What grounds it?
(iii) Under what conditions can the potency here become act?
(iv) How far does this capacity extend?

(i) The Encyclical may refer to attempts in epistemology towards describing the basic human capacity for knowledge, but focusses only on how these present themselves as critiques of metaphysics. It only discounts these as unjustified suspicion, or as false, reductive views of the capacity for knowledge inherent in human nature.[25] Against such empiricist reductionism, the Encyclical (correctly) points out that the very fact of reflection and theorizing on human powers of knowledge, and on the *possibilities* thereof – goes beyond what the senses can know, and as such is either meaningless (on the assumption that the truth must be sensorily accessible), or else in itself a proof that our knowledge goes beyond the sensory.[26] The most this proves, however, is that we cannot but avoid presupposing the existence of such a capacity. We have not yet made any progress towards understanding or describing the actual constitution of such a capacity that would enable us to understand objective truth, not only regarding sensory realities, but also 'metaphysical', 'invisible' ones.

Now, it is precisely the epistemologies developed in modernity that have attempted such descriptions, in great detail, and Christian theology has played a part. It follows that the Roman Catholic Church's teaching office needs somehow to take an explicit stand on these. *Fides et ratio* does not get beyond mentioning that it is argument, deductive thought, that moves beyond the sensorily-given to metaphysical truth, attributing such an ability to 'reason' or to 'speculative thought'.[27] In the long run, however, this is not enough: it simply says that we can attain knowledge of objective truth, implicitly restricted to whatever sort of reality happens to be given to us to understand. We need more: we need to *show* that

[25] *Fides et ratio*, §§44, 55, 61.
[26] See esp. *Fides et ratio*, §22.
[27] See e.g. *Fides et ratio*, §40.

what is given to our capacities for knowledge (however construed) goes beyond the sensory, includes something beyond the sensory.

All of which leads one to suggest that the Encyclical may need to develop a more complex view of 'experience' and 'phenomenon'. The text presents 'experience' simply as a medium through which the non-Absolute becomes present,[28] and 'phenomenon' as denoting merely the sensorily given[29] – although the latter also sometimes describes the given in general, not necessarily confined to the sensory.[30] A positive account of how human beings, as naturally constituted, can know truth must surely extend and differentiate these concepts, bringing out the mutual causal relationships between the unitary structure these concepts indicate and the plurality of what is given us. Such an account would also show how this unitary structure is included within the givenness that provides us, such as we are, the possibility (NB – the *natural* possibility) of objective truth about the Absolute also – in other words, in what we have just been talking about: the foundational givenness of the Absolute as a reality to be understood by us.

(ii) What grounds this natural capacity? The Encyclical neither contains nor hints at a detailed account of the range of possible objects of human knowledge, but in effect it presupposes that only through this foundational givenness of the Absolute as something to be understood by us is this scope of our knowledge opened up to the objective truth of the Absolute.

Humanity's natural striving for the 'ground of all things', for 'being, the transcendent and the Absolute' is not in vain, because this search and striving is already founded by, motivated by, grounded in, and orientated towards an already existing basic certainty. 'The very capacity to search for the truth and make inquiry about it has of itself created the initial response. Man would never embark on the search for anything he knew nothing about or which he supposed to be quite beyond his reach. Even the hope of arriving at some answer can set a man on the first stage of his journey.'[31] At first sight, this basic certainty seems only that of our own existence – over and above that its content seems only negative (certainty of one's own necessary mortality), and the form it takes is interrogative. However, it really does ground humanity's natural openness for the universal and the transcendent, as ancient philosophers show who were 'concerned with teaching a method by which the mind, freed from all external constraints, could emerge from the constrictions of

[28] As in *Fides et ratio*, §§80, 83.
[29] *Fides et ratio*, §§82, 83.
[30] See *Fides et ratio*, §§67, 81.
[31] *Fides et ratio*, §29.

fables and so be able to open itself up to a higher realm. The mind, therefore, purged and made righteous could rise to the higher degrees of meditation and so provide intelligent creatures with strong grounds for a transcendent and absolute being.'[32]

None of our acts of moving beyond or above in this way are made possible by themselves; they are rooted in this logically prior reality that is given to them. The point is made quite explicitly clear when the philosophy of being is described as follows: 'the philosophy of being is an active or dynamic philosophy, which presents truth by means of structures which are at the same time ontological, causal, and capable of being shared with others. It discovers its impetus and continual impulse in the very fact that it is upheld by the act of "being", and as a result it possesses a complete and general access to a solid universe of things and goes beyond every limit to arrive at him in whom the consummation of all things is attained.'[33] The possibility of our natural knowledge and recognition of the ground and origin of all things is grounded in the foundational givenness of the Absolute as something to be understood by us. Paul talks about this in the first chapter of his Letter to the Romans, as does the old saying concerning God's revelation in the book of nature.[34]

(iii) However, this understanding of how our natural potency to know the Absolute is grounded leaves open the question of *how* this potency is *actualized*. The answer emerges from the fact that humanity is not only the being that searches for the objective truth of the Absolute, but also the being that is social. Thus, humanity's natural ability to know the objective truth of the Absolute can only develop into actual knowledge only through *dialogue* with others.[35]

This principle expresses a general prerequisite for knowledge rooted in human nature. It applies not only to knowledge of the Absolute, but also to knowledge of all truth. According to the Encyclical, the activity of knowing the truth always occurs as man accepts truths that have already been known by the community into which he was born and in which he grew up, on which he depends and for which he is responsible. This acceptance happens as follows: individuals receive statements claimed to be true, then 'believe' ('credit') them for themselves, 'instinctively' and because they trust those who passed them on to them. Because all real knowledge of truth is mediated through dialogue in society, man is not merely a being asking about truth, but also a being of faith: 'the one who

32 *Fides et ratio*, §41.
33 *Fides et ratio*, §97.
34 *Fides et ratio*, §§19, 22.
35 *Fides et ratio*, §§31–3.

lives trusting in others'. 'Believe' here (*credere*, *fidere*) means 'to accept as true statements that have been handed down as claiming to be true, on the basis of instinct and the trustworthiness of the one handing down'. The Encyclical gives precedence to the various forms of knowledge itself for two reasons. Firstly, this faith exists before knowledge in the proper sense; only subsequently – as part of the process of personal growth and maturity – does one start critically to question truth-claims handed down, and either discard them or reappropriate them. Secondly, this subsequent process occurs only with some of the claims handed on as true. Believed truths (in this sense) remain always far greater in number than the ones we question.[36]

In many respects, these points are unexceptionable. The fact that dialogue and the acceptance of truth-claims handed down are permanent prerequisites for the activity and process of human knowledge of truth is something that it is possible to overlook, but one cannot consistently deny it. So too the point about what is accepted without being tested as far greater in quantity than what one thinks through for oneself. The Encyclical is right in its claim that the social quality of our existence makes our knowledge of truth always knowledge of 'the truth of the person', knowledge of the person's 'self-giving and fidelity' in relationship with others. Above all it is right in stating that the acceptance of a truth-claim 'on the basis of trust between people', though *supported* by the known truth regarding the reliability of the person making the claim, is nevertheless *ordered to* the truth itself pointed out by this person.[37]

(iv) These considerations suggest that we also have to be more specific about the *limitations* of humanity's natural capacity to know objective truth. The text makes an obvious and clear distinction between such limitations that arise from original sin and other limitations inherent in the sheer fact of being created.[38] The question arises as to how such a distinction should be drawn. Since limitations arising from sin are made possible by the limitations inherent in created human nature, we will begin by considering the latter. The natural human capacity for knowledge includes the capacity to know realities beyond the sensory (for example, realms of possibility). It follows, therefore that it is aware of its own *natural* limitation.[39] What does this limitation consist in? There are two possibilities.

This primal limitation could be primarily one of power (and then secondarily one of extent). In other words, the limitation would arise

[36] *Fides et ratio*, §31.
[37] *Fides et ratio*, §32.
[38] *Fides et ratio*, §§22, 80–1.
[39] *Fides et ratio*, §42.

mainly from how the human capacity for knowledge is constituted: it is fundamentally passive, receptive, grounded on a condition of possibility which is distinct. This would mean that it could never appropriate this condition through its knowledge – from which would arise the limitation on the extent of this power: the foundational givenness of the Absolute as a reality to be understood by us would be from beginning to end more than what we, such as we are, could draw into our understanding.

Such an account of our epistemic limitation as primarily one of power can without contradiction be set alongside the Encyclical's dominant account of objective truth as absolute, total and unitary. Our recognition of natural limitation coincides with our knowledge of the Absolute as in its essence 'source and origin'. So construed, the limitation of our natural capacity for knowledge lies in the relationship of dependence between all knowledge possible to us and its condition of possibility: the foundational givenness of the Absolute as a reality for us to understand. From this, two consequences would follow. Any act of knowledge on our part would be made possible only by this foundational givenness of the Absolute as something for us to understand, as a reality that is reliably accessible to us. The natural autonomy of our knowledge would be grounded in a theonomy. There would be nothing we can know on the basis of our own power. Also then, it would follow that our knowledge would never exhaust the objective truth of the Absolute. However, everything we know would be patient of addition by virtue of the Absolute's free gift until such time as we attained the unsurpassable objective truth about the intrinsically unsurpassable (namely eternal) being (*Wesen*) of the Absolute.

Alternatively we could construe the limitation as primarily one of content, and as one of power derivatively. Our natural power to recognize objective truth, the correspondence between thing and intellect, would be limited to certain things; for example, to material and sensory things, or universals within this world, or merely the fact *that* the world has been set in being by the Absolute. This would contradict what the Encyclical says about how our natural power can be aware of the Absolute's objective truth in its totality and unity, and leads to a tri-lemma. We can deny that we have a natural capacity for the *totality* of objective truth; we can deny that we can be aware of its *unity*; or we can deny that we have a natural capacity for knowing objective truth *at all*. For either the truth accessible to us (limited one way or another in terms of content) forms a totality, in which case it would not be a unity, but rather a duality comprising two different kinds of truth (one naturally accessible to us, one requiring that we have some kind of supernatural power). If, by contrast, we attempt to salvage the unity of truth by claiming that it is united in its ground and ultimate object, then we are

nevertheless conceding that such unity is not accessible to our natural power of knowledge.

So much for the two possible ways of understanding how our natural powers (independent of any considerations about sin) for knowing absolute truth are limited. How does the Encyclical handle the issue? The question is whether such a limitation of content is the primary one, or whether it is derivative from some limitation on the *power* of our natural capacity. A decision on this matter requires us to consider what it says about our ability to know truth on the basis of revelation, what revelation is, and its relationship to reason.

Supernatural Revelation in Christ

As explained before, the Encyclical reserves the term 'revelation' only for that knowledge of objective truth about the Absolute which, owing to its dependence on special kinds of condition, goes beyond our own natural powers of recognition. It is these conditions which specify the essence of knowing objective truth from revelation. The Encyclical cites the teaching of the two Vatican Councils, referring to the gift of God's own speech.[40] But what these conditions amount to is something that stands in need of being worked out clearly, through some kind of analysis of what it is for God to speak to humanity, or for humanity to be addressed by God. Only then could we begin to clarify the relationship between revealed truth and the foundational givenness of the Absolute that already grounds our natural capacity to know objective truth about the Absolute. But the Encyclical is no more forthcoming about such a structural account of our capacity to know revealed objective truth than it is regarding our natural powers. Quotation from Vatican I poses rather than solves the problem: that of showing the unity (or unity-in-difference) of the Creator's work, the unity-in-difference between the conditions of possibility for the knowledge of objective truth arising from the foundational givenness as a reality for us to understand, and the special or revelation-related givenness.[41] Vatican II speaks of how revelation in deed and word go together, but this does not help us here.[42] It represents an advance on Vatican I only in so far as it specifies in terms of salvation history the way we look at revelation – a development which the Encyclical takes further by specifying that historical revelation in Christ comes to fullness precisely at Easter.[43]

The Encyclical synthesizes the salvation-historical idiom of *Dei*

---

[40] *Fides et ratio*, §§7, 10, 13.
[41] *Fides et ratio*, §§34, 43.
[42] *Fides et ratio*, §10, citing *Dei Verbum*, §2.
[43] *Fides et ratio*, §§2, 11.

Verbum with the differentiation in Vatican I between reason and revelation. From the way the themes are structured within the whole text, it seems the task requires some sphere 'where the two may come together'.[44] Where is this sphere? Natural knowledge of the truth? Revelation? Or some *tertium quid*? The Encyclical repudiates any *tertium quid*; the answer given is revelation in Christ, and any idea that the truth of revelation or its relationship to natural knowledge can be known and assessed in terms of natural knowledge is firmly excluded.[45] It is through *revelation* that we know of how our natural potential for knowing the truth enables a dialogue with non-believers or believers other than Christians; only through revelation is the proper use of natural reason, in keeping with its true and in-built goal, possible, with neither too much nor too little being attributed to it. Only faith, drawing on the light of revelation, can recognize the true capacity of our natural potential for knowledge and our natural language.

At the same time, the Encyclical takes up Vatican II's emphasis on salvation history. The revelation given in Christ is revelation in the specific, full and unsurpassable sense – but therefore, obviously, not the only instance of revelation. On the contrary: God's revealing work includes also the Old Testament and the revelation in the 'book of Nature'.[46] The Encyclical gives no ground for supposing that this refers only to the external world. It at least does not exclude the possibility that it includes the whole of human nature, with the implication that human nature itself counts as a revelation, as a self-imparting of God. And the Encyclical is quite clear that even our natural power for truth cannot do without 'the knowledge which clearly comes from God', with the context making it quite clear that the reference is to revealed truth in the narrow sense – a knowledge that has pertained to human nature from the beginning, at all times and places.[47]

The Encyclical is therefore sending a complex message. On the one hand, the natural capacity of human nature itself includes a striving – unconsciously – for the knowledge of the Absolute's objective truth precisely in its absoluteness, unity and totality.[48] This, however, finds its fulfilment only in the revelation granted in the full sense only by God, in the revelation that occurs in Christ.[49] On the other hand, however, our natural potential for knowing the truth is accompanied, from the very

---

[44] *Fides et ratio*, §23.

[45] See *Fides et ratio*, §§7–15, 37, 70–1. For particular application to the Church's teaching office, see §§49–63.

[46] *Fides et ratio*, §§18–19.

[47] *Fides et ratio*, §22.

[48] *Fides et ratio*, §41.

[49] *Fides et ratio*, §§24–35.

beginning and at all times, by a simultaneous revelation-knowledge (a foundational givenness of the Absolute as a reality to be understood by us), indeed grounded in this revelation-knowledge and enabled by it.[50] Do these two sets of claims cohere? If so, how? An answer to this question depends obviously on the precise sense in which the claims about revelation are to be understood as implying limitations regarding our natural capacity for knowing the truth, as considered above.

There are some indications that the Encyclical sees the limitation in terms primarily of content. Most significantly, the truths accessible through revelation are presented as extensions of what we can know naturally: thus, the Fathers of the Church 'fully accepted reason as open to the absolute, and then introduced the riches of Revelation into it'.[51] The traditional formula – 'grace both presupposes and perfects nature' – would then be understood as a perfection in terms of completing the content of our knowledge.[52] A further, negative consideration in favour of this interpretation is that nowhere do we hear an account of how our natural knowledge can be at once limited by its reference to revelation and on the other sustained by *revelation* in the pursuit of its proper goal *as natural*. This would have to be present were there to be any plausibility in the claim that the Encyclical understands the limitation on our natural knowledge primarily in terms of power.

However, the claim that the limitation is primarily one of content leaves us with a range of difficult questions and problems, as set out above. Nor will it do to invoke society and dialogue as furnishing solutions. For, as has already been shown, the acceptance of statements on the basis of trust in the reliability of the speaker is only possible if the matter known, the one handing it on, and the one receiving it are all operating on the same epistemic level. A version of 'trust' can be operative within nature or within revelation, but it cannot license the leap from one to the other. We might suppose that both spheres somehow had something in common: for example, if we supposed that nature was *de facto* conditioned by factors that only grace, as *the fulfilment of nature*, or revelation as *the fulfilment of the natural knowledge of truth*, subsequently brought to light. And this would imply that the very idea of nature involved an openness to fulfilment through grace (and therefore a claim that grace is constitutive of nature), or when the natural capacity for truth in itself was understood as including the possibility of being fulfilled by revelation (and therefore a claim that the natural capacity for truth is constituted by revelation).

All of this would imply, however, that the limitations on our natural

---

[50] *Fides et ratio*, §29.
[51] *Fides et ratio*, §41.
[52] *Fides et ratio*, §43.

power for truth were limitations primarily of power, and only secondarily and consequently limitations of content. As has been said, the Encyclical's explicit formulations do not run along these lines. Nevertheless, we should not rule out too quickly the possibility that its teaching could be deepened and clarified by invoking such a concept. There are some basic intuitions in the Encyclical which make sense only if we understand it in these terms: for example, the idea of grace perfecting nature, or revelation perfecting our natural knowledge of the truth, the different steps of revelation. Nor, if such an account of the limitations on our capacity for truth were postulated, would any of the Encyclical's explicit teachings have to be revoked. In particular, to my mind, all the statements the Encyclical makes in terms of difference of content regarding reason and revelation could be preserved. After all, this account of the matter still allows for a secondary, derivative limitation in terms of content. However, such a reading of what the Encyclical says on this topic would have two important consequences. The first concerns the role of dialogue and tradition as humans appropriate truth historically; the second is about what constitutes human certainty.

We begin with the first of these consequences, regarding truth's transmission in history. Clearly, the ongoing development of human awareness of truth depends on objective truth being communicated – on people witnessing to it, and on others who accept this witness. Moreover, such acceptance involves some kind of surrender regarding this absolute, objective truth. What, however, enables those receiving the truth to surrender themselves in this way? This can only happen if it is not just a witness to the truth that is present to the hearer, but the truth itself. This principle applies especially regarding truths about the perennial constitution of the world and humanity, what it is in the grace of God, in God's assured will to create, reconcile and consummate, that makes them the way they are. This truth is obviously not present to every person foundationally: it is given them through disclosures which they do not control as something to be understood, and then conceptualized in thought, communicated in language. Through this witness, the attested truth can then become present to those who hear it. Indeed, this truth in its very self must be what is present to them as evident if it is to be a proper focus of their surrender. In other words, the communication of truth, truth that has already become evident, is a necessary (though not sufficient) condition for truth becoming evident in such a way as to enable surrender to it. But it is not a sufficient condition: this truth that has become evident to the witness handing it on must become evident to the one receiving it.

All this applies regarding Jesus's witness to the coming of the reign of God in the present. What for Jesus was evident became evident to his

disciples only at Easter – a principle which applies all the more to other witnesses of how the truth of Jesus's witness, of his gospel, became evident at Easter. It follows, therefore, that true and reliable witnesses may affirm their witness to others and assure them subjectively of its truth, but they cannot guarantee it – this in the sense of making through their witness alone the truth present in such a way that the others can surrender themselves not just to them and their witness, but to the very truth itself as something present to them.[53] The principle applies also to the Church's office-holders. Their witness is a task laid on them by the Church; through their conformity with the Church, their witness is true and reliable; it constitutes a necessary condition for the truth becoming evident to those receiving the witness. Nevertheless, the witness itself, just by being there, does not make the truth witnessed actually present in itself. It is the truth itself which makes itself present, in the presence of the reliable witness, but within the receivers' own freedom.

The other issue raised concerns certainty. It is only when this witnessed truth thus becomes evident in freedom that all further doubt is excluded, and a certainty is reached in which the human longing for ultimate objective truth in its unity, totality and absoluteness attains its goal.[54] The Encyclical is quite right in its denial that human life could ever exist without some level of participation in such certainty, and also quite rightly stresses the indissoluble connection between such assurance and human freedom.[55] However, it describes this connection in terms of a free act of knowledge itself creating this unshakable certainty. 'And thus by believing, the human person accomplishes the most meaningful act of her life, for here the certainty of truth is attained in that one who decides to live by it.'[56] In the same vein, it is claimed, '[a] moment arrives for everyone, whether admitted or not, when his individual existence must be supported by absolute truth, which confers a certitude not subject to wider doubt'.[57] This means: certainty is grounded on knowledge – knowledge first, assurance second. But if such acknowledgment is not to be arbitrary, if it is to be grounded on truth and have truth as its object, then it must be grounded on the fact that truth itself has become evident, in a way that of itself excludes all doubt. So, for example, because for Paul the truth of the Easter message had become evident, this truth brought about certainty in him – a certainty which he acknowledged and let work through all he did and all that happened to him.[58] In other words, it is not

[53] *Fides et ratio*, §33.
[54] *Fides et ratio*, §27.
[55] *Fides et ratio*, §91.
[56] *Fides et ratio*, §13, cf. §32.
[57] *Fides et ratio*, §27.
[58] See 2 Cor 4:6 and Rom 8:38.

that freedom creates certainty, but that certainty creates and orientates freedom.

It is only on the basis of *this* argument that we can reach the point that the Encyclical presents as the ideal: that human beings are governed only by the authority of a truth which has become evident to them in itself; that on the basis of this truth they have attained freedom with regard to what is within the world, and maintain this freedom only through obedience to this truth.[59]

Sin

These reflections all concern the foundational – we might even say ontological – relationship between our natural capacity for knowing truth and the capacity we have as a result of revelation. They deal with this relationship, so to speak, in terms of 'nature' – in the sense of its being something set foundationally by the source and origin of creation. We have not yet considered how sin and its consequences might affect this foundational relationship, nor what the effects of God's reconciling act might be. We have been talking more about what such sin and such reconciliation must presuppose, and setting out conditions for a proper understanding of sin and reconciliation.

Everything, therefore, the Encyclical says about human sin and God's reconciliation – and it confines itself to hints – needs to be interpreted in terms of one or the other accounts of how revelation relates to our natural capacity for knowledge: either in terms of revelation primarily extending our power to know, or in terms of its primarily extending the content of what we know. In my opinion, the Encyclical's statements in this regard are susceptible to both interpretations. At any rate, a fully adequate account of sin and reconciliation would require a full development of one or other interpretation.

The task cannot be attempted here. Nevertheless, what has been said enables us to foresee which interpretation is more likely. If revelation is understood as extending our natural capacity for knowledge primarily in terms of *power*, in other words in terms of an act of revelation even in the creation encompassing our natural power, then the perfect goodness of God's foundational creation can consist only in its being *ordered* from the beginning to its goal of perfection, but not in its already in some sense being there. It would follow that sin can no longer be understood as simply an arbitrary human act within the perfect creation, but only as a culpable act of freedom, for which the agent is responsible, within conditions that are orientated towards perfection but which are not yet

[59] *Fides et ratio*, §90.

perfect, conditions of a primal fallibility, a primal susceptibility to frustration. For people coming into the light of Christian revelation, such fallibility would then be set aside. The above suffices to show how our understanding of sin and reconciliation, and therefore justification, depends on how we understand the foundational relationship between our natural capacity for truth and revelation. The Encyclical reminds us of this point, and thereby becomes a document that is significant for ecumenical discourse. Any appropriate discussion about sin, reconciliation and justification depends on an in-depth analysis of issues of reason and revelation. In particular, it is clear that an appropriate understanding of reconciliation and justification must rest on a proper account of just how the authority of the objective truth of the Absolute itself comes to affect us such as we are, in its acts of reconciliation, liberation and consummation.

‘*Visio Unica et Ordinata Scientiae*’?

NICHOLAS LASH

‘Concepts have dates’: a parable

In the late 1840s, the establishment in the University of Cambridge of honours examinations in the Moral Sciences (comprising moral philosophy, political economy, modern history and law) and the Natural Sciences (comprising anatomy, physiology, chemistry, botany and geology) was resisted chiefly on the grounds that ‘undergraduates would be diverted from the serious pursuit of mathematics if by acquiring an ordinary degree they could indulge a bent for the natural or the moral sciences’.[1] (Some surprising absences from that list of natural sciences are explained by the fact that astronomy, geometry and ‘natural and experimental philosophy’ – roughly: physics – were deemed branches of mathematics.) There exist in Cambridge, to this day, a ‘Moral Sciences Club’, consisting exclusively of philosophers, and a ‘Philosophical Society’, established in 1819, to which only natural scientists are admitted.

These local eccentricities may serve as a reminder that, as Bernard Lonergan remarked to my uncle Sebastian Moore, on the occasion of their first meeting: ‘Concepts have dates’. This is no less true of the concepts of ‘philosophy’, or ‘science’, or ‘reason’, than it is of any other. My aim in this essay is twofold: first, to argue that the notion of the history of philosophy largely presumed in the Encyclical *Fides et ratio*, and in the commentaries on it that I have seen, is, in important respects, insufficiently historical and, secondly and in consequence, that the contributions which theologians and philosophers can hope to make to overcoming what the Pope calls ‘an increasing fragmentation of knowledge’ are immeasurably more modest than he seems, in this Encyclical, to suppose.

[1] D. A. Winstanley, *Early Victorian Cambridge* (Cambridge: Cambridge University Press, 1955), p. 211.

In what sense of 'philosophy' is philosophy so important?

Confronted as we are by 'an increasing fragmentation of knowledge', and a widespread loss of nerve in the capacity of human beings to understand themselves and the world in which they live, John Paul II wrote *Fides et ratio* in order 'to reaffirm the intense interest the Church has in philosophy', to reiterate that 'the Church is utterly persuaded that faith and reason "contribute to each other"', and because 'It is often the case that only in the discipline of philosophy do we find mutual understanding and dialogue with those who do not share our faith', an understanding 'all the more important' if we are effectively to address 'the pressing questions which face humanity – [such as] ecology, peace and the co-existence of different races and cultures'.[2]

Against the background of my experience of more than thirty years' participation, as a theologian with philosophical interests, in the bewilderingly varied range of conversations which constitutes the life of a modern university, I confess to being unconvinced that the climate in which such conversations operate, in which we learn things from each other, and more or less fruitfully agree and disagree, could, for the most part, be described as pertaining to or derived from 'the discipline of philosophy'. It is, at least, worth noting that, if 'philosophical' is the appropriate description of the ground on which we meet, its appropriateness would remain unrecognized by many, perhaps most, of the participants in serious conversation concerning 'the pressing questions facing humanity'.

Twenty years ago, the philosopher Edward Craig gave a series of radio talks 'directed to an audience supposedly puzzled by the relationship between philosophy, the subject currently practised, taught and studied in most universities of the English-speaking world, and what I called 'Philosophies', those sweeping maps of reality which the traditional philosopher figure of the popular intellectual image used to provide for our guidance in thought and behaviour'.[3]

Perhaps one of the reasons why it is quite difficult to identify the sense, or senses, of 'philosophy' with which the Pope is working is that he seeks admirably to sustain the connection between philosophy in the somewhat diffuse sense of the rendering explicit of implicit world-views, grand narratives and 'sweeping maps of reality', and philosophy in the sense of a craft or 'discipline' sufficiently specific for it to make sense to appoint 'Professors of Philosophy' alongside professors of

---

[2] *Fides et ratio*, §§81, 63, 100 (citing Vatican I's Constitution *Dei Filius*), 104.

[3] Edward Craig, *The Mind of God and the Works of Man* (Oxford: Clarendon Press, 1987), p. 1.

earth sciences, comparative law, molecular biology and ancient Chinese literature.

The same connection was invoked in a fascinating exchange, occasioned by the Encyclical, between the Austrian philosopher Clemens Sedmak and the English theologian Philip Endean. Sedmak produced a vigorous and provocative account of the relations between philosophy and Magisterium. He defended four theses: that a normative understanding of philosophy has characterized Christian faith from the beginning; that 'the Catholic magisterium has repeatedly established criteria for what it calls a *sana philosophia*'; that magisterial texts cannot be formulated without implicit philosophical assumptions; and that philosophy has a special role, recognized by the Magisterium, in interdisciplinary work.[4]

In a measured and beautifully crafted response, Endean showed that, at least where the English-speaking world is concerned, there are no grounds for the suspicion, voiced by Sedmak (and perhaps underlying the Pope's lament that 'to a large extent . . . modern philosophy . . . gives a wide berth to the metaphysical search for man's ultimate questions in order to concentrate attention upon matters which are of particular and localised interest and are perhaps even merely formal') that some Catholic philosophers turn to the analytic tradition as a way of gaining emancipation from magisterial control.[5] Acknowledging that Sedmak had important points to make 'about magisterial authority and philosophy', Endean regretted that he undermined an important case by arguing it 'in a one-sided and insufficiently nuanced fashion'. Sedmak, he said, is being 'inexact when he identifies his target as "Oxford", as analytic philosophy as such; his real concern is with an anti-realism, a relativism, and a loss of belief in metaphysics, that are by no means universal among analytic philosophers'.[6]

In an eirenic and constructive reply, Sedmak generously acknowledged that his earlier contribution bore signs 'of the rigidity of youth and reveals a certain immaturity', urged that 'The concept of philosophy is . . . an ongoing task rather than an achievable definition', and offered the following description of philosophical knowledge: it 'does not produce encyclopedic or empirical knowledge . . . and it does not produce symbolic or religious knowledge . . . The "Unique Selling Proposition" of

---

[4] Clemens Sedmak, 'Rom, Athen und Oxford. Katholisches Lehramt und Philosophie', European Society for Catholic Theology *Bulletin ET* 10 (1999), pp. 139–48. I have cited the English translation of his second thesis from Endean's reply, p. 41.

[5] *Fides et ratio*, §61.

[6] Philip Endean, 'Philosophy and the Magisterium. A Contribution from "Oxford"', *Bulletin ET* 11 (2000), pp. 39–54, p. 51.

philosophy is the generation of categorial or grammatical knowledge . . . The main tool of philosophy is the distinction'.[7] That description of philosophy's task is not far from Aristotle's notion of ontology, as expressed by Peter Geach: 'Certain concepts, like existence and truth and thing and property, are used, and cannot but be used, in all rational discourse whatsoever; and ontology is an attempt to scrutinize our use of them.'[8] Aristotle may have called this 'first philosophy', and later writers may have named it 'metaphysics', because it is treated by him in a volume of that name; it remains, however, but one 'branch' of a considerably larger 'tree' known, until quite recently, as 'philosophy' or 'science'.

The question that I now want to put to the Encylical is this: when Pope John Paul II speaks of 'philosophy', is it the tree, or is it the branch, that he has principally in mind?

Dramatis personae

Papal encyclicals are written according to well-established literary conventions, one of which is to populate the text with dramatic personifications of key themes and concepts: the style is one which might not unreasonably be called 'baroque'. In the present case, characters called 'Faith' and 'Reason' begin as limbs, but soon take on a life of their own: 'Faith and reason seem to be like two wings by which the human spirit is raised up toward the contemplation of truth'; a little later: 'reason itself, intent upon investigating man from one angle only . . . seems to have forgotten that the same man is always invited to progress toward a truth which transcends himself'.[9] Notice that, according to this convention, it is 'reason', not human beings, that has 'forgotten'.

Even though such rhetorical devices may not mislead people trained to read these texts (and although, near the end, the Pope addresses 'theologians', 'philosophers' and 'scientists',[10] the Encyclical's primary audience is 'the bishops of the Catholic Church'), they do make it dangerously easy to imagine that 'faith' and 'reason', 'theology', 'philosophy' and 'science' are, as it were, the names of individuals which, although they have a history (about which the Encyclical has quite a lot

---

[7] Clemens Sedmak, ' "How Many Idiots?": The Idea of the Catholic Magisterium and its Relation to Philosophy', in *Bulletin ET* 11 (2000), pp. 132–51, esp. p. 138.

[8] Peter Geach, 'Symposium: On What There Is', in *Freedom, Language and Reality*, Aristotelian Society Supplementary Volume XXV (London: Harrison, 1951), p. 136. This description was much loved, and used, by my Cambridge predecessor, Donald MacKinnon: see, for example, D. M. MacKinnon, *Themes in Theology. The Threefold Cord: Essays in Philosophy, Politics and Theology* (Edinburgh: T&T Clark, 1987), p. 147.

[9] *Fides et ratio*, Preface, §5.

[10] *Fides et ratio*, see §§105, 106.

to say) nevertheless retain, through that history, a more or less constant identity through all the adventures that they undergo.

Laurence Hemming, noting that 'One of the criticisms advanced in Anglophone reception of this Encyclical has been that it to a certain extent hypostatises "reason" and "faith"', defends the Encyclical on the grounds that, when well read, its insistence that it is 'the human person as such' that is 'the "place" of truth' safeguards us 'from hypostatising either faith or reason'.[11] I have no doubt that, philosophically, Hemming is correct. My criticism is stylistic: as any student of rhetoric from St Augustine onwards should be well aware, the forms of what we say shape understanding and imagination against the grain of good intentions.

What I have called the 'baroque' tradition shaping the rhetoric of *Fides et ratio* has its origins in early modern thought, certain habits of which, it seems to me, tend to obscure the Encylical's admirable central thrust and argument. By rhetorically attributing to certain concepts a stability of identity which only individuals enjoy, we generate conceptual confusion and mis-narrate these concepts' history. I now propose briefly to amplify and illustrate this twofold charge.

The tangled roots of 'faith and reason'

'Despite the fact that more than a hundred years have passed since the appearance of Leo XIII's encyclical *Aeterni Patris*', says the Pope, in the opening paragraph of the Encyclical's conclusion, 'we think it imperative to insist more clearly on the close link between faith and philosophy . . . we have judged it both appropriate and necessary to underline the importance of philosophy for the understanding of faith, as well as the limits philosophy faces when it forgets or denies the truths of revelation. The Church is utterly persuaded that faith and reason "contribute to each other"; since both at the same time exercise a critical and purifying critique, while also providing a stimulus for further inquiry and deeper understanding.'[12]

Does not the drift of that paragraph, taken in conjunction with the title of the Encyclical, give the impression that there are, as it were, two camps: one populated by 'faith', 'revelation' and (implicitly) 'theology', the other by 'reason' and 'philosophy', even if the thrust of the Encyclical's argument is to urge their mutual indispensability?

It is not, I think, the distinction between 'theology' and 'philosophy'

---

[11] Laurence Paul Hemming, 'Unreasonable Faith', *New Blackfriars* 81 (2000), pp. 389–400, esp. pp. 389 and 398.

[12] *Fides et ratio*, §100 (citing *Dei Filius*).

that is the problem although, even here, to draw that distinction too rigidly would seem prematurely to exclude the possibility of a philosophical theology that was as philosophically rigorous as it was theologically devout. One might do better to distinguish, as Anselm did, between 'monologion' and 'proslogion' – between thoughts thought in apparent, or attempted, or provisional autonomy, and thoughts thought, in principle, and in intention, on one's knees before the crucifix, responsive to the silent mystery of God.

Nor is it the fluidity of the connotations of 'philosophy' (a fluidity admittedly in tension with the tendency, when considering the history of philosophy, unduly to harden the contours of the concept) that, in itself, necessarily causes the confusion – for reasons that I indicated earlier, when I mentioned the work of Edward Craig. Sometimes, philosophy is a 'gift' or task; sometimes it is that which assists the construction of 'a logical coherence of assertions . . . distinguished by a firm body of teachings'; sometimes it is instinct in us all: 'man is naturally a philosopher'.[13]

It is the eponymous team captains, 'Faith' and 'Reason', that are the problem, because the roots of the indispensable distinction between 'proslogue' and 'monologue', thus drawn, lie deep in that disjunction between 'believing' and 'reasoning' which is at the very heart of Enlightenment rationalism. The confusions which this generates, for the consideration of that cluster of absolutely fundamental problems with which the Encyclical is concerned, are twofold.

On the one hand, notwithstanding the widespread recognition that, except as a tactical device, any such disjunction is entirely fictional, because all good reasoning expresses and proceeds from prior commitments and beliefs, and relies, at every step along the way, on believing – albeit cautiously and not uncritically – the testimony of others engaged in this and similar collaborative enterprises, it is still possible to hear distinguished persons say (as I heard Professor Lewis Wolpert say on BBC Radio not very long ago) that science proceeds by reason and religion by faith.

On the other hand, it is perfectly clear that the 'faith' of which the Pope speaks is not belief in general, or habits of believing, but Christian faith in God: that credence 'in Deum' which Augustine memorably characterized as: 'in believing to love, in believing to delight, in believing to walk towards him, and be incorporated amongst the limbs or members of his body'.[14] But surely that which is to be contradistinguished from such believing, such 'faith', is not 'reason' but sin, the creature's

[13] *Fides et ratio*, §§3, 4, 64.

[14] My somewhat free translation from 'quid est ergo credere in eum? Credendo amare, credendo diligere, credendo in eum ire, et eius membris incorporari'. Augustine, *Commentary on John*, in *Patrologia Latina* 35, col. 1631.

refusal to be a creature, refusal to exist in obedient and absolute dependence upon the mystery of God?

I am suggesting, in other words, that the Pope would have served his purposes more effectively and straightforwardly if, instead of urging that mutual suspicion between 'faith' and 'reason' be replaced by trust and co-operation, he had deployed the rich resources that are available, both theological and philosophical, to subvert the foundations on which the endlessly misleading early modern disjunction between faith and reason was established.

Of what is the history of 'philosophy' the history?

Before making some remarks about the history of the 'tree', a few words concerning that 'branch' of philosophy known as metaphysics or ontology. John Paul II is deeply disturbed by 'the lack of trust in reason itself displayed to a large extent by modern philosophy itself, in that it gives a wide berth to the metaphysical search for man's ultimate questions'; and he emphasizes 'the need of a *truly metaphysical* philosophy of nature, able to go beyond empirical evidence in such a way that, seeking the truth, it arrives at something absolute, ultimate and grounded'.

The Pope insists that he is not speaking of 'metaphysics as about some particular school or historical tradition'.[15] Nevertheless, the emphasis on ultimacy, absoluteness and transcendence, suggests that the concept of metaphysics with which, in fact, he works possesses a high degree of specificity.

Commenting on this section of the Encyclical, Francis Selman says that 'When we go *beyond* physics, we come to *meta*physics . . . physics leads to metaphysics as we have to go *beyond* physics to answer some of its questions'.[16]

At first sight, all these metaphors of spatial distance, of 'transcending' and 'going beyond', may appear quite harmless. It is, for example, true that, in order profitably to consider questions such as: 'What, then, does or does not count as a "thing"? Is gravity a thing, is grace, and is the human mind?',[17] it is useful to have considered, in as much detailed specificity as possible, a very great variety of different kinds of thing. In this sense, metaphysical enquiry undoubtedly 'comes second', spreads its wings at dusk, 'goes beyond' particular enquiries.

---

[15] *Fides et ratio*, §§61 (cf. 55), 83.

[16] Francis Selman, 'The Recovery of Metaphysics', *New Blackfriars* 81 (2000), pp. 376–88, esp. pp. 378 f. (The first two stresses are Selman's, the third is mine).

[17] Cf. Nicholas Lash, *On What Kinds of Things There Are: The Beginning and End of 'Religion'* (Cambridge: Cambridge University Press, 1996), pp. 93–111, esp. p. 96.

And yet, in early modern thought (including, of course, the neo-scholasticism which was an aspect of it) such spatial metaphors often played a much more substantial and questionable part. To put it very crudely: in the traditions that I have in mind, it sometimes seems as if concepts such as 'existence', 'being', and 'substance' denote a layer of reality lying deeper than, 'beyond', the familiar world of our experience. And, near the heart of these strange habits of imagination is the belief that God is to be sought at the most 'absolute' and 'ultimate' layer of all, 'beyond' the world.

But such a god, the god of early modern theism or deism (we should never forget that these two terms, when first coined, were, for some time, interchangeable in sense), has little in common with that incomprehensible and holy mystery which spoke through the prophets, took flesh in Jesus, and has – in the outpouring of the Spirit – come closer to us than our own most private thoughts. To say this is not to opt for 'Jerusalem' rather than for 'Athens'; it is merely to suggest that bad metaphysics makes a poor partner for theology. To take up again Peter Geach's account of Aristotle's metaphysics, it would seem very strange to say that 'existence and truth and thing and property' do not pertain to the reality of the everyday, familar world, but only to some mysterious other territory that lies 'beyond'.

There are affinities between mediaeval distinctions of 'material' and 'formal' modes of predication, Kantian distinctions between the 'categorial' and the 'transcendental', and Wittgenstein's distinction between 'empirical' and 'grammatical' investigations. The tendency of much early modern thought to substitute for such distinctions a distinction between two levels or layers of reality (a tendency exemplified in the disastrous shift in the grammar of the 'supernatural') has little to commend it.

Now let me turn to the larger question: of what is the 'history of philosophy' the history? In one sense, of course (and it is a sense which the Encyclical acknowledges) it is simply the history of the human quest for wisdom, a history which therefore includes, but is by no means exhausted by, the history of the sciences, much of the history of religion and ethics and theology, as well as the history of what we might now call 'philosophy'. There are, however, a number of passages in which it seems as if, for the Pope, the focal sense of 'philosophy' is, and has always been, the enterprise in which those whom we would now call 'philosophers' have been engaged.

Thus, for example, to say that 'Among the ancients the study of natural sciences was not divorced from philosophical knowledge' seems, historically, a curious way of putting it. Similarly, when speaking of the need for philosophy to 'rediscover its *fullness of wisdom*', the Pope says

that this will give 'philosophy a useful spur to conform to its proper nature'. (The last six words are my translation of *ut suae ipsius naturae accommodetur*, which the translation used in this volume renders, somewhat obscurely, as 'to bring itself into its own genius'.)[18] But in what sense of 'philosophy' does philosophy have a 'nature', let alone a 'proper' nature?

'Saint Albert the Great and Saint Thomas . . . were the first learned men to admit the necessary autonomy that philosophy and the sciences needed, so that each should depend upon arguments belonging to their own sphere.'[19] But is this not anachronistically to read back into the thirteenth century distinctions between 'philosophy' and 'science' which were (as my opening parable indicates) only laboriously worked out during the nineteenth century?

'It should', says the Pope, 'also not be forgotten that in our modern culture the place of philosophy has been transformed. Rather than as wisdom and universal knowledge, it has been reduced to a position of one among many in the fields of knowledge. Indeed in some ways it has been consigned to a quite marginal role.'[20] But what is the 'it' which has been thus 'reduced'? We could hardly reply 'philosophy', for that would beg the question! After all, it would be equally correct to say that, in point of terminology, 'science' has gradually been 'reduced' (especially in the English-speaking world) from 'universal knowledge' to only a few of the many fields of human knowing. But, although labelling only some branches of knowledge 'sciences' does have disadvantages, these do not include depriving the other branches of appropriate criteria of rigorous procedure and hence, on another account of what 'science' means, of their scientificity.

Insisting that 'the discipline of philosophy has great importance, which must not be removed from any programme of theological studies or the training of students in seminaries', John Paul II says that the Fifth Lateran Council's confirmation (in 1517) of the decision that 'before the study of the theological *curriculum* begins, a period of time must be allotted to the special study of philosophy', had 'its roots in the experience of the Middle Ages'.[21] But surely the Council was simply stipulating that students for the priesthood, before they entered into the study of theology, should have received a good general education?

---

[18] *Fides et ratio*, §§19, 81 (my stress).
[19] *Fides et ratio*, §45.
[20] *Fides et ratio*, §47.
[21] *Fides et ratio*, §62.

'Under the shade of wisdom'

My concern about the Pope's tendency to restrict the range of reference of what 'reason' does to that branch of serious enquiry and ordered knowledge which we now call 'philosophy' is that he risks inadvertently understating the scale and gravity of the challenge which confronts us.

Writing in *New Blackfriars* after the death of Elizabeth Anscombe, Fergus Kerr said: 'She will be remembered for her resistance to the utilitarianism which now almost completely dominates our culture (consequentialism, as she renamed it).'[22] It is against this dominance of consequentialism, and other diseases of our reasoning, that John Paul II makes his plea for the need for philosophy to rediscover 'its *fullness of wisdom*' (although 'its sapiential breadth' might perhaps be an inelegant but more accurate translation of *sapientialem amplitudinem*, because what he is surely driving at is the need to recognize that cleverness and erudition are simply not enough).[23] And yet, in my experience, although our universities are now infected, from outside, by the view that their purpose is to make the country rich, it is not amongst academics, and certainly not amongst academic philosophers, that the homelands of consequentialism are to be found, but in the broader commanding heights of our pagan and individualist late capitalist culture.

That, I think, is the first thing that needs to be said. But the second (and I do not suppose that the Pope would disagree with this) would be that it is by no means only, or even primarily, amongst philosophers that the need to recover a sense of the sapiential is so urgent, but across the whole sweep of what Newman called 'the circle of the sciences'. And it is here, it seems to me, that the Pope's concentration on 'philosophy' may be misleading.

In an address to university teachers, on 9 September 2000, Pope John Paul II said that they 'must make universities "cultural laboratories" in which theology, philosophy, human sciences and natural sciences may engage in constructive dialogue'.[24] That is a noble ambition and an urgent need, but it would be difficult to overestimate the obstacles that stand in the way of its achievement.

'We therefore wholeheartedly declare ourselves convinced', says the Pope, 'that man can reach a single, ordered vision of knowledge.'[25] This declaration seems to me central to the concerns of the Encyclical, but it is

---

[22] Fergus Kerr, 'Comment: A Great Philsopher', *New Blackfriars* 82 (2001), pp. 54–5, esp. p. 55.

[23] *Fides et ratio*, §81.

[24] Quoted from *Osservatore Romano* (English or Italian edition) (13 September 2000), p. 2.

[25] *Fides et ratio*, §85.

not easy to interpret or assess. On the one hand, I take John Paul II to be declaring that the world – the whole of God's creation, from the beginning to the end, in all the vastness of its temporal reach and complexity of structure, and not withstanding the bewildering diversity of human cultures and traditions – is one in such a sense as to entail the unity of truth. To put it in terms of contemporary philosophical discussion: the Pope is, I take it, rejecting the notion of wholly incommensurable conceptual frameworks; the notion that there are or might be languages which are such as to be, in principle, incapable of being translated into one another.[26] Notwithstanding the immense difficulty which participants in different cultures and traditions, or different academic schools and styles and disciplines, regularly experience in reaching common understanding, to insist, in this sense, on the unity of truth is to insist that failure to reach such understanding is not, in principle, inevitable.

On the other hand, it does not follow from the oneness of the world, and the unity of truth, thus understood, that there is or could be some one true story of the world in the sense of a unified and unifying comprehensively explanatory 'theory of everything'. There are two reasons why the currently fashionable quest (in certain scientific circles) for such imperial explanation is to be resisted. In the first place, as the American lawyer, Joseph Vining, has argued in a powerful critique of total theories: 'there is a deep connection between totalitarian social and political thought . . . and total theories of the nature of the world', because both total theories and totalitarianism reduce the human person to the status of an 'instance'.[27] In the second place, the imperialist project is unfeasible because, as Karl-Otto Apel saw, 'the fact that a natural science requires the existence of a linguistic community of communication as an a priori for its own existence cannot be grasped scientifically but must be understood hermeneutically'; an observation convergent upon the Nobel Prize-winning neuroscientist Gerald Edelmann's claim that it follows, from what we now know about the processes of the human brain, about the 'recursive symbolic properties of language', and about the historical irreversibility of specific 'symbolic and artistic realisations in society and culture', that 'there can be no fully reducible description of human knowledge'.[28]

---

[26] See Fergus Kerr's discussion of Donald Davidson and Wittgenstein in *Theology After Wittgenstein* (Oxford: Blackwell, 1986), pp. 105–9.

[27] See Joseph Vining's inaugural lecture to the Erasmus Institute at the University of Notre Dame, *On the Future of Total Theory: Science, Antiscience and Human Candor*, private publication for the Erasmus Institute, 1999, p. 6.

[28] Kurt Müller-Vollmer, 'Introduction' in Kurt Müller-Vollmer (ed.), *The Hermeneutics Reader* (New York: Continuum, 1985), p. 44; Gerald M. Edelman, *Bright Air, Brilliant Fire: On the Matter of Mind* (London: Penguin Press, 1992), p. 177.

In the passage from which I set out, the Pope speaks, however, not of humanity reaching a single *explanation* of the world, but a 'single, ordered *vision* of knowledge'.[29] What kind of 'vision' does he have in mind? We should not, I think, exclude the possibility that the attainment, by the whole of humankind, of such a 'vision', is better understood as an expression of eschatological hope, of the goal of our ceaseless cognitive striving, than as historical expectation.

But in what forms might this vision find interim, provisional expression? Two related possibilities come to mind: on one hand, the dramatic or symbolic forms that we associate with liturgy and public ritual; on the other, Christianity and Judaism are by no means the only cultural traditions to draw upon narrative, parabolic and (in a non-pejorative sense) mythic expressions of such a goal and vision.

The invocation of such general, cultural considerations clearly does not go nearly far enough to meet the urgency of the Pope's insistence that 'the interior unity of modern man is severely frustrated by the fragmentation of human knowledge'.[30] And yet, to be brutally frank, the nearer we come to the 'academic coal-face', the less realistic seems his plea that universities should be so transformed as to become ' "cultural laboratories" in which theology, philosophy, human sciences and natural sciences . . . engage in constructive dialogue'.[31]

Having begun with one Cambridge parable, I will end with another. For over thirty years, I have been a member of a dining club, the 'Triangle Club', which we created in order to promote the kind of dialogue which *Fides et ratio* sees as 'all the more important' in our day.[32] The members of the Triangle (the three corners being: philosophy, theology, the sciences) meet once a term and one of their number, or a guest, reads a paper. I have learnt much, over the years, from our meetings. And one of the things that I have learnt is that the numbers of scholars and scientists able and willing, for a variety of reasons, to engage, in a sustained way, in such conversations, are so minute as to have almost no impact whatsoever on the broader culture of a university. There is no disputing the desirability of the 'dialogue' for which the Pope pleads. But where are the educational, political, religious, economic and cultural pressures which might facilitate its promotion, and the radical transformation of institutions and attitudes (to say nothing of budgets and timetables!) which this would require? And yet, unless some movement is made in this direction, the attainment of the kind of common understanding necessary if we are fruitfully to address 'the pressing questions which face humanity' seems ever more elusive.[33]

---

[29] *Fides et ratio*, §85 (my stress).

[30] *Fides et ratio*, §85.

[31] See above, n. 24.

[32] *Fides et ratio*, §104.

[33] *Fides et ratio*, §104.

Reasonable Faith and a Trinitarian Logic: Faith and Reason in Eastern Orthodox Theology[1]

ARISTOTLE PAPANIKOLAOU

With the entire theological enterprise in the West being aimed primarily at constructing an *objective* or *scientific* theology, it was both natural and essential for it to establish itself on an equally objective and clearly defined foundation. Hence, the identification of faith, in theological terms, with 'propositions'; hence also the rejection from the theological process of any reference to or dependence upon *experience*. Yet it is precisely faith *as experience*, the total and living experience of the Church, that constitutes the source and the context of theology in the East, of that theology which characterized the patristic age.[2]

The first heretical differentiation which not merely survives historically, but has transformed radically the course of human history is one which denies the fundamental presupposition of orthodoxy, the apophaticism of truth . . . Augustine is surely the first great stage in the theoretical foundation of the rejection of apophaticism . . . And so, for the first time in history, truth is identified with its formulation and knowledge or the possession of truth with the individual understanding of this formulation. The truth is separated from the dynamic of life, it is identified with the concept, with right reasoning . . . Right reasoning replaces the dynamic indeterminacy of life; life enters the forecourt of 'logic' (*ratio*), logic is raised to a final authority, either in the form of moral rules or as a command of social and political practice.[3]

---

[1] I would like to express my gratitude to John Behr, John Fotopoulos, Joseph Lienhard, SJ, and Bernard McGinn for their comments on this essay. Omissions, mistakes and incoherences are entirely of my own doing.

[2] Alexander Schmemann, 'Liturgy and Theology', in *Liturgy and Tradition*, Thomas Fisch, (ed.), (Crestwood, NY: St Vladimir's Seminary Press, 1990), p. 54.

[3] Christos Yannaras, *Elements of Faith: An Introduction to Orthodox Theology*, trans. Keith Schram (Edinburgh: T&T Clark, 1991), pp. 154–5 [*ἀλφαβητάρι τῆς πίστης* (Athens: Domos, 1983), pp. 230–2]: '*Ἡ πρώτη αἱρετικὴ διαφοροποίηση ποὺ ὄχι ἁπλῶς ἐπιβιώνει ἱστορικά, ἀλλὰ μεταβάλλει ριζικὰ τὴν πορεία τῆς ἀνθρώπινης Ἱστορίας, εἶναι αὐτὴ ποὺ ἀρνεῖται τὴ θεμελιώδη προϋπόθεση τῆς ὀρθοδοξίας,*

A reasonable faith

If history is any guide, one might expect a theologian within the Eastern Orthodox tradition to offer a negative response to *Fides et ratio*. Even a cursory reading of the works of contemporary Eastern Orthodox theologians would reveal an attitude that one could charitably describe as suspicious toward any theological attempt to relate faith and reason. The mistake of Roman Catholic theology, most of these theologians would argue, is to rationalize that which is beyond reason. Knowledge of God, the goal of theologies, does not consist in 'objective' propositions resulting from rational processes and rules of logic, but is an event of mystical union or 'experience' with the living God. For these theologians, what distinguishes Eastern Orthodox from Roman Catholic theology is the priority of experience over reason. For Georges Florovsky, 'dogma presupposes experience, and only in the experience of vision and faith does dogma reach its fullness and come to life'.[4]

Eastern Orthodox sentiments on the 'rationalism' of the Roman Catholic tradition are discernible in their own assessments of the history of Orthodox theology. Since the Enlightenment, Orthodox theology has been subjected to 'Scholastic Captivity', in which the content of Orthodox theology was determined by scholastic methodology.[5] According to

---

τὸν ἀποφατισμὸ τῆς ἀλήθειας . . . Ὁ Αὐγουστίνος εἶναι σίγουρα ὁ πρῶτος μεγάλος σταθμὸς στὴ θεωρητικὴ θεμελίωση τῆς ἄρνησης τοῦ ἀποφατισμοῦ . . . Ἔστι, γιὰ πρώτη φορὰ στὴν Ἱστορία, ἡ ἀλήθεια ταυτίζεται μὲ τὴ διατύπωσή της καὶ ἡ γνώση ἢ κατοχὴ τῆς ἀλήθειας μὲ τὴν ἀτομικὴ κατανόηση αὐτῆς τῆς διατύπωσης. Ἡ ἀλήθεια χωρίζεται ἀπὸ τὴ δυναμικὴ τῆς ζωῆς, ταυτίζεται μὲ τὸ ἐννόημα, τὴν ὀρθὴ συλλογιστική . . . Ἡ ὀρθὴ συλλογιστικὴ ὑποκαθιστα τὴ δυναμικὴ ἀπροσδιοριστία τῆς ζωῆς, ἡ ζωὴ μπαίνει στὸ νάρθηκα τῆς «λογικῆς» (ratio), *ἡ λογικὴ ἀνάγεται σὲ τελικὴ αὐθεντία, εἴτε μὲ τὴ μορφὴ ἠθικῶν κανόνων εἴτε ὡς πρόσταγμα κοινωνικῆς καὶ πολιτικῆς πρακτικῆς.*' Such rhetoric against the 'rationalism' of the Roman Catholic tradition is present throughout Yannaras's work, most notably *De l'absence et de l'inconnaissance de Dieu d'après les écrits aréopagitiques et Martin Heidegger*, trans. Jacques Touraille (Paris: Editions du Cerf, 1971); *The Freedom of Morality*, trans. Elizabeth Briere (Crestwood, NY: St Vladimir's Seminary Press, 1984); *Orthodoxy and the West: Theology in Greece Today* (Athens: Domos, 1992 – in Greek); and *Personhood and Eros*, 4th edn., trans. Peter Chamberas (Brookline, MA: Holy Cross Orthodox Press, forthcoming).

[4] Georges Florovsky, 'Revelation, Philosophy and Theology', in *Creation and Redemption*, Vol. 2 in *The Collected Works of Georges Florovsky*, p. 35. See also, John Zizioulas, 'The Ecumenical Dimensions of Orthodox Theological Education', in *Orthodox Theological Education for the Life and Witness of the Church* (Geneva: World Council of Churches, 1978), p. 36; also, Schmemann's comments in n. 2 above.

[5] Zizioulas, 'The Ecumenical Dimensions of Orthodox Theological Education', p. 33. Though the phrase is Zizioulas's, the sentiment is evident throughout the works of Orthodox theologians, most notably Christos Yannaras and Alexander Schmemann. See especially, Christos Yannaras, 'Theology in Present-Day Greece', *St*

Christos Yannaras, 'An Orthodox people suffered the imposition from above of the western way of organizing and administering theology and popular piety.'[6] The contemporary Eastern Orthodox theologians who are critical of Western 'rationalism' and of the Orthodox captivity to 'scholastic methodology' are primarily those who heeded the call of Georges Florovsky for a *neo-patristic synthesis* within Eastern Orthodox theology.[7] At the centre of contemporary Orthodox attempts toward a *neo-patristic synthesis* is Gregory Palamas, the fourteenth-century Byzantine theologian. Palamas's thought is characterized as the culmination of Eastern patristic thought.[8] His apophaticism, distinction between God's essence and energies, understanding of knowledge of God in terms of mystical union beyond reason, and theology of the uncreated light have come to be identified as constitutive factors of a contemporary Orthodox theology. They have also become categories used to distinguish Eastern Orthodox approaches to theology from Roman Catholic rationalism.[9] Whatever the reason for Palamas's centrality in the contemporary Orthodox attempts toward a *neo-patristic synthesis*,[10]

Vladimir's Seminary Quarterly 16 (1972), pp. 195–214; Alexander Schmemann, 'Russian Theology: 1920–72: An Introductory Survey', *St Vladimir's Seminary Quarterly* 16 (1972), pp. 172–93, esp. pp. 172–4. See also, Georges Florovsky, *Ways of Russian Theology*, Part One, trans. Robert Nichols, Vol. 5 of *The Collected Works of Georges Florovsky* (Belmont: Nordland, 1979).

[6] Yannaras, *Elements of Faith*, p. 162 [p. 240]: '*Ἕνας ὀρθόδοξος λαὸς νὰ ὑφίσταται τὴν ἄνωθεν ἐπιβολὴ τοῦ δυτικοῦ τρόπου ὀργάνωσης καὶ διοίκησης τῆς Ἐκκλησίας, μὲ συνακόλουθη ἀλλοτρίωση τῆς θεολογίας καὶ τῆς λαϊκῆς εὐσέβειας.*' See also, Yannaras, *The Freedom of Morality*, p. 133 and *Orthodoxy and the West: Theology in Greece Today*.

[7] Georges Florovsky, 'Patristics and Modern Theology', in Hamilcar S. Alivisatos, (ed.), *Procès-verbaux du premier Congrès de Théologie Orthodoxe* (Athens: Pyrsos, 1939), pp. 238–42.

[8] See Vladimir Lossky, *The Vision of God* trans. Asheleigh Moorhouse (Crestwood, NY: St Vladimir's Seminary Press, 1983). It would be difficult to locate an Orthodox theologian that does not rely on the thought of Gregory Palamas as a basis for expressing a contemporary Orthodox theology. The sole exception is John Zizioulas who is critical of what he sees as a one-sided emphasis on the apophaticism of the neo-Palamite tradition in contemporary Orthodox theology, which threatens to negate the personal ontology of Cappadocian Trinitarian thought. For Zizioulas, Vladimir Lossky is the person responsible for the neo-Palamism of contemporary Orthodox thought.

[9] Christos Yannaras, commenting on the work of the Roman Catholic scholar Juan-Miguel Garrigues, argues that 'the acceptance or rejection of this (essence/energies) distinction will determine either the abstract or the real character of theological knowledge, the attribution of theological truths to either rational certainty or existential experience'. 'The Distinction between Essence and Energies and its Importance for Theology', *St Vladimir's Seminary Quarterly* 19 (1975), pp. 232–45. He is responding to Juan-Miguel Garrigues's 'L'énergie divine et la grace chez Maxime le Confesseur', *Istina* 19 (1974), pp. 272–96.

[10] It may have been a response to criticisms levelled against aspects of Palamas's thought by some Western scholars such as, Dom Clément Lialine, 'The Theological Teaching of Gregory Palamas on the Divine Simplicity', *Eastern Churches Quarterly*

the importance of his thought for contemporary Orthodox theology explains in large part the Orthodox attitudes of 'anti-rationalism'.[11]

One of the leading figures of the neo-palamite school is the Russian émigré theologian Vladimir Lossky. As such, Lossky was also at the forefront of Orthodox criticism of the 'intellectualism' of the Roman Catholic tradition, which is why his inclusion among 'recent thinkers' whose 'generous researches' resulted in a 'fruitful relationship between philosophy and the Word of God' is baffling.[12] It was indeed this way of understanding the theological enterprise that Lossky himself found, without exaggeration, perilous.

The fundamental problem of the intellectualism of the Roman Catholic tradition, according to Lossky, is that it precludes experience with the living, personal God by misconceiving the purpose of theology. The goal of theology for Lossky is not true, objective propositions about God, but to know God through a union with God.[13] Lossky's criticisms of the intellectualism within theology are most evident in his interpretation of the *filioque* in Western trinitarian theology.

The *filioque*, Lossky argues, is the result of a faulty theological method that precludes divine–human communion and depersonalizes the Trinity.

---

6 (1946), pp. 266–87. Vladimir Lossky was clearly aware of such criticisms. See *The Vision of God*, especially the first chapter entitled 'The Tradition of the Fathers and Scholasticism'. See also his 'The Theology of Light in the thought of St. Gregory Palamas', in *In the Image and Likeness of God*, eds. Thomas F. Bird and John H. Erickson (Crestwood, NY: St Vladimir's Seminary Press, 1974), pp. 45–69. For more on the debate over Palamas, on the Eastern Orthodox theologians' use of Palamite thought against the intellectualism of the West, together with additional references, see Rowan Williams, 'The Philosophical Structures of Palamism', *Eastern Churches Review* 9 (1977), pp. 27–44; also Kallistos Ware's response, 'The Debate about Palamism', pp. 45–63.

[11] The sole exception, to my knowledge, to this 'anti-rationalism' is Dumitru Staniloae, who distances himself from what he describes as the one-sided apophaticism of Lossky and Yannaras. Although for Staniloae 'rational knowledge' and 'apophatic knowledge' complete each other, priority is still given to apophatic theology as a 'direct experience' of God. See *Orthodox Dogmatic Theology: The Experience of God*, Vol. 1, trans. and ed. Ioan Ionita and Robert Barringer (Brookline, MA: Holy Cross Orthodox Press, 1998), pp. 95–124. See also, 'The Problems and Perspectives of Orthodox Theology', in *Theology and the Church*, trans. Robert Barringer (Crestwood, NY: St Vladimir's Seminary Press, 1980), pp. 213–26. Here and throughout his work Staniloae is uncharacteristically positive about 'Western theology', meaning the so-called 'rational' approach to theology in the Roman Catholic tradition.

[12] *Fides et ratio*, §74. On the puzzling nature of this list see Fergus Kerr, 'Comment: *Fides et ratio*', *New Blackfriars* 81 (2000), pp. 358–9.

[13] 'God no longer presents Himself as object for it is no more a question of knowledge but of union.' 'The way of knowledge of God is necessarily the way of deification.' Vladimir Lossky, *The Mystical Theology of the Eastern Church* (Crestwood, NY: St Vladimir's Seminary Press, 1976), pp. 28, 39.

For Lossky, knowledge of God is an encounter with the living, uncreated God. As such, it is an *ekstatic* mystical experience, one which transcends the limitations of created existence, including all human forms of knowing. When speaking about the *filioque*, Lossky usually refers to Thomas Aquinas's attempt to understand the Trinity in terms of Aristotelian categories. According to Aquinas, distinctions within God's essence are grounded in relations of mutual opposition. Aquinas's own argument for the *filioque* is based on the need to distinguish between the Son and the Spirit through a relation of mutual opposition (spiration–procession). On Lossky's reading, Aquinas affirms the *filioque* because of a rational demand that distinctions within God's essence must be based on relations of mutual opposition.[14] The *filioque* is then the result of a form of theology which defines knowledge of God in terms of Aristotelian understandings of theology as science, and hence, reduces the living God to an object of human understanding. If knowledge of God is defined in such a way, then divine–human communion is rendered impossible since knowledge of God as an object of human understanding does nothing to transcend the gulf between the uncreated and the created. Human modes of knowing are inevitably finite and limited. The *filioque* is then a result of a way of doing theology which precludes divine–human communion.

The doctrine of the Trinity best expresses the reality of divine–human communion not by resolving the antinomy of the one and three, which is what Lossky thinks the Thomistic interpretation of the *filioque* attempts to accomplish, but through an apophatic approach that maintains the antinomy between the one and the three. The goal is not to make comprehensible the incomprehensible, but to express the antinomy of the transcendent yet immanent God. The apophatic approach to the Trinity is one which affirms the reality of divine–human communion as an event of participation in the uncreated existence of God, and as such, an *ekstatic* transcendence of the limitations of created existence. Such an apophatic approach simply affirms as 'fact'[15] that God is Trinity without further attempting to understand *how* God is Trinity. The distinctions between the Son and the Spirit are simply expressed through distinct relations of origin from the Father, which themselves are biblically based.

The second problem is the depersonalization of the Trinity and the affirmation of a monistic conception of God, which, according to

[14] See Lossky, 'The Procession of the Holy Spirit in Orthodox Trinitarian Doctrine', in *In the Image and Likeness of God*, esp. p. 76.

[15] 'Here apophaticism finds its fulfilment in the revelation of the Holy Trinity as primordial fact, ultimate reality, first datum which cannot be deduced, explained or discovered by way of any other truth; for there is nothing which is prior to it' (Lossky, *The Mystical Theology*, p. 64).

Lossky, is the inevitable result of a theological rationalism.[16] In so far as the Spirit proceeds from the Father and the Son 'the two persons represent a non-personal unity, in that they give rise to a further relation of opposition'.[17] If one accepts that the Holy Spirit proceeds from both persons, then the distinction between the Father and the Son is confused, and the Trinity is in jeopardy. The Father and the Son become 'a single principle' and the diversity in the Trinity is 'relativised.'[18] Moreover, in that the Holy Spirit proceeds from both, the Holy Spirit becomes the bond which unites the Father and the Son, or 'the unity of the two in their identical nature'.[19] Not only is the personal diversity of the Son and the Father threatened by being 'a single principle', but also that of the Spirit in being reduced 'to no more than a reciprocal bond between the Father and the Son'.[20] In being the love which the Father and the Son share, the Holy Spirit is no longer a person but an attribute. No matter which way one turns, the 'relations of opposition' ultimately leads one, according to Lossky, back to the essence of God.[21] For Lossky, as the principle of

---

[16] Yannaras and Zizioulas also affirm the link between rationalism and the depersonalization of the Trinity, with the Western culprit being not so much Aquinas as Augustine. For Yannaras see *The Elements of Faith* and *Personhood and Eros*. For Zizioulas, see *Being as Communion* (Crestwood, NY: St Vladimir's Seminary Press, 1985), 'Human Capacity and Human Incapacity', *Scottish Journal of Theology* 28 (1975), pp. 401–48, 'The Doctrine of God the Trinity Today: Suggestions for an Ecumenical Study', in *The Forgotten Trinity: A Selection of Papers Presented to the BCC Study Commission on Trinitarian Doctrine Today*, ed. Alasdair I. C. Heron (London: BCC/CCBI, 1991), pp. 19–32, 'On Being a Person: Toward an Ontology of Personhood', in *Persons, Divine and Human*, eds. Christoph Schwöbel and Colin E. Gunton (Edinburgh: T&T Clark, 1991), pp. 33–46, and 'The Doctrine of the Holy Trinity: The Significance of the Cappadocian Contribution', in *Trinitarian Theology Today: Essays in Divine Being and Act*, ed. Christoph Schwöbel (Edinburgh: T&T Clark, 1995): pp. 44–60. For criticism of Orthodox interpretations of Augustine's Trinitarian theology, see Rowan Williams, '*Sapientia* and the Trinity: Reflections on the *De Trinitate*', in *Collectanea Augustiniana. Mélanges T. J. Van Bavel*, eds. B. Bruning, et. al. (Leuven: Uitgeverij Peeters 1990), pp. 317–32. See also Michel René Barnes, 'Augustine in Contemporary Trinitarian Theology', *Theological Studies* 56 (1995), pp. 237–50.

[17] Lossky, 'The Procession of the Holy Spirit in Orthodox Trinitarian Doctrine', p. 77.

[18] Lossky, 'The Procession of the Holy Spirit in Orthodox Trinitarian Doctrine', p. 77.

[19] Lossky, 'The Procession of the Holy Spirit in Orthodox Trinitarian Doctrine', p. 77.

[20] Lossky, *The Mystical Theology*, p. 62.

[21] Rowan Williams in dealing with Lossky's misinterpretations of Aquinas strongly disagrees with Lossky's interpretation and ultimately concludes that 'the understanding of persona which emerges', from Thomistic trinitarian theology, 'is one which *does* allow for a measure of real trinitarian pluralism, a plurality of consciousnesses, and for a genuine analogy between human and divine personality' ('The Theology of Vladimir Nikolaievich Lossky: An Exposition and Critique' [unpublished PhD thesis, Oxford University, 1975], p. 154).

personal communion with the living God, the personal distinctiveness of the Holy Spirit is essential to maintain, and can only be done through a theological apophaticism.[22]

Rowan Williams puts it well in asserting that 'it is, of course, Lossky's attack on the *filioque* which is the most immediately striking feature of his polemic against Western theology'.[23] Lossky himself would say that the *filioque* is no trifling matter but 'the sole dogmatic grounds for the separation of East and West'. He adds further that 'the difference between the two conceptions of the Trinity determines, on both sides, the whole character of theological thought. This is so to such an extent that it becomes difficult to apply, without equivocation, the same name of theology to these two different ways of dealing with divine realities.'[24] The two different ways, of course, are the rational approach versus the apophatic approach. For Lossky, the *filioque* results from an intellectualization of the Trinity, and in so doing, echoing Pascal, he argues that 'the God of the philosophers and savants is introduced into the heart of the Living God'.[25] The rational approach inevitably leads to a monistic God, a conception that does not allow for real communion between the divine and the human.

The rhetoric of the contemporary Eastern Orthodox theologians might give one the justifiable impression that there is no place for reason within the Eastern Orthodox tradition.[26] The anti-intellectualism of the

---

[22] For more on Lossky and the *filioque* see Rowan Williams, 'The Theology of Vladimir Nikolaievich Lossky', esp. pp. 129–56; see also Aristotle Papanikolaou, 'Apophaticism versus Ontology: A Study of Vladimir Lossky and John Zizioulas' (unpublished PhD thesis, The University of Chicago, 1998), esp. pp. 148–57.

[23] Williams, 'The Theology of Vladimir Nikolaievich Lossky', p. 129.

[24] Lossky,'The Procession of the Holy Spirit in Orthodox Trinitarian Doctrine', pp. 71, 80.

[25] Lossky, 'The Procession of the Holy Spirit in Orthodox Trinitarian Doctrine', p. 88. Elsewhere he says, 'The positive approach employed by *Filioquist* triadology brings about a certain rationalization of the dogma of the Trinity, insofar as it suppresses the fundamental antinomy between the essence and the hypostases. One has the impression that the heights of theology have been deserted in order to descend to the level of religious philosophy. On the other hand, the negative approach, which places us face to face with the primordial antinomy of absolute identity and no less absolute diversity in God, does not seek to conceal this antinomy but to express it fittingly, so that the mystery of the Trinity might make us transcend the philosophical mode of thinking and that the Truth might make us free from our human limitations, by altering our means of understanding. If in the former approach faith seeks understanding, in order to transpose revelation onto the plane of philosophy, in the latter approach understanding seeks the realities of faith, in order to be transformed, by becoming more and more open to the mysteries of revelation' (p. 80).

[26] Except for the limited use of categories whose meaning is transformed. See Georges Florovsky, 'Revelation, Philosophy and Theology', in *Creation and Redemption*, esp. p. 33; also Lossky, *The Mystical Theology of the Eastern Church*,

contemporary Eastern Orthodox theologians, however, tends to ignore the more positive uses of reason in relation to faith in the Eastern Christian patristic tradition.[27] The emphasis on a mystical union with God beyond reason did not necessarily entail the rejection of rationality in the life and expression of faith. A cursory reading of apologetic texts and those commenting on the ascetical life reveal the importance of the role of reason for the Eastern Christian tradition.

The ascetical life for Gregory Palamas includes an effort to 'keep watch over and correct our reason by a rigorous sobriety'.[28] This link between ascetical practices and right thinking or correct reasoning is affirmed throughout the Eastern patristic tradition, in no less a thinker than Maximus the Confessor. According to Maximus: 'The one who has had success with the virtues and has become rich in knowledge as at last discerning things by their nature does and considers everything according to right reason and is in no way misled. For it is on the basis of whether we make use of things rationally or irrationally that we become either virtuous or wicked.'[29] Throughout Maximus's writings and those of other Eastern Christian writers, the virtue of discernment, which involves the rational capacity of the soul, is a necessary condition for growth in the spiritual life. Even in the ascetical life, which leads to the union of God beyond reason, the rational capacity of the soul clearly has its function.

---

esp. p. 50; also, John Meyendorff, 'Greek Philosophy and Christian Theology in the Early Church', in his *Catholicity and the Church* (Crestwood, NY: St Vladimir's Seminary Press, 1983): esp. p. 42. *Fides et ratio* itself rejects such a limited view of the relation between faith and reason. Commenting on the early Christian fathers it asserts that 'This means that it is grossly unfair to try to interpret their work as an attempt to reduce the truths of faith to philosophical categories' (§41).

[27] Even in Palamas, the main concern was not the opposition between faith and philosophy, but the proper use of philosophy. 'If one says that philosophy, in so far as it is natural, is a gift of God, then one says true, without contradiction, and without incurring the accusation that falls on those who abuse philosophy and pervert it to an unnatural end. Indeed they make their condemnation by using God's gift in a way pleasing to Him' (*The Triads*, trans. Nicholas Gendle [New York: Paulist Press, 1983], 1.1.19 [p. 27]; see also 1.1.22 [p. 30]). For more on Palamas's thought on philosophy, see John Meyendorff, *A Study of Gregory Palamas*, 2nd edn., trans. George Lawrence (London: The Faith Press, 1974), pp. 116–33. Such sentiments echo *Fides et ratio*: 'Reason, bereft of revelation, runs into devious paths which deprive it of the ability of discovering its ultimate goal.' (*Fides et ratio*, §48).

[28] Palamas, *The Triads*, 1.2.3 (p. 43).

[29] Maximus the Confessor, *The Four Hundred Chapters On Love*, trans. George C. Berthold (New York: Paulist Press, 1985): 1:92 (p. 45). See also 4:91 (p. 85). See also John Climacus, *The Ladder of Divine Ascent*, trans. Colm Luibheid and Norman Russell (New York: Paulist Press, 1982), step 26 (p. 229): 'discernment is . . . a solid understanding of the will of God in all times, in all places, in all things . . . an uncorrupted conscience. It is pure perception.'

One can further discern that the use of reason is also necessary for the expression of faith itself. Such a view of reason is especially evident in a late apologetic work by Athanasius of Alexandria, *On the Incarnation*.[30] Throughout the treatise, Athanasius is concerned to show that the way in which God has saved humanity is indeed 'fitting'. He is even bold to say that any other way would have been 'unfitting' (ἀπρεπής) and 'unworthy' (ἀνάξιος) of God:

> For it would not have been worthy of the goodness of God that what had been brought into existence by him should be corrupted on account of the deceit which the devil had played on men . . . So it was not right that he should permit men to be destroyed by corruption, because this was neither *proper* nor *fitting* for the goodness of God. But as this had to be, so again on the other hand lies opposed to it what was *reasonable* for God.[31]

Athanasius gives reasons why salvation involved the death and resurrection of the Word, ultimately concluding that 'his death for us on the cross was suitable and fitting, and its cause appeared to be *eminently reasonable*'.[32] As Khaled Anatolios argues, 'The systematic task of demonstrating a rational coherence between the doctrine of God and the doctrine of the incarnation is thus integral to the apologetic design of this treatise.'[33] Athanasius is rejecting the path of fideism and accepting the challenge that once revealed, God's salvific action in history can indeed be shown to be more reasonable than any of the alternatives.[34]

Although it appears that *Fides et ratio* is directed primarily to the philosophical community, it also has ecumenical relevance as it challenges the 'sister church', and especially the contemporary Eastern Orthodox theologians to go beyond the rhetoric of 'anti-intellectualism', which includes labelling all the ills of modernity, such as the notion of the autonomous self, as the logical end of scholasticism,[35] and to think more

---

[30] One could also mention Justin Martyr, Clement of Alexandria, Origen, among others, as *Fides et ratio* reminds us (§§ 36–39).

[31] Athanasius, *On the Incarnation*, trans. Robert W. Thomson (Oxford: Clarendon Press, 1971), 6–7 (p. 149); emphasis mine. Similar passages can be found in 1, 10, 19, 22, 26, 33, 41, 44.

[32] Athanasius, *On the Incarnation*, 26; emphasis mine.

[33] Khaled Anatolios, *Athanasius: The Coherence of His Thought* (New York: Routledge, 1998), p. 39.

[34] For additional Eastern patristic references, including Gregory Nazianzus, Gregory of Nyssa, John Chrysostom, Dionysius the Areopagite and Gregory Palamas, reflecting positive attitudes toward 'rational knowledge' of God and the rational capacity of the soul, see Staniloae, *Orthodox Dogmatic Theology: The Experience of God*, esp. pp. 95–124.

[35] This view of modernity is especially evident in the works of Christos Yannaras

critically about the relation of faith, reason and the mystical life in their own tradition. In an age where European and American cultures can no longer be labelled as 'Christian', Christianity has entered a second apologetic period in its history. As with the first apologetic period, theologians are required to articulate how the Christian faith is reasonable, that is, makes sense in response to questions that test its credibility. As Avery Dulles has well said,

> The Church itself needs to be well armed with rational grounds for believing, so that she can proclaim the gospel in a persuasive way, as did the apostles. For believers who are troubled by difficulties, the arguments frequently serve to remove obstacles or deterrents to faith and to assure them that the objections are not valid.[36]

Contemporary Orthodox theologians should not have a problem supporting the spirit of the document's claim that 'the Church judges philosophy to be an indispensable instrument for gaining understanding of faith and for communicating the truth of the Gospel to those who do not yet know it'.[37]

A trinitarian logic

Beyond the anti-intellectualism, however, one can detect a genuine concern over the effect a relationship between philosophy and theology may have on the Christian faith. Lossky's own claim that with the *filioque*, 'the God of the philosophers and savants is introduced into the heart of the Living God' echoes not simply Pascal, but Tertullian, 'What does Athens have to do with Jerusalem?' The issue of the relation between philosophy and theology has been an ongoing discussion within the Christian tradition almost since its inception. In relating philosophy to theology, the question inevitably is raised whether the content of faith is transformed in such a way that one sees something other than what is revealed in Jesus Christ. The anti-intellectualism of the contemporary Eastern Orthodox theologians may appear extreme, but it does raise the legitimate question of whether theology needs to be related to philo-

---

and Alexander Schmemann. See Yannaras's 'Scholasticism and Technology,' *Eastern Churches Review* 6 (August 1974), pp. 162–9. For an extreme view of the relation between European secularism and Roman Catholicism, see Justin Popovich, 'Humanistic and Theanthropic Education', 'Reflection on the Infallibility of European Man', and 'Humanistic Ecumenism', in *Orthodox Faith and Life in Christ*, ed. and trans. Asterios Gerostergios, et. al. (Belmont, MA: Institute for Byzantine and Modern Greek Studies), pp. 51–116, 169–96.

36 'Reason, Philosophy, and the Grounding of Faith: A Reflection on *Fides et ratio*', *International Philosophical Quarterly* 40 (December 2000), p. 488.

37 *Fides et ratio*, §5.

sophy, or if the particular way in which the relationship is conceived may give rise to a primacy of reason over faith. As Rowan Williams himself says of Lossky, 'his unfairness and inaccuracy in particular criticism of the West are not of primary significance; the essential complaint about Western intellectualism and subordination to philosophy remains unaffected, raising the whole question of rival conceptions of precisely how God is known, and how His activity is mediated in the world to created subjects'.[38]

It is clearly not the intent of *Fides et ratio* to subordinate theology to philosophy. Instead it speaks of the need of the one for the other, their complementarity, and compatibility.[39] The Encyclical is emphatic, however, on the primacy of faith, philosophy's need of faith and revelation, and the role of faith in restoring philosophy's integrity and giving it the right direction. There is no lack of criticism for philosophies that have lost their way, particularly those which have abandoned philosophy's original purpose – the pursuit of truth. 'Reason, bereft of revelation, runs into devious paths which deprive it of the ability of discovering its ultimate goal.'[40] What is needed is reason with 'the outlook provided by faith', 'purged and made righteous' and 'enlightened by faith'.[41] Only through faith can one hope to 'enter the inner mystery' of God revealed in Jesus Christ, and revelation itself presents signs 'to help reason, which seeks to understand the mystery'.[42]

If the Encyclical is clear on the primacy of faith in relation to reason, it is less so on what is actually meant by reason. The *ratio* in *Fides et ratio* seems to intend more than simply the natural human capacity to reason. Throughout the Encyclical speaks of reason as a particular 'degree of knowledge' and affirms its 'autonomy'.[43] It enjoys this autonomy because 'reason by its nature tends towards truth, and moreover is equipped with the necessary means to arrive at it'.[44] Philosophy is the 'way of knowing those principal truths which touch upon the life of man' and it does so 'observing its own laws', with 'the powers of reason alone', and by remaining faithful to its 'own character and rules'.[45] These particular methods are then brought in critical relationship to the propositions of faith for the sake of greater understanding. Philosophy then brings to faith 'a reason that is both educated and formed by reflection and by argument' in order for theology to do its work, because 'in the light of faith there is need of critical reason'.[46] It is exactly the relationship between faith and a philosophy with its own 'rules' and 'powers of

[38] Williams, 'The Theology of Vladimir Nikolaievich Lossky', p. 156.
[39] *Fides et ratio*, §§48, 5, 67.
[40] *Fides et ratio*, §48.
[41] *Fides et ratio*, §§16, 41, 20.
[42] *Fides et ratio*, §13.
[43] *Fides et ratio*, §§34, 75.
[44] *Fides et ratio*, §49.
[45] *Fides et ratio*, §§5, 73, 76, 49.
[46] *Fides et ratio*, §77.

reason' that raises the concern for contemporary Eastern Orthodox theologians, among others within the Christian tradition, of the subordination of faith to philosophy, and hence, the loss of content of the salvific revelation in Jesus Christ. This concern can be illustrated further through an analysis of the relationship between the *auditus fidei* and the *intellectus fidei* as discussed in *Fides et ratio*.

According to the Encyclical, the task of the *auditus fidei* is the right interpretation of the truth of revelation in Jesus Christ. Theology 'makes its own the content of revelation, illustrated in the progress of time by Sacred Tradition, Holy Scripture and the living Magisterium of the Church'.[47] The goal of the first part of the twofold task of theology is to arrive at the correct expression of the truth of the revelation in the form of propositions. For this to occur, 'a first and urgent necessity is imposed upon us of carefully exploring the texts: above all of Holy Scripture, and subsequently those in which the living tradition of the Church is expressed'.[48] Such an analysis with the guidance of the Church's Magisterium will allow for the expression of what is actually believed, the content of faith for Christians.

The second aspect of the 'two established methodological principles' is the *intellectus fidei*, the attempt to give understanding to faith.[49] At this point the role of philosophy, with its own rational methods and rules, becomes crucial. The *intellectus fidei* is the process of giving 'rendering more easily intelligible ecclesial tradition, the pronouncements of the Magisterium, and the opinions of the distinguished masters of theology: for these latter often express themselves by means of thoughts and forms of thinking, which derive in their turn from a particular philosophical tradition'.[50] The *intellectus fidei* illustrates that the truth articulated in the *auditus fidei* 'enjoys its own natural intelligibility, which is so logically coherent that it stands as *an authentic wisdom*'.[51] Through the help of philosophy, the *intellectus fidei* expresses the knowledge of the 'divine Truth' by 'reflection and by argument'.[52] 'Speculative dogmatic theology presumes and embraces the philosophy of man, and of the world, and more profoundly of "being" itself, which rests on objective truth.'[53] A bit more emphatically toward the end, the Encyclical asserts:

> the *understanding of faith* demands the assistance of a philosophy of being, which allows *dogmatic theology* to perform its task in an appropriate fashion . . . If the *understanding of faith* wishes to enfold

[47] *Fides et ratio*, §65.
[48] *Fides et ratio*, §93.
[49] *Fides et ratio*, §65.
[50] *Fides et ratio*, §65.
[51] *Fides et ratio*, §66, emphasis mine.
[52] *Fides et ratio*, §§66, 77.
[53] *Fides et ratio*, §66.

within itself all the treasures of the theological tradition, it must have recourse to a philosophy of being.[54]

An analysis of the relationship between the *auditus fidei* and the *intellectus fidei* would thus confirm that by *ratio* the Encyclical is referring not simply to the natural human capacity to reason, but to an autonomous and independent philosophy, with its own rational method and rules, which then serve to give coherency to the truths of faith, demonstrate their intelligibility and authenticate the content of faith as a body of knowledge.

This understanding of the relation between faith and reason comes under question when examining further the distinction between the *auditus fidei* and *intellectus fidei*. The basic issue is whether the distinction makes any sense, and whether it fails to acknowledge adequately that an *intellectus fidei* is already operative in the *auditus fidei*. In other words, the *auditus fidei* already expresses an *intellectus fidei*. Since *Fides et ratio* often mentions the doctrine of the Trinity, it is to the development of the trinitarian doctrine of God that we will now turn to examine further this distinction.

The doctrine itself is the culmination of centuries of reasoned responses to particular questions concerning the gospel message of salvation in Jesus Christ. The response to such particular questions is the establishment of the Christian tradition itself and a particular Christian mode of rationality. As Eric F. Osborn points out, much of early Christian thought was dedicated to establishing a 'canon' or 'rule of faith'. Such a rule of faith was not for the purpose of excluding reason, but for making reason possible.[55] He adds that 'the rule was a matter of logic and that Christian truth, because of its exclusive revelation, generated argument from the beginning. To abandon it was not merely wrong but unreasonable.'[56] The rule did not exclude argument, but was the logic by which argument within the Christian tradition proceeded. As John Behr argues, the 'canon' constituted the 'first principles' of Christian reflection.[57] Moreover, 'the point of the canon is not to stymie inquiry and reflection, but rather to make it possible'.[58]

---

[54] *Fides et ratio*, §97.

[55] Eric F. Osborn, 'Reason and the Rule of Faith in the Second Century AD', in *The Making of Orthodoxy: Essays in honour of Henry Chadwick*, ed. Rowan Williams (Cambridge: Cambridge University Press, 1989), pp. 40–61. My thanks to John Behr for suggesting this essay.

[56] Osborn, 'Reason and the Rule of Faith in the Second Century AD', p. 48.

[57] 'These first principles, grasped by faith, are the basis for subsequent demonstrations, and are also subsequently used to evaluate other claims to truth, acting thus as a "canon"' (John Behr, *The Way to Nicaea*, Vol. 1 of *The Formation of Christian Theology* [Crestwood, NY: St Vladimir's Seminary Press, 2001], p. 33).

[58] Behr, *The Way to Nicaea*, p. 38. See also Osborn, 'Reason and the Rule of Faith

A cursory reading of the development of Christian thought in the first four centuries, with special attention to the doctrine of the Trinity, reveals that the *auditus fidei*, the expression of the Christian faith, is not simply a matter of exegesis and interpretation of the datum of Christian revelation. It is itself an embodiment of an *intellectus fidei*, an ongoing understanding of the central elements of the gospel of Christ according to the Scriptures. The process of expressing, and hence, understanding the Christian faith is also the formation of a particular Christian tradition of reasoning with its own principles and rules of logic. In asserting the independence and autonomy of philosophical reasoning *Fides et ratio* may be forgetting that reason itself has a history.[59] As Alasdair MacIntyre argues, there is no conception of rationality that is not constituted within a particular tradition. Traditions themselves are particular modes of rational enquiry that are 'tradition-constituted' and 'tradition-constitutive'.[60] This leads to the inevitability of incommensurable and incompatible modes of rational enquiry. Such incommensurability does not necessarily mean that traditions 'do not share some standards. All the traditions with which we have been concerned agree in according a certain authority to logic both in their theory and in their practice . . . But that upon which they agree is insufficient to resolve those disagreements.'[61] Highlighting the rule of non-contradiction as amongst 'a sort of nucleus of philosophical ideas, which are regularly present in the history of human reflection' (§4), *Fides et ratio* is simply pointing to the rules of logic which various forms of rationality may have in common but which are not sufficient for overcoming their incompatibility and incommensurability. Furthermore, in affirming that philosophy, with a particular conception of being, is needed to give understanding to the propositions of faith, the Encyclical may be suggesting a need to relate two incompatible forms of tradition-constituted rational enquiry.[62] Although *Fides et ratio* may express some concern that such a view of rationality may lead to relativism, MacIntyre argues that a view of rational enquiry that is tradition-constituted and tradition-constitutive does not necessarily mean that the traditions are not making truth claims, nor does it mean that such a view of truth is relativist or perspectivist.[63]

---

in the Second Century AD', p. 57: 'The rule did not limit reason to make room for faith, but used faith to make room for reason. Without a credible first principle, reason was lost in an infinite regress.'

[59] Alasdair MacIntyre, echoing Hegel, in *Whose Justice? Which Rationality?* (Notre Dame, IN: University of Notre Dame Press, 1988), p. 9.

[60] MacIntyre, *Whose Justice? Which Rationality?*, pp. 349–69.

[61] MacIntyre, *Whose Justice? Which Rationality?*, p. 351.

[62] As Zizioulas suggests in rejecting the attempt to understand God as Trinity within the framework of a 'substance ontology'.

[63] MacIntyre, *Whose Justice? Which Rationality?*, pp. 352–69.

An analysis of the history of the doctrine of the Trinity reveals the development of a particular Christian mode of rationality. This history has traditionally been presented as an attempt at finding the proper language for expressing coherently a God who is three yet one. The development of the doctrine itself, according to the traditional view, is then one of intelligibility, conceptual clarity and coherency of the three-and-one God that is presented in the Scriptures as the Father, Son and Holy Spirit. Early Christian thinkers, such as Justin Martyr and Origen, who do not clearly affirm the co-equality of the Son with the Father are, anachronistically, labelled subordinationist. It is anachronistic to label them as such because in the early period of Christianity there is no question of God as Trinity or of the one and the many within the life of God. There can be no subordinationism in the formative period of Christianity simply because the central question is not how God is three-and-one, or even how the Father and Son are distinct yet one God. The very identity of Jesus Christ is itself under question.

The explicit affirmation of the Trinity comes with Athanasius in response to particular positions held by Arius. Athanasius's own trinitarian theology is the culmination of centuries of reasoned reflection on the initial faith in the gospel about Jesus Christ, crucified and risen, according to the Scriptures,[64] which is forced to clarify itself as it encounters questions from pagan intellectuals who find absurd the notion, among others, of a crucified messiah.[65] Who is Jesus and what is the nature of the salvation accomplished and offered in his person?[66] These two questions are never separated from each other in early Christian thought, and they are the central questions that drive Christian thought eventually to affirm the Trinity. As Bernard Lonergan himself states, Athanasius set out to establish that 'the Father is God, that the Son is also God, and that there is only one God'.[67] Athanasius's primary concern, however, was not the elimination of the contradiction of how the Son and the Father could be distinct yet one God. Missing is why Athanasius was concerned with affirming that Christ is of the same

---

[64] For how this gospel proclamation constituted the core of early Christian thought, see Behr, *The Way to Nicaea*, pp. 1–48.

[65] 'But an answer cannot stand alone, without being an answer to a specific question; the question provides the context within which the answer has its meaning' (Behr, *The Way to Nicaea*, p. 6).

[66] ' "Who do you say I am?" (Matt 16:15). This question, posed by Jesus Christ, is the one that Christian theology seeks to answer.' Early Christian theology is nothing less than 'the reflection provoked by this question in the formative years of the history of the Christian Church' (Behr, *The Way to Nicaea*, p. 1).

[67] Bernard Lonergan, *The Way to Nicaea: The Dialectical Development of Trinitarian Theology*, trans. Conn O'Donovan (Philadelphia: Westminster Press, 1976), p. 47.

divinity as God the Father. This 'why' has to do with the question of salvation and is essential to understanding the doctrine itself.

To establish the point that the *auditus fidei* of Christian faith is also an *intellectus fidei* there is no need to go into the details of the already well-known Arian controversy. It is enough to remind ourselves that Arius rejected the notion that the Son is of the same substance of the Father for the simple reason that it threatened the notion of the one God, one that is scripturally sound and that enjoyed wide support in Greek philosophical circles for more than a few centuries.[68] It simply was more reasonable to assert that there is only one God, and one could not reasonably affirm the principle of the one God with talk of the Son being of the same substance as the Father. Athanasius defied such logic, because something more was at stake than a particular philosophical notion of the one God. For Athanasius Christ must be divine because our salvation requires him to be so. If salvation consists in freedom from death and corruption, as it does for Athanasius, then it must consist in the unity of the uncreated and the created.[69] The by now familiar axioms that God 'became man so that humans can become divine',[70] and 'only the uncreated can save the created'[71] are essential to understanding Athanasius's trinitarian theology. If salvation is accomplished and given in Jesus Christ, and if salvation consists in freedom from death and corruption inherent in created nature and actualized because of sin, then Jesus Christ must be divine, otherwise there is no salvation.

In broad terms, Athanasius's own thought is implying that the monistic conception of God that Arius was affirming is inadequate to resolving the question of the immanence and transcendence of God.[72]

---

[68] Some would argue that Arius was also soteriologically motivated. See Robert C. Gregg and Dennis E. Groh, *Early Arianism: A View of Salvation* (Philadelphia: Fortress Press, 1981).

[69] See Athanasius, *On the Incarnation*, 9.

[70] Athanasius, *On the Incarnation*, 54. 'but being God, he later became man, that instead he might deify us' ('Orations Against the Arians, Book I', in *The Trinitarian Controversy*, trans. and ed. William G. Rusch, [Philadelphia, PA: Fortress Press, 1980], 39 [p. 102]). Also, 'It is as one who is God that he took on flesh, and it is as one who was in flesh that he divinised the flesh' ('Oration Against the Arians, Book III', in *The Christological Controversy*, trans. and ed. Richard A. Norris, Jr [Philadelphia, PA: Fortress Press, 1980]: 38 [p. 97]).

[71] Different patristic writers express this axiom in different ways. See Irenaeus, *Against the Heresies*, 3.19.1, 4.33.4. It is expressed throughout Athanasius's writings. As an example, 'But a creature could never be saved by a creature, any more than the creatures were created by a creature, if the Word was not Creator' (*Ad Adelphium*, 8. Cited in Anatolios, *Athanasius: The Coherence of His Thought*, p. 125).

[72] On the relation of Athanasius's trinitarian theology to the question of the immanence and transcendence of God, see Anatolios, *Athanasius: The Coherence of His Thought*, esp. pp. 85–163.

Both poles of God's being are necessary for the sake of human salvation, and in order for this relation between the uncreated and the created to be adequately expressed a new conception of God is required. Plurality needs to be thought of in the very being of God and such plurality need not threaten the unity of God's being, that is, the notion of the one God. Moreover, divine–human communion, the immanence and transcendence of God require a mediator who is fully divine and human, who manifests a God who is above all yet in all, and who unites the uncreated and the created, the universal and the particular.[73] Athanasius forges a new, trinitarian logic, one of divine–human communion against the monistic logic of the Greek philosophers. The Trinity is an expression of divine–human communion and the Christian response to the question of the transcendence and immanence of God, to the one and the many.

The development of the doctrine of the Trinity in early Christianity is thus the development of a mode of rationality. This is especially clear if one investigates the reasons why Athanasius affirmed the divinity of the Son over Arius's objections. In doing so, Athanasius is affirming a trinitarian rationality, a logic of divine–human communion against a monistic conception of God. Athanasius's own formulation also reveals that although the doctrine of the Trinity is puzzling, it is not illogical or irrational.[74] Simply because it cannot be arrived at through the traditional rules of logic implies that the Trinity embodies its own logic that either transforms or supplements the traditional rules of logic. As a result, the doctrine itself cannot constitute a first principle which gives guidance to reason, as is suggested in *Fides et ratio*. It may express principles incompatible with certain first principles of philosophy, as Athanasius's dispute with Arius would suggest.

Attention to the development of the doctrine of the Trinity also reveals that the heart of the doctrine itself is divine–human communion. Theological speculation on God as Trinity that also attempts to relate faith and reason must preserve the core of the doctrine, which is divine–human communion. As an example of such speculation, it may be helpful to turn to Aquinas's treatment of the Trinity since he is highlighted in *Fides et ratio* as a model for a creative synthesis between faith and reason, and since he is often cited by contemporary Orthodox theologians as the representative figure of a faulty scholastic method. It would be a mistake, as contemporary Orthodox theologians are apt to make, to treat necessarily Aquinas's trinitarian theology in the *Prima Pars* in

---

[73] On Athanasius's understanding of Christ as mediator between the uncreated and the created, see Anatolios, *Athanasius: The Coherence of His Thought*, pp. 109–16.

[74] A position held by many contemporary Eastern Orthodox theologians.

isolation from his treatment of salvation in the *Tertia Pars*.[75] Second, it would also be a misinterpretation of Aquinas to read him as not concerned with divine–human communion.[76] It is legitimate, however, to question whether Aquinas's method of attempting to understand God as Trinity within the framework of an ontology of *esse* answers not simply the question of how God is one and three, but how the Trinity adequately resolves the problem of God's immanence and transcendence and of divine–human communion.

The question must also be posed as to why for Aquinas and for *Fides et ratio* the 'philosophy of man, and of the world, and more profoundly of "being" itself' needs to be established in order to understand the doctrine of the Trinity.[77] Does not the doctrine itself imply its own philosophy of being, the human being and the world? Might it also imply a philosophy of being that is necessarily incompatible with philosophies of being that do not begin with the first principle that the truth of God is revealed in the person of Jesus Christ? The Eastern Orthodox theologian John Zizioulas affirms such a position.[78] For Zizioulas, a preconceived ontology of substance is incompatible with the 'ontological revolution' implied within the trinitarian theology of the fourth century. Although Zizioulas's interpretation of the fourth-century trinitarian theology is not without its detractors,[79] it does not weaken the force of his assertion that trinitarian theology implies a relational ontology that defines being in terms of personhood, otherness, particularity and difference, a position opposed to the argument in *Fides et ratio* that a philosophy of being is needed to understand the intelligibility of the Trinity.[80]

---

75 As Wayne J. Hankey reminds us in *God in Himself: Aquinas' Doctrine of God as Expounded in the* Summa Theologiae (Oxford: Oxford University Press, 1987).

76 As both Hankey and Anna Williams remind us. For Williams see, *The Ground of Union: Deification in Aquinas and Palamas* (New York: Oxford University Press, 1999).

77 *Fides et ratio*, §66.

78 For references to Zizioulas's Trinitarian theology, see above, n. 16.

79 See in particular the criticism of André de Halleux, 'Personalisme ou essentialisme trinitaire chez les Pères cappadociens? Une mauvaise controverse', *Revue théologique de Louvain* 17 (1986), pp. 129–55, 265–92; also, '"Hypostase" et "Personne" dans la formation du dogme trinitaire (ca. 375–81)', *Revue d'histoire ecclésiastique* 79 (1984), pp. 313–69, 625–70.

80 It is also worth noting Zizioulas's own conception of the relation of philosophy to theology. For Zizioulas there can be no philosophical justification of theology, but rather the reverse, 'a *theological justification of philosophy*' (*Being as Communion*, p. 46). Philosophy is able to identify the problems theology alone can resolve (see 'On Being a Person: Towards an Ontology of Personhood', esp. p. 44.). For a similar view of the relation between philosophy and theology, one that at least merits comparison, see Jean-Luc Marion, '"Christian Philosophy": Hermeneutic or Heuristic?', in *The Question of Christian Philosophy Today*, ed. Francis J. Ambrosio (New York: Fordham University Press, 1999), pp. 247–64. See also, idem, 'The Face: An Endless Hermeneutics', *Harvard Divinity Bulletin* 28 (1999), pp. 2 f., 9 f.

Conclusion

Fides et ratio is a challenge to the theologians of the 'sister church', to go beyond the rhetoric of 'anti-intellectualism', and to reconsider the more positive relation of reason to faith portrayed within the writings of the Eastern Fathers. It does not, however, dispel the concerns of these theologians that a particular way of conceiving this relationship may, in fact, lead to a subordination of theology to philosophy, and thus, affect the content of Christian faith. Part of the problem is that the Encyclical itself is not clear on what it means by reason and on the relation between reason and faith. The confusion is expressed well by John Webster:

> So, we have a circle, a movement from a to b, an elliptical motion, a path and a move to an horizon. I suppose it could be post-modern geography, the triumph of spatial indeterminacy; but to me, at least, it just seems like good old pre-modern confusion. And it offers almost no clarification of just what the relation of theology and philosophy is, beyond securing that there is a relation which needs to be taken very seriously.[81]

It is clear in its affirmation on the autonomy and independence of philosophy. The autonomy of philosophy, the distinction between the *auditus fidei* and the *intellectus fidei*, and the failure to recognize that the expression of faith embodies also a particular mode of reasoning leads to an a-historical account of reason and faith, one which seems to support the modern break between reason and faith that the document itself adamantly opposes.[82]

---

[81] '"Fides et ratio", articles 64–79', *New Blackfriars* 81 (February 2000), p. 74.

[82] Cf. *Fides et ratio*, §48. Webster expresses a similar sentiment that the Encyclical is a '*modern* document', but for different reasons. See *Fides et ratio*, §76.

The Integrity of Human Experience: Cultural Dimensions and Implications of the Encyclical *Fides et ratio*

ANGELO SCOLA

The inescapable question of anthropology

Desire and nostalgia

'I am filled with a question to which I do not know the answer . . . Who can tell what kind of scream I am screaming?'[1] This profoundly human plea of the Italian poet and director Pier Paolo Pasolini finds a glimmer of a response in George Steiner, who, writing against today's regnant 'scientific universalism', perceptively states: 'If only I could cast overboard the dead weight of the religious vision of the world. If only I could put this "childhood disease!" behind me once and for all.'[2] But 'neither science nor logic has the power to resolve or banish the highest of all questions, which Leibniz posed when he asked "Why is there not nothing at all?" The positivist decree that the adult mind shall ask of the world and of existence only "How?" and not "Why?" is among the most obscurantist forms of censorship. For me there exists the absolutely undeniable pressure of a presence foreign to all explanation.'[3] 'We need a witness – even if his judgment is harsh – of our little heap of dust. In our sickness, in our psychological or physical terror, before the cadaver of a child, we cry out.'[4]

Question and presence (mystery): Are these not the distinctive features of the *humanum*, which, cutting across all cultures, express their common centre of gravity? It would be extremely difficult, not to say impossible, to grasp the cultural implications of *Fides et ratio* apart from

[1] P. P. Pasolini, *Teorema* (Milano: Garzanti, 1968) [ET *Theorem*, trans. Stuart Hood (London: Quartet, 1992), pp. 175–6].

[2] G. Steiner, *Errata*, trans. Claude Béguin (Milano: Garzanti, 1998), p. 194 [originally published in English, *Errata: An Examined Life* (London: Weidenfeld & Nicolson, 1997), p. 162].

[3] G. Steiner, *Errata*, pp. 199–200. [p. 167].

[4] G. Steiner, *Errata*, pp. 190–1. [p. 159].

this anthropological root, which is simultaneously personal and social. Indeed, the Encyclical takes its starting point precisely from 'these questions . . . which flow from that common investigation concerning meaning itself by which the spirit of man is never left undisturbed'.[5] They give voice to the experience of 'its burning desire' for fulfilment that constitutes the human heart. They describe its *drama*. As *capax Dei*, men and women do indeed bear deep within this urgent need for fullness, yet they are not able, by themselves, to satisfy it fully. Their desire therefore becomes a nostalgia: not only for 'something' that has been lost but, above all, for 'someone' to *trust* as a source of 'true and coherent knowledge', in which 'there is indeed an appropriate reply to questions which as yet are without answers'.[6]

Man's nature is *enigmatic*: he is a being that *exists*, yet *does not contain the foundation of its own existence*; a being that is, yet *receives its being from another*. Because of this enigmatic nature, *man's existence unfolds dramatically*. Nothing is decided in advance, and every circumstance, every situation, and every relation always involves our freedom. This state of affairs can be rather dizzying, especially when one perceives the (far from abstract) risk of determining one's freedom contrarily to one's own good. Using a limit concept, we can say that, as he journeys towards self-consciousness, man intuits not just his inability to attain fulfilment by his own powers alone, but nothing less than the intrinsic possibility of self-destruction.[7]

On this anthropological *humus*, the Encyclical introduces its critical dialogue between faith and reason, which passes through the inseparable pair 'culture-cultures'. In *Fides et ratio* we readily find the essential dimensions of the Magisterium's recovery (beginning especially with *Gaudium et spes*)[8] of the original relation between faith, reason and culture.[9] We hasten to add, of course, that it would be extremely reductive simply to restate these dimensions. We do not want to use a net that lets the biggest fish get away. Yet a quick review of the main points is not out of place. These appear in rapid succession mainly in paragraphs 69–71 of Chapter VI, 'The Interaction between Philosophy and Theology'.

---

[5] *Fides et ratio*, §1.

[6] *Fides et ratio*, §§33, 17.

[7] For this reason, the Encyclical dedicates brief but illuminating remarks to the problem of sin, which burdens man's search for truth. Cf. §22.

[8] Cf. *Gaudium et spes* §§53–62.

[9] Cf. *Fides et ratio*, §§70–71.

Cultural Dimensions

Against those who 'take their starting point from a mistaken notion of the pluralism of cultures, and in consequence reject the universal good of a philosophical patrimony, which the Church accepts', and those who, in order to emphasize the importance of 'the relationship between faith and culture . . . maintain that theology should be translated into a form of so called "common wisdom" rather than into a philosophy which arose in Greece and is therefore Eurocentric', *Fides et ratio* maintains that a correct examination of the nexus between culture and cultures reveals the necessary and intrinsic orientation of these cultures to philosophy. In the end, we cannot limit ourselves to 'what people think' but we must ascertain 'the very nature of truth in itself'.[10] This suggests an enhancement, rather than a diminishment, of philosophy's role within theology.

For the time being, however, let us content ourselves with enumerating the six dimensions that, according to *Fides et ratio* (above all in paragraphs 63–71), chiefly constitute the relation between culture and cultures:

(i) First, when one speaks of culture, one must be aware of its plurality: culture lives concretely in cultures tied to space, time, and the particularities of the peoples that created them. This particularity can sometimes prove to be an obstacle to communication.

(ii) Nevertheless, 'Cultures, which make their roots deep in human nature, carry with themselves proof of an openness to universality and transcendence which is proper to humanity. Therefore they express the diverse approaches to the truth, which are of great use to us inasmuch as they provide values which are capable of rendering our existence more and more human.'[11]

(iii) Cultures are by nature dynamic, in a process of development (which, however, need not be linear): 'These cultures, simply because they are yoked to men and women and their history, share the same tendencies which are manifested in the human condition. These transformations and advances are accounted for from the communality which men in their convergences produce when they meet and share amongst themselves their ways of life.'[12]

(iv) As a reality expressive of the *humanum*, cultures are structurally

---

[10] *Fides et ratio*, §69 (citing a passage from St Thomas Aquinas, *De Caelo*, in *Exposition of Aristotle's Treatise on the Heavens*, trans. R. F. Larcher and P. H. Conway, 2 vols. (Columbus, OH: College of St Mary of the Springs, 1964), 1, 22 §8).

[11] *Fides et ratio*, §70.

[12] *Fides et ratio*, §71.

open to fulfilment: 'Every man is bound to some culture, depends upon it and in some measure moulds it. He is at the same time both child and parent of the culture he finds himself in. In all important things of life, he always bears with him what marks him out from all other creatures; that is an enduring openness to mystery and the insatiable desire for knowledge. This means that every culture contains within itself and displays an indestructible urge for some sort of fulfilment. We can therefore say that culture contains within itself the capacity for receiving divine revelation.'[13]

(v) While the proclamation of the Gospel in diverse cultures reveals its unifying and universalizing potency, it is no obstacle to the maintenance of cultural identity: 'In this common vision, far from cultures being in any sense rejected, on the contrary they are encouraged to open themselves to the truth of the Gospel and from this find the incentive to further developments.'[14]

(vi) 'The consequence is that a culture can never become the norm, and much less the ultimate criterion of truth, for judging the divine revelation.'[15]

In sum, we can say that this catalogue of citations gives evidence of a profound realism. On the one hand, we should always speak of 'cultures' in the plural, because they are the necessary, multiple expressions of the variegated experiences of human beings situated in history. On the other hand, cultures share in common the characteristic of being an expression of the *humanum*. They possess, in other words, a structural openness to mystery. This makes them capable of welcoming, through a necessary process of maturation, the universal message of Jesus Christ.

Fides et ratio hearkens back, then, to an anthropological conception of *culture* spread out over the entire Magisterium of John Paul II. It will be sufficient for our purposes to recall the famous speech of 2 June 1980 at UNESCO.[16] The Pope in turn looks especially to *Gaudium et spes*[17] and *Evangelii nuntiandi*.[18]

Faith, reason and culture

The relation between culture and cultures, in all its dimensions, is thus a significant expression of the *humanum* in its historical concreteness.

[13] *Fides et ratio*, §71.
[14] *Fides et ratio*, §71.
[15] *Fides et ratio*, §71.
[16] John Paul II, 'Allocuzione all'UNESCO', 2 June 1980, in *Insegnamenti* III/1 (1980), pp. 1636–55.
[17] Cf. *Gaudium et spes*, §§53–62.
[18] Cf. *Evangelii nuntiandi*, §20.

These dimensions result from a twofold, indivisible dynamic played out between the universal and the particular. It is for this reason that, in order not to lose the essential logic of the incarnation or to blunt the force of its universal salvific scope, faith in Jesus Christ requires an *intellectus fidei* (theology) in which reason (philosophy) bears the burden of responsibility for culture-cultures.

Having recalled the cultural dimensions of *Fides et ratio*, we can now ask about the Encyclical's implications. These implications follow directly from its underlying anthropology, yet they also suggest a fruitful method for reading the contemporary situation.

So as not to betray our own emphasis on the particularity of cultural phenomena, it behoves us to say that our point of reference will be the dominant cultural climate of the West that, despite variations in customs, styles, and traditions, is still shared by Europeans and Americans alike.

I would like, then, to undertake a three-stage journey through anthropology and culture. In each stage, I will attempt to show how some particular foundational element of Christian anthropology, together with its cultural implications, both flows from the right relation between faith and reason and, at the same time, enables us to understand decisive elements of the socio-cultural context in which many Christian communities of the North of the planet live.

The question of meaning and the desire for truth

In numerous paragraphs of the Encyclical, the Holy Father describes the core of the *humanum* in terms of the desire for truth[19] and of the question of meaning.[20] In both cases, he is referring to ineradicable characteristics that constitute man's uniqueness and open him to transcendent mystery: 'The desire to know is so great and so dynamic that the spirit of a man, although aware of its own limits, even so aspires to an infinite richness that lies beyond, because he already perceives that there is indeed an appropriate reply to questions which as yet are without answers.'[21] In this way, human beings, moved by the wonder through which reality brings to explicit awareness in them the questions that lie at the very core of their being, inexorably tend toward truth, even if they cannot reach its fullness by their own power alone.[22]

---

19 Cf. *Fides et ratio*, §§1, 3–4, 16–17, 24–5, 28, 42.

20 Cf. *Fides et ratio*, §§1, 3, 27, 33, 81.

21 *Fides et ratio*, §17.

22 *Fides et ratio*, §§4, 26. Cf. §§1, 13, 19, 28, 51.

The human capacity for truth

The question of meaning and the desire for truth are the very apex of human reason:

> as the poetic genius of every time and every people clearly shows, this genius, like a kind of prophetic voice of humanity, asks again and again the serious question that makes human beings truly what they are . . . [W]hen human reason explores why things are with integrity and in order to find the ultimate, most exhaustive answer, it attains its zenith and opens to the religious impulse. Indeed, the religious impulse is the highest expression of the human person, because it is the high point of his rational nature. It springs from man's profound human aspiration towards truth, and it is the basis of his free and personal search for the divine.[23]

What does this anthropological core imply for the relation between faith and reason? Ultimately, *Fides et ratio* invokes it in order to legitimate its insistence on the need to search for ultimate truth without succumbing to the siren call of those who claim that reason is powerless to attain it: 'it is vital not to abandon the desire for ultimate truth, the eagerness to search for it or the audacity for discovering new paths in the search'.[24] 'There is a great demand upon us as the present millennium draws to a close that we be able to make a transition, both necessary and urgent, *from appearance to foundation*.'[25]

The Encyclical's insistence on the human being's 'metaphysical capacity' does not, however, privilege any one school of thought: 'We are not speaking here about metaphysics as about some particular school or historical tradition. What is important to stress is that reality and truth transcend empirical facts and origins. It is vital to defend man's power of arriving in a true and certain way at this transcendent and metaphysical reason, even though that way may be imperfect and analogical.'[26] This brings fully to light the objective significance of philosophy. Especially in its quality as a sapiential science, which as such opens human beings to the ultimate meaning of life, philosophy is able to play a powerful role in facilitating the encounter between cultures and the Christian faith: 'Philosophical thought is often the only ground for understanding and

---

[23] John Paul II, 19 October 1983, general audience for the Holy Year, 1–2, in *Insegnamenti* VI/2 (1983), pp. 814–15.

[24] *Fides et ratio*, §56. See also §§5, 27, 102.

[25] *Fides et ratio*, §83. See also §§22, 97.

[26] *Fides et ratio*, §83.

dialogue with those who do not share our faith . . . [with] the followers of other religions and all those who, while not sharing a religious belief, have at heart the renewal of humanity.'[27]

The impossibility of analogy?

Fides et ratio forcefully affirms human reason's capacity for truth, which it founds upon the inescapable (religious) question of meaning. In this way, it does full justice to the importance of philosophical thought and its indispensable contribution to a culturally situated *intellectus fidei.*

By the same token, the Encyclical obliges us to come to terms with a feature of Western culture that has been particularly accentuated by the rise of so-called post-modernity. Since the dawn of modernity, in fact, there has been an ever more vigorous tendency to deny, in various ways, the possibility of expressing the Face of Being through a conjunction of the One and the many.

Some of the secular commentators on *Fides et ratio*, at least in Italy, have remarked that the Encyclical's critical interlocutor should be sought not so much among the spokesmen of a more or less nihilistic[28] 'weak thought'[29] – which, they say, does not deserve that level of attention – as among those who insist upon the radical *aporia* of thought itself. This *aporia*, it is claimed, entails the impossibility of analogy. In this view, the One does indeed manifest itself, but nothing can be said about it on the basis of the many. But man, for his part, is structurally confined to the realm of multiplicity. Accordingly, the objection continues, we are ontologically dependent upon an unresolvable *di-aporein*. In other words, the

[27] *Fides et ratio*, §104, cf. §§81, 85, 106.

[28] Cf. *Fides et ratio*, §90. For the sake of clarity, I shall try to state in simple terms what I understand by nihilism. Each one of us, when we consider reality in all its manifestations (the other, a sunset, a good action, an object, etc.), perceives it as something positive, as a good. But, on the natural plane, it is in and of itself contingent. In other words, even if it exists now, it can also cease to exist. The nihilist concludes from this contingency that, since reality can come to an end, it is in itself nothing. Montale, perhaps the greatest of contemporary Italian poets, has expressed this tendency well: 'Forse un mattino andando in un'aria di vetro,/ arida, rivolgendomi, vedrò compirsi il miracolo:/ il nulla alle mie spalle, il vuoto dietro/di me, con un terrore di ubriaco./ Poi come s'uno schermo, s'accamperanno di gitto/ alberi case colli per l'inganno consueto./ Ma sarà troppo tardi; ed io me n'andrò zitto/ tra gli uomini che non si voltano, col mio segreto.' E. Montale, 'Ossi di seppia' in *L'opera in versi* (Turin: Einaudi, 1980), p. 40

[29] On this subject, see S. Grygiel, 'Socrate e l'infelicità del pensiero debole', *Il Nuovo Aeropago* 3 (1989), pp. 7–19; G. Penati, 'Modernità e postmoderno nel pensiero filosofico attuale', *Communio: Rivista internazionale di teologia e cultura* 110 (1990), pp. 16–32; T. Gadacz, 'La provocazione del Nichilismo', *Il Nuovo Areopago* 3 (1995), pp. 5–17; G. Dalmasso, 'Immagini della scienza. Dalla conscienza moderna al nichilismo', *Il Nuovo Areopago* 2 (1982), pp. 106–13.

ineffability of being is as basic as its capacity for self-disclosure. By the same token, there is no way to untie this problematic knot without falling into a violent *gnosis* that ends up transferring to the very heart of thought the nowadays undisputed logic of scientific and technological dominion, of the very scientific universalism that cannot tolerate the existence of questions without answers. Being, by contrast, is by its very nature a question without an answer.

Moreover, this *Destruktion* of the fortress of Western thought as the inheritor of classical Christian thought is not – once again according to these commentators – the work of 'vandals' attacking from the outside. On the contrary, the majestic intellectual architecture that Thomas brought to completion on the basis of the analogy of being collapsed, they insist, under its own weight when Ockham boldly asserted that everything is a mere *name* because even analogy tells us nothing about the *thing*. Digressing somewhat, I would add that this position not only aims to explain the restless unease of a Heidegger or the lucid folly of a Nietzsche, but goes so far as to claim atheism as the natural heir of the Judaeo-Christian tradition.[30]

How, then, do we respond to this unsparing criticism, which perhaps gives us the key to deciphering a number of contradictory cultural, political, and social phenomena, at least in the West? Think, for example, of the passionate debates surrounding birth and death, the split between personal freedom (or ethics) and civil freedom (or ethics), or the dialectic between rights and the economy. Must we really abandon analogy as the primary condition for thinking the real? Or should we not – taking our cue from a number of perceptive observers closer to our own tradition – rethink analogy in such a way as to secure it from the intellectualist reduction, still noticeable in Barth and perhaps even in Przywara, that is the actual target of this critique?[31]

---

[30] The pages of *Gaudium et spes* on the question of atheism remain extraordinarily relevant! Cf. *Gaudium et spes* §§19–21.

[31] Cf. Hans Urs von Balthasar, *Theology of Karl Barth*, trans. Edward T. Oakes SJ (San Francisco, CA: Ignatius Press, 1992), pp. 381–5, cf. pp. 136–55 [*La teologia di Karl Barth*, trans. Giovanni Moretto (Milan: Jaca Book, 1985), pp. 405–13]; Erich Przywara, *Analogia entis. Metafisica. La struttura originaria e il ritmo cosmico* (Milan: Vita e pensiero, 1995), pp. 250–302. Among the more recent studies that examine the results of the decisive debate between Przywara, Barth and Balthasar, the following are worth noting: G. De Schrijver, *Le merveilleux accord de l'homme et Dieu; Etudes de l'analogie de l'être chez H.U. von Balthasar* (Leuven: Uitgeverij Peeters, 1983); A. Scola, 'La logica dell'Incarnazione come logica sacramentale: avvenimento ecclesiale e libertà', in AA. VV., *Wer ist die Kirche? Symposium zum 10 Todesjahr von Hans Urs von Balthasar* (Einsiedeln: Johannes Verlag, 1999), pp. 99–135; Nicola Reali, *La ragione e la forma* (Milan: Mursia, 1999). On the philosophical plane, one can find important justifications for the doctrine of analogy in Virgilio Melchiorre, *La via analogica* (Milano: Vita e pensiero, 1996); Franco Riva, *L'analogia metaforica. Una questione logico-metafisica nel tomismo* (Milan: Vita e pensiero, 1989).

The way to a rediscovery of the One's capacity, not only to display itself in the many, but to make itself known therein, hence, the way to knowledge of the truth, passes through a reformulation of the *analogia entis* within the context of what we can call an *analogia libertatis*. We do not, of course, propose the submission of this rediscovery to the norm of an *ab-solute* reason that, arrogating to itself cosmic centrality, presumes to measure reality in an immediate way. Our point is rather that this rediscovery occurs through the medium of each person's free cognitive self-abandonment to the manifestation of the foundation that, in fact, shines out in all things.[32] It is just here, moreover, that we begin to see the import of the gratuitous event of Jesus Christ. For it is Christ who, in his singular person, achieves the *analogia entis* within the *analogia libertatis*. Jesus' theandricity is not a gnostic construction of a chimerical being that holds together God and man in an impossible dialectical sublation. On the contrary, it is nothing less than the ontological basis of his free (*sponte*) correspondence to the trinitarian foundation, which is then the source of our salvation. The import of soteriology is that the supreme *ponti-fex* accomplishes a substantive, and not merely nominal, analogy (the idea of analogy has to do, after all, with the notion of a bridge), in order, through his death and resurrection, to enable my act of freedom to be just that, truly free. The interweaving of faith and freedom may be the key to the flourishing of the latter even in the midst of our current cultural crisis. This seems to be the burden of *Fides et ratio*: 'Therefore, it is not that in faith freedom merely happens to be present: it is required by it. In fact faith itself gives to each of us the power of expressing individual freedom on far better grounds . . . And thus by believing, the human person accomplishes the most meaningful act of her life, for here the certainty of truth is attained in that one who decides to live by it.'[33]

Closely related to this critique of analogy is the claim that thought is weak, that it therefore has little to say about reality, and that this is actually a good thing. A number of authors, including some Catholics, are even convinced that this limitation of reason is a boon to Christianity, which, they think, could step in to supply whatever reason is unable to tell us! This is a trap, because faith in Jesus Christ is more than just a bare wager. Even if reason cannot lay claim to faith, faith itself must be reasonable, that is, deeply in accord with the human heart. As *Fides et ratio* reminds us in several of its paragraphs, those who would be Christian today must, more than ever before, struggle for reason.[34]

---

32 Cf. *Fides et ratio*, §83.
33 *Fides et ratio*, §13.
34 Cf. *Fides et ratio*, §§5, 27, 56, 90, 102.

The return of the gods

Man's religious sense is ineradicable. But it is always open to ambiguity and, therefore, to cooption by its parasite, ideology. The cult of the idols is either the first, ingenuous approach to God, typical of man's beginnings, or it is sheer *hybris* (violence) by which man fancies himself to be the God and Lord of the universe. In this case, the true religious ideal is replaced by utopia and ideology – even in the case of that 'noble', but very rare thing called theoretical atheism, since, as Dostoevski perceptively noted, all atheists are 'idolaters, but they are not godless.'[35]

All of which helps to explain the frequent recurrences of polytheism throughout history. For years, the culture of nihilism had predicted the demise of the religious sense and its definitive replacement by a 'worldly world' (secularization). More recently, however, it has had to confront the evidence of an explosion of a wild form of sacrality. Yet, as the Encyclical states, it accounts for this phenomenon by taking refuge in new forms of esotericism.[36] We are thus witnessing the resurgence, at least in the West, of a new kind of pagan polytheism that does not hesitate to assert the need for a 'return to the gods'.

In the spring of 2000, a major exponent of the European intelligentsia, Roberto Calasso, head of the sophisticated Italian publisher Adelphi, gave a series of lectures at Oxford under the title, 'Literature and the Gods'. Armed with erudite and perceptive references to various returns to paganism throughout history, Calasso, drawing mainly on Heine and Baudelaire, speaks of the gods who already inhabit our workaday world:

> they are like a massive crowd thronging the streets of a vast metropolis. They no longer live in huge mansions spread out over the slopes of a mountain. The important point is not that their names are as exotic and unpronounceable as those we read by the doorbells of immigrant households. The power of their story continues to exert its influence. The real novelty of the situation is that that motley tribe of the gods now exists only in its history and in its scattered idols. The path to cultic worship is barred. '– Secularism is affecting even neo-pagan polytheism!' – Oh, who can explain why there is no longer a devout people to perform the ritual deeds? Or, if such a people should exist, why have the deeds been cut short? The statues of Diva or Vishnu are still moist with homage, but Varuna is already an indistinct and remote entity for the Indian of today. And Prajapati is found only in books, often in books that but a few may ever open. Is this perhaps a

[35] F. Dostoevski, *L'adolescente*, trans. Rinaldo Küfferle (Milan: Editoriale Opportunity Book, 1995), p. 455 [ET: *The Adolescent*, trans. Andrew R. MacAndrew (New York: W.W. Norton, 1981)].

[36] Cf. *Fides et ratio*, §37.

> prelude to extinction? Only in appearance . . . When all is said and done, the world – and now is the time to say it even if the news will be disagreeable to many – has no intention of being disenchanted. If for no other reason than that disenchantment would be a crashing bore.[37]

I do not believe that Calasso is giving his readers a mere taste of what he calls elsewhere 'absolute literature'. He himself has said in a recent newspaper article that 'today it's not just a matter of habit, but also of taste – a mischievous taste, no doubt – for me to write only what is guaranteed to drive every sort of hasty folk insane'. Be that as it may, Calasso's point is that human beings find refuge from boredom in the sacred. The kind of sacred he means is an untamed sacrality whose pagan polytheism, anaemic through lack of flesh and blood participation in ritual, can do no more than powers that be to hold society together. In societies, such as those of Europe, in which millions of people filter reality through a never ending succession of acts of 'reading' (television, the Internet, and so forth), the religious sense is, once again, in the clutches of its great parasite, ideology. Nor does the growing importance of multi-religiosity, multi-culturalism, and multi-ethnicity, which has not been spared the experience of bloody violence, seem able to restore the religious sense to its former dignity.

Someone might object that Calasso's remarks are a sort of luxury for intellectuals that has as much to do with real life as the most extravagantly expensive Rolex. But this impression is false. In the great melting pot of cultures (*bouillon de culture*) in which the media have placed us to boil, all of us are more or less conscious victims of the empty religiosity in which one faith is as good as any other, and the true, the good, and the beautiful dissolve with the help of scientific universalism. We need to see that the return to the gods, with its neo-pagan renewal of polytheism, reveals the direction in which our culture is really headed: 'away with the infamous Galileo', as the young intellectual of the *l'École païenne* of Baudelaire would say. Present limits do not allow us to explore to what degree this orientation is an immediate consequence of the religious and cultural apostasy of the West or is a strategy employed by a certain intelligentsia convinced of the need for radical secularization. Like the insistent pounding of the waves upon the rocks, this cultural soup, whose true nature is revealed in the return to polytheism, wears away, and finally effaces completely, the Christian identity of the peoples brought into being by baptism.

There is no point in rending our garments over this state of affairs. What we must do instead is ask ourselves *whence* and *why* a cultural

[37] R. Calasso, 'La letteratura e gli dei. La scuola pagana', *Il Corriere della Sera* (4–5 May 2000).

tendency of this sort could be so influential in a civilization like ours that would never have existed without Christ. What, in the end, is the root cause of this general climate? If Christianity is the extraordinary event in which being, in its self gift, declares to us its nature as a loving Father; if, in Jesus Christ, grace takes us by the hand and enables us to do what we had always yearned to do, namely, *to be like gods*,[38] how can we write off as a negligible loss this tragic confinement of men and peoples to one dimension of life only (*one* soup made of *many* ingredients)? How can a process of this nature have prevailed?

We are in the midst of a new rejection of the 'Christian claim' that, in Jesus Christ, God, without ceasing to be God, is made man. By the power of the Father acting in the Spirit, the Archetype becomes the image without losing its character as Archetype. The 'Christian claim' reaches its highpoint in Christ's death and resurrection, through which the exchange between the human and divine natures is offered to the freedom of each and all.[39] But, as *Fides et ratio* forcefully reminds us, to follow Christ, the perfect image of the Father, is to respect the undiminished consistency of the real, reason's capacity for the truth, and the (religious) question of meaning as the apex of the *humanum*.

We are witnessing, then, yet another in the interminable series of rejections of God's absolutely unprecedented initiative. Once again, human beings are succumbing to the same, tired objection: *why am I not a God?* This objection, in turn, sums up and appropriates the major questions of philosophy, which come under the heading of Leibniz's *why is there being rather than nothing?* This prometheanism appears heroic only at first sight. However, as Lewis reminds us, it is in danger of using the power of science and technology to abolish the *humanum*. It may seem easier to abandon ourselves to the recurring temptation to pretend to be God. Compassion for the innate fragility common to all human beings and peoples may appear to argue in favor of patterning ourselves after the demigods of the new cosmopolitan Olympus rather than clinging to the demanding embrace of the Father. Yet we see how inhuman this is when we realize that every fibre of our heart, in the daily rhythm of affections and work, calls for a freedom that is willed and kept in being by the mysterious, but real presence of the *rerum tenax vigour*. Surely his loving eyes and hands, portrayed so beautifully in Rembrandt's famous painting of the prodigal son, will once more pardon the lost sinner. Surely we, the weary dwellers of the North of the planet, will be taught

[38] Cf. Gen 3:5.

[39] Hans Urs von Balthasar, *Theologik*, Vol. I (Einsiedeln: Johannes Verlag, 1985), 'Is it possible, to invoke the limit concept that arises in this context, to conceive a being that in itself could realize the transposition of the exemplar into an image without falsifying the former?', p. xvii.

once more to grieve over our sin in surrendering ourselves to the Father's embrace.

'Found in Him' (Philippians 3:9)

What, then, enables men and women to refrain from abandoning the quest for meaning? What can satisfy the fabric of the human heart?

Only the encounter with truth for, as the Pope recalls, 'Opinions may fascinate the mind, but not satisfy it'. For two thousand years the Church has indefatigably repeated its message: the Church 'from within the Paschal Mystery . . . received the ultimate truth about human life as a gift'. In fact, 'Through this revelation the ultimate truth about his own life and the end of history is displayed before us'.[40]

This claim begins to make sense when situated within the Christocentric horizon in which *Gaudium et spes* places anthropology. The famous paragraph §22 of the Pastoral Constitution of the Second Vatican Council has marked the Magisterium of John Paul II from its inception. In *Fides et ratio*, the Pope gives new expression to this longstanding conviction of his: 'The mystery of the Incarnation remains like a fixed point to which everyone should be referred in order to comprehend the secret of human life, the created universe and God himself.'[41]

Faith as a resource for reason

Fides et ratio also makes a point of underscoring a crucial implication of this teaching for the method governing the relation between faith and reason. If, because man has been created in Him, Jesus Christ definitively reveals man to himself, revelation is a great resource for, but never a limitation upon, human reason.[42]

The Pope highlights this inference in several paragraphs of the Encyclical: 'Therefore Revelation introduces into our history a truth which is both universal and ultimate, and which spurs on the human mind and prevents it from coming to a standstill; instead it forces it continually to expand the limits of its knowledge until it recognizes that it has completely realized all its full potentiality.'[43] The Pope thus valorizes, but does not overvalue, reason,[44] thus protecting it from the consequences of the Enlightenment's one-sided emphasis that, paradoxically, succeeded only in engendering sceptical mistrust in relation to the truth.[45] Moreover, Christian revelation – by virtue of its role not only in purifying reason (the subjective aspect), but also in enlarging the scope of

[40] *Fides et ratio*, §§27, 2, 12.
[41] *Fides et ratio*, §80. Cf. §60.
[42] *Fides et ratio*, §§23, 79.
[43] *Fides et ratio*, §14. Cf. §21.
[44] Cf. *Fides et ratio*, §20.
[45] Cf. *Fides et ratio*, §§45, 47, 55, 91, 124.

knowledge (the objective aspect of content) – offers enrichment for philosophy and extraordinary possibilities of growth for cultures.[46]

The 'good life'

The proposal of *Fides et ratio* must, of course, also deal with the increasingly prevalent tendency to set up 'consensus' as the criterion of truth.[47] The Pope speaks directly to this point: 'In particular there is growing support for a concept of democracy without any reference to the changeless bases of rights and duties: the honesty or dishonesty of certain moral practices is decided by reference solely to the view of the parliamentary majority. The consequences of this method of decision are quite clear: bit by bit moral decisions and pronouncements are made dependent upon the discussions of particular institutions.'[48]

This conception lies at the root of today's rigid separation between the public and private spheres, which in turn continues to cause many insuperable political and social problems, especially in Western countries. According to Ross Poole, the division between public and private in today's market society is here to stay.[49] Private life *must* be kept out of public life. Public life is supposedly governed by (above all juridical) rationality and thus functions as the domain of ethics in the proper sense, while private life, centred on domestic relations, on the bearing and education of children, is seen exclusively as the transitory locus of subjective desires, irrational emotions and selfish affections. The result is an exclusion of the subject that not only is not involuntary or surreptitious, but actually tends towards its abolition.

Clearly, this view of things rules out *a priori* any proposal of what the classical Christian tradition has called the 'good life'. This expression refers ultimately to the Aristotelian doctrine (see the *Nicomachean Ethics*) developed by St Thomas (above all at the beginning of the *Secunda Pars* of the *Summa Theologiae*). For these authors 'it is necessary to consider the action of man as a rational agent in terms of life as a totality, which is therefore ordered according to the ends and goods that define its essential character'.[50]

But without a realistic pursuit of the good life, it is impossible to harmonize personal conduct with the common good.

We are all familiar with the objection that this approach is likely to

46 Cf. *Fides et ratio*, §76.
47 Cf. *Fides et ratio*, §§56, 92.
48 *Fides et ratio*, §89.
49 See Ross Poole, *Morality and Modernity* (London: Routledge, 1991).
50 Angelo Scola, *Il mistero nuziale*, Vol. 2. *Matrimonio-famiglia* (Rome: *Pontificià uiversità lateranense*, 2000), p. 187.

encounter. A conception of the good life, it will be said, must be anchored in objective criteria of truth. But the question of truth is very much bound up with the question of freedom of conscience. At best, then, it is only the individual, and then only in his private life, who may affirm an objective and necessary connection between the good and the true. In public life, by contrast, such an affirmation would inevitably lead to the abolition of pluralism and to intolerance. Hence the pragmatic principle 'all forbidding forbidden' that, unfortunately, is uncritically bandied about everywhere today. But to rule out the good life, which is to say, to rule out the possibility of a single, internally differentiated end of both public and private life, is, in the final analysis, to render impossible the building up of the *polis*. This issue is always a timely one because of the enduring link between faith, reason, and cultures. As we have seen, this link enables the freedom of the person in society through a fruitful enactment of analogy. In the language of Lévinas, the 'I', the 'other', and the 'third' are the necessary, 'asymmetrical' foundation of society.

'The most civic of men'

Charles Péguy, in his inimitable style, affirms that Christians are 'the most civic of men . . . heirs to the ancient citizens, universally, eternally civic men'.[51] Also, and perhaps especially in the West, our task is to display the fruitful resources that the experience of faith of God's people can bring to the building up of a civil society that does not merely tolerate differences, but accords them their full value in a kind of symphony. Of course, this task cannot succeed without a considerable dose of heroism (and perhaps even martyrdom). One cannot help thinking here of the fruitfulness of the Judaeo-Christian matrix that – to limit ourselves to the recent past – has given us the Bonhoeffers and the Kolbes, the Simone Weils and the Edith Steins, or, to return to our own day, the abbot of the Algerian monastery of Tibhirine.

If, in fact, the edification of the *polis* consists in pursuing that 'good life' that is asked both of the individual and the community, the achievement of this goal can be conceived only as a practical consequence of the positive value that being, whose face is ultimately that of the Triune reality, irradiates within all things. But precisely this is the case: in every thing, being shows itself (*pulchrum*), gives itself (*bonum*), and speaks itself (*verum*), thereby calling to the freedom of the individual.

In spite of the development of law, neither the refined Greek *polis* nor the well-crafted Roman *civitas* broke through to an understanding society as a *family* (a home). Both versions, in fact, regarded men as

---

[51] Charles Péguy, *Lui è qui. Pagine scelte* eds. Davide Rondoni e Flora Crescini (Milan: Biblioteca universale Rizzoli, 1997), p. 80.

citizens only in so far as the State accorded them at birth legal rights resting on various conditions. As citizens they were then defined as so-called 'free men'. What was missing was the figure of the father, the *source* that guarantees *a priori* the sacred dignity of every person and continuously engenders a unity between siblings that grounds authentic social development. What was lacking, in other words, was a source capable of regenerating freedom, which, therefore, cannot be defined as the absence of all ties. Once again, we see the relevance of the relation between faith and freedom.

Christianity integrates the notion of citizen with that of person, understood at one and the same time as a being endowed with freedom and as the subject of relationships. Christianity thereby holds together individual and community in their original dual unity that issues from a conception of the person as a communal being and as the social craftsman (*artifice*) of 'this' culture and of 'this' civilization: 'We are not speaking of "abstract" man, but of the real, "concrete", "historical" man.'[52] In this view, the state agrees to exist for the sake of a civil society animated by a pluriformity of intermediary bodies. We can trace back to the diversified societies of the Middle Ages an awareness of the original unity that transcends the task that each of the so-called three states (nobility, clergy, people) were summoned to carry out. Even the idea that governance has something to do with the divine will (as, for example, in the Christian European conception of kingship) does not create distance between persons, for – and here we perceive an echo of the Old Testament – this connection means precisely that governance is an election for service of the whole.

The birth of the modern nations, fuelled precisely by this enlargement of the concept of *civis* (citizen and person), is the *novum* that Christianity brought to European civilization. We can no longer afford to confine the *civis* to the mere proclamation of equality among men and to a formal conception of human rights. Human beings are not only equal, but also jointly responsible, in freedom, for one another. The dismaying words of Cain: 'Am I my brother's keeper?'[53] may increasingly capture the self-image of the modern citizen, who is ever more concerned to defend his own individual rights and, correspondingly, ever less aware of his responsibility for the *body* to which he in fact belongs. But they are utterly foreign to the mind of the 'civic person' who is a member of the kind of *societas* that reflects the deepest desires of the human heart touched by the Christian faith.

---

[52] Cf. John Paul II, *Redemptor hominis* (Encyclical Letter promulgated on 4 March 1979), §13.

[53] Gen 4:9.

Jesus Christ, enigma and drama

Imago Dei, faith and reason

Christian anthropology, following Scripture, has used the expression *imago Dei* to give a synthetic account of the human person that takes as its starting point the indivisible pair formed by the (religious) question of meaning *and* faith in Jesus Christ.

In the two accounts of the Book of Genesis, which agree precisely in affirming that man is created in the image and likeness of God, the Old Testament brings to light the singularity of human beings with respect to all other creatures.[54] The notion of *image* exhibits this irreducible singularity in light of human beings' relation with God, with one another, and with the world. To comprehend this notion fully, however, we need to keep in mind that the New Testament attributes the *imago Dei* in the full sense to Jesus Christ, whom it confesses to be the perfect image of the invisible God.[55] Biblical revelation thus gives us an anthropology founded upon the understanding of man *ad imaginem Imaginis*. This formula expresses the fact that man is both a creature of God and a son of God. The creative act of the Father reveals the unity of the divine plan centred on Jesus Christ and the vocation of men and women to become *filii in Filio*. The primary referent of every authentic reflection on man is thus Jesus Christ and not Adam: Jesus Christ alone reveals the human enigma without determining in advance the outcome of its drama.[56]

The Holy Father presents this understanding of the *imago* as the key to anthropology: 'from the pages of the Bible it is very clear that the species of man is as it were *in the image of God*, and bears upon himself signs of his being, and freedom, and not least the immortality of the soul'.[57] Precisely because being *imago* is characteristic of human beings, it is possible to maintain that 'It is God himself who implanted in the minds of men and women an inclination for knowing the truth and an inclination for loving him, so that knowing and loving him, they may likewise attain the whole truth about their very selves'.[58]

Once again, the anthropological starting point governs the relation between faith and reason seen in light of the relation between culture and cultures. Drawing particularly on a conception of the *imago Dei* in

---

[54] Gen 1:26–27; 2:18–25.

[55] 2 Cor 4:4 and Col 1:15.

[56] See Hans Urs von Balthasar, *Theo-drama*, Vol. III, trans. Graham Harrison (San Francisco, CA: Ignatius Press, 1998, pp. 33–40 [*Theodramatik* (Einsiedeln: Johannes Verlag, 1983)].

[57] *Fides et ratio*, §80.

[58] *Fides et ratio*, Preface.

terms of the dual unity of faith and the religious sense, the Encyclical demonstrates that freedom is co-original with, and not derivative from or extrinsic to, the relation between faith and reason. Only if freedom is seen in light of its ontological and gnoseological foundation can we correctly grasp its relation to the truth. The Encyclical speaks illuminatingly of this relation in the following text: 'Once the truth about man has been removed he is often deluded in supposing he can make himself free, for truth and freedom are either joined together or together they perish miserably'.[59]

Nature and freedom

The Pope's reflection brings us dramatically face to face with a dominant feature of the contemporary pragmatic and utilitarian mentality. This feature is one that is intimately bound up with 'scientific universalism'.[60] I am referring to the attempt to eviscerate the concept of nature of all meaning. Human freedom as a created reality is objectively referred to a given that, at least in the Western cultural tradition, has been called 'nature'. The freedom of the 'I' cannot be separated from its existence as a unity of 'body and soul', of 'man and woman', and of 'individual and community'. Finite freedom grows up on a soil (nature) that possesses certain definite characteristics. Freedom is constituted by certain polarities, and these lie at its very origin. This does not mean that we must subscribe to a 'biologistic' conception of nature that would simply rule out the kind of dynamic evolution that 'cultures' may introduce in various ways. We must, however, recognize that culture cannot produce nature *ex nihilo*, since contingency inevitably binds men and women to an original polarity of nature and culture.[61] Thomas's treatment of the 'inclinations' contains an extremely important teaching on this score. The freedom of man (of *Dasein*: dramatic anthropology) is awakened by constitutive inclinations that surface as biological instinct and, through the unconscious and the 'spiritual pre-conscious',[62] press forward to full consciousness. But however we decide the complex issue of nature, we cannot, in the end, deny that it does indeed function as an objective rule for freedom.

It is just this function that has been ignored by so-called 'scientific

[59] *Fides et ratio*, §90.

[60] Cf. *Fides et ratio*, §§5, 15, 47, 88.

[61] Cf. Angelo Scola, *L'alba della dignità umana* [At the Dawn of Human Dignity] (Milan, 1982), pp. 182–5.

[62] Scola, *L'alba della dignità umana*, p. 145. On the notion of 'spiritual pre-conscious', see Jacques Maritain, *Quattro saggi sullo spirito umano nella condizione di incarnazione* trans. Luciana Vigone (Brescia: Morcelliana, 1978) [*Quatre Essais sur l'esprit dans sa condition charnelle* (Paris: Desclée de Brouwer, 1939)].

universalism',[63] which in the present phase of globalization and media domination conditions human self-consciousness on an even more massive scale. The expression 'scientific universalism' is meant to refer to the now dominant cultural trend that would extend to all levels of the *humanum* an objective and universally valid discourse – based upon the abolition of the subject. Scientific universalism, ensconced in the narrow, but impregnable fortress of technical jargon, is the concentrated expression of a philosophy of man centred on two principles: the physicalist principle that the knowable is exhaustively reducible to the empirically measurable, and the subjectivist principle that the possible is the licit. The subject, swept up in a kind of maelstrom, no longer finds any limits to cling to for support.[64]

The weight of difference

The anthropological consequences of this position become particularly apparent in the delicate domain of the second anthropological polarity, namely, that of man and woman. The experience of unity is constitutive of anthropology. Of course, this unity is not static, but dramatic. Indeed, in creatures, that is, in contingent reality, unity occurs always as a *dual unity*. As noted above, man's unity is always a unity of body and soul, man and woman, individual and community. Could we not say, then, that the failure to come to terms with this anthropology of dual unity is the root cause of the often radical misunderstandings of the essence of Christianity that abound in our culture today? What we are calling dramatic anthropology is the ground on which the Christian is called to enter into critical dialogue with all comers if, that is, he wishes to communicate the fullness of the *humanum* that he has experienced in faith. But today this terrain is blocked by the *climate of eroticism* that pervasively colours our social and personal life. Scientific universalism and the false opposition between desire and duty – which is often accompanied by a fierce dialectic between the freedom of the person and the good of society, between morality and law – only aggravate this state of affairs by confusing, often uncritically, issues that ought to be treated with more clarity and distinction. Recent debates regarding gay pride, reproductive technologies, and paedophilia provide macroscopic illustrations of the situation.

Not a few scholars have observed that the conflict between Christian experience and an eroticist culture has today assumed the importance

---

[63] Cf. M. Binasco, *Un contributo clinico-psicoanalitico alla questione dell'omosessualità machile*, pro manuscripto.

[64] Cf. L. Lombardi Vallauri, 'Il pensiero moderno sulla sessualità umana', *Rivista di sessuologia* 8–9 (1984–5), pp. 14–35.

once held by the contrast between Christianity and revolution. In fact, eroticism attacks the heart of the nuptial mystery, which weaves sexual difference, love as reciprocal gift, and fecundity into an inseparable unity.[65] In this way, eroticism radicalizes modernity's disfigurement of the face of the man–woman relation.[66]

Even a superficial glance is enough to convince that this culture of eroticism bases its claim on the supposedly self-evident belief that the natural given of sexual difference can be eliminated. The result is one of the gravest wounds inflicted on elementary human experience that, given the possibility of the wholesale transfer of techniques of fertilization from animals to humans (cloning), threatens, for the first time in history, to abolish man himself.

We thus have greater need than ever to give an adequate account of the difference at the heart of identity itself. We must, however, avoid confusing the pair identity and difference – by its nature always intrapersonal – with the pair equality and diversity, which is always inter-individual. To speak of identity and difference is to say that the other emerges within the 'I', while the pair equality and diversity always begins with a relation between the two. Etymologically, 'difference' (*dis-ferre*) means to bring the same thing to another place, while diversity is based by its very nature on multiplicity and plurality.[67]

It may seem somewhat foolish to speak of the abolition of difference a mere thirty years after the death of Martin Heidegger, given the importance generally thought to attach to his inquiry into the ontological difference. But, as Paul Ricoeur has helpfully shown,[68] not even

[65] Cf. Angelo Scola, *Il mistero nuziale*, Vol. I, *Uomo–donna* (Rome: Pontificià università lateranense, 1998), pp. 91–116.

[66] Libertinism is the 'first coherent attempt to sever sexuality from fecundity (whether biological or social), to abolish the difference of the sexes, and in particular, to abolish woman. The body loses its value as the sacrament of the whole person. The body – one's own and others' – is reduced to a machine that must always keep the flame of pleasure burning. The libertine insistence on the licitness of every sexual relation initiated by the stronger party gives way to the liberal claim of the licitness of every sexual relation between consenting adults. Romanticism, reacting against the resulting elimination of any passion or compassion from love, envisages sexuality as the ecstasy produced by the fusion of the lovers. Sexuality, where love and death meet, takes on a mystical flavour that supposedly gives it its highest meaning. Beginning in the Sixties, the so-called sexual revolution extended libertine love to the masses, judiciously mixing it with elements drawn from the other theoretical postures just mentioned. It is helpful to point out that this denatured conception of erotic ecstasy is not only an attack on a bourgeois form of Christian society, but strikes at a fundamental aspect of Christianity's very essence, namely, the nuptial mystery' (Scola, *Il mistero nuziale*, Vol. 2, *Matrimonio*, pp. 83–4).

[67] Cf. Scola, *Il mistero nuziale*, Vol. 2, pp. 85–6.

[68] Cf. Paul Ricoeur, *Oneself as Another*, trans. Kathleen Blamey (Chicago: University of Chicago Press, 1992), pp. 56–87 [*Sé come un altro* ed. (Daniella Iannotta (Milan: Jaca Book, 1993), pp. 75–102].

Heidegger could halt the modern tendency to abolish the original difference between 'I' and 'self' that began with Descartes. Now, this difference, among other things, is precisely what accounts for the insuperability of sexual difference that, according to psychoanalysis (certainly not biassed in favour of Christian experience), is indefinable because impossible to deduce from some other principle.

Thinking difference adequately, that is to say, thinking difference at all levels of anthropology, ontology, and theology is the principal way to the rediscovery of identity itself. We can overcome discrimination (as we must) precisely because difference in the strong sense (anthropological, ontological, and theological) is never in itself inequality. The pair identity and difference can comprehend, and respect all the way down, the pair equality and diversity – but not vice versa. Here we see the sleight of hand to which the prevailing eroticism resorts. It introduces difference under the guise of a diversity that generates discrimination in order then to eliminate difference itself. Saving, not eliminating, difference is the indispensable condition for safeguarding elementary human experience.

Integral human experience: against nihilism and the will to power

The journey that we undertook at the beginning is now at an end. We began with a synthetic exposition of the cultural dimensions of *Fides et ratio*. This led us to analyse certain implications of the Encyclical bearing on the importance of the relation between culture and cultures. For the Encyclical, this relation holds faith and reason in balance, inasmuch as it gives historical proof of the importance of a dramatic anthropology that respects the inseparable binomial (dual unity) of the question of meaning, that is, of the religious sense, and Christian revelation, that is, faith in Jesus Christ. The Encyclical thus sets forth a method of Christian life (a culture) that makes possible a persuasive proclamation of Jesus Christ to men and women in our society today.

A faith that trivializes the religious sense becomes formal (moralistic) and sterile, and a religious sense that does not encounter faith becomes enfeebled or, as we have seen, withers away entirely. By contrast, the method proposed by the Encyclical enables Christians to live out the Christian life in all its splendour with each passing day. But it also serves as a salutary provocation for the so-called 'secular humanists' (*laici*). *Fides et ratio* invites both Christians and 'secularists' to examine themselves against the horizon of their question. This will enable them to avoid allowing their nostalgia to degenerate into nihilism and their desire to become a promethean will to power, whether it be social (the reduction of anthropology to ethics and politics) or scientific (the universalism of science and technology).

The Autonomy of Philosophy in *Fides et ratio*

ROBERT SOKOLOWSKI

The title of the Encyclical names the two things that are to be brought together, faith and reason.[1] This essay will attempt to clarify each of the terms and to discuss the kind of autonomy reason, and specifically philosophical reason, enjoys within Christian faith.

Reason as intelligent articulation

Reason in its widest scope can be considered to be the insertion of syntax or categoriality into human experience.[2] To move from simple experience into rational experience is to introduce – and to become explicitly aware of – distinctions between wholes and their parts. Instead of just perceiving an object, such as a tree, and reacting to it, we come to register articulated facts involving the object: we register *that* this object is a tree, *that* the tree is blossoming, and *that* we could climb out on one of its branches; we move from sensibility to intellection, from things to their intelligibility. Reason brings articulation and syntactic form into human consciousness and into the things we are aware of.

Reasoning is often considered to be the activity of moving from one statement or proposition to another, from premises to conclusions or from effects to causes, but it is also true that the original registering of a situation is a rational act, an act of intelligence. Reason is exhibited not only in propositional logic but also in predicational logic, when an object of any sort is taken as a whole (as a subject) and a feature or a part is declared to belong to it: that is, when *S* is said to be *p*. Reason does not

---

[1] Encyclical Letter *Fides et ratio* of the Supreme Pontiff John Paul II to the Bishops of the Catholic Church, trans. as *On the Relationship between Faith and Reason* (Vatican City: Libreria Editrice Vaticana, 1998).

[2] This is how Edmund Husserl describes and defines reason in *Logical Investigations*, Vol. II, trans. J. N. Findlay from the second German edition (London: Routledge, 2001), Investigation VI 'Elements of a phenomenological elucidation of knowledge' [*Logische Untersuchungen*, 2 Aufl. (M. Niemeyer, Halle, 1913–22)].

just draw inferences, but also manifests by articulating. Reason is at work when a whole is unfolded for us into its various parts. In fact, this manifesting role of reason is much more elementary than the inferential; we cannot move from one proposition to another until we have accumulated a store of convictions. The inferential work of reason simply introduces further syntactic forms into what we intend: we present not only individual but also concatenated states of affairs, and their linkage with one another is but a more complicated kind of syntax.

Our rational articulation normally takes place in language, in predication and its various elaborations, but there can be other kinds of articulation that disclose the truth of things: the composition of a picture, for example, is also a 'syntactic' manifestation with its own kind of logic, its own way of being consistent and inconsistent, coherent and incoherent. Picturing is an act of reason, and so are compositions and performances in music, dance, cooking and gardening, as well as architectural constructions. They, too, are forms of conviction and they are humanly structured wholes. Practical conduct and moral action are also made rational by their categorial forms.[3]

Linguistic and mathematical exercises of reason can take place on a rather small scale, in rather localized articulations and collections, but they can also occur on a grand and systematic scale. We can achieve not only episodic bits of knowledge; we can also build up the various sciences, which have been defined as 'organized knowledge'.[4] In the Encyclical, the Holy Father recognizes the wide range of reason and includes a moving tribute to scientists, 'expressing our admiration and . . . offering encouragement to these brave pioneers of scientific research'.[5]

Philosophy as the comprehensive form of reason

The Encyclical is primarily concerned with one particular form of rational thinking, namely, philosophy: in the Introduction, John Paul II says, 'we also wish to turn our gaze toward this particular work of human reason', and he says that by 'insisting on the truth of faith' he and his brother bishops 'can both restore to contemporary men and women a true confidence in their capacity for reflecting and can also inspire philosophers to regain and develop the proper dignity of their

---

[3] See Robert Sokolowski, *Moral Action: A Phenomenological Study* (Bloomington, IN: Indiana University Press, 1985), pp. 1–6; and 'What is Moral Action?', in *Pictures, Quotations, and Distinctions: Fourteen Essays in Phenomenology* (Notre Dame: University of Notre Dame Press, 1992), pp. 261–76.

[4] See Joseph Owens, CSsR, *Cognition: An Epistemological Inquiry* (Houston: The Center for Thomistic Studies, 1992), pp. 291–309.

[5] *Fides et ratio*, §106.

discipline'.[6] Faith is to confirm our confidence in our natural power to understand, and it is to remind philosophy of its noble role in human affairs.

How is philosophy different from other forms of thinking? All the others, even the organized forms of knowledge that we call the sciences, are partial. Each of them is limited to one particular domain of the world, and each realizes that there are other domains that have their own claims on truth. Each science, and each localized expression of truth, marks off a part of the whole for its attention, and, moreover, it knows that it restricts itself in this way. It is conscious of its limitations. It *knows* that to some extent it is specialized. It has its own expertise and it can be proud of it, but it also knows that other people have other kinds of expertise. This limitation is reassuring. It draws borders on what the specialist is responsible for. He is obliged to know what is important within his domain, but he can defer to others in regard to their professional competence.

Philosophy, however, is the 'specialty' that knows no borders. It is the attempt to formulate the whole, the big picture. By definition it takes on the challenge of trying to say something, not about a part, but about the comprehensive whole. In principle, the philosopher cannot make any disclaimers; he cannot say, 'Well, that's outside my field'. If, for example, a given philosopher tries to specialize in the philosophy of language, he cannot say, to a questioner, 'You are asking me about change and stability, and about images and memories; I don't know anything about such things. I can only talk about language.' Such a reply would indicate that the speaker has become a linguist, not a philosopher, because if he presents himself as a *philosopher* of language he cannot in principle refuse to entertain questions from any quarter. He has to be able to show how language fits into the whole of things, and to do so he will have to take into account how it is related, in the case of these particular questions, to stability, change, and representation. The philosopher of language might acknowledge his limitations by saying, 'I haven't thought about that yet; I have been occupied with other things', but these are his personal limitations, not restrictions on his 'field'. He cannot disavow the effort by saying that it is outside his responsibility. He is responsible for the whole, and on this level everything is related to everything else.

The philosopher will know that it is a tricky business to think and speak about the whole. He will also know that language begins to act strangely when you apply it to this encircling domain, just as the natural elements behave oddly when they approach absolute zero.[7] One of his

[6] *Fides et ratio*, §5, 6.

[7] To draw out the analogy, it would be interesting to ask what in philosophical

tasks, therefore, is to show how words become transformed, in both their semantics and their syntax, when they are taken from their birthplace in partial domains and applied to the most comprehensive context. Furthermore, sometimes one of the partial sciences tries to become the science of the whole: physics might try to provide the theory of everything, or history, psychology, or evolutionary biology may claim to be the encompassing science, but if any such partial science tries to take over the whole show, if it tries to become philosophy, it, too, will fall prey to the same difficulties that face philosophy. It will have to answer questions from all quarters and it will be unable to make any exclusions. It will have to absorb everything into itself. Physics, for example, if it tries to become the science of the whole, will have to account for such things as quotation, picturing, memory and political decisions.

It is not the case that only professional philosophers take a position toward the whole of things. Every thinking person has some opinions about the whole, and every person inevitably gets into subjects that are philosophical: whenever anyone uses words such as *truth*, *falsity*, *change*, or *time*, he enters into issues that can be properly treated only in the context of the whole. Also, whenever a person becomes involved in moral debate, he activates terms, such as *virtuous* and *vicious*, *responsible* and *innocent*, that engage the widest context, that of the whole, because they get into the issue of moral truth.[8] Socrates perplexed his interlocutors by showing that they cannot avoid philosophical questions. Generally, the opinions people have about the whole are just taken over from what others say, or they are projected from one particular special field. Only the philosopher sets out explicitly to think about the whole as such, on terms that are appropriate to it.

There is a fundamental veracity that is part of every human being; the Encyclical says, 'Man may be defined, therefore, as *the one who seeks the truth*', and it quotes St Augustine in saying that while there are people who try to deceive others, no one wants to be deceived himself.[9] This inclination to truth develops into the individual and regional understandings of the way things are, but the philosopher lets this veracity expand without confinements, into its widest setting, that of the whole of

---

language corresponds to superconductivity and to Bose–Einstein condensation as matter approaches absolute zero, when it has almost no thermal energy.

[8] The Encyclical often restates the claim found in *Veritatis splendor*, and in other teachings of John Paul II, that freedom and morality must be based on truth: 'Once the truth about man has been removed he is often deluded in supposing he can make himself free, for truth and freedom are either joined together or together they perish miserably.' In the same section he writes that without truth human beings are led 'either to the destructive desire for power or to the despair of isolation' (§90).

[9] *Fides et ratio*, §§28, 25.

things. The philosopher reads authors who are judged to have explored this field with some success, and he spends much time reflecting on how difficult it is to think without the restrictions that mark out a domain to be cultivated. The Encyclical also observes that no particular philosophical achievement can ever conclude human thinking: 'the *body* of philosophy . . . must recognize that which is the basis of all philosophical *reflection*, from where it draws its origin and which it must serve appropriately'.[10]

Philosophy as the inquiry into the first and highest things

Philosophy does not only move into the most comprehensive context; it is also concerned with the first principles of that context. One cannot think about the whole of things without having some inkling of what is first and best and original in the whole. The whole is not a flat, undifferentiated collection of particular issues. It is ordered around a first and best, around something that governs the whole. A concern with the divine has always been part of the philosophical impulse. All classical philosophers have thought about the first and ultimate principle or principles of the world. They did not think only about particular issues, or even about the cosmos as a whole; they also thought about the first principle of the universe.

Thus, Parmenides and Heraclitus, Plato and Aristotle, the Stoics and Epicureans, all thought about the divine, the first and the best. To think about the divine was part of their philosophy. However, both the philosophical and religious thinkers of antiquity took the whole of things, the cosmos, as the ultimate setting for their thought. They did not conceive of the possible non-existence of the cosmos; its factual givenness was quite properly taken for granted, and the divine principles, the god or the gods, were thought of as the highest and best entities within that setting. And because pagan thinking accepted the world as the final, unquestioned context, the two approaches to the whole, religion and philosophy, offered competing versions of how the whole and the divine principles should be understood. The philosophers considered the poetic stories about the gods to be inadequate and unworthy, and thought that their own interpretation of the divine, and consequently of the whole, should purify the inherited religious tradition: Plato is to refine Homer as the educator of the Greeks, and Aristotle demythologizes the poets. Philosophy claimed to offer a more appropriate expression of ultimate truth, but it did not try to replace religion, it only claimed the right to monitor it; the attempt to replace religion by philosophy – the attempt

[10] *Fides et ratio*, §4.

that defines the modern Enlightenment – would in this view destroy philosophy, because philosophy has to remain the concern of relatively few people, not of everyone.

In such a pagan setting, it is hard to avoid what was later called an Averroistic understanding of the relationship between theology and philosophy, between faith and reason. Religious belief and human reason each attempt to think about the whole of things, and they have rival views of what is highest and best in it. Religious belief and reason are in competition because both view the cosmos as the final setting for reason, and consider the divine to be the best, highest and governing principle in the cosmos.

We should also observe that the philosophical search for the first and the divine occurs not only in ancient philosophy but in contemporary thinking as well. In our intellectual culture, the role of the governing, 'divine' principle is usually played by evolution, on both the cosmic and biological scale. People may say that the evolution of living things is based on purely accidental mutations, but when they speak more generally about it they attribute to it a providence and a superior intelligence that strongly resembles the Mind (*Nous*) that the Presocratic philosopher Anaxagoras said was part of nature.[11]

It is easy to see that philosophy enjoys a great autonomy in the pagan understanding of things. There, philosophy stands in judgment on poetic and religious truth, distinguishing the valid from the invalid and retaining only what it considers acceptable to human thinking. Aristotle gives a philosophical interpretation of the ancient legends and concludes, 'Only thus far, then, is the opinion of our ancestors and of our earliest predecessors clear to us.'[12] He accepts what he can reformulate philosophically and discards the rest as poetic fictions added in order to persuade the multitude.[13] And Plato, after criticizing Homer, says that 'only so much of poetry as is hymns to gods or celebration of good men should be admitted to a city'.[14] Philosophy, in this conception, is obviously the governing knowledge.

The autonomy of philosophical thinking in the Encyclical

The Encyclical *Fides et ratio* also acknowledges the autonomy of philosophical evidence and truth. One of the places it does so is in the course

[11] See Aristotle, *Metaphysics* I 3, 984b15–18, trans. Hugh Tredennick (Cambridge, MA: Harvard University Press, 1933).

[12] Aristotle, *Metaphysics* XII 8, 1074b13–14, trans. Hugh Tredennick (Cambridge, MA: Harvard University Press, 1935).

[13] Aristotle, *Metaphysics* XII 8, 1074b3–8.

[14] Plato, *Republic* X, 607a, trans. Allan Bloom (New York: Basic Books, 1968).

of its recommendation of the work of St Thomas Aquinas, which it praises not only for its intrinsic value but also for Thomas's willingness to learn from Jewish and Muslim thinkers. It also endorses and recommends Aquinas because he is such a good conduit of the classical tradition.[15] However, the Encyclical insists that 'the Church does not have a philosophy of her own, nor does she select a particular one to the detriment of others'. The reason for this reserve is very interesting: 'philosophy, even when it has a connection with theology, must act in accordance with its own character and rules: there is no other way of being sure that it tends toward the truth and makes its way forward by a course plotted by reason'.[16]

In other words, the Church refrains from making any philosophy official *because she does not want to endanger the autonomy of philosophy.* Her restraint is based on a respect for philosophy and natural wisdom, and for the truth that they can attain. A philosophy based on authority would not rest on its own evidence, and hence it would not be philosophy. It is to protect philosophy that the Encyclical allows it to function on its own: 'Any philosophy which does not proceed under the guidance of reason in accordance with its own principles and its particular methodology would be of little assistance.'[17] The major reason for the Pope's reluctance to canonize a philosophy is this respect for the autonomy of the discipline, but there may be a historical and practical reason as well: having lived under an ideological regime in Poland and having seen how artificial, empty and inauthentic an 'official philosophy' inevitably becomes, he is all the more sensitive to the nature of philosophical evidence. A third reason why the Pope acknowledges the independence of human intelligence is the confidence in reason that his Christian faith gives him. Christian belief understands itself to be based on truth, and therefore it does not need to fear any other expressions of truth. In its view, the more understanding the better.

Does this acknowledgment of the autonomy of philosophy mean that reason can set itself up as the tribunal for faith, as it does in pagan thinking? Obviously not; in fact, there are passages in the Encyclical that seem to make the opposite claim, to subordinate reason to faith, and to restrict the autonomy of philosophy.

Christian faith as deeper than reason

The most dramatic passage that declares the priority of faith is the following: 'The preaching of Christ crucified and risen is the reef upon

[15] Aquinas is mentioned often in the Encyclical; see §§43–4, 57–9, 61, and 78.
[16] *Fides et ratio*, §49.
[17] *Fides et ratio*, §49.

which the reach between faith and philosophy can break up, but beyond which the infinite horizon of truth lies open.'[18] The phrase, 'the preaching of Christ crucified and risen', is somewhat ambiguous. First, it can mean the preaching that was accomplished by Christ in his death and resurrection; this decisive action of Christ, his death and resurrection, is the ultimate word that was uttered, the ultimate statement that was made, by the incarnate Word of God. It was a statement made through an action and not merely through words. Second, the phrase can mean the preaching carried on by the apostles and by the Church, who proclaim the death and resurrection of Christ through their words and actions. This second sense is probably the one intended by the Encyclical, but the first sense is certainly a welcome overtone.

Still, if reason stands in need of the revelation that took place in the death and resurrection of Christ, how can it be autonomous?

The phrase, 'Christ crucified and risen', does not signify only the particular truth of the death of Christ and his rising from the dead; it also implies the incarnation, and consequently the mystery of the Holy Trinity. That is, it signifies the understanding of God that is revealed through the death and resurrection of Christ. These events do not just reveal *Christ*; they also reveal *God*. The death and resurrection of Jesus are not simple facts that stand alone; they both manifest and presuppose a certain background, a certain understanding of God, which was revealed gradually through the words and events of the Old Covenant and brought to its final manifestation in the words and actions of Christ, as well as in the words and actions of the Church, enlivened by the Holy Spirit, in the aftermath of Christ. Biblical revelation did not take place against a neutral, universal sense of the divine that is common to all religious thinking, or common to all monotheisms. It did not merely confirm a generic understanding of the divine. It manifested a new sense of the divine, a new name for God.

In the Old Testament, God is revealed as radically different from the world. He is not just the best and highest entity within the world, as divinity is understood in paganism; rather, he is the one who created the world and is totally different from anything in it. He cannot even be represented by an image in the world. Israel was different from other nations because its God was different from theirs. It was not just that the Jews had the right divinity while the other nations had the wrong ones; rather, the very meaning of the divine was changed through the pedagogy and disclosure of the Old Covenant. The other 'gods' were not gods at all, not in the sense of *God* that was now being revealed.

This revealed sense of the divine is then perfected in Christ, who

[18] *Fides et ratio*, §23.

shows, by his words and actions, and especially by his death and resurrection, that the God of the First Covenant is not only radically other to the world, but that he is so other to it that he could become part of it without diminishing his divinity. The Father of Jesus Christ is the same God as Jahweh, but more deeply revealed and understood. Through the Old and New Covenants, God is understood to be so different from the world that he could exist, in undiminished goodness and greatness, even if the world had not existed; that is, God created the world out of sheer generosity and benevolence, not out of any need to perfect himself or to bring about any increase in the goodness and greatness of being itself. The charity of creation is manifested by the even greater charity of the incarnation, death, and resurrection of the Son of God.

This deepening of the sense of the divine makes possible a harmony between *this* kind of faith and human reason. In paganism, the religious or poetic grasp of the whole is necessarily at odds with philosophy, because both consider the cosmos as the ultimate context, and take the divine to be the greatest and best principle within the cosmos. Both religion and reason were able to reach this far by their own efforts. In biblical and Christian faith, which understands itself not as an achievement of reason simply but as the reception of the Word of God, the cosmos is no longer seen as the ultimate context, the encompassing whole. The cosmos is now understood as possibly not having been. The whole that served as the final and unshakable setting for human thinking is now seen as possibly not having come into being. God is now understood as not having had to create; he could have been all that there is, with no lessening of goodness and greatness. He is not just the best and highest entity in the whole of things. A new sense of the whole, a new sense of the divine, a new sense of the cosmos, as well as a new sense of the human person, are revealed to us in this kind of faith.[19]

In this new understanding of the whole and the divine, philosophy is not seen as an alternative or a rival to religious faith. Here, philosophy cannot see the religious formulation of the divine as inadequate or unworthy. It cannot demythologize the narrative that presents the action of God, as Plato and Aristotle could demythologize the stories of the poets. Philosophy could not say of biblical revelation what Aristotle, in a quotation, says about Simonides and other writers, 'Poets tell many a lie'.[20] In fact, St Anselm's argument for God's existence in the *Proslogion*

[19] See Robert Sokolowski, *The God of Faith and Reason: Foundations of Christian Theology* (Washington, DC: The Catholic University of America Press, 1995 [1982]); also, *Eucharistic Presence: A Study in the Theology of Disclosure* (Washington, DC: The Catholic University of America Press, 1993), chapters 5 and 10.

[20] Aristotle, *Metaphysics* I 2, 983a3.

shows that reason can attain the insight that when God is understood as he is in Christian faith, he cannot be understood not to exist.[21]

This new understanding of God and the world was, historically, not reached by human rational inquiry.[22] However, once it is presented to us, through God's own Word, reason can rejoice within it and exercise itself to its fullest capacity: 'What a challenge this offers to our reason, or rather what advantage is gained by those who embrace it' (§23). Reason can be autonomous in the space opened by biblical revelation and Christian faith. Reason does not turn into credulity or mere acceptance of poetic legends, because the Word of God proposes an understanding and not just a statement, an insight and not just a legend or a tale.

In Christian faith, the world is no longer taken as the ultimate setting, with the divine as the best, highest, original, and governing principle in it. The world is to be understood as possibly not having existed, with God understood as undiminished in goodness and greatness even if he had not created. Creation becomes an act of unnecessitated generosity, confirmed and more deeply revealed by the even greater generosity of redemption. This modification, this 'gestalt shift' in the understanding of the whole, is not simply one among many of the teachings of Christian faith. It stands at the intersection of faith and reason, and serves as the pivot on which the meaningfulness of all the other mysteries depend. What Christians mean by salvation, for example, or grace, or the sacraments, or the role of the Blessed Virgin, cannot be properly understood if the new context is not introduced. The syntax and semantics of Christian belief presupposes this adjustment in reason's grasp of the whole. And finally, we must also remember, as the Encyclical often reminds us, that this new understanding of God was not reached by an appearance that was glorious in the eyes of the world; it did not come to light through spectacular celestial phenomena or acts of earth-shaking terror. Rather, it was revealed through a shameful execution: 'Man cannot understand how death can be the fountain of life and love: even so God chose to use what human reason regards as "foolishness" and a "stumbling block" in order to make clear the mystery of his saving purpose.'[23]

---

[21] For this interpretation of St Anselm, see Sokolowski, *The God of Faith and Reason*, chapter 1.

[22] The Encyclical mentions the concept of 'a personal God who is both free and Creator', as one of the 'truths, which, though available to reason, would never have been discovered by it were it left to its own resources' (§76).

[23] *Fides et ratio*, §23.

The human person and Christian faith

If reason can be defined as intelligent articulation, Christian faith can be defined as the acceptance of this new understanding of God and the whole of things, with the conviction that it was presented to us by God himself, in Christ and through his Church. Through faith, the final truth about God and the world is disclosed to us. Christian reasoning or Christian theology is then the articulation that can be carried out within the context opened by this new understanding.

Faith also presents us with the truth about ourselves, about the human person. In doing so, it responds to another aspect of philosophical inquiry. We have described philosophy as the form of thinking that examines the whole and the divine principles in the whole, but it is also the inquiry into what we ourselves are. We are not merely components of the whole; as persons, we are questions to ourselves that cannot be answered merely by discussing cosmic and natural principles. From its beginnings the search for wisdom was also an attempt to know ourselves, as the Encyclical observes while quoting the admonition at the temple of Delphi.[24]

To shed light on the place of the human person in Christian faith, I would like to draw on a remark made by the Catholic philosopher from Munich, Robert Spaemann. He draws a very interesting contrast between Socrates and Christ. When we consider the way each of these men reacted to people who were hostile to them, we immediately notice 'the difference between the harsh speech of Jesus against his adversaries and the friendly, ironic speech of Socrates'.[25] Socrates is friendly and ironic, often playful, because he appeals to the evidence of the ideas, of the things he is conversing about. He tries to give reason its full exercise. His role is instrumental, in the service of the forms. His mission is to bring his interlocutors to the point at which reason and philosophy take over in them. He tries to help them overcome their ignorance, the confusion in their minds that keeps them from accepting the truths that they themselves would desire if only they were able to grasp them.

The opposition to Christ, however, is not grounded merely on confusion and ignorance, but on a steadfast resistance to the truth, on a love of darkness instead of light. Spaemann says that the New Testament introduces another dimension into human being, which it calls 'the

---

[24] *Fides et ratio*, §1.

[25] Robert Spaemann, *Personen: Versuche über den Unterschied zwischen 'etwas' und 'jemand'* (Stuttgart: Klett-Cotta Verlag, 1996), p. 30: 'der Unterschied zwischen der harten Sprache Jesu gegenüber seinen Gegnern und der freundlich-ironischen Sprache des Sokrates'.

heart'. He says that this concept is the foundation of the later concept of the person, and in fact its use in the New Testament 'signifies something like the discovery of the person'.[26] It is 'the ground for the turning away from the good',[27] and it is also, conversely, the ground for the turn toward the good and toward truth. Furthermore, according to Spaemann, this turning toward or turning against is not just a response to an argument or to an idea, but a response to someone – God, and in the more immediate situation, Christ – who discloses the truth: '. . . the decision between good and evil, between light and darkness, is not a decision made before an idea, but before a person, who comes forth as the ineluctable (*unhintergehbare*) revelation of the truth'.[28] Socrates knows that he himself may have been only a historical contingency, but Christ is the only way to the truth that he himself brings to light; there is no possibility of taking another route or somehow 'going around' him.

Spaemann also says that this introduction of 'the heart' is not only a theological teaching, but also a philosophical one: 'What is expressed here is an anthropological discovery, because it corresponds to something we experience'.[29] This concept of the heart is an ultimate 'explanation' for the turn toward truth or darkness, and it is original in the New Testament: 'The heart is the unfounded foundation in a sense for which there is no thinkable or conceptual equivalent in antiquity.'[30]

I would like to observe that this 'unfounded foundation' is not a Nietzschean will or a blind desire for pleasure or power, but the impulse for or against truth, the inclination that makes a person to be what he is. It is not just a power but the responsibility we have to let the truth of things disclose itself. The heart is not something that unfolds spontaneously; receptivity to the truth – or its correlate, the love of darkness – is not a merely natural process. Our relation to the truth cannot be automatic or necessary; it must be free, responsible and most deeply our own doing. It would be misleading, however, to speak of it as a choice, because it is much more basic than that; it is not one choice among many, but the movement toward truth that underlies all our choices. It also underlies all our specific exercises of truthfulness, all our particular disclosures, as well as all our true or false statements and scientific

---

[26] Spaemann, *Personen*, p. 30: 'Er bedeutet so etwas wie die Entdeckung der Person'.

[27] Spaemann, *Personen*, p. 30: 'Der Grund für die Abwendung vom Guten'.

[28] Spaemann, *Personen*, p. 30: 'Die Entscheidung zwischen gut und böse, zwischen Licht und Finsternis [ist] nicht eine Entscheidung gegenüber einer Idee, sondern gegenüber einer Person . . . , die als unhintergehbare Offenbarung der Wahrheit gilt'.

[29] Spaemann, *Personen*, p. 30: 'Was hier zum Ausdruck kommt, ist eine anthropologische Entdeckung, weil es einer Erfahrung entspricht'.

[30] Spaemann, *Personen*, p. 30: 'Das Herz ist grundloser Grund in einem Sinn, für den es in der Antike kein gedankliches und begriffliches Äquivalent gibt'.

endeavours. It underlies both reason and will; it is not one act of the will among many. It establishes us as agents of truth. The way this impulse is exercised will determine what kind of person each of us becomes before God. It can be either cultivated or blighted, and whichever occurs is our doing, which is why Christ so severely reprimanded those who refused the truth to which he bore witness.

The kind of manifestation that is at issue in Christian faith depends on the central and powerful authority of Christ. In the Old Covenant, God himself spoke to his people, but he did so through Moses and the prophets. In the New Covenant God spoke as a human being. The tone of Christ's words reflects this difference. He does not merely bear witness to the truth and point out the way, but asserts that he *is* the way, the truth, and the life, that no one comes to the Father except through him, and that whoever has seen him has seen the Father.[31] Christ is an unsurpassable and irreplaceable speaker. Socrates was the midwife who helped others discover the truth of things through their own powers, but Christ reveals the truth. When we were children, other people introduced us to the syntax of human intelligence, which we then took over and exercised on our own. Christ gives us the syntax and semantics we need to call God our Father, to understand the world as his creation and ourselves as his adopted children. This understanding in faith, however, is not one that we can take over on our own; we can possess and exercise it only in union with 'Christ crucified and risen', with whom we must remain affiliated in the Church, his body. Our willingness to accept the disclosure of God as our Creator and Father depends on our willingness to listen to Christ, to respond to the human presence that God has assumed in order to speak to us: 'the Eternal enters time, Who is Whole is concealed in the part, God takes on human face'.[32]

The fact that we depend on other persons for the disclosure of things does not constrict the autonomy of reason. Every human being enters into reason – becomes elevated into syntax and language – only by being introduced to it by other human beings. Without the help of others we would never be able to introduce syntactic structure into our experience; we could never intelligently articulate our experiences and the things we know. The flowering of our reason requires the intervention of others; it does not occur by itself. It is not like the growth of our muscles and bones.

It is true that philosophy aims at a final responsibility for the truth and that it subjects our experience to a kind of relentless verification. It desires the most comprehensive truth of things, and it keeps rethinking,

[31] Jn 14: 6, 9.
[32] *Fides et ratio*, §12.

in the light of further truth, whatever we may know at any moment. However, in this very attempt at complete verification, we may come to realize that a certain kind of truth would be entirely unavailable to us had not someone else registered it for us and with us. The understanding that comes from Christian faith is like this. No philosopher did in fact grasp the radical transcendence of God that biblical revelation made known to us; still less could anyone have arrived at the mysteries of the Holy Trinity and redemption. But when we reflect on these mysteries, and see how they extend beyond the context of the world, we can see with insight that they are beyond us. Our autonomy consists in recognizing our own limitations, in coming to know what we do not and what we could not know on our own.

And by knowing what we cannot grasp on our own – by knowing what we believe, and seeing that we can possess it only by believing it – we become much more aware of what we do know on our own. We become much more aware of and confident in our reason precisely in contrast with our faith. Faith justifies our reason. By going beyond reason we more vividly appreciate it for what it is.

Autonomy and limitation

Limitation need not be a deficiency, and the recognition of it need not be humiliating. In several places, the Encyclical points out that limitation and dependence need not destroy human autonomy, but that they make possible certain perfections that are appropriate to human beings. It reminds us that in our natural exchanges with others we often 'place our confidence in the knowledge of other persons'. We believe what they tell us. Such confidence in others permits us to develop 'an even more profound capacity for trusting other persons'. We are also told that 'the capacity and willingness for committing oneself and one's life to another person, anthropologically speaking, are among the most significant and expressive of human acts'.[33] Such remarks clearly reflect moral and religious intuitions made possible by the Holy Father's personalist philosophy and by his dealings with people in a lifetime of pastoral care. They are similar to thoughts expressed by Alasdair MacIntyre in his book, *Dependent Rational Animals*, which discusses 'the virtues of acknowledged dependence'.[34]

Such confident dependence on others, furthermore, extends even into the philosophical life; the Encyclical calls to mind 'the teaching of the earliest philosophers, who held that friendship was among the more

[33] *Fides et ratio*, §§32, 33.

[34] Alasdair MacIntyre, *Dependent Rational Animals: Why Human Beings Need the Virtues* (Chicago: Open Court, 1999), p. 8.

appropriate contexts for sound philosophizing'. It calls upon the Old Testament to warn us, in a phrase that might be considered an implicit critique of Machiavelli, that the path to human knowledge is not for the proud 'who supposes that everything is achieved by his own power'.[35] The discovery of truth involves reception as well as initiative. The Kantian desire for pure autonomy stems in part from too radical a disjunction between the spontaneity of reason and the passivity of sense, between the kingdom of ends and the kingdom of nature. Our moral excellence depends not only on the imperatives we legislate for ourselves, but also on what we give and receive to and from others in friendship. Likewise, the dependence of philosophy on Christian faith, and ultimately its dependence on Christ as the Word of God, can also be seen not as a deficiency but an opportunity that discloses a truth about things that could not have been attained in any other way.

In closing, I wish to return to Spaemann's remark about the difference between Socrates and Christ. The serious discourse of Christ is now part of the life of thinking, but there still remain situations in which Socratic irony is appropriate. Christian revelation elevates but does not replace human reason, and it leaves intact not only reason's power to discover the truth, but also its dialectical and playful manner of doing so.

---

[35] *Fides et ratio*, §§33, 18.

Fides et ratio: The Post-modern Pope

JANET MARTIN SOSKICE

Fides et ratio may be about faith and reason, but it is also about nihilism and despair (not the same things), and the relation of metaphysics to ethics. As such it is an essay in philosophical and theological anthropology. One might summarize its distinctive contribution by saying that whereas so much English-language philosophy of religion takes the issue of *faith and reason* to be *au fond* epistemological, the Pope sees it as anthropological in the Catholic sense – that is, to do with our concept of the human person.

In terms of this unified vision, the Encyclical's endorsement of Aquinas is striking but not surprising. When the Encyclical first came out there was debate as to which 'Aquinas' this might be – was it Aquinas as reconfigured by twentieth-century, and primarily French, scholarship and now influential in many mainstream universities? Or was it the Aquinas of 'textbook' Thomism such as the Pope might have met in his seminary days? It seems likely that it is both, although the Pope goes out of his way to mention the twentieth-century *ressourcement* which has been so influential in the academy. 'The more distinguished of the Catholic theologians of this century, to whose reflections and researches Vatican II owes so much, are children', he reminds us, 'of the restoration of the philosophy of Saint Thomas.'[1]

The Encyclical presents us with many familiar Thomistic and Augustinian themes. There can be no conflict between faith and reason. Truth is one, the believer has nothing to fear and much to gain by its pursuit.[2] All people desire knowledge and '[b]y means of intellect, everyone, believer as much as non-believer, is granted the capacity to plumb "the deep waters" of knowledge (cf. *Prov* 20:5)'.[3] Yet reason cannot do without faith, especially when it comes to matters of salvation.[4] The highest truth is revealed truth and pre-eminently that revealed in Christ. Revelation does not abolish reason but rather, in the familiar tag, faith

[1] *Fides et ratio*, §58.
[2] *Fides et ratio*, §53.
[3] *Fides et ratio*, §16.
[4] With reference to St Thomas Aquinas, *Summa Theologiae*, Ia, Q. 1.

perfects reason.[5] This restatement of classical Thomism shows how very attractive it is, and gives some indication why interest in Aquinas has soared amongst non-Catholic theologians in recent years. Aquinas is not held up as having all the correct answers, but rather as a theologian whose work can be a template for those who, in our time, seek to bring faith and reason in their own ways while nonetheless retaining the same passionate conviction that the two can and must be held together.

Paragraph 67 also provides a concise definition of the nature and purposes of *fundamental theology*, not a term in general parlance amongst non-Catholic theologians and one which may, for the uninitiated, misleadingly suggest 'fundamentalism'. Far from it. *Fundamental theology*, in this Catholic sense, is rather the branch of theology which has as its task 'producing an account of faith' and 'explaining the relationship between philosophy and philosophical knowledge'.[6] As such, *fundamental theology*, while truly philosophical, is not quite the same as *philosophy of religion* whose efforts in the academy are in parallel with those of *philosophy of music* and *philosophy of science*. Philosophy of science, for instance, has little or no impact on the practice of science and the same may be said for much philosophy of religion. These are second-order reflective disciplines. *Fundamental theology*, however, is central to the theological enterprise in so far as that is 'faith seeking understanding'. As such it is concerned with meaning, truth, language, science, doubt and diffidence, amongst other things, and integrates theology, philosophy and apologetics. (In British and American universities we sometimes make a distinction between *philosophy of religion* on the one hand and *philosophical theology* on the other, with the second akin to what the Catholic church calls *fundamental theology*.) A Thomistic precedence is given, by the Encyclical, to faith – which nonetheless does not proceed without reason: 'Thus faith, the gift of God, though it in no sense rests upon reason, can never proceed without it; a similar need exists for reason to derive its strength from faith and thus pursue new ends which it could not arrive at by itself.'[7]

Welcome in this endorsement of Aquinas, and especially in these days when many without and within the Catholic communion think Rome

---

5 Cf. *Fides et ratio*, §42, where, after some discussion of Anselm, he says 'The fundamental harmony between philosophical knowledge and the knowledge of faith is once again confirmed: faith demands that its object be understood with the help of reason; reason, in attaining the summit of its search, unavoidably points to what faith makes plain'; and, following Saint Thomas, 'Faith, therefore, is not afraid of reason; rather it seeks it out and places its trust in it. Even as grace both presupposes and perfects nature, so too faith presupposes and perfects reason', §43. See also §§67–9.

6 *Fides et ratio*, §67.

7 *Fides et ratio*, §67.

overly confident of its unique grasp of truth, is the restatement of Thomas's beautiful idea that a matter may be objectively certain in itself and yet remain subjectively uncertain to us, a truly objective knowledge, which nonetheless 'can be further perfected'.[8] This 'Christian realism' is enunciated in a paragraph which criticizes 'radically phenomenalist or relativist philosophy'.[9]

The document is ostensibly targeted more at philosophers than theologians – and at all philosophers whether they be believers or not. However it emerges that the Pope believes that 'All men and women . . . are in some sense philosophers and have their own philosophical conceptions with which they direct their lives'.[10] The Pope raps professional philosophers over the knuckles – not for neglecting theology or Christian faith but for not doing philosophy bravely enough. They have contented themselves with philosophical trivia while the *big questions are left unanswered or unaddressed*. The philosophers have made themselves marginal in a world that more than ever needs their honest deliberations, and here we arrive at the nihilism.

The big questions are those of metaphysics – questions about Being and the meaning of life. The Pope, we know, was a professional philosopher and these words at the twentieth year of his pontificate, while perhaps not entirely his own, seem nonetheless to come from his heart. Nor does he think the matters he is dealing with are abstruse or unimportant to ordinary people today. Quite the opposite – our current era, he says, is marked by a 'crisis of meaning'. We find ourselves with more and more information – a 'mass of data and facts' – yet constantly told that, faced with this 'plurality', it doesn't make sense to ask questions about meaning and truth any more.[11] The result is scepticism, indifference and ultimately nihilism. Here we have the 'Post-modern Pope' – for while post-modernity is often taken as a synonym of nihilism, the term itself, as the Pope notes, is ambiguous and indicates an evangelical opportunity. If Nietzsche is right in insisting on a connection between the Death of God and the Death of Man (that is, of all transcendent values by which we can guide our lives), then it is also the case that modern men and women, staring into this abyss of meaninglessness, may well with integrity want to reconsider metaphysics – and even God.

---

[8] *Fides et ratio*, §82. Cf. St Thomas Aquinas, *Summa Theologiae*, Ia, Q. 1.

[9] *Fides et ratio*, §82 in the first English translation. Although our present translation is more transparent to the non-philosopher, the earlier one uses terms which are more recognizably those of the philosophical trade here.

[10] *Fides et ratio*, §30, first English translation. Our translation has here 'Every man . . . is in some sense a philosopher and possesses philosophical conceptions by which he directs his life.' I prefer the earlier translation here because, while perhaps less elegant, it at least mentions that women are called to be philosophers, too.

[11] *Fides et ratio*, §81.

Indeed as a university teacher I find this is common amongst students, many of them second or third generation un-Churched: they are ready to ask about God. The Pope is not asking that philosophy 'prove' Christian faith to be true – as he has said, that conviction comes only with acceptance of the truths of revelation – but a truly reasonable philosophy will acknowledge that faith cannot be ruled out as an option. It is, in short, not unreasonable to believe.

Some particular philosophers (not all of them Catholics) receive the Pope's praise, some philosophical tendencies (historicism, positivism, nihilism) receive his censure, but throughout, his concern is to find a balance between two opposing and equally unsatisfactory extremes – both all too evident in late modernity. Already in the nineteenth century the Magisterium rightly sought to balance, on the one hand, the rationalism which makes claims for the powers of human reason too bold to be sustained, and on the other (and here those critics who say the Pope advocates a blind faith may pause for thought) the *fideism* and *radical traditionalism* which distrusts reason altogether.[12] *Fideism* is a philosophical position (though it sometimes disguises itself as faith) that claims that religious assertions cannot be subject to critical scrutiny. 'Don't ask questions, just believe.' This, too, from the Pope's perspective is a form of nihilism – a counsel of despair which fails furthermore to value highly enough the gift of reason as well as of faith – 'two wings by which the human spirit is raised up toward the contemplation of truth'.[13] Quoting Augustine he says 'belief itself is nothing other than thinking with assent . . . whoever believes, thinks by believing and believes by thinking . . . for unthinking faith is nothing'.[14] Faithful thinking will lead us to the truth which can only be one and which is found most fully in sharing the life of the Triune God.

So we are all called to be philosophers but, above all, those in positions of intellectual responsibility are encouraged to ask boldly the big questions of 'the true, the good, and the beautiful, to which the word of God gives access'.[15] The *dis-ease* of our somnolent culture, the Pope suggests, lies not in the fact that such questions cannot be answered but rather we are increasingly told such questions cannot even be asked. (Indeed we are sometimes told as much by our philosophy departments.) Science and modernity are not the difficulty, but rather the pressures of the 'immanentist mind-set and the narrow straits of a technocratic-

[12] *Fides et ratio*, §52.

[13] *Fides et ratio*, Preface.

[14] *Fides et ratio*, §79. The reference is to St Augustine, *On the Predestination of the Saints*, Book 2, Para. 5.

[15] *Fides et ratio*, §103. This will be perceived as a shot across the bows to some schools of philosophy.

logical approach'.[16] An unwillingness to ask any big questions (on the grounds that each one should please himself or herself) leads ineluctably to a distrust of reason itself with corrosive effect on our understanding of the human being as a reasonable and reflective creature. Philosophy becomes increasingly peripheral when rationality is regarded as not directed towards ultimate goals or 'the meaning of life' but is deployed instead, as instrumental reason, towards the promotion of utilitarian ends, towards enjoyment or power.[17]

If these big questions of meaning go unaddressed, in a culture of relativism which suggests that they cannot even be formulated much less addressed, then the result is a default to the pragmatic mode: a world driven only by need and greed. We become imprisoned by what the Pope sees (in ways that echo Heidegger) as the worst aspect of technocratic mentality and its alliance with a crude pragmatism – that is, since we can no longer ask what is true or good or beautiful we ask only *what works*.[18] In this, human beings become profit-and-loss automatons, failing to see their own beauty and that of their neighbours as free creatures, graced with reason by a loving God. We fail to see ourselves and others as truly we are – *in imago dei.*

---

[16] *Fides et ratio*, §15. In neglecting the search for ultimate truth, and a one-sided investigation of human subjectivity, we can forget that 'men and women are always called to direct their steps towards a truth which transcends them. Sundered from that truth, individuals are at the mercy of caprice, and their state as person ends up being judged by pragmatic criteria, based essentially upon experimental data, in the mistaken belief that technology must dominate all' (§5, first English translation). Again, the language of this first translation, while in many ways less felicitous, catches the sprit of the Heideggerian critique of 'technologization' that seems to lie behind the Encyclical.

[17] These sentiments seem to echo Charles Taylor's Sources of the Self (Cambridge, MA: Harvard University Press, 1989).

[18] See *Fides et ratio*, §§5, 15.

Index of Modern Authors

Index of Subjects